P9-DWK-283

FOOD AND MOOD

The Complete Guide to Eating Well and Feeling Your Best

ELIZABETH SOMER, M.A., R.D.

A HENRY HOLT REFERENCE BOOK
HENRY HOLT AND COMPANY · NEW YORK

A Henry Holt Reference Book
Henry Holt and Company, Inc.
Publishers since 1866
115 West 18th Street
New York, New York 10011

Henry Holt® is a registered
trademark of Henry Holt and Company, Inc.

Published in Canada by Fitzhenry & Whiteside Ltd.,
195 Allstate Parkway, Markham, Ontario L3R 4T8.

Library of Congress Cataloging-in-Publication Data
Somer, Elizabeth.
Food and mood: the complete guide to eating well and feeling
your best/Elizabeth Somer.—1st ed.
p. cm.
Includes index.
1. Nutrition. 2. Mood (Psychology).
3. Nutritionally induced diseases. I. Title.
RA784.S647 1995 94-6000
613.2—dc20 CIP

ISBN 0-8050-3125-1

Henry Holt books are available for special promotions
and premiums. For details contact:
Director, Special Markets.

First Edition—1995

Designed by Paula R. Szafranski

Printed in the United States of America
All first editions are printed on acid-free paper.∞

1 3 5 7 9 10 8 6 4 2

For Patrick,
my one true and lifelong love

The nutritional and health information presented in this book is based on an in-depth review of the current scientific literature. It is intended only as an informative resource guide to help you make informed decisions; it is not meant to replace the advice of a physician or to serve as a guide to self-treatment. Always seek competent medical help for any health condition or if there is any question about the appropriateness of a procedure or health recommendation.

Contents

Acknowledgments

I am deeply indebted to many people for their help with this book. Without their advice, feedback, and hard work, it never would have reached completion. In addition, without the excellent research being conducted around the country and world, and the willingness of those researchers to explain their findings to me, I never would have grasped the complexity and interconnectedness of the food and mood issues.

In particular, I would like to thank Paula Kakalecik, my editor, for her commitment to excellence and her patience with my anxiety attacks during the writing of this book. I also would like to thank Sandra Gleason, M.A., Karen Newton, R.D., M.P.H., and Kathy Schwab, R.D., for their painstaking time and attention in reading the manuscript and providing feedback. Also, thank-yous to Victoria Dolby, Elise Goodness, and the Reference Department staff at Salem Public Library, in their relentless search for the hundreds of research studies I requested.

There are not enough pages to thank all of the scientists, physicians, and researchers whose work contributed to this book. However, a few took extra time to talk with me and answer my numerous questions. A special thank-you to Dr. Richard Anderson at the USDA Human Nutrition Research Center in Beltsville; Dr. Jeffrey Blumberg at the USDA Human Nutrition Research Center at Tufts University in Boston; Elizabeth Burrows at the Fred Hutchinson Cancer Research Center in Seattle; Dr. C. Wayne Callaway at George Washington University in Washington, D.C.; Dr. Larry Christensen at the University of South Alabama in Mobile; Dr. Fergus Clydesdale at the University of Massachusetts in Amherst; Dr. Douglas Darr at Duke University Medical Center in Durham; Dr. Adam Drewnowski at the University of Michigan in Ann Arbor; Dr. Helen Gensler at the University of Arizona in Tucson; Dr. Douglas Heimburger at the University of Alabama in Birmingham; Dr. Robert Jacob at the USDA Agricultural Research Service in the Presidio in San Francisco; Dr. Jan Johnson-Shane at Illinois State University in Normal; Dr. Darshan Kelley at the USDA Agricultural Research Service in the Presidio in San Francisco; Dr. Robert Labbe at the University of Washington in Seattle; Dr. Sarah Leibowitz at Rockefeller University in New York City; Dr. Alan Levy at the Food and Drug Administration in Washington, D.C.; Dr. Wayne Miller at Indiana University in Bloomington; Dr. Daniel Nixon at the American Cancer Society in Atlanta; Dr. James Penland at the USDA Human Nutrition Research Center in Grand Forks; Dr. William Pryor at Louisiana State University in Baton Rouge; Dr. Judith Rodin at Yale University in New Haven; Dr. Robert Sack at the Oregon Health Sciences University in Portland; Dr. Adria Sherman at Rutgers University in New Brunswick; Dr. Barbara Smith at Johns Hopkins University in Baltimore; Evelyn Tribole, R.D., in Beverly Hills; Dr. David Williamson at the Centers for Disease Control in Atlanta; Dr. Judith Wurtman at the Massachusetts Institute of Technology in Cambridge; and Dr. Gary Zammit at the Sleep Disorders Institute of St. Luke's Hospital in New York City.

PREFACE

It Doesn't Have to Be This Way!

It always amazes me what people will put up with. We tolerate feeling tired day in and day out. We suffer in silence with mild depression that interferes with enjoying life. We give in to food cravings, then blame ourselves for being weak willed. We're grumpy or irritable and assume we were born that way. We think that because we can't think clearly or remember details that we must not be very smart. We endure feeling sluggish as if it were our lot in life.

We also create elaborate excuses to justify these problems. From blaming our fatigue on the fact that "we're getting older" and "can't do what we used to do" to assuming that feeling blue or stressed is a natural consequence of juggling so many responsibilities, we rationalize our bad moods or low energy as being normal.

But why put up with second best? Why settle for less than feeling good, or even great? Why tolerate the fatigue and depression that undermine your quality of life? There is much more to life than just getting by. Life can be filled with joy, adventure, and vitality when you feel your best, your healthiest, your youngest—regardless of your age. Pizzazz is a basic human right, but no one will hand it to you. You must reach out and grab it, and the first step is to change your motto to "It doesn't have to be this way!"

You Are What You Eat/You Eat What You Are

Granted, extreme depression, fatigue, or other emotional stumbling blocks often are signs of a more serious underlying illness that requires medical attention.

However, for many of us, mood and energy problems are a result of what we eat and how we live. In most cases, making a few simple changes in what and when we eat could be all it takes to feel better. Combined with physical activity, a positive mental attitude, and relaxation, eating right could make the difference between getting by and feeling great!

Most people recognize that "they are what they eat." That is, what they eat affects their health today and their future risk for diseases. We know that eating a high-fat diet increases our chances of developing heart disease and that not including enough calcium in our diets today could increase our risk for developing osteoporosis later on.

However, many people ignore the profound effects that food can have on mood, intellect, and energy level. In fact, not eating right will affect your memory, mood, and vitality long before it will affect your heart and bones. It takes decades of eating a calcium-poor diet before your bones become fragile; however, what you eat this morning (or don't eat) could affect how you feel this afternoon. What you ate for dinner could affect how well you sleep tonight. When and what you last ate could determine whether or not you give in to a food craving or lose the weight-control war. Even something as simple as not eating enough iron-rich foods could result in chronic fatigue, poor concentration, and mild depression. It is much like filling your car's tank with dirty gas. You may get to work, but it won't be a smooth ride. On the other hand, using high-quality fuel keeps your car running efficiently and smoothly.

The link between food and mood, however, goes further: you also eat what you are. In other words, your mood (often created by the foods you choose) determines what you eat at your next meal. Imbalanced eating habits trigger a vicious cycle where you feel worse and worse and turn repeatedly to the wrong foods for a quick fix. These foods only perpetuate the fatigue and depression. In essence, you create a mood monster by repeatedly making food choices that drag you down. In contrast, when you make the right food choices, you're providing fuel for a healthy body, a good mood, an active mind, and a high energy level.

Getting Your Mood Back on Track

Everything you need to know to break the cycle and get your mood, mind, and energy level back on track is in *Food and Mood*. This handbook blends the current research from thousands of scientific studies on how what you eat affects how you feel with easy-to-follow dietary guidelines—tailored to your individual concerns—for revitalizing your life.

Compared to other diets, the Feeling Good Diet, included in the following pages, is a breath of fresh air. It promotes mental, emotional, and physical health instead of counting calories or grams of fat and helps you gradually develop a personal eating style that will help you feel your best.

For example, emerging research sheds light on two ways that food functions as a mood regulator. First, people suffering from negative moods—from mood swings during premenstrual syndrome to depression and food cravings—seek out foods to self-medicate and provide relief from the negative mood. Second, certain foods, such as sugar and caffeine, or certain eating habits, such as skipping meals, may aggravate or even generate negative moods; consequently, eliminating these foods and habits is an effective solution for improving mood. The Feeling Good Diet will explain why and how you can make these dietary changes simply, painlessly, and realistically.

Out of the Dark Ages and into the Future

The link between food and mood is not new. In ancient times, onions were recommended to induce sleep, lemons to protect against the "evil eye," and salt to stimulate passion. While these food-mood connections are more fiction than fact, others, such as drinking a cup of warm milk before bed to ensure a restful night's sleep, recently have been proven to have a scientific basis. The commonsense eating habits outlined in this book are a compilation of tried-and-true recommendations and hot-off-the-press recent findings based on scientific evidence that could change your life. Rather than put up with chronic fatigue, erratic moods, or sleepless nights, rather than let your life slip through your fingers because you couldn't muster the energy to live it to the fullest, I hope that reading this book and following the Feeling Good Diet will help you take the first step toward feeling your best for the rest of your life.

INTRODUCTION

Why Most Diets Make Us Crazy

- "I think I was born tired. But I look well and all the medical tests came back negative, so no one takes my fatigue seriously."
- "I've battled the blues for years. I've been told I bring these mood swings on myself, but I'm sure there's another reason, I just don't know what it is."
- "I used to sleep like a baby. Now I spend many nights tossing and turning. What's wrong with me?"
- "The more I diet to lose weight, the stronger are my urges to eat. I must not have what it takes when it comes to willpower."
- "I just wish I could think, concentrate, and remember like I used to."

Depression. Fatigue. Insomnia. Food cravings. Poor concentration. These and other emotional or mental problems plague just about every person at one time or another. In many instances it's a simple case of the blues or a temporary lull in energy. In others, the fatigue, mood swings, food cravings, or memory loss persists, disrupting daily life, straining relationships, and even jeopardizing careers.

Often symptoms are vague. You feel "under the weather," "not up to par," like you're "idling in neutral." You don't feel bad enough to seek medical help, or if you do, often you are told there is nothing physically wrong. The diagnosis can leave you feeling more hopeless or frustrated, and it implies that you have brought these changes on yourself, that it is "all in your head" or, worse yet, that there is no cure.

Anyone who has struggled with low energy or mood problems will admit that the "just do it" cure is easier said than done. The frustration of not being able to control a craving or a mood only adds insult to injury and increases the risk of developing other problems, such as depression. Self-esteem, self-control, mood, and eating become intertwined, so that what a person eats or feels is wrongly used to define who that person is. For example, food cravings are mistakenly thought to be only a matter of the lack of willpower. Mood swings associated with PMS or seasonal affective disorder (SAD) are often dismissed with a simple "get a grip!" If you are tired all the time, you're labeled a complainer or just plain lazy.

People can function despite mild fluctuations in mood, energy, or mental function. Some can live with the ups and downs of repeated weight loss and regain. Women suffering from PMS can blame their monthly mood transformations on hormones and learn to live with them. We can assume life is supposed to be this stressful. We can make lists and blame our poor concentration on the natural consequence of getting older. We can get used to anything, if we have to.

But why settle for less? Granted, how we feel, sleep, or eat and what our energy level is are complicated issues. However, feeling good—even feeling great—might be a lot easier than you realize. In fact, there might be a common thread among many seemingly unrelated mood and energy problems. The solution could be something as simple as diet. In other words, there might be a scientific basis for something once thought to be "all in your head."

Are You Eating for Better or Worse?

The food-mood link is not new. Most people at one time or another have turned to food for solace, relaxation, or a quick pick-me-up. A person may snack from the refrigerator upon returning home from work as a way to relax. Someone else might find comfort in a pint of ice cream when alone on a Friday night. A coworker says her midafternoon doldrums are relieved by a candy bar. In the past, no one gave it much thought. Scientists thought the brain was relatively impermeable to diet and dietary changes. A "blood-brain barrier" supposedly shielded the brain from changes in the chemical composition of the blood caused by diet, drugs, or other substances.

It now appears that what we eat can affect whether we are happy, sad, irritable, moody, alert, calm, or sleepy. Some nutrients in food might improve memory, give a boost of energy, or satisfy an otherwise insatiable appetite. For some people, diet alone might be the cause of or solution to their waning energy levels or plummeting moods.

Stress, depression, or low energy can leave people with little time or desire to eat right. Or they might turn to all the wrong foods for solace. Consequently, when nutritional needs are at an all-time high, the quality of food intake is at its lowest. A vicious cycle develops whereby a mild change in sleep, mood, or energy interferes with eating an optimal diet, which in turn aggravates the insomnia, depression, or fatigue.

Even if you know there is another reason besides diet for your negative mood, improving your nutritional status *always* will help you feel better, give you more energy, and help you fend off colds, infections, and illnesses. In short, if you want to feel your best, you have to eat your best.

Most people understand that what they eat affects their physical health. Eating a high-fat diet increases the risk of developing heart disease. A low-fiber diet is linked to colon cancer. A diabetic must avoid excessive amounts of sweet desserts. Osteoporosis might be avoided by drinking more milk throughout life. So it makes sense that diet has just as great an impact on how we feel, think, act, and sleep.

Take sugar, for example. A graph showing sugar consumption in America during the past 150 years looks like the upward trajectory of a missile. Whereas a typical person in 1840 consumed a scant 4 teaspoons of sweeteners daily, today the average American heaps 43 teaspoons (or almost 1 cup) of sugar onto his or her daily plate. The U.S. Department of Agriculture's 1992 Continuing Survey of Food Intakes showed that most people are two to four times more likely to reach for a glass of soda pop, a cookie, or a doughnut than for a whole wheat bagel.

On the surface, the only proven harm posed by eating too much sugar is tooth decay. Many researchers suspect, however, that a sugar-laden diet is a factor in the development and progression of heart disease, hypoglycemia, diabetes, kidney disease, gallstones, and ulcers. Limited research has shown a connection between high sugar consumption and excessive calorie intake (a 20 percent increase above normal) resulting in obesity. However, until the research shows a consistent trend, no verdict can be reached.

The sugar issue goes much deeper than disease, however. During the past fifteen years, there has been a veritable explosion of interest in the relationship between diet and behavior. In many cases the scientific findings converge at the juncture of nutritional and emotional or mental health. As discussed in this book, America's addiction to sugar is linked to food cravings, energy level, premenstrual syndrome (PMS) and seasonal affective disorder (SAD), depression, stress, brain power, and sleep patterns.

Studies from Rockefeller University, Johns Hopkins University, Yale University, Cornell University, the University of Michigan in Ann Arbor, and many more research centers have uncovered fascinating links between sugar and the brain chemicals that influence who we are, what we do, and how we think. The combination of sugar and fat (that is, what I call sweet-and-creamy combinations, such as ice cream, chocolate candy, and cookies) might reprogram our brains, our emotions, or our behaviors in ways only recently begun to be explored.

The link between sugar and mood is but one example of how what we eat can affect how we feel. Other nutritional factors—from too little of certain vitamins and minerals to too much caffeine—can influence a person's mood, sleep patterns, and behavior. Even when and how much you eat could be causing your afternoon doldrums or interrupting a good night's sleep. That's why the premise of this book is that you not only are what you eat but that your moods may dictate what foods you choose.

How to Break the Cycle

Your daily food choices fuel your body and your mood. That is, they affect your energy, your sleep habits, and your ability to cope with stress. Likewise, your food choices reflect your body's needs and your moods. For example, people tend to turn to sweets, chocolate, or carbohydrates when they are depressed. However, these food choices help fuel the depression from which they stem and establish a potentially destructive cycle. Repeated poor food choices can set fundamental patterns in the production of the brain chemicals that regulate appetite and mood, so that you become a victim of mood swings, food cravings, poor sleep habits, and other emotional problems—not because they are inherent in your personality but because of poor eating habits. This intricate link between food and mood is discussed in chapter 1.

The good news is that you can change all of this and, more important, the change can be relatively painless. The Feeling Good Diet described in chapter 13, and discussed in practical terms in chapter 14, is the way to put your energy level, mood, and emotions back on track. It combines all the recommendations for a healthful diet with the specific foods, eating habits and patterns, and optimal nutrient intake necessary to improve your mood. How the Feeling Good Diet can be tailored to correct specific mood, sleep, stress, and other problems is discussed in detail throughout this book.

Take It Slow

Whether used for weight loss or better health, rigid diets don't work. For decades, Americans have fallen prey to every kind of get-thin-quick scheme. Millions of people have lost weight, but fewer than 5 percent of them maintain that weight loss, while most regain the weight *plus* extra pounds at the end of the dieting attempt. In fact, the average woman is five pounds heavier today than fifteen years ago. The same failure rate holds true for low-fat diets. Despite two decades of education on the ills of eating fat, Americans have reduced their fat intake by only a few percentage points, from 42 to 37 percent of total calories (the recommended level is less than 30 percent). It seems we can't live with fat—but *why* can't we live without it?

The problem might not be what but *how* we attempt to cut out the calories and change our eating habits. In short, "too much, too fast" is likely why people can't stick with a diet. For example, recent research shows that sugar and fat intakes are regulated not only by willpower but also by a stew of brain chemicals that rebel against drastic changes in food intake. Elliott Blass, Ph.D., at Cornell University and other researchers have found a link between cravings for sweet-and-creamy foods and the brain's morphinelike chemicals—called endorphins—that produce pleasurable feelings. He speculates that when people attempt restrictive diets or reduce their fat or sugar intake too quickly, they may throw these and other appetite-regulating brain chemicals into chaos, setting up a pendulum effect whereby dieters swing from abstinence to binge eating. A similar response may hold true for sugar alone. Chapter 1 explains how these brain chemicals are at the helm, controlling your appetite.

Research on the brain's appetite-control center has shown that making gradual changes in your diet is the most effective way to work with your brain's appetite-control chemicals and thus to avoid the pendulum effect. The Feeling Good Diet (chapter 13) and the sample menus in chapter 14 are based on this slow approach to dietary change. With these dietary guidelines, you'll learn how to make gradual changes that result in a personalized eating plan for feeling better.

I.

THE FOOD-MOOD LINK

CHAPTER ONE

How Food Affects Your Mood

What a miracle you are! With little or no effort you can remember simple and complicated facts and events, so that by the time you reach adulthood you are a rich canvas of experiences, memories, and relationships. You can feel a wide array of emotions, from ecstasy to grief to boredom to apathy. You can solve problems, untangle puzzles, develop plans, and form opinions. You have a unique sense of humor, a one-of-a-kind personality, and personal dreams and hopes for the future. At the very foundation of these traits and talents is an orchestra of cells and chemicals that allow your basic nature to develop and interact with the world. Who you are depends on how well that orchestra, called your nervous system, plays its music.

Getting to Know Your Neurons

The smallest functioning unit of the nervous system is the nerve cell, or *neuron*. This cell "talks" to other neurons and tissues by relaying electrical messages within the brain and between the brain and the rest of the body. To instinctively pull your hand away from a hot burner on the stove, blink an eye, think a thought, hear a noise and recognize its origin, memorize a song, walk, or perform one of the millions of other functions you do every day requires that thousands of neurons communicate efficiently. In fact, the adult brain has more than one hundred billion neurons and an equivalent number of "support cells" to help those neurons function.

The neuron is not your typical cell. While most cells in the body are relatively spherical, the neuron is shaped more like a tree. On one end are its branches, called dendrites, that reach out and allow the neuron to receive incoming messages from other nerve cells. These messages are relayed down the "trunk" of the neuron, called the axon, much as phone messages are carried on telephone wires. Nerve cell axons can vary in length from a fraction of a millimeter to three feet long. For example, the pressure-sensitive neurons in the feet send information to a neuron with an axon that travels all the way to the spinal cord in the lower back (see Illustration 1.1).

The messages eventually reach the roots, or *axon terminals*, of the neuron, which in turn bump up against dendrites on other nerve cells. The tiny space between two communicating nerve cells (the axon terminal of the sending neuron and the dendrites of the receiving neuron) is called the *synapse*.

To relay a message from one nerve cell to the next, the sending neuron must find a way to jump the gap, or synapse, to get to the other side. Without some way to cross this gap, messages would stop dead at the end of the sending neuron and all processes dependent on the nervous system would come to a halt.

To ensure that this does not happen, nerve chemicals called neurotransmitters are stored in tiny sacs at the end of the axons. The electrical message (a thought or feeling) traveling down an axon arrives at the terminal and causes some of these sacs to release their neurotransmitters. These nerve chemicals cross the synapse and send the electrical message to the next neuron, much as a baton is passed to the next runner in a relay race. Once the neurotransmitters have relayed the message, they are broken down by enzymes in the synaptic gap or are absorbed intact into the receiving neuron's storage space to be used again.

In this way, neurons communicate with each other and send "state-of-the-union" messages from the body to the brain. The brain processes this information by sending messages among its billions of neurons and then issues orders for action to the muscles and organs of the body—all within a split second and with no conscious effort on your part. Emotions, feelings, thoughts, hunger, and all other moods and behaviors are orchestrated by these neurons and their neurotransmitters.

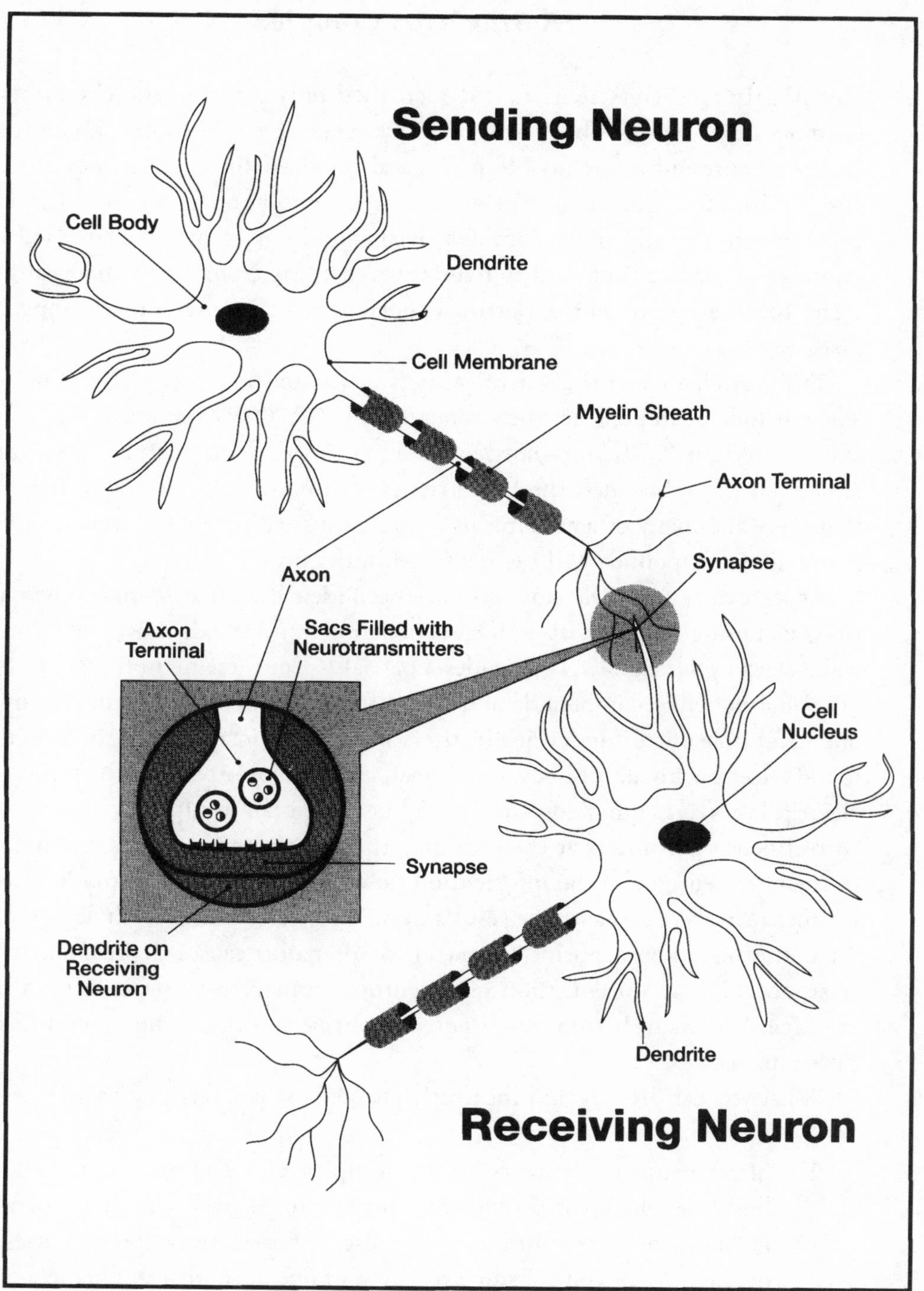

ILLUSTRATION 1.1

A *Star Wars* Complex

Until fairly recently scientists had identified only a few of the chemicals and hormones that regulate body and brain processes. Everyone knew about insulin and adrenalin and a few people had heard of adrenalin's cousin, noradrenalin, and insulin's foil, glucagon. But in the past twenty years the chemical story has become considerably more complex, with hundreds of newly identified compounds that have been found to regulate everything from mood and eating patterns to whether or not a person experiences headaches or develops heart disease.

The participants in this chemical network sound like a cast from *Star Wars*. They include neuropeptides such as neuropeptide Y (NPY, for short) and galanin, cholecystokinin (CCK, for short), amines, prostaglandins such as the prostacyclines and thromboxanes, the leukotrienes, and numerous hormones. It is likely that these and many other chemicals represent just the tip of the iceberg and that many more compounds will be identified in the future.

At least forty neurotransmitters have been identified that regulate nerve function, including memory, appetite, mental function, mood, movement, and the wake-sleep cycle. Table 1.1 provides a partial list of these neurotransmitters and other hormonelike compounds and their effects on appetite. Disruption of even one neurotransmitter dramatically alters nerve cell function and can have a profound effect on any or all body, emotional, and mental processes. In essence, if an electrical message comes down the axon but there is an insufficient amount of the correct neurotransmitter at the terminal, then the message is not communicated to the next neuron and the information flow stops. For example, too little of the neurotransmitter acetylcholine results in memory loss, while too little of the neurotransmitter norepinephrine (a cousin to adrenalin) causes depression. In contrast, too high a concentration of a neurotransmitter may overcommunicate a message. For example, too much norepinephrine results in the mental disorder called mania.

What you eat directly and indirectly affects how you feel in a variety of ways:

1. Many neurotransmitters are made up of either amino acids—the building blocks of protein that are obtained from the diet—or a fatlike substance called choline, also obtained from food. Consequently, when you consume too little of one or more of these dietary

TABLE 1.1 Hormones, Neurochemicals, and Other Chemicals That Influence When and What You Eat

CHEMICAL	LOCATION	INFLUENCE
Cholecystokinin	GI tract	Reduces food intake
Bombesin	GI tract	Reduces food intake
Gastrin-releasing peptide (GRP)	GI tract	Reduces food intake
Somatostatin	GI tract	Reduces food intake? (research inconclusive)
Litorin	GI tract	Reduces food intake
Motilin	GI tract	Increases food intake
Thyrotropin-releasing hormone (TRH) & derivatives	GI tract	Reduce food intake
Insulin	Pancreas	Increases food intake
Glucagon	Pancreas	Decreases food intake
Satietins	GI tract	Reduce food intake
Opioids (endorphins)	Brain	Increase fat intake (may be triggered by taste on tongue)
Serotonin	Brain	Low—increases carbohydrate intake; high—decreases carbohydrate intake
Norepinephrine	Brain	Increases intake of sweets
Neuropeptide Y (NPY)	Brain	Increases carbohydrate intake
Galanin	Brain	Increases fat intake
Corticotropin-releasing hormone	Brain	Inhibits appetite
Calcitonin gene-related peptide	GI tract	Inhibits appetite
Neurotensin	GI tract	Inhibits appetite
Dopamine	Brain	Inhibits appetite
Pancreatic polypeptide	Pancreas	Stimulates appetite
Neuropeptide YY	Brain	Stimulates appetite

building blocks, your body limits production of the neurotransmitter dependent on their availability and you experience changes in mood, appetite, and other behaviors.

2. Vitamins or minerals, such as vitamin B1, vitamin B2, vitamin B6, vitamin B12, folic acid, vitamin C, and magnesium, function as assembly-line workers in the manufacture of neurotransmitters; some aid neurotransmitter activity, as is the case with iron; and some protect neurotransmitters from damage, as is the case with selenium. If the diet does not supply ample amounts of these helpers, the neurotransmitters are not made or stored in sufficient amounts and you experience changes in mood, thinking, and behavior.

3. Neurotransmitters become more or less active depending on dietary intake. Either overconsuming or dramatically restricting a particular food, such as fat or carbohydrates, may trigger imbalances in neurotransmitters that then affect mood, eating habits, and other behaviors.

4. Nutrients such as protein, zinc, vitamin B6, iodine, folic acid, and vitamin B12 are essential for the normal development of the nervous system. Insufficient intake of these essential nutrients during development (from conception through the early years of life) can result in potentially irreversible damage to the nervous system, thus altering personality, mental function, and behavior.

5. Food additives such as monosodium glutamate (MSG) and chemicals such as tyramine, found in aged cheeses, can influence brain activity and result in mood changes or can interfere with the manufacture or release of neurotransmitters. Other additives may block the neurotransmitter so that the receiving neuron is unable to understand the message. Still other additives may increase the release or alter the structure of a neurotransmitter or affect the enzymes that normally regulate how much neurotransmitter remains in the gap between nerve cells. Any of these changes can have profound yet sometimes subtle effects on mood, behavior, and thinking processes.

The Diet-Made Compounds: Serotonin, Norepinephrine, and Acetylcholine

The four neurotransmitters that are manufactured directly from food components are serotonin, dopamine and norepinephrine, and acetylcholine. The levels and activity of these neurotransmitters are sensitive to food intake, and changes in dietary patterns can have profound effects on behavior, eating patterns, sleep, and energy level.

Serotonin: General Mood Regulator

Serotonin is one of those catchall neurotransmitters that performs a variety of functions. Ample amounts of serotonin in the nerve cells help regulate everything from sleep to mood to food intake to pain tolerance, while low serotonin levels produce insomnia, depression, food cravings, increased sensitivity to pain, aggressive behavior, and poor body-temperature regulation.

Serotonin levels are directly related to diet. This neurotransmitter is manufactured in the brain from an amino acid called tryptophan, which is found in protein-rich foods, with the help of vitamins B6 and B12, folic acid, and other nutrients. Serotonin levels are directly related to the amount of tryptophan in the blood and the availability of these vitamins. That is, as blood and brain levels of tryptophan rise and fall, and as vitamin intake fluctuates between optimal and deficient, so does the level of serotonin.

Ironically, eating a protein-rich meal *lowers* brain tryptophan and serotonin levels, while eating a carbohydrate-rich snack has the opposite effect. Tryptophan is a large amino acid that shares an entry gate into the brain with several other large amino acids such as tyrosine. When you eat a protein-rich meal you flood the blood with both tryptophan and its "competing" amino acids, and they all fight for entry into the brain. Only a small amount of tryptophan gets through the blood-brain barrier (the gatekeeper between the body and the brain), so serotonin levels do not rise appreciably. As a result, a person may crave carbohydrate-rich foods such as desserts or starches, feel more depressed, sleep less soundly, or experience a lower tolerance to pain (see Illustration 1.2).

From Food to Mood
Dietary protein→↑blood amino-acid levels, including tryptophan→variety of amino acids compete for entry into the brain→relatively low amounts of tryptophan enter brain→moderate to low serotonin levels→stored in the axon terminal of the nerve cell.

ILLUSTRATION 1.2 Food, Mood, and the Blood-Brain Barrier

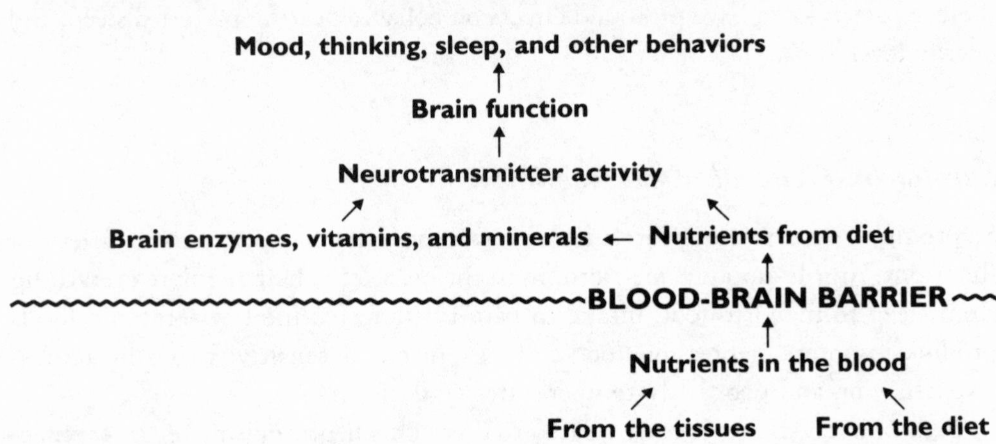

In contrast, a carbohydrate-rich meal triggers the release of insulin from the pancreas. This hormone causes most amino acids floating in the blood to be absorbed into the body's (not the brain's) cells—all, that is, except tryptophan, which remains in the bloodstream at relatively high levels. With the competition removed, tryptophan can freely enter the brain, causing serotonin levels to rise. The high serotonin levels, in turn, increase feelings of calmness or drowsiness, improve sleep patterns, increase pain tolerance, and reduce cravings for carbohydrate-rich foods (see "Diet and Serotonin Levels," page 17).

From Food to Mood
Dietary carbohydrate→↑blood insulin levels→↓blood amino-acid levels and↑blood tryptophan levels→↑brain tryptophan levels—(vitamin B6, B12, folic acid, and enzyme)→↑serotonin→stored in the axon terminal of the nerve cell.

Diet and Serotonin Levels

Different food components have different effects on serotonin.

- *Sugar:* Triggers release of insulin, which lowers blood levels of most large amino acids and increases blood levels of tryptophan. As a result there is a short-term increase in brain serotonin levels.
- *Starch:* Triggers release of insulin, which lowers blood levels of most large amino acids and increases blood levels of tryptophan. As a result there is a long-term increase in brain serotonin levels.
- *Vitamin B6:* Aids in the manufacture of serotonin. A deficiency of this B vitamin reduces serotonin production and affects mood and food cravings.
- *Estrogen:* May inhibit vitamin B6 status and decrease brain serotonin levels by its effects on NPY.
- *Tryptophan:* Raises blood, then brain levels of tryptophan, which increases serotonin production.
- *Protein:* Raises blood levels of large amino acids and decreases blood levels of tryptophan. As a result there is a decrease in brain serotonin levels and increase in cravings for carbohydrates.
- *Fat:* There is no documented effect of fat on serotonin levels.

Dopamine and Norepinephrine: Mood and Energy Elevators

Dopamine and norepinephrine (also called noradrenalin) are manufactured from the amino acid called tyrosine with the help of several other nutrients, including folic acid, magnesium, and vitamin B12. Low levels of dopamine and norepinephrine are associated with an increased incidence of depression and other mood disorders, while increasing the levels of these neurotransmitters by consuming more tyrosine might improve mood, alertness, ability to cope with stress, and mental functioning.

From Food to Mood
Dietary protein→↑blood tyrosine levels→↑brain tyrosine levels—(enzyme)→↑dopa—(vitamin B6, magnesium, and enzyme)→↑dopamine→stored in the axon terminal of the nerve cell *or*—(vitamin C and enzyme)→↑norepinephrine→stored in the axon terminal of the nerve cell.

Like tryptophan, tyrosine is found in protein-rich foods. But unlike tryptophan, tyrosine levels in the blood and brain rise when a person consumes pure tyrosine or, to a lesser extent, eats a protein-rich meal. The same conditions that lower tryptophan levels—that is, high levels of competing amino acids and no insulin—are the very conditions that favor tyrosine. Consequently, tyrosine and tryptophan are at odds with each other: for tryptophan-serotonin levels to rise, tyrosine levels must be low; conversely, when tyrosine and its neurotransmitters are in full swing, tryptophan levels are moderate to low (see "Amino Acid Supplements," page 19).

This seesaw relationship between tyrosine and tryptophan has a similar effect on appetite. A person who eats a carbohydrate-rich breakfast such as pancakes or waffles will experience a rise in serotonin levels that shuts off the desire to eat more carbohydrates. At the next meal, the person is likely to select a low-carbohydrate, high-protein selection such as a tuna fish sandwich with milk, which will raise dopamine-norepinephrine levels. And so a person swings back and forth from carbohydrates to proteins throughout the day, in part because of fluctuations in these neurotransmitters. To examine your own mood swings and energy levels, try the quiz on page 20.

While raising blood levels of tryptophan always increases the manufacture of serotonin in the brain, raising blood levels of tyrosine increases dopamine and norepinephrine levels only if (1) the nerve cells are using these neurotransmitters and need more; or (2) the nerve cell numbers are reduced, as in aging. In the latter case, fewer cells are working harder (that is, they are sending more messages and need more neurotransmitters) in an attempt to compensate for the dwindling numbers of cells.

Amino Acid Supplements: A Word of Caution

Just because an amino acid is safe when consumed in food, that does not mean it is safe when consumed alone in large quantities. In fact, amino acid supplements are more like drugs than nutrients. In foods, amino acids are present in small amounts and in proper ratios to each other. However, these building blocks for powerful neurotransmitters could possibly have far-reaching effects on a person's mental function and overall health. Michael Trulson, Ph.D., a professor of anatomy at Texas A&M University College of Medicine, reports, for example, that large supplemental doses of tryptophan can cause liver damage unless carefully monitored by a physician.

In addition, there is much more to be learned about how these amino acids function. For example, the amino acid phenylalanine was once thought to increase brain levels of norepinephrine, but later it was discovered that this amino acid had the opposite effect of lowering neurotransmitter levels.

Finally, another danger of self-medicating with amino acid supplements is their potential interaction with other medications. Tryptophan should not be taken with mood-elevating medications such as Prozac or the MAO inhibitors. These drugs function by allowing serotonin to linger longer at the receiving nerve cell, thus increasing the length and strength of the stimulation to that nerve cell. Further elevating serotonin levels by supplementing with tryptophan could intensify the effects of these drugs to potentially dangerous levels.

Acetylcholine: The Memory Manager

When it comes to choline, the food-mood link is straightforward. Unlike amino acids, which must compete for entry into the brain, the fatlike substance choline has no competitors. Consequently, the more you consume, the more gets to the brain, where it is used as a building block for another neurotransmitter called acetylcholine. This nerve chemical is important in memory and in general mental function, while dwindling acetylcholine levels, which are common with aging, result in memory loss and reduced cognitive capability. A study at the University of Massachusetts at Worcester showed that healthy people who took a drug that blocks acetylcholine flunked a memory test, but when they took a drug that increased acetylcholine levels, they passed the test. Other studies have shown that maintaining optimal choline levels in the brain is associated with increased acetylcholine levels, improved learning ability, and a slowing, if not a halting, of certain forms of age-related memory loss.

QUIZ 1.1 What Do You Eat and How Do You Feel?

Rate your mood before and after you eat, to monitor how your diet might affect even temporary mood and energy levels. Rate each mood from 0 (does not apply) to 5 (strongly applies) before you eat lunch. Then rate yourself again within one hour of eating.

MOOD	BEFORE LUNCH	AFTER LUNCH
Agreeable		
Alert		
Calm		
Clearheaded		
Clumsy		
Contented		
Coordinated		
Discontented		
Drowsy		
Energetic		
Excited		
Feisty		
Friendly		
Full		
Happy		
Hostile		
Hungry		
Interested		
Lethargic		
Muddled		
Quick-witted		
Relaxed		
Sad		
Sluggish		
Tense		
Tired		
Tranquil		
Troubled		
Withdrawn		

What did you eat for lunch? ______________________________

From Food to Mood
Dietary choline→↑blood choline→↑brain choline→↑manufacture of acetylcholine.

The Survival Chemicals

While single nutrients in the diet can make or break a person's mood, so can an army of nerve chemicals produced by the hypothalamus, which is the appetite-control center in your brain. According to Sarah Leibowitz, Ph.D., a professor of neurobiology at Rockefeller University in New York City, it is no coincidence that this region of the brain is also the control tower for reproduction. The ability to reproduce, and thus keep our species alive, requires that the body maintain well-stocked energy and fat stores.

Consequently, the neurons that regulate sexuality and the neurons that control eating are in constant communication. When these cells receive messages that fuel stores are threatened (as a consequence of strict dieting or even after an overnight fast), they send out an array of appetite-stimulating neurotransmitters, including neuropeptide Y (NPY) and galanin, to perk up our desire to eat. As far as these nerve cells are concerned, making sure you eat enough is essential to survival.

The Role of NPY

NPY, in combination with blood glucose levels, serotonin, noradrenalin, and another nerve chemical called GABA (gamma-amino-butyric acid), turns on your desire for carbohydrate-rich foods. In essence, as NPY levels go up, so does your desire for sweet or starchy foods. The link is clear. Inject NPY into the hypothalamus of animals and they start munching carbohydrates and ignoring fatty foods. Measure NPY levels in the brains of animals and, sure enough, the higher their NPY levels the more they enjoy their carbohydrates, while carbohydrate cravings dwindle as NPY levels decrease.

NPY jump-starts the eating cycle in the morning. Sugar stores (called glycogen) in the muscles and liver are drained during the night as we sleep, so waning blood-sugar levels send a message to the brain to release NPY. This neurotransmitter may be why we prefer waffles, pancakes, toast, jelly, doughnuts, and other carbohydrate-rich foods in the morning.

From Mood to Food
↓glycogen (sugar) stores→↓blood-sugar levels→brain→hypothalamus→↑NPY→↑desire for and consumption of carbohydrate-rich foods→ ↓NPY.

Stress and strict dieting also trigger NPY production, probably as a survival mechanism to get more quick-energy carbohydrates into the system. In this case, a stress hormone called corticosterone from the adrenal gland triggers NPY production and activity.

From Mood to Food
Stress, dieting, etc.→↑corticosterone from adrenals→brain→hypothalamus→↑NPY→↑desire for and consumption of carbohydrate-rich foods.

Galanin at a Glance

A different set of nerve chemicals from the hypothalamus regulate your intake of dietary fat. These include galanin and the endorphins. As galanin levels rise, so does your desire to eat foods that contain fat. The more galanin produced, the more fat you eat. For example, when galanin is injected into the hypothalamus of laboratory animals, they select more fat-laden and less carbohydrate-rich foods. In contrast, drugs that turn off galanin activity also reduce an animal's desire for fats.

Besides increasing our craving for fat, galanin affects how much of that dietary fat is stored as body fat—again, probably as a result of the body's ensuring that long-term energy stores are maintained for survival and reproduction.

What causes galanin to be released? The breakdown of body fat, as occurs during dieting or when several hours have passed between meals, releases fat particles into the blood that travel to the hypothalamus and trigger the release of galanin. Your cravings for fat-containing foods, from chocolate to a hamburger, are your body's way of safeguarding its fat (that is, its long-term energy) supply. Reproductive hormones such as estrogen, and possibly the endorphins, also turn on galanin, while the neurotransmitter dopamine might turn off galanin release.

From Mood to Food
Dieting, food restriction, estrogen, etc.→↑galanin→↑desire for and consumption of foods that contain fat→↓galanin.

NPY and galanin levels fluctuate during the day. While NPY levels are highest in the morning, galanin levels begin to rise by early afternoon and peak in the evening. The NPY-induced desire for carbohydrates is a call for quick-energy fuel in the morning, and the galanin-induced desire for fattier foods later in the day is possibly the body's attempt to store long-term energy in anticipation of the overnight fast (see Illustration 1.3).

The Natural High of Endorphins

The endorphins are the body's natural morphinelike chemicals that help boost your tolerance to pain, calm you during times of stress, and produce feelings of

ILLUSTRATION 1.3 The Ups and Downs of NPY and Galanin

Under ideal conditions—when NPY and galanin are functioning in balance—these two neurotransmitters rise and fall in a seesaw fashion during the day. NPY levels are highest in the morning and drop off in the afternoon as galanin levels are rising. Stress, strict dieting, and other conditions can throw off this balance, triggering changes in eating habits and mood.

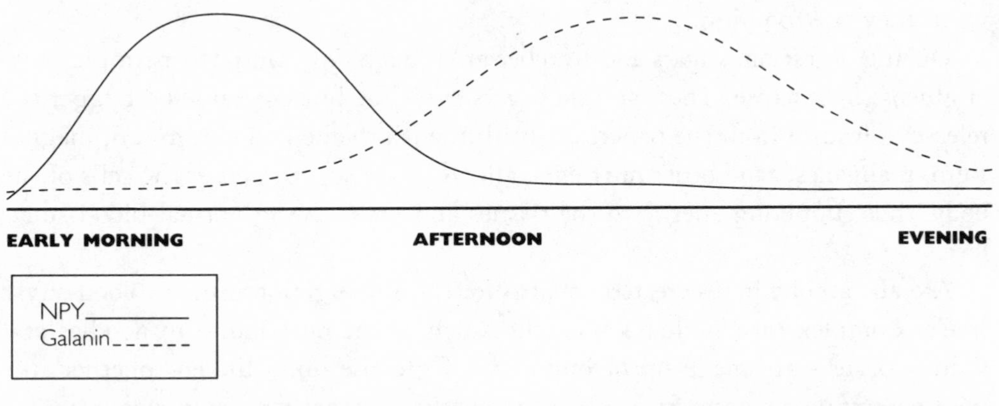

euphoria and satisfaction. They are released during intense exercise and are the underlying cause of "runner's high"—that feeling of joy and of being at peace with the world that many athletes experience during and following exercise. Laughter, soothing music, meditation, and other pleasurable experiences also raise endorphin levels. Endorphin levels are at an all-time high during times of stress—possibly the body's attempt to regain calm.

These mood-elevating nerve chemicals are linked to appetite. When laboratory animals are injected with a medication that increases endorphin levels, they eat more. In contrast, medications that block endorphins are associated with a reduced desire to eat. Endorphin levels also might be related to body weight—that is, as endorphin levels increase, so does body weight. Finally, endorphins are suspected to trigger cravings for sweet-and-creamy foods, possibly in combination with galanin. On the other hand, even the taste of something sweet on the tongue is suspected to release endorphins in the brain, making the sweet treat doubly pleasurable.

The Highs and Lows of Your Blood Sugar

Blood sugar is at the helm of appetite and mood control. An army of hormones, including glucagon from the pancreas, epinephrine and the glucocorticoids from the adrenal glands, and thyroxin from the thyroid gland, are involved in raising blood-sugar levels when they fall below normal concentrations. In contrast, insulin balances the effects of these hormones by lowering blood-sugar levels when they rise too high.

During digestion, sugars and starches are broken down into their simple units of glucose or fructose. These simple sugars enter the bloodstream and trigger the release of insulin from the pancreas. Insulin, with the help of chromium, magnesium, manganese, and other nutrients, allows blood sugar to enter the cells of the body, thus supplying energy to the tissues and maintaining normal blood-sugar levels.

Are all carbohydrates created equal? No. Insulin secretion mirrors blood-sugar levels. Complex carbohydrates—starches such as the ones found in noodles and kidney beans—are made up of hundreds of glucose units linked together like high-energy pearls on a string. In general, they are broken down slowly in the digestive tract and enter the bloodstream gradually, producing a mild and progressive elevation in blood-sugar and insulin levels. In contrast, concentrated sugars—such as table sugar or sugary foods—enter rapidly into the blood and trigger a large release of insulin from the pancreas. Insulin funnels the excess sugar out of the blood and into the cells. Consequently, blood-sugar levels drop quickly, sometimes to below normal levels, while elevated insulin levels linger for hours. The sugar-induced rapid rise in insulin might arouse hunger signals, according to Judith Rodin, Ph.D., professor of psychology and psychiatry at Yale University in New Haven. Her research shows that people are hungriest and like sweet tastes more when insulin levels are high (see "A Sugar by Any Other Name," below).

Interestingly, blood insulin levels also correspond to body-fat stores. The more often and the longer blood insulin levels remain high, the more likely a person is to accumulate excess body fat and battle a weight problem. Since body fat is

---

A Sugar by Any Other Name

To most people, sugar is what you sprinkle on cereal, put into your coffee, or mix into a batch of cookies. Although this type of sugar—called white, granulated, or table sugar—is the most common, there actually are more than 100 substances that have a sweet taste and are classified as sugar.

The simple sugars, or monosaccharides—glucose, fructose, and galactose—are the fundamental units of sugar and other carbohydrates. *Glucose* is the primary sugar in corn syrup. *Fructose*, or fruit sugar, is found in apples, cherries, pears, grapes, and other fruits; honey; and high-fructose corn syrup (HFCS), an increasingly popular processed sugar used in soft drinks and other foods. *Galactose* is not found alone in foods.

These simple sugars also combine in foods to form double sugars, or disaccharides, such as sucrose (1 glucose unit + 1 fructose unit), lactose (1 glucose unit + 1 galactose unit), and maltose (2 glucose units). *Sucrose* is processed from sugar cane or sugar beets. White table sugar, brown sugar, turbinado sugar, and the sugar in molasses are sucrose. Sucrose is also found naturally in fruits such as bananas, apples, and oranges; cooked dried beans and peas; and vegetables such as peas, onions, and carrots.

Lactose is the sugar in milk products, while *maltose* is more commonly called malt sugar. Complex carbohydrates (or polysaccharides), found in grains and vegetables, are formed when between 10 and 1,000 glucose units are strung together much like beads on a string.

---

linked to galanin activity (and fat intake), and insulin is linked to serotonin activity (and carbohydrate intake), it is likely that these tissues, hormones, and brain neurotransmitters (and possibly hormones from the adrenal glands, such as the stress hormones) work as a team, with imbalances resulting in powerful urges to eat too much and weight gain (see "The Effects of Dietary Habits on Blood Glucose," below).

Nature Versus Nurture

Just as you are born with a particular shape to your nose and a unique color in your eyes, and are destined to reach a certain height (assuming you are not significantly malnourished), you also are born with an inherent neurotransmitter profile. In the laboratory, rats with individual "personalities" select different combinations of foods. Some rats love fat and, if allowed to eat all they want of whatever they want, choose up to 60 percent of their calories from fat. Most of these fat-craving rats are obese, but not all of them. Other rats love their carbohydrates and ignore the fat. Most of them are lean, unless their preference is for the sweet

The Effects of Dietary Habits on Blood Glucose

Skip a meal	Blood glucose slowly drops and, in the case of breakfast, may only partially rise to normal levels if food intake is delayed too long.
Skip two meals	Limited glycogen stores are mobilized to maintain blood-sugar levels. These stores are exhausted within twenty-four to forty-eight hours of fasting.
Eat simple sugars	Blood sugar quickly (within ten to fifteen minutes) rises to above-normal levels, followed within twenty-five to forty minutes by a dramatic drop in blood sugar to subnormal levels.
Eat starches	Blood-sugar levels slowly, steadly rise for up to four hours.
Eat protein and fat	Blood-sugar levels are stabilized for up to four hours.
Drink alcohol	Blood-glucose levels may be slightly reduced for a short time—less than one hour.
Drink caffeine	Blood-sugar levels rise in the first hour, followed by a drop in glucose to subnormal levels.

carbohydrates such as sugar, in which case they are more likely to be overweight. These and other experiments lend credence to the theory that all people do not have the same food preferences and responses to foods.

You may not be able to change your genes, but you can coax your neurotransmitters a little through a few simple dietary and lifestyle habit changes. Even slight changes in your appetite- and mood-control chemicals can have dramatic effects on your mood, eating habits, sleep patterns, ability to think and remember, and personality. If your eating habits are fueling your mood problems, even minor changes in when and what you eat could help you feel and think your best.

How Are You Eating? A Self-Assessment

You can't decide where you are going until you know where you have been. So before reading further, take a few minutes to complete the following dietary self-assessment. Keep in mind that the more honest and accurate you are, the more valuable feedback you will have on your current eating habits, which will help you decide what eating patterns need changing and which ones support feeling good. The results of this assessment can be used in conjunction with the Food and Mood Journal on page 297 to help you tailor the Feeling Good Diet (see chapter 13) to your personal food preferences, lifestyle, and nutritional needs.

QUIZ 1.2 A Self-Assessment of Your Diet

Choose the answer that most closely describes your eating habits, even if it is not a perfect fit. There are no right or wrong answers. This self-assessment should provide feedback on your current eating habits, so you can compare them to the Feeling Good Diet described in chapter 13. This feedback can be used to plan how and what you want to change.

Dietary Questions

1. What is the best example of your most typical eating style?
   a. I eat five or six mini-meals and snacks evenly divided throughout the day.
   b. I eat three square meals a day.

c. I nibble all day, perhaps eating eight or more times in a day.

d. I eat sporadically. One day I may skip breakfast and lunch, then eat a large dinner. The next day I may eat breakfast and several snacks, but skip dinner.

2. What is your average calorie intake?

a. More than 2,500 calories a day.

b. 1,600 to 2,500 calories a day.

c. 1,000 to 1,600 calories a day.

d. Because I diet frequently, my calorie intake varies from fewer than 1,000 calories to more than 2,500 calories a day.

3. Do your eating habits fluctuate?

a. Rarely. I usually eat about the same types of foods at about the same time during the day.

b. Somewhat. I might skip a meal or eat larger or smaller meals a couple of times during the week.

c. Often. My eating habits vary almost daily.

d. Always. I regularly skip meals, grab snacks on the run, forget to eat all day, then eat a large dinner, and/or switch from one eating style to another.

4. Do you eat breakfast?

a. Yes, always.

b. Usually, at least four days a week.

c. Sometimes (fewer than four days a week).

d. Seldom.

5. If you eat a morning meal, which of the following best represents your typical breakfast?

a. Cereal or toast, milk, fruit.

b. Eggs, bacon, toast with butter, coffee.

c. Doughnut and coffee.

d. Coffee.

6. Do you eat lunch?

a. Yes, always.

b. Usually, at least four days a week.

c. Sometimes (fewer than four days a week).
d. Seldom.

7. If you eat a midday meal, which of the following best represents your typical lunch?

a. A grain such as pasta or bread, meat, and a vegetable, or a large salad that contains some meat or cheese and a roll.
b. A large meal, such as a hot roast beef sandwich with gravy and mashed potatoes.
c. A fast-food lunch, such as a hamburger, French fries, and a beverage.
d. Coffee, a candy bar, or soda pop.

8. Do you eat an evening meal?

a. Yes, always.
b. Usually, at least four days a week.
c. Sometimes (fewer than four days a week).
d. Seldom.

9. If you eat an evening meal, which of the following best represents your typical dinner?

a. I keep dinner light and usually have small portions of fish, salad, pasta, and/or fruit.
b. Dinner is my biggest meal and may include generous portions of meat, vegetables, and bread or potato.
c. A frozen entree or a meal-replacement drink.
d. I usually skip dinner or grab something from a fast-food restaurant.

10. What do you eat most frequently for a snack?

a. Fruits and vegetables, yogurt, whole-grain breads.
b. Cookies, potato chips, or granola bars.
c. Candy bar, doughnut, or French fries.
d. Nothing. I seldom or never eat between meals.

11. What types of foods do you eat between dinner and bedtime?

a. Fresh fruits and vegetables, whole grains, or low-fat milk products.
b. Snack foods such as popcorn, crackers, potato chips, or other convenience foods.
c. Chocolate, cola soft drinks, hot cocoa, or spicy snacks.

d. I do most of my overeating in the evening, including large bowls of ice cream with chocolate sauce or second servings of leftovers from dinner.

12. How frequently do you have strong cravings for starchy or sugary foods?

a. Seldom.

b. Only during certain times of the month or year, such as the week before my menstrual period or in the winter.

c. Frequently.

d. Daily, and the urges often lead to overconsumption of the craved food.

13. How many servings of unsweetened fruits and plain vegetables (fresh fruit and vegetables or fruits canned in their own juice and plain frozen vegetables) do you eat in an average day (one serving = one piece or ½ cup)?

a. Eight or more.

b. Five to seven.

c. Three or four.

d. Fewer than three.

14. Of those fresh fruits, how many are vitamin C–rich selections, such as oranges, grapefruit, or cantaloupe?

a. Three or more.

b. Two.

c. One.

d. Fewer than one each day.

15. Of those fresh or plain frozen vegetables, how many are dark green, such as romaine lettuce, spinach, or broccoli, or dark orange, such as sweet potatoes and carrots?

a. Three or more.

b. Two.

c. One.

d. Fewer than one each day.

16. How many servings of grains, such as bread, cereal, pasta, rice, or tortillas, do you typically eat each day (one serving = one slice of bread, one tortilla, or ½ cup cooked grains)?

a. More than eight.

b. Six to eight.

c. Five to six.

d. Fewer than five.

17. Of these grains, how often are the choices whole grain?

a. All the time.

b. One out of every two choices is whole grain.

c. Occasionally I select whole grains.

d. Seldom or never.

18. Of these grains, how often do you choose crackers, waffles, sugar-coated cereals, tortilla chips, buttered popcorn, or other grains that contain fat and/or sugar?

a. Seldom or never.

b. Occasionally—two or three times a week.

c. Frequently—once a day.

d. Most of the time—more than once a day.

19. How many servings daily of extra-lean red meat, chicken, fish, and cooked dried beans and peas do you eat (one serving = 3 ounces of meat or ¾ cup of beans)?

a. Three to four.

b. Two.

c. One.

d. None.

20. How often do you trim the visible fat from red meat before cooking, remove the skin before cooking chicken, and cook without using oils and fats such as butter and margarine?

a. Always.

b. Usually.

c. Sometimes.

d. Seldom or never.

21. How many 8-ounce glasses of milk or 8-ounce servings of yogurt do you consume in a day?

a. Three to four.

b. Two.

c. One.

d. None.

22. What type of milk products, including milk, yogurt, and cheese, do you usually consume?

a. Nonfat—nonfat milk; nonfat yogurt; fat-free cheeses.

b. Very low-fat—1 percent low-fat milk; yogurt made from a mixture of nonfat and low-fat milk; low-fat cheeses.

c. Low-fat—2 percent low-fat milk; yogurt made from 2 percent milk; reduced-calorie or "light" cheeses.

d. Whole milk—yogurt made from whole milk; regular cheeses.

23. How often do you snack on cookies, candy, fruit-flavored yogurt, and other sweets (one snack serving = two small cookies, one small candy bar, one 8-ounce yogurt)?

a. Once a day or less.

b. Twice a day.

c. Several times a day.

d. Several times a day and often in large amounts; I'll eat half a bag or more of cookies in the evening.

24. What do you usually eat for dessert?

a. I seldom eat dessert, and if I do it is fresh fruit.

b. Small servings of nonfat ice cream or sorbet, oatmeal cookies, or angel food cake.

c. Moderate-size servings of ice cream, pie, pastries, cake, or cheesecake.

d. Large servings of pie or cake and ice cream, candy, or other sweets. Sometimes I eat right from the cake or pie without portioning off a serving.

25. How often do you add sugar to your foods, including coffee or tea, cereal and fruit?

a. Never.

b. Sometimes.

c. Frequently.

d. All the time.

26. What is your typical weekly consumption of soda pop, including diet sodas?

a. None to three 12-ounce cans each week.

b. Four to six 12-ounce cans each week.

c. Seven to ten 12-ounce cans each week.

d. More than ten 12-ounce cans each week.

27. How many cups (5-ounce servings) of caffeinated coffee do you drink on a typical day?

a. I don't drink caffeinated coffee.

b. Two to three 5-ounce cups or fewer.

c. Four 5-ounce cups or fewer.

d. Five or more 5-ounce cups.

28. What is your average alcohol consumption for the week? (One drink is a 6-ounce glass of wine, 1 ounce of hard liquor, or a 12-ounce can of beer.)

a. I average fewer than five drinks a week or do not drink at all.

b. I average a drink a day.

c. I average ten drinks a week.

d. I average two drinks or more each day.

29. How often do you bake, steam, broil, poach, or grill food, rather than fry, sauté, or use sauces and gravies that contain fat?

a. Always.

b. Usually.

c. At least 50 perent of the time.

d. Seldom or never.

30. How often do you cook in water, broth, or other no-fat liquids?

a. Always.

b. Usually.

c. Often.

d. Seldom or never.

31. How often do you use tomato-based or no-fat sauces on pasta, rather than creamy sauces or sauces with fatty meats?

a. Always.

b. Usually.

c. Often.

d. Seldom or never.

32. How much salad dressing do you use?

a. I use nonfat salad dressing or use 2 teaspoons or less of oil-based dressing on my salads.

b. I use low-fat dressing and limit the serving to 2 tablespoons.
c. I use regular salad dressing and limit the serving to 3 tablespoons.
d. I use generous servings of regular salad dressings (more than 3 tablespoons) and eat salads regularly.

33. How often do you eat in fast-food restaurants?
a. Less than once a week.
b. Once a week.
c. Twice a week.
d. More than twice a week.

34. How often do you use butter, margarine, oils, whipping cream, sour cream, whipped toppings, mayonnaise, and shortening?
a. Seldom.
b. Once a day.
c. Several times a day.
d. I couldn't cook or eat without these foods.

35. How often do you read labels and select foods that contain 3 grams of fat or less for every 100 calories?
a. Always.
b. Usually.
c. Often.
d. Seldom or never.

36. How many glasses of plain water do you drink daily?
a. Six or more glasses.
b. Four to five glasses.
c. Two to three glasses.
d. I seldom drink water.

37. How often do you limit intake of salty foods and avoid using salt in food preparation or at the table?
a. Always.
b. Usually.
c. Often.
d. Seldom or never.

38. What is your current weight?

a. I'm within 10 percent of my desirable body weight.

b. I'm approximately 15 pounds or more overweight.

c. I'm approximately 15 pounds or more underweight.

d. I'm more than 20 pounds overweight.

39. How often have you dieted to lose weight in the past?

a. I've been on fewer than three weight-loss diets in my life.

b. I've been on four to six weight-loss diets in my life.

c. I've been on seven to ten weight-loss diets in my life.

d. I've lost count. I'm always trying new diets to lose weight.

40. What type of supplement(s) do you take?

a. When my diet is less than optimal, I've taken a moderate-dose multiple vitamin and mineral supplement.

b. A moderate-dose vitamin supplement.

c. I'm not sure what to take, so sometimes I supplement and sometimes I don't.

d. I know my eating habits are not the best, but I don't take supplements or I fluctuate between not taking anything to taking large doses of single-nutrient supplements.

General Health Questions

41. How often do you feel, look, act, and function your best?

a. Most of the time.

b. At least 50 percent of the time.

c. I'm down more often than I'm up.

d. I seldom feel good.

42. How frequently do you engage in planned exercise?

a. Five or more times a week for at least 30 minutes each time.

b. Three or more times a week for at least 30 minutes each time.

c. Fewer than three times a week.

d. I don't exercise.

43. How frequently do you take time out for yourself—read a book, take a walk in the woods, visit with a friend, take a hot bath, work on hobbies?

a. Daily.

b. At least a couple of times a week.

c. Once a month.

d. I don't remember the last time I had a moment's peace.

44. How often do you discuss your personal concerns with a close friend or family member?

a. Daily or at least several times a week.

b. Occasionally, when things get bad.

c. Seldom.

d. I have no one to talk things out with.

The following questions will not affect your score on the above quiz. Your answers to these questions will help you assess your eating habits.

45. Do your eating habits change when you are sad, irritable, depressed, or lonely; when you are happy, excited, stressed, or with friends; or when you are tired, lacking in sleep, or not feeling up to par? Yes_____ No_____

If yes, when and how do your eating habits change? ______________________________

____

46. What foods do you avoid?____

____

47. Why do you avoid these foods? ____

____

48. Are you currently seeing a physician for any disease or problem? Yes_____ No_____

If yes, explain. ____

____

49. Do you have a personal or family history of depression, insomnia, stress-related health problems, weight problems, PMS, seasonal affective disorder, or other emotional or mood disturbances? Yes_____ No_____

If yes, explain. ____

____

If yes, were the symptoms serious enough to require medical attention?
Yes_____ No_____

50. Do your eating habits change during certain times of the month or during the winter? Yes_____ No_____

51. Do you frequently develop colds, infections, or other signs of a weakened immune system? Yes_____ No_____

52. Do you take any medications, including aspirin, birth control pills or estrogen, antibiotics, or heart disease or blood pressure medications? Yes_____ No_____

If yes, which ones?____

____

53. Do you use tobacco or are you frequently around people who smoke?
Yes_____ No_____

Scoring:

Review your answers and tally your score for questions 1 through 44, giving yourself:

2 points for every *a* answer
1 point for every *b* answer
0 point for every *c* answer
-1 point for every *d* answer

Remember, this assessment is feedback on your current eating and lifestyle behaviors. As you read this book, return to this assessment to compare how you have been eating to the dietary recommendations for each emotional or mental problem. What eating habits need changing? Which ones can stay the same? After following the Feeling Good Diet, complete this assessment again (give yourself at least six months) and see how far you have come!

If you scored:

70 to 88: Congratulations! Your dietary habits are excellent. Review those questions on which you scored fewer than two points and see if you still can find room for improvement.
51 to 69: Very good. Your diet is in the ballpark. However, a few changes could do wonders for your emotional and physical well-being.
37 to 50: Caution. Your dietary habits are average, which means you probably consume too much of the wrong foods and not enough of the right ones. Your diet is likely to be a contributing factor to your mood problems.
Fewer than 37: Warning: what and how you are eating are major contributing factors to how you feel. The good news is you have lots of room for improvement!

For questions 45 through 53:
45. If you answered yes, read chapters 4, 6, 7, 8, and 9.
46 and 47. Read chapters 10, 11, and/or 12.
48, 49, and 52. Many emotional problems stem from physical ailments or even nutrient-drug interactions. Your physician can explain how a medication, illness, or treatment might affect your eating habits and mood.
49 and 50. For information on PMS and SAD, read chapter 5.
51. If you answered yes, read chapter 7.
53. Smoking is a primary factor in stress and insomnia. If you answered yes, read chapters 7 and 9.

Chapter Two

Do You Crave Carbohydrates?

- Do you find it impossible to eat just one cookie?
- Are you unable to concentrate on work knowing there is a candy bar in your desk drawer?
- Is the thought of fresh bread or a warm bagel too tempting to resist?
- When faced with a box of chocolates, a glazed doughnut, or a blueberry torte, do you find yourself in a tug-of-war between the angel of good intentions and the devil of desire?

Most people occasionally find it hard to "just say no" to a sweet treat or other carbohydrate-laden snack. For example, you may have craved a milkshake or fantasized about ordering French fries after vacationing in Mexico, been willing to die for a bagel after completing a "protein-only" weight-loss diet, or given in to a craving for ice cream on a hot day.

Some people, however, battle cravings daily and are virtually addicted to carbohydrate foods. Seemingly level-headed people can become anxious or irritable if they don't have their morning doughnut or afternoon soda pop. Nothing will stand in the way of their satisfying a chocolate craving. This is not necessarily a sign of a lack of willpower or a split personality, so put aside the guilt. Research is uncovering a far more complex and deep-seated cause of those irresistible urges. Are you plagued by carbohydrate cravings? Take the brief quiz on page 40.

QUIZ 2.1 Are You a "Carbo Craver"?

Answer yes or no to the following questions.

______ **1.** It is difficult to resist sweets and desserts.

______ **2.** I would rather snack on bread, a granola bar, cookies, cakes, or other starchy or sweet foods than on peanuts, sliced meats, yogurt, or crunchy vegetables.

______ **3.** When I am tired, depressed, or irritable, I feel like eating something sweet.

______ **4.** I have a hard time stopping once I start eating sweets, starches, or snack foods.

______ **5.** I am not satisfied after eating a meal or snack that contains only meat and vegetables.

______ **6.** A breakfast of eggs, bacon, and toast is likely to leave me feeling tired and hungry for something sweet by midmorning.

______ **7.** I feel better (more relaxed, more calm, or uplifted) after eating something sweet.

______ **8.** After being on a strict diet, I indulge in sweets or starchy foods.

______ **9.** I feel lethargic and irritable when I don't have a midmorning or midafternoon snack.

______ **10.** I would prefer a simple meal with a dessert to a gourmet meal with no dessert.

______ **11.** I feel more energetic after eating a starchy or sweet snack.

______ **12.** I have a craving for something sweet or starchy almost every day.

______ **13.** My cravings for sweets or starchy foods are so strong I often am unable to resist giving in to them.

______ **14.** The urge to eat sweets or starchy foods is greatest after a meal that contained only meat and vegetables.

______ **15.** I've tried lots of diets but have not had long-lasting success with any of them.

Scoring:

Total the number of yes answers to the above self-assessment. A score of 5 or less reflects a low probability that you are carbohydrate sensitive. A score between 6 and 9 suggests that you might be moderately carbohydrate sensitive, but you often can control your cravings. Following the Feeling Good Diet may be all you need to get back on track, although you might benefit from some of the dietary recommendations in this chapter (see "Carbohydrate Cravings Control Guidelines," page 57). A score of 10 or greater indicates that carbohydrate cravings might be a problem for you, so adapting the Feeling Good Diet based on the dietary recommendations in this chapter will be helpful.

The Biological Basis for Cravings

Women have known for millennia that there is more to cravings than meets the eye. Pregnant women are flooded with food cravings, especially during the first trimester. A woman who ate only whole-grain breads and a low-fat diet prior to pregnancy suddenly craves what she calls "1950s foods"—macaroni and cheese, sandwiches made with white bread, and TV dinners. Another pregnant woman can't get enough deviled-egg sandwiches, even though she disliked eggs prior to pregnancy. The most frequently documented cravings among pregnant women are for chocolate, milk, citrus fruits, ice cream, and salty snacks. On the other hand, women commonly report an aversion to fried foods, meat, coffee, alcohol, and Italian food during the first trimester. Menopausal women also report food cravings and aversions. It doesn't take a scientist to put two and two together and come up with a connection between changes in body chemicals (hormones, nerve chemicals, and more) and food cravings.

Perhaps the biggest surprise is that there is such a large supporting cast in these cravings. In fact, willpower might play only a minor role in control of cravings. Instead, each person rides a wave of body and brain chemicals, fueling his or her basic instincts. Imbalances in these chemicals can produce a drive so strong it might be easier to walk across hot coals than to control a craving.

For example, nutrients in the blood, such as glucose, hormones from the stomach, such as cholecystokinin (CCK), or the pancreas, such as insulin, switch hunger on and off. Also, the brain is a stew of appetite-triggering chemicals with names such as noradrenalin, dopamine, serotonin, and GABA. To complicate matters, there is a newly discovered family of chemicals called neuropeptides. These are small proteins that trigger nerve impulses and include neuropeptide Y (NPY), galanin, and the endorphins. The quantities of these chemicals ebb and flow throughout the day, and also fluctuate from day to day and from season to season. Thus your appetite, hunger, and cravings are essentially the result of riding internal chemical swells, much as a surfer skims precariously along on a massive wave. (See chapter 1 for an in-depth look at these chemicals.)

Serotonin Secrets

A desire for sweets may be hard-wired in the brain. As discussed earlier, a carbohydrate-rich meal or snack stimulates the release of the hormone insulin from the pancreas, which in turn lowers blood levels of all amino acids except tryptophan. Normally, tryptophan must compete with other amino acids for entry into the brain, but when insulin eliminates the competition, tryptophan levels in the brain rise. Tryptophan is then converted into serotonin, the neurotransmitter that regulates sleep, reduces pain and appetite, calms you down, and improves your mood.

Richard Wurtman, Ph.D., a professor of brain and cognitive science at the Massachusetts Institute of Technology in Cambridge, postulates that some people crave carbohydrates not because they lack willpower but because of an imbalance in serotonin. This theory is supported by evidence that obese people and people who crave carbohydrates often have lower serotonin levels than do lean people or people who prefer protein-rich snacks. Their extra-low serotonin levels leave them feeling anxious, irritable, and craving a serotonin "fix."

From Mood to Food
↓serotonin levels→↑cravings for and consumption of carbohydrate-rich foods→↑serotonin levels and ↓ carbohydrate cravings.

In essence, cravers turn to cookies, cakes, doughnuts, and other pastries, or even pasta and breads, to relieve dwindling energy levels, hunger, depression, and stress brought on by their low serotonin levels. The carbohydrate-rich snack raises serotonin levels, curbs the craving, and energizes the craver. Cravers are "rewarded" each time they indulge their cravings because the food increases their serotonin levels and makes them feel better. Just as Pavlov's dog salivated in anticipation of food whenever a bell rang, carbohydrate-sensitive people become conditioned to crave desserts, breads, or other carbohydrate-loaded foods whenever they are tired, depressed, or anxious.

Several medical or health conditions associated with depression and fatigue are linked to increased cravings for carbohydrate-rich foods, suggesting that people unknowingly regulate their moods with food. For example, people with a condition called seasonal affective disorder (SAD) crave carbohydrates during their cyclical bouts of depression, lethargy, and inability to concentrate. The carbohydrate-rich snack soothes and calms them. In addition, cravers given a drug called d-fenfluramine, which increases serotonin levels, report that their cravings subside. Apparently, the physiological need to increase serotonin levels leads to an uncontrollable urge to eat starchy or sugary foods. (See chapter 5 for more information on SAD and related conditions.)

While the carbohydrate-rich meal or snack alters brain chemistry and provides temporary relief from mild depression or tension, a high-protein diet, by supplying more of the competing amino acids, reduces tryptophan and serotonin levels in the brain. Consequently, carbohydrate-sensitive people who eat a high-protein breakfast such as eggs and bacon might experience fatigue or mood swings and crave a carbohydrate-rich midmorning snack in an effort to raise brain serotonin levels and feel better. The low-carbohydrate weight-loss diets of the past failed these people. Within days of going cold turkey on carbohydrates, the carbohydrate cravings were amplified and the dieter was almost powerless against succumbing to an all-out binge (see "Yo-Yo Dieting and Weight Control" later in this chapter).

Candy Is Dandy, But . . .

The serotonin theory provides an interesting connection between carbohydrates and cravings, but it is not the whole picture. For one thing, people report feeling an immediate calm when they give in to a food craving, but it takes at least an hour for the diet-triggered release of serotonin to go into effect.

Therefore, it is not surprising to find that food cravings might be fueled by an addiction to pleasure. Much like the high experienced after intense exercise, a good laugh, or good music, a euphoric or calming response is produced by certain foods that release the morphinelike chemicals in the brain called endorphins. While the serotonin response from eating carbohydrates would take some time to occur, the mere touch of sugar on the tongue produces an immediate endorphin rush. Thus, eating a doughnut produces an immediate endorphin-triggered rush followed by a lingering good mood induced by the slow-acting increase in serotonin.

Barbara Smith, Ph.D., an assistant professor of psychology at Johns Hopkins University in Baltimore, has researched the calming effects of sugar on newborns. "Healthy infants generally stop crying rather quickly when given small amounts of a [diluted sugar solution], and the calming effect persists over time, even when the sugar is removed," says Dr. Smith.

Dr. Smith's research suggests that sugar affects the endorphins that ease stress and discomfort. "The sweet taste might stimulate the release of these endorphins and result in a calming effect," says Dr. Smith. As discussed in chapter 1, the endorphins probably enhance what is called a hedonic or pleasurable response to eating. In short, they make eating fun, which can put them at odds with your willpower. The effects of endorphins on fat cravings (or more specifically on sweet-and-creamy cravings) are discussed in chapter 3.

Endorphins are powerful regulators of your appetite clock. Inject a rat with endorphins and it will heartily devour fats, proteins, and sweets. Inject it with an endorphin-blocking drug, and the snack attack subsides. Endorphins probably also play a role in regulating when and what you want to eat. For example, endorphins probably influence a person's preference for carbohydrates in the morning and for fats, proteins, and sweets later in the day.

Sarah Leibowitz, Ph.D., a professor of neurobiology at Rockefeller University in New York City, suspects that imbalances in endorphins might underlie obesity and other eating disorders. For example, obese people have elevated endorphin levels and eat less when they are given an endorphin-blocking drug, while both anorexics and bulimics have abnormal endorphin levels. Obese people are more sensitive to the appetite-stimulating effects of endorphins than are lean people. Dr. Leibowitz also theorizes that endorphins help control cravings during stress or starvation, which would explain why some people can't eat when they are stressed and why the desire for food often subsides after a few days of fasting.

The sugar-endorphin theory has not been thoroughly tested in adults, but it does provide an interesting link between sweet cravings and several health conditions. For example, people with premenstrual syndrome (PMS), bulimia, or seasonal affective disorder (SAD), or those who quit smoking or drinking also have more frequent cravings for sweets than is normal and report almost immediate relief from depression, tension, or fatigue after satisfying the craving. These people often explain the cravings by saying, "I need something to calm myself." The sugary snack provides a temporary quick fix that may aggravate future food cravings.

On the other hand, while simple carbohydrates such as sugar may contribute to the problem, complex or starchy carbohydrates can be part of the cure. Nutrient-packed complex carbohydrates such as whole-grain breads and crackers and starchy vegetables do not aggravate brain chemicals or blood sugar, but they do satisfy endorphin and/or serotonin needs. These nutritious foods can help see you through periods of craving. Later in the chapter you'll find guidelines on how to curb your carbohydrate cravings.

Sweet Addictions

The link between cravings and chemicals may extend beyond food to other compulsive behaviors. For example, people who are breaking the tobacco habit report a range of symptoms, from fatigue to sleep disturbances to increased appetite to mood changes. To counteract these symptoms many people use food, especially sugary or refined carbohydrates, as a substitute for tobacco. In essence, the sweet cravings are an attempt to improve mood and diminish withdrawal symptoms. Bonnie Spring, Ph.D., a professor of psychology at Chicago Medical School, found that ex-smokers in nicotine withdrawal are less likely to crave sweets and are more likely to stay off cigarettes if they consume a high-carbohydrate diet—that is, lots of pasta, breads, cereals, and starchy vegetables as outlined in the Feeling Good Diet (see chapter 13).

There also may be links between alcohol abuse, food cravings, and mood. While light drinkers usually consume alcohol for social reasons, heavy drinkers often do so to feel better or relieve feelings of tension, depression, and loneliness or to combat fatigue. They may use alcohol to improve their mood. Withdrawal from alcohol for heavy drinkers is associated with increased cravings for substances such as coffee, candy, sweets, and other carbohydrates. The sweets help counteract the depression, fatigue, and irritability associated with alcohol withdrawal.

Carbohydrate cravings during tobacco and alcohol withdrawal are probably influenced by imbalances in body chemicals, including blood sugar, serotonin, endorphins, and other hormones and nerve chemicals. For people undergoing withdrawal, turning to sugary foods produces a temporary high, but within a few hours they feel tired, anxious, and irritable again (a condition called dysphoria) and return for another jolt of sugar and caffeine. The chemical roller coaster that results makes recovery that much more difficult and painful (see "Sugar and Caffeine" below).

In contrast, an eating plan based on the Feeling Good Diet, with small, frequent meals that contain some protein and some complex carbohydrates—such as whole-grain breads and cereals, crackers, pretzels, flavored rice cakes, and starchy vegetables—will satisfy the cravings while helping to balance the body's appetite-regulating chemicals. In short, a person can use carbohydrates to fuel his or her recovery rather than to sustain poor mental and physical health. (See "A Dozen Carbohydrate-Rich Snacks," page 47, for ways to satisfy cravings without compromising health.)

Sugar and Caffeine: The Temporary Fix

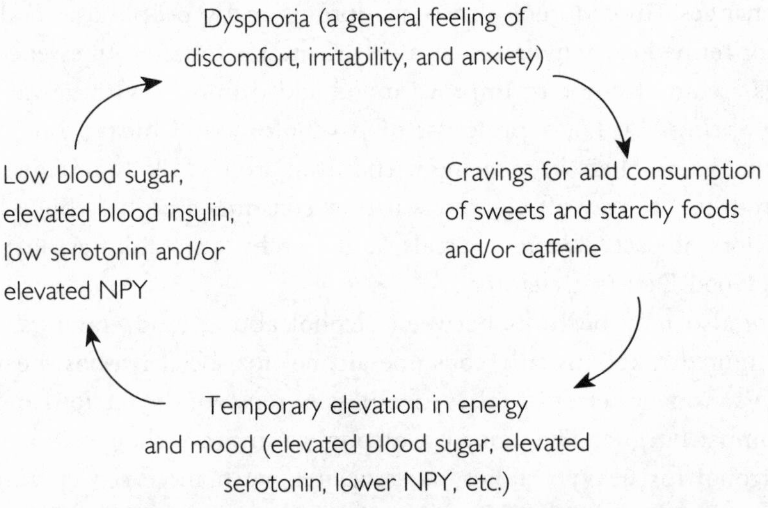

A Dozen Carbohydrate-Rich Snacks

SNACK	CARBOHYDRATE CONTENT (G)
1. One cup vanilla low-fat yogurt with ½ cup fresh strawberries	40
2. Apple-Pineapple Salad, 2 cups*	50
3. One slice whole wheat bread topped with ½ cup nonfat cottage cheese and ¼ cup crushed pineapple	25
4. Air-popped popcorn, 3 cups	19
5. Fig bars, 3	30
6. One-half cup no-fat refried beans with 1 ounce oven-baked tortilla chips	48
7. Six graham crackers with 1 tablespoon peanut butter and ½ banana, sliced	49
8. One corn tortilla filled with ¼ cup black beans, 1 ounce low-fat cheese, ¼ cup chopped cilantro, and salsa to taste	26
9. One whole wheat, raisin bagel with 1 tablespoon nonfat cream cheese and 2 teaspoons all-fruit spread	41
10. One medium baked potato, topped with 1 tablespoon chopped green onions, ¼ cup no-fat cottage cheese, and 1 tablespoon salsa	53
11. One-half cup dried fruit with 2 tablespoons nuts	47
12. Baked apple, plain, 1 large	30

*See "Recipes for Feeling Your Best" at the back of this book.

Your Basic Instincts

The desire to eat forbidden fruits might stem from an even deeper internal need than just to relieve anxiety or to feel good. The nerve cells in the brain that control eating are part of the body's elaborate plan for regulating energy balance and, fundamentally, for survival of the species. It is no coincidence, therefore, that the appetite-control center in the brain is next door to the reproductive center, according to Dr. Sarah Leibowitz. She believes the cycle of fat and sugar cravings coincides with reproductive needs.

"Nature is seeking reassurance that we have enough energy and body fat for survival of the species," says Dr. Leibowitz. For example, with their high estrogen levels, women consistently report more cravings than do men and are more likely to crave sweetened fats such as doughnuts, cakes, and pies, especially during puberty and following ovulation (the cravings experienced with PMS). These calorie-packed foods are ideal for building up energy stores in preparation for pregnancy. Men, with their species-survival need for greater muscle mass, prefer protein-fat mixtures such as a roast beef sandwich, a hamburger, or other meat dishes.

Dr. Leibowitz's research has uncovered a consistent daily cycle in two brain chemicals that whisper sweet cravings in our ears—NPY and galanin. Both people and other animals have elevated NPY levels in the morning, which apparently jump-start the day's eating by dictating a preference for carbohydrates (possibly with help from the endorphins). For example, laboratory animals eat more carbohydrates when NPY levels are high or when NPY is injected into their brains. Waffles, toast, pancakes, cereal, and fruit satisfy this NPY-induced craving and replenish the carbohydrate stores drained after an overnight fast.

From Mood to Food
An overnight fast→↓glycogen (sugar) stores→↓blood-sugar levels→ brain→hypothalamus→↑NPY→↑desire for and consumption of carbohydrate-rich foods→↓NPY.

NPY levels are highest not only in the morning after an overnight fast but also during times of stress or dieting. According to Dr. Leibowitz, these are the times a person is most likely to crave carbohydrates, which explains why people crave sweets after dieting and during PMS, depression, and other stressful times (unless the elevated NPY levels are subdued by an imbalance in endorphins). NPY is also linked to serotonin, estrogen, and stress hormone levels, and the combined effect can be overpowering.

Stress adds to food cravings. Many people report that everything from boredom to anxiety can set off a craving. Interestingly, stress hormones such as norepinephrine (a cousin of adrenalin) and corticosterone, both secreted from the adrenal glands during stress, raise NPY and galanin levels, which in turn increase food cravings, overeating, and weight gain.

From Mood to Food
Stress, dieting, etc.→↑corticosterone adrenals and/or↑norepinephrine from the adrenal glands→brain→hypothalamus→NPY→↑desire for and consumption of carbohydrate-rich foods.

Doing the Blood-Sugar Boogie

The most clearly defined connection between sugar and food cravings involves blood sugar (glucose) and insulin, its regulating hormone. Here's how it works: As discussed in chapter 1, during digestion, sucrose and other sugars, such as lactose, and starches are broken down into their simple units of glucose or fructose. These simple sugars enter the bloodstream and trigger the release of insulin, a hormone that regulates blood sugar levels. A mixed meal of protein, complex carbohydrates, and fats, such as a roast beef sandwich, causes a moderate release of insulin and maintains a steady blood-sugar level. On the other hand, sugary foods raise blood-sugar levels too high and trigger a large release of insulin from the pancreas. This, in turn, causes blood-sugar levels to drop, sometimes below normal, while elevated insulin levels linger for hours.

Judith Rodin, Ph.D., a professor of psychology and psychiatry at Yale University in New Haven, believes that the sugar-induced elevation in insulin might stimulate the appetite and induce repeated sugar cravings. Her research shows that people are hungriest and like sweet tastes more when insulin levels are high. When people snack on sugary foods, their insulin level rises and they eat more food and calories at the next meal than do people who snack on other foods or drink water.

Why, then, isn't everyone a carbohydrate craver? Dr. Rodin states that some people are "hyper-responders" and are more sensitive to insulin. In these people, the insulin level jumps even at the sight or smell of food, as if their bodies are gearing up for a meal even before the food reaches their mouth. This unique response might explain why some studies have found a link between sugar and mood, while other studies report that sugar intake does not affect either blood-sugar levels or mood.

Fortunately, a taste for sugar is often learned, which means it can be unlearned or replaced by a new habit. "You see a doughnut, you eat one, and your insulin level jumps to the occasion. Before long, you expect a doughnut at the morning break and your body learns that its insulin level goes up when pastries are around, much like Pavlov's dog learned to salivate when a bell was rung," reports Dr. Rodin. People who have developed this insulin response can curb it by following the Feeling Good Diet (see chapter 13) and the guidelines outlined on page 57.

The Fructose Fix

Fructose may be a sweet alternative to sugar. This simple sugar found in fruit does not trigger the insulin response and the food cravings. For example, in one study, people drank a beverage sweetened with either fructose, glucose, or aspartame (also called NutraSweet). Those who drank the fructose-sweetened beverage ate fewer calories overall and consumed less fat than did the other people.

Why? Apparently fructose is absorbed more slowly than glucose or sucrose and must travel to the liver to be converted to glucose before it can enter the bloodstream. Thus, fructose alone or with a meal stimulates insulin release, but not as dramatically or as rapidly as glucose or table sugar. These three differences—slower absorption, the stopover in the liver, and a more gradual release of insulin—mean that you can help curb cravings and avoid overeating at the next meal by switching from a sucrose-laden doughnut to a fructose-filled orange.

But don't get carried away. Concentrated fructose—which can be purchased in health food stores, is found in honey, and is also labeled as high-fructose corn syrup (HFCS) in processed foods and soda pop—is no substitute for the more nutritious, naturally occurring fructose in fruits or the complex carbohydrates in grains and vegetables. The latter carbohydrates come packaged with vitamins, minerals, fiber, water, and other essential nutrients. In addition, although fructose is sweeter than sucrose—and thus less is needed to obtain the same sweet taste—the effect is noticeable only in cold beverages such as iced tea or lemonade. There is no appreciable reduction in amount or number of calories when HFCS or honey is added to baked items.

Some people have trouble digesting fructose and develop diarrhea, gas, and abdominal pain when even small doses of the concentrated fructose in honey or the HFCS in soda pop are consumed. The fructose in fruits is diluted with water, vitamins, and fiber and does not cause these health problems. Fructose in excess of 20 percent of total calories also might raise blood triglyceride, cholesterol, and LDL-cholesterol levels, thus increasing the risk of developing heart disease. The bottom line is that lots of fruit and a little honey are one way to avoid the blood-sugar roller coaster produced by most commercial sweets and desserts. Just be careful not to overload on HFCS-sweetened processed foods, pure fructose from the health food store, or excessive amounts of honey.

How Sweet It Is

The artificial sweetener story is complicated. Saccharine and cyclamates are on the hazardous-to-your-health list, having produced cancer in laboratory animals. And while aspartame (more commonly known as Equal or NutraSweet) may be relatively harmless, it has been a flop at weight management.

Weight-loss hopes were high when aspartame hit the marketplace. Aspartame is a nonnutritive sweetener composed of two amino acids—phenylalanine and aspartic acid—and an alcohol-like compound called methanol. It is several times sweeter than sugar, so one packet of Equal, supplying 4 calories, is as sweet as two teaspoons of sugar, which has 32 calories.

Since the early 1980s, aspartame has been used in dry foods and soft drinks with U.S. Food and Drug Administration approval. However, some researchers are not convinced aspartame is safe. Dr. Richard Wurtman, a professor at the Massachusetts Institute of Technology, reported that seizures and abnormal concentrations of brain chemicals, including neuropeptides and neurotransmitters, developed when he fed laboratory animals large doses of the sweetener. Small amounts of aspartame were safe, but the cumulative effect of moderate to large quantities in soft drinks, especially if consumed with a high-carbohydrate–low-protein snack, might cause nausea, headaches, or moodiness in sensitive people.

As much, if not more, evidence shows that aspartame is safe even in moderate to large doses. In these studies, concentrations of brain chemicals and behavior were unaffected by aspartame ingestion. A report published by the American

Medical Society stated that aspartame produces no serious adverse health effects. Finally, a summary report of an international conference on aspartame concluded that "aspartame at 50 mg/kg body weight [the equivalent of more than 3 grams for a 135-pound person] given acutely or chronically is far below a level for a pharmacological effect and is therefore safe." All groups agree that aspartame, and all dietary sources of phenylalanine, could be harmful to children and adults with the metabolic disorder called phenylketonuria (PKU).

With more than 34 million people—including one out of every two women—dieting at any given time, it is no wonder diet soft-drink sales have more than tripled in the past twelve years. The thought of consuming a sweet drink that allows you to save 160 calories each day—a reduction that could theoretically result in a seventeen-pound weight loss in one year—is too tempting to ignore. Nevertheless, obesity rates have soared. Evidently, America's weight problems require a solution more potent than artificial sweeteners.

In fact, some studies report that aspartame-sweetened beverages increase appetite and food intake, possibly contributing to cravings and weight problems. The reasons are poorly understood, but it may be that the sweet taste triggers an unconscious sugar-anticipation response that increases the craving for food when not satisfied. In other words, the body craves a certain amount of calories or sugar, and it is not tricked by artificially sweetened drinks and food. It is not surprising, therefore, that researchers report artificial-sweetener users to be no more likely than nonusers to lose weight; in fact, they might be more prone to weight gain.

Aspartame is also suspected of interfering with weight loss and weight maintenance. Dr. Wurtman theorizes that the sweetener increases cravings for carbohydrate-rich foods by producing a chemical in the brain that triggers appetite. Some studies show that aspartame stimulates appetite more than sugar does. For instance, one study showed that people who ate chocolate sweetened with aspartame had a higher rise in endorphin level than did people who ate chocolate sweetened with sugar. Since elevation in these pleasurable nerve chemicals is associated with increased food intake, it could be that artificially sweetened foods and beverages stimulate the appetite by upsetting the brain's chemistry. Other studies, however, have not found this appetite-stimulating effect. Although the findings are controversial, there is no evidence that aspartame either suppresses appetite or significantly aids in weight control.

So what is the bottom line on aspartame? The number of health complaints against this sweetener are minute compared to the estimated 100 million Americans who regularly consume the sweetener. In addition, the complaints often are of common ailments such as headaches and nausea, and it is difficult to identify a specific syndrome characteristic of aspartame toxicity. Until the controversy is resolved, it is wise to avoid aspartame if you have phenylketonuria, are pregnant, have experienced any adverse side effects when consuming the sweetener, or are an infant or young child. For others, consume moderate to low amounts and pay attention to the number of foods that contain the sweetener. For the weight manager, an occasional diet soft drink can temporarily satisfy a sweet tooth, but it probably won't help you lose weight.

Yo-Yo Dieting and Weight Control

At any one time, more than half of all adult Americans are trying to lose weight. Most are initially successful, but as many as 95 percent of dieters regain the weight they lost within five years. In fact, the weight of the average woman is five pounds more than it was 15 years ago.

The message that diets don't work comes across loud and clear; diets can also create havoc with your food cravings. In addition to putting a damper on your metabolic rate and promoting increased body fat, restrictive diets or even very low-fat diets disrupt the natural cycle of nerve chemicals, especially serotonin, NPY, and galanin. "These peptides, hormones, and [nerve chemicals] go totally berserk when a woman goes on a quick-weight-loss diet," says Dr. Leibowitz. Laboratory studies show that when you force rats to eat a very low-calorie diet and then give them unlimited access to food, they gorge, increasing their consumption of fat from a typical 35 percent of calories to as much as 60 percent of calories.

Adam Drewnowski, Ph.D., the director of the Human Nutrition Program at the University of Michigan at Ann Arbor, has found in his research that people who repeatedly gain and lose weight also prefer sweet-and-creamy foods more than do people who maintain their weight. It is likely that severe calorie-restricted diets raise NPY, galanin, or endorphin levels (and/or lower serotonin levels), setting up a rebound effect and swinging the eating pendulum from fasting to bingeing.

Interestingly, people who have been obese since childhood—that is, whose obesity is probably influenced more by nature than by nurture—do not have the same uncontrollable food cravings. Thus, it is likely that repeated dieting scrambles the body's normal chemical cycles, increases a person's preference for sweets, and results in a fast-and-feast scenario that encourages weight gain.

In short, dieting or erratic eating habits are counterproductive. Restrictive eating patterns such as cutting back severely on calories in an effort to get thin quick, repeated dieting attempts, low-carbohydrate diets, or skipping breakfast disturb the body's chemical routine. In addition, the chemicals that turn cravings on and off are also the chemicals that regulate mood, state of mind, physical energy, and even sex drive. It is easy to see that you can't mess with mother nature!

Eat and Be Merry

The diet and mood picture is far from complete; many questions remain to be answered. Are a person's responses to diet and carbohydrates contained in the genetic code or developed in infancy, or even in the womb? Why do some people react to small amounts of sugar while others can eat cups of sugar with no apparent side effects? And what are the nonchemical causes for cravings?

It's in Our Genes

People may be born to crave sweets. Of the four types of taste buds (sweet, sour, bitter, and salty), those for sugar hold the most prestigious spot: on the tip of the tongue. Children are born loving sweets. It is only as we age that the craving for sweets dulls, so that by adulthood we prefer the sweet-and-creamy taste of fudge, while a child prefers a sugary sucker.

Paleolithic cave dwellers made rock paintings that show how they robbed bees' nests of their sweet nectar. This preference for sweets was an important survival mechanism, since sweet foods tend to be nourishing (high in calories) and safe, while many bitter foods are toxic or poisonous. The taste preference allowed our ancestors to gather sweet-tasting foods such as fruits, which are also rich in vitamins, minerals, and calories. However, our cave-dweller bodies now live in affluent societies where easy and unlimited access to highly processed and concentrated sugar has resulted in each American's eating his or her weight in sugar annually. In short, our genetically programmed taste buds run headfirst into a glut of sugar.

Deconditioning a Conditioned Response

It is likely that some cravings are mere habits. Much like Pavlov's dog, humans seek rewards. If a midafternoon sweet snack makes you feel good, you are likely to have it again. Repeating the behavior over and over results in a habit or even a craving.

Controlling cravings in these situations is a matter of changing the behavior by substituting a more nutritious snack—replacing the midmorning doughnut with a whole wheat bagel or exchanging the afternoon candy bar with a piece of fresh fruit or a custard-style nonfat yogurt, which provides sweetness and a creamy texture. Or it can mean developing a new habit to replace the old one—taking a walk during a time you usually experience cravings or riding an exercise bicycle rather than eating potato chips while watching television in the evening. The craving should subside within two weeks of the change in your behavior.

Cravings, Old Tapes, and Other Memorabilia

Cravings can be the result of childhood food associations, memories, cultural beliefs and traditions, or other powerful emotional cues. For example, women who regularly experience food cravings also report more frequent bouts of boredom and anxiety than do women who are less prone to such cravings. In these "chicken-or-egg" cases, it is difficult to determine whether the craving is triggered by a nerve chemical or the desire to eat is a conditioned response to an uncomfortable situation.

In either case, keeping the Food and Mood Journal in chapter 13—where you record when, what, and how much you eat and how you felt before and after eating—can pinpoint the internal signals that are causing the cravings. Information from the food journal can help you plan a strategy for making healthier food choices or finding a nonfood alternative to inappropriate eating, such as exercise, visiting a friend, or gardening. (See chapter 12 for more information on how to identify and avoid emotional eating.)

Listen to Your Body—It's Trying to Tell You Something

Food cravings sometimes are the body's way of correcting a deficiency. For example, people who are protein-deficient crave protein-rich foods, while people who are well nourished select diets that contain a modest 15 percent of total calories from protein. Pica, or the craving for nonfoods such as soil (a source of iron), is common in people who are iron-deficient. Glycogen stores (the short-term supply of sugar stockpiled in the liver and muscles) depleted by dieting, intense aerobic exercise, or skipping meals can lead to cravings for carbohydrates as the body attempts to restock.

Cravings Control Basics

You can subdue your cravings and stay on track, even when you face a battle between your willpower or good intentions and a stew of appetite-triggering body chemicals (see "Carbohydrate Cravings Control Guidelines," page 57).

First, if you are a carbohydrate craver, realize you cannot "will away" your craving, so work with it instead. Make sure every meal contains some foods rich in complex carbohydrates, such as bread, cereals, or crackers. In addition, plan a complex-carbohydrate snack during that time of the day when you are most vulnerable. Pinpoint your true craving. Is it for something cold and sweet? Crunchy? Chewy? Once you have identified exactly what you want, find a low-fat food that will satisfy that craving. Keep in mind that by following the Feeling Good Diet, including eating four to six small meals and snacks throughout the day, and slowly weaning yourself from sweets, your cravings for fatty or overly sweet foods will slowly dwindle (see "Cravers Versus Non-Cravers," page 58).

Carbohydrate Cravings Control Guidelines

The trick is to work with your cravings and appetite-regulating chemicals, not against them. The Feeling Good Diet (chapter 13) is the foundation for keeping your neurotransmitters, hormones, and peptides happy and balanced. Here are a few important considerations when designing your eating plan.

1. Eat small meals and snacks that include some complex carbohydrates, such as whole-grain breads, starchy vegetables, and legumes, throughout the day. This will keep NPY and serotonin levels in the normal range.
2. Eat breakfast and include at least one serving of grains and one serving of fruit. Skipping breakfast will only escalate NPY levels and increase cravings later in the morning.
3. Avoid fatty meals and snacks at midday, since they may give galanin an extra boost and set you up for more fat cravings at night. Snack on fresh fruits and vegetables, low-fat yogurt, pretzels, or a bagel with fat-free cream cheese, rather than on candy or cheese in the late afternoon. See chapter 3 for more on fat cravings.
4. Use alternative flavorings such as vanilla, nutmeg, spearmint, cinnamon, and anise to appease a sweet tooth.
5. As outlined in the Feeling Good Diet, gradually make dietary changes to reduce fat, sugar, or calories, allowing time for your body to adapt.
6. Plan your snacks. Allot a certain number of calories for a small sweet snack and make it low in fat—nonfat frozen yogurt, fruit ices, vanilla wafers, or fig bars. Abstinence leads to binge eating, while allowing small servings of your favorite food helps curb the cravings.
7. If habit, not chemicals, is at the root of your cravings, find nutritious, low-calorie foods to substitute or develop a new habit that provides a similarly pleasurable or rewarding effect. For example, take a brisk walk, soak in a hot bath, or play ball with the dog during your vulnerable time of the day.
8. Exercise. While couch potatoes are likely to make regular trips to the refrigerator and struggle with their weight, people who exercise regularly maintain their weight and are less prone to bingeing and cravings. Also, exercise is an alternative to sugary foods for getting the pleasurable endorphin rush and reducing stress.
9. Drink plenty of water. Often a desire for sweets in the evening is actually a signal that the body needs fluids. Some people report their craving for ice cream subsides within a few minutes after they drink one or two glasses of water. Try drinking water as you clean up the kitchen and prepare dessert; you may feel less of an urge to indulge as a result.

Cravers Versus Non-Cravers

People who crave carbohydrates are energized by these carbohydrates, while a plate of pasta will put other people to sleep. Consequently, plan carefully when to have carbohydrates so as to provide energy when you need it and to enhance your work performance.

CARBOHYDRATE-CRAVER'S EATING PATTERN	**STANDARD EATING PATTERN**
BREAKFAST	
Cereal and low-fat milk, fruit	Egg substitute; whole wheat toast, fruit
SNACK	
Oatmeal-raisin bagel, fruit, water	Toasted bagel with fat-free cream cheese, water
LUNCH	
Spaghetti with marinara sauce, salad, low-fat milk	Tuna sandwich, carrot-raisin salad, low-fat milk
SNACK	
Rice cakes, pretzels, other carbohydrate-rich snack, water	Nonfat cheese and crackers, vegetables or fruit, water
DINNER	
If you want to relax: Meat, vegetable, potato, low-fat, milk	Linguini with clam sauce, French bread, tossed salad, water
If you want to exercise or work: Meat, vegetable, potato, low-fat milk	Cold chicken, rice, steamed vegetables, water

Another way to work with a craving is to "urge surf." G. Alan Marlatt, Ph.D., a professor of psychology at the University of Washington in Seattle, in his book *Relapse Prevention*, suggests that cravings are similar to a wave that builds, then breaks on the beach. Overcoming the temptation to indulge is much like riding the wave as it builds, crests, breaks, and subsides. Even though the initial relief of satisfying a craving might appear to end the urge to eat, in the long run it encourages stronger and more frequent temptations and leaves you more vulnerable to the next snack attack. The temptation to give in to a craving becomes less frequent and progressively weaker when you outlast the urge. Visualize yourself riding the urge like a wave until it crests and then subsides. (See chapter 12 for information on how emotions affect cravings and what to do about it.)

Second, people who know they are sensitive to sugar should avoid sweets or eat them in small doses and always with other, more nutritious foods. Most people know that cakes, cookies, candies, sweetened cereals, and soda pop are high in sugar. However, many people are surprised to find sugar listed on the labels of catsup, salad dressings, commercial spaghetti sauce, even frozen entrees. Table 2.1 provides a partial list of commonly used foods and their added sugar content.

Third, any dramatic change in normal eating patterns can alter brain chemistry. Bingeing on sweets, skipping meals such as breakfast, imposing an overzealous fat restriction (less than 20 percent of total calories), and following other unusual eating habits affect neurotransmitter levels and, consequently, mood and behavior. In contrast, the Feeling Good Diet—which provides approximately 25 to 30 percent of calories from fat and supplies at least 2,000 calories of nutrient-packed, wholesome foods—provides ample nutrients to sustain mental, emotional, and physical health. Consuming several small meals or snacks throughout the day rather than two to three big meals helps maintain steady blood sugar and neurotransmitter levels.

Fourth, don't diet, at least not in the traditional sense of the word. Drastic diets and diet pills that radically alter normal eating patterns don't work in the long run and also interfere with brain-chemical production. Instead, develop a weight-management plan based on the Feeling Good Diet and daily exercise, with a goal to lose no more than two pounds per week. A gradual shift in eating habits and a slow-and-steady approach to weight loss helps "down regulate" your body's appetite-controlling chemicals. Gradual weight loss also helps burn body fat and keep the weight off (see "A Weight-Loss Plan for Carbohydrate Cravers," page 62).

TABLE 2.1 Sweet Surprises: The Sugar Content of Certain Foods

Most people know candy bars, cakes, and cookies are sweet treats. But did you know how much sugar is also in the following foods?

FOOD	SERVING SIZE	TEASPOONS OF ADDED SUGAR	% CALORIES FROM SUGAR
Pecan pie	1 medium slice	12.0	35
Orange soda	12-ounce glass	11.8	100
Coca-Cola	12-ounce glass	9.3	100
Low-fat fruited yogurt	1 cup	8.8	54
Tang	8-ounce glass	7.6	100
Cranberry juice cocktail	8-ounce glass	6.4	73
Coffee cake	1 medium slice	6.4	44
Angel food cake	1 medium slice	6.8	61
Sherbet	½ cup	6.7	80
Kool-Aid	8-ounce glass	6.0	100
Cranberry sauce	½ cup	6.0	96
Applesauce, sweetened	½ cup	4.3	60
Ovaltine mix	4–5 teaspoons	4.3	77
Instant oatmeal:			
cinnamon-spice	1.5 ounces	4.3	40
maple and brown sugar	1.5 ounces	3.5	35
Low-fat flavored yogurt	1 cup	4.2	33
Gingerbread	1 medium slice	4.1	31
Peaches, canned in heavy syrup	½ cup	4.0	64
Nestea Light	8-ounce glass	3.7	100
Gatorade	8-ounce glass	3.5	100
Beans and franks	¾ cup	3.3	19
Dessert wine	3.5-ounce glass	3.0	35
Pineapple, canned in heavy syrup	½ cup	3.0	54
Frozen yogurt	½ cup	2.8	50

Peaches, canned in light syrup	½ cup	2.3	50
Quaker Honey & Oat granola bar	1	1.8	20
Oatmeal cookies	2	1.7	22
Chewing gum	1 stick	0.6–1.5	92
Jelly or jam	½ tablespoon	1.5	88
Danish pastry	1 medium	1.5	9
Corn, cream-style	½ cup	1.5	23
Peanut butter	2 tablespoons	1.3	11
Bran muffin	1 medium	1.2	17
Graham crackers	2 large	0.9	25
Catsup	1 tablespoon	0.6	63
French dressing	1 tablespoon	0.4	9

Many fad diets restrict carbohydrate-rich foods and emphasize protein-rich foods such as meats, eggs, chicken, cottage cheese, and fish. These diets can be disastrous for people who crave carbohydrates because protein foods lower brain levels of serotonin, stimulate a craving for carbohydrates, and increase the likelihood of depression and binge eating. For these people, a diet balanced in protein and carbohydrates, the latter preferably from unrefined complex sources such as whole wheat breads and pasta, with some protein and some complex carbohydrates at each meal and snack, will help subdue the cravings while promoting weight loss and optimal nutrition (see "A Sample Weight-Loss Diet for Carbohydrate Cravers" on page 63.)

Fifth, exercise at least five times a week. Daily movement, especially aerobic activities such as walking, jogging, swimming, or bicycling, helps regulate blood-sugar levels and other nerve chemicals and provides an endorphin rush without the calories. You are not likely to curb your cravings unless you also exercise!

Finally, effective coping skills; a strong support system; and limited or no alcohol, cigarettes, and medications that may compound an emotional problem are important considerations for controlling your cravings.

A Weight-Loss Plan for Carbohydrate Cravers

1. Identify the number of calories required to maintain your desired weight and that will allow no more than a two-pound weight loss each week.
2. Based on this calorie allotment, plan four to six moderate meals and snacks balanced in protein and starch and low in fat.
3. As part of your calorie allotment, plan a small carbohydrate-rich snack for the time of day when cravings are most likely to occur.
4. Plan an aerobic exercise break during your high-risk time of day to divert attention from snacking and help change your body's chemistry so you will be less prone to snacking later in the day.
5. Monitor your weight loss. If you are losing more than two pounds a week, increase your calorie intake by 100 to 200 calories a day. If you are not losing at least one pound a week, reduce your daily calorie intake by 100 to 200 calories (but not below 1,200 calories) and increase your daily exercise.

Work with your cravings—don't try to will them away. Diet is not shaped by food cravings alone; it also takes an attitude of acceptance and an accommodating environment. You can offset unhealthy cravings by tailoring your home and work environments to support healthful eating. For example, plan ahead how you will handle risk-prone situations, eliminate tempting foods from your environment, and encourage support from friends and family.

A Sample Weight-Loss Diet for Carbohydrate Cravers

This menu supplies approximately 1,200 calories. Optimal levels of all vitamins and minerals cannot be guaranteed when calorie intake is this low, so choose a moderate-dose multiple supplement when following any low-calorie diet.

BREAKFAST

Whole wheat toast, 1 slice
All-fruit jam, 2 teaspoons
Nonfat yogurt, 1 cup
Strawberries, ¾ cup
Tea

MIDMORNING SNACK

Orange, 1 small

LUNCH

Turkey sandwich, open-faced:
2 ounces turkey, 1 slice rye bread, and 1 teaspoon mayonnaise
Spinach salad:
2 cups spinach, ¼ cup mushrooms, 1 medium tomato, 2 tablespoons green onions, ¼ cup jicama, and lemon or nonfat salad dressing
Nonfat milk, 1 cup

MIDAFTERNOON SNACK (HIGH-RISK TIME)

Two of the following:
Oyster crackers, 20
Cherries, 12 medium
Vanilla wafers, 6
Angel food cake, 1½-inch slice
Nectarine, 1
Raisins, 2 tablespoons

DINNER

Broiled salmon, 3 ounces
Brown rice, ⅓ cup
Green beans, ½ cup
Crunchy raw vegetables, 1 cup

EVENING SNACK

Nonfat yogurt, 1 cup

CHAPTER THREE

Other Food Cravings: Fats and Chocolate

- An irresistible urge for a candy bar
- A passion for chocolate
- The desire to spend the evening with a half-gallon of ice cream
- A longing for a glazed doughnut
- An obsession with French pastry

No one can explain exactly why we crave foods, yet 97 percent of women and 68 percent of men indulge a craving now and then. Certainly we all can vouch for how hard it is to ignore a craving once it hits. Women in particular often feel guilty or angry with themselves when they give in to a craving. Yet with just about every aspect of life triggering your appetite, from your body's chemistry and basic instincts to seductive television commercials and the aroma of warm cinnamon rolls from a local bakery, it is understandable how cravings can happen. That's why it is so important to develop a plan to control such cravings.

Your "Fat Tooth"

Although many people assume they crave sweets and claim they have a sweet tooth, in reality they may be searching for fat. Adam Drewnowski, Ph.D., director of the Human Nutrition Program at the University of Michigan at Ann

Arbor, disagrees with Richard Wurtman's theory that people crave carbohydrates because of the effect these foods have on levels of serotonin, a neurotransmitter that has a calming effect (see chapter 1). Drewnowski's research shows that it is a desire for fat—or, more specifically, for sweetened fat—that leads people to indulge in chocolate, ice cream, and cookies.

"These so-called carbohydrate-rich foods derive as much, if not more, of their calories from fat than from sugar; the sugar just makes the fat taste better," says Dr. Drewnowski. For example, 54 percent of the calories in some ice cream comes from fat, while a chocolate chip cookie is up to 40 perent fat calories and a Hershey's Special Dark chocolate bar is 51 percent fat calories (see Table 3.1).

Fat alone is unpalatable. But add even a little sugar and you have a sweet-and-creamy combination that brings out cravings in even the most ardent dieter. Dr. Drewnowski's studies on food preferences using a varying amount of sugar and fat show that people are least likely to choose a high-sweet, low-fat food such as jelly beans or a Popsicle, and they are most likely to choose a sweet-and-creamy food with a taste and texture similar to sweetened whipped cream. In other words, the combination of fat and sugar is what dictates cravings for some people.

Sugar masks the fat in foods. When people are asked to taste foods containing various amounts of sugar and fat, their perception of the fat content decreases as the sugar content increases. For example, commercial cake frosting contains 70 percent sugar and 15 to 20 percent fat, which is too sweet for most adults. However, these frostings gain in appeal if the fat content is increased to 25 percent or more. In other studies, few adults place sweetened skim milk (high sugar, low fat) or unsweetened cream (low sugar, high fat) at the top of their list of cravings. Yet the majority of adults respond favorably to sweetened heavy cream (high sugar, high fat). So sweet and creamy is the dynamic duo: fat makes the food desirable and sugar makes the fat invisible. Consequently, people often have no idea how much fat they are eating, and they unjustly accuse the sugar of prompting an uncontrollable urge to eat.

Granted, few people drool at the thought of greasy foods. The craving for fat is mostly unconscious and has a lot to do with texture, smell, and brain chemicals. Dietary fats are largely responsible for the texture, flavor, and odor of foods, which means they make foods mouth-watering, delectable, tantalizing, and palat-

TABLE 3.1 The Fat in Food

Often cravings for sweets might be cravings for fat. The fat content of the following sweets might surprise you.

FOOD	AMOUNT	TEASPOONS OF FAT
General Mills Chocolate Angel Food Cake	1 slice	0
Peach sorbet	1/2 cup	0
Fruit-flavored sherbet	1/2 cup	1/2
Hydrox chocolate sandwich cookie	1	1/2
Vanilla ice cream	1/2 cup	1/2 to 1 1/2
Oatmeal-raisin cookie	1	1
Pepperidge Farm Brownie Chocolate Nut cookie	1	1
Chocolate chip cookie	1	1 to 2
Cake doughnut	1	1 1/2
Weight Watchers German Chocolate Cake	1	1 1/2
Peanut butter cookie	1	1 1/2 to 3
Cherry pie	1/8 pie	2 to 4
Glazed old-fashioned doughnut	1	2 to 4
Drake's Apple Pie Snack	1	2 1/2
Avocado	1	3
Fruit Danish	1	3
Hershey's Bar None candy bar	1	3
Krackel chocolate bar	1	3
Pumpkin pie	1/8 pie	3
Sara Lee Light Classic Strawberry French Cheesecake	1/8 cake	3
Snickers candy bar	1	3
Pepperidge Farm Chocolate Fudge Cake	1/8 cake	3 1/2
Ben & Jerry's Chocolate ice cream	1/2 cup	4
Mrs. Smith's Old Fashioned Apple Pie	1/8 pie	4
Mr. Goodbar chocolate bar	1	4 1/2
Carrot cake with cream cheese icing	1/8 cake	5

able. For instance, the butterfat in ice cream makes it creamy and smooth. The marbling in meat makes it tender. The fats used in deep-frying make French fries and onion rings crisp and crunchy.

For example, notice the first one or two words that come to mind to describe each of the following foods:

croissant	fresh orange
chocolate pudding	potato chips
carrot stick	peanut butter

If words such as *flaky, smooth, creamy, rich, crunchy, juicy, crisp, gooey*, or *sticky* came to mind, you are not alone. When asked to describe foods, most people use texture terms rather than color (did *brown* come to mind when you thought of chocolate?) or flavor (did *citrusy* come to mind when you thought of oranges?). And more often than not, it is the fat that gives those foods their appealing texture.

People also turn to "creamy" foods for their taste. In one study at Duke University, normal-weight, nondieting women were given several meals that varied in taste, including a bland-fat meal, a tasty-fat meal, a bland-carbohydrate meal, and a tasty-carbohydrate meal. The tasty versions of both the carbohydrate and the fatty meals were more satisfying and satisfied hunger better than did either of the bland meals. Since fat carries the aroma and much of the taste in food, a craving for something sweet-and-creamy could really be a desire for something tasty. If this is the case, adding no-calorie flavorings such as cinnamon, vanilla, or nutmeg to foods like nonfat yogurt, low-fat cereals, or angel food cake can sometimes appease the "fat" tooth without adding calories.

If you crave the taste and texture of sweet-and-creamy foods, feed your "fat tooth" without sacrificing your health or waistline. Try custard-style low-fat and nonfat yogurt or use fat-free cream cheese. Replace butter and sugar with applesauce or pureed prunes in brownie recipes. Low-fat vanilla yogurt can replace half the butter in some dessert recipes. And the new nonfat foods, such as those made with fat substitutes like Simplesse, also might be helpful in curbing your fat cravings. These foods provide the same rich, creamy "mouth feel" without the fat or calories.

Fat and Your Body's Chemistry

According to Dr. Drewnowski, endorphins—the natural morphinelike substances in the brain that produce euphoric or pleasurable feelings—might be the culprit in sweet-fat cravings. "Few theories on food cravings take into account the importance of the pleasure response," says Dr. Drewnowski. Both sugar and fat are suspected to release endorphins in the brain and produce a natural painkilling effect.

These suspicions are supported by several studies, including those conducted by Elliott Blass, Ph.D., at Cornell University. Dr. Blass has found a similar link between the endorphins and cravings for sweet-and-creamy foods. He speculates that when people go on restrictive diets or quickly and drastically reduce their fat intake, they set up a rebound effect whereby they swing from abstinence to binge eating. In contrast, avoiding very restrictive weight-loss diets and slowly lowering your dietary fat—perhaps taking a year or more to reach your goal of 30 percent or less calories from fat—is the most effective way to work with the endorphin levels and avoid the rebound effect.

Fat for Survival

Sarah Leibowitz, Ph.D, a professor of neurobiology at Rockefeller University, has pioneered research on the body's control center for food cravings. As mentioned in chapter 2, it may be no coincidence that our brain's cravings center is next door to its reproduction center. Dr. Leibowitz believes that the body's fundamental drive to survive—to reproduce—rests on the body's ensuring that it receives enough food to meet energy demands today and during times of potential famine. Dr. Leibowitz's research has found that elevated levels of a brain chemical called NPY in the morning jump-start the day's eating pattern by dictating a preference for carbohydrates (see chapter 1).

The body has a built-in appetite for fat, its long-term fuel. This appetite is regulated by a brain chemical called galanin, which rises as the day progresses and triggers a desire for fatty foods such as meats, cream sauces, and salad dressing for lunch, or a chocolate truffle or bowl of ice cream for a midafternoon or late-night snack.

The connection between fat cravings and galanin has been clearly identified in laboratory animals. For example, in an experiment where galanin was injected into the hypothalamus—the appetite-control center—of the brain, research animals selected a fat-rich diet. Galanin had no effect on appetite when it was injected into other centers of the brain, whereas injecting a galanin-blocking drug into the appetite-control center caused research animals to switch from a high-fat to a low-fat diet.

Galanin is closely connected to the pleasure response triggered by the endorphins. "Galanin and the endorphins co-exist in the same nerve cells and work together," says Dr. Leibowitz. So while galanin is triggering a craving for ice cream, the endorphins are making that experience pleasurable.

Galanin works with other hormones to convert dietary fat into body fat. As galanin levels go up, so do fat intake and body weight. In laboratory animals, the more galanin produced, the more weight the animal is likely to gain in the future. Perhaps this is why obese people prefer fatty foods and, although they may consume the same number of calories as lean people, more of those calories come from fat. Combined with a disturbance in the hormonelike compounds that usually turn off appetite—such as insulin from the pancreas and cholecystokinin (CCK) from the digestive tract—Dr. Leibowitz speculates that an excess of galanin or NPY could escalate a craving into a weight problem.

What turns on the galanin system? As mentioned, galanin levels rise naturally as the day progresses; therefore, they are lowest in the morning and highest from late afternoon until bedtime. Galanin levels also rise when estrogen levels are high, which might explain the cravings for sweet-and-creamy foods associated with premenstrual syndrome (PMS). In essence, estrogen, by way of galanin, makes a woman want to eat and deposit fat in preparation for childbearing.

Fad diets interfere with galanin levels. Strict diets and quick weight loss generate a flood of metabolic debris that signals the appetite-control center in the brain to raise galanin levels. This in turn triggers a fat craving—probably a survival mechanism to safeguard the body's fuel stores.

Stress adds to the food cravings. Everything from boredom to anxiety can set off a fat craving. Interestingly, stress hormones such as norepinephrine (cousin to adrenalin) and corticosterone, both secreted from the adrenal glands during stress, raise galanin levels, which in turn increase food cravings, overeating, and weight gain.

Adding further support to the link between survival of the species and food cravings, Dr. Leibowitz points out that cravings for fatty foods correspond to increasing galanin levels at puberty. Preadolescent children prefer sweet foods to fatty foods. They like the icing on a cake, a candy sucker or Popsicle, and sugar-coated cereals. Beginning with puberty, their taste buds get a facelift, and the preference for sweets decreases while the desire for fat increases. Young men prefer protein-rich fat foods and list meat and potatoes among their favorite foods, probably reflecting the body's attempt to build muscle and perpetuate the species. On the other hand, with their escalating estrogen levels, young women consistently crave sweet-and-creamy foods such as ice cream and chocolate, which stock the fuel stores and prepare them for pregnancy.

In short, some cravings may reach the root of your being, originating in your genetic code. Trying to override these cravings may lead to a binge. (See chapter 11 for more on cravings and eating disorders.) Restrictive diets, erratic eating habits, and very low-fat diets are the worst thing for a person, because they disrupt the natural cycle of nerve chemicals, sending the system into a tailspin. The only way to curb a fat craving is to work with it.

A Calorie Is Not Just a Calorie

There is more to fat than taste and texture. An ounce of fat is over twice as calorie dense as an ounce of carbohydrate or protein. For example, a tablespoon of a fat-rich food such as butter contains more calories than an entire baked potato. Often, removing fat from the diet means that a larger quantity of food can be eaten with fewer calories. Substituting half a baked chicken breast for half a fried chicken breast saves almost 100 calories, with no loss of taste or amount of food. Replacing regular cream cheese with nonfat cream cheese saves 75 calories per ounce. A half-cup serving of Breyer's Inspirations frozen yogurt in place of a half-cup Häagen-Dazs Vanilla Swiss Almond ice cream saves 175 calories and more than a tablespoon of fat (see Table 3.2 for similar examples).

Although most people think that a calorie is just a calorie, in reality calories from fat are more "fattening" than calories from either protein or carbohydrates. As fat intake increases, so do body weight and body fat. One reason for this is the shape of fat. Dietary fat is perfectly shaped for storage as body fat, so only about 3 percent of the calories in a tablespoon of butter or other dietary fat are used to convert it into hip and belly fat. In contrast, carbohydrates and protein are not shaped correctly for storage as fat, so the body uses up almost 25 percent of their calories to convert them to body fat. Even then, the body resists converting car-

TABLE 3.2 Ways to Trim the Fat Without Sacrificing Taste

Cutting the fat means you can eat the same or more food and maintain or even lose weight. Not to mention the benefits to your health!

INSTEAD OF	CHOOSE	CALORIES SAVED	FAT SAVED (IN TEASPOONS)
Chocolate fudge with nuts (3 ounces)	Low-fat fudge made with pureed prunes and nonfat milk (3 ounces)	181	3.0
Yoplait Soft-Frozen Yogurt (6 ounces)	Simple Pleasures frozen dessert (4 ounces)	80	2.0
French vanilla soft ice cream (6 ounces)	American Glacé Soft Serve frozen dessert (4 ounces)	235	4.0
Devil's food cake (1 slice)	Angel food cake (1 slice)	218	2.0
Duncan Hines Oatmeal Raisin cookies (from mix) (3)	Entenmann's Fat-Free Oatmeal Raisin cookies (3)	81	2.0
Pepperidge Farm Tahiti Cookies (3)	Fig bars (3)	74	2.0
Fruit-filled Danish pastry (1 piece)	Whole wheat toast with jam (1 slice)	245	3.5
Croissant (1)	Plain whole wheat bagel (1)	35	2.0
Glazed doughnut (1)	Angel food cake (1 slice)	110	3.0
Premium ice cream (1/2 cup)	Nonfat frozen yogurt (1/2 cup)	175	4.0
Hot cocoa with whole milk (1 cup)	Hot cocoa with water (1 cup)	115	2.0
Vanilla milkshake (10 ounces)	McDonald's Low-Fat Shake (10 ounces)	60	2.0
Hershey's Milk Chocolate candy bar (1.6 ounces)	York Peppermint Patties (0.5 ounce)	186	2.2
French fries	Baked potato	135	4.0
Chicken drumstick, fried	Chicken breast, baked	96	2.5
Ranch dressing (2 tablespoons)	Nonfat ranch dressing (2 tablespoons)	85	3.0

bohydrates and protein to fat, since these fuels are better used as quick-energy stores, such as for glycogen in the muscles and liver or for building tissue. A person must consume an excessive amount of calories as carbohydrates before the body will convert those calories to fat.

The higher the fat content of the diet, the more lipoprotein lipase the body produces. This is an enzyme that converts fats in the blood to fat fragments called fatty acids, which are then stored in fat tissue. With more lipoprotein lipase, the body becomes more efficient in storing body fat. According to a study conducted at the University of Tennessee, the most consistent predictor of body weight in women is the amount of fat in the diet. The body can handle excessive intakes of protein or carbohydrate, but has no way to handle excessive fat intake other than increased storage. Therefore, a person who eats a high-fat diet will gain more weight than a person who eats a high-calorie, high-carbohydrate diet.

The inverse is also true. Overweight women report eating the same number of calories as do lean women, but more of their calories come from fat. Another study showed that, given a choice between a low-fat and a high-fat version of the same food, overweight people choose the high-fat version. Dr. Drewnowski reports that overweight women who repeatedly diet and regain weight also prefer the sweet-and-creamy combination more than do women who are lean or who have been overweight since childhood with no history of weight cycling.

These and other findings suggest that fat cravings sustain a vicious cycle. Whatever makes people fat also contributes to a craving for fatty foods, and fatty foods make people fatter. The good news is that as you lower your fat intake, your fat cravings should subside. Researchers at the Cancer Research Center in Seattle surveyed 448 women who had participated in nutrition classes to lower their fat intake, and 56 percent of them reported that being on a low-fat diet made them dislike the taste of fat. More than 60 percent said they actually felt physical discomfort after eating high-fat foods. Thus, following a low-fat diet can reprogram the body's chemistry and help you maintain a more desirable weight.

Why We Crave Fat: A Simple Explanation

Sometimes food cravings are spurred by a period of abstinence, such as during a strict diet. Much as an alcoholic craves alcohol during withdrawal from the drug, a dieter can experience food cravings because of deprivation. A restrictive diet will catapult most people to the edge of desire for forbidden foods, just as focusing on *not* running into a pothole while riding your bike usually results in falling headfirst into the hole. Dieters can eat diet-friendly foods such as cottage cheese, skinless chicken, and fruit for just so long before the sensory deficit entices them to indulge.

Cravings also are triggered by their positive-reward nature. A preoccupation with chocolate may be the result of months, years, or even decades of having eaten chocolate in positive situations. The chocolate tasted good, the experience was pleasant, and you return for more—sometimes with a vengeance.

Coffee is a good example of how well-established associations of food and good times (positive reinforcers) can lead to future cravings. A person who drinks coffee while sharing special moments with a friend, who has sipped a warm cup of coffee on a lazy morning, or whose welcome break in the hectic day is a cup of coffee is likely to associate the brew with many of life's most cherished moments. Subsequent cravings for coffee are intertwined with feelings of love, peace of mind, refreshment, and escape. On the other hand, people may continue to drink coffee to avoid the unpleasant feelings associated with coffee withdrawal (here coffee is acting as a negative reinforcer). See chapter 12 for a detailed look at the psychology behind food choices.

Of course, the mind can play tricks on you. Knowing how much fat is in a meal may influence how much you eat. At the National Center for Toxicology in Jefferson, Arizona, people were fed similar meals, but were told that some were higher in fat than others. People ate more calories when they thought the meal was low in fat and significantly less food when they believed they were eating a high-fat meal. In short, eating habits are based on beliefs about foods in addition to being influenced by chemicals in the brain that control appetite. The trick is to reeducate yourself about food and reprogram your brain chemicals and taste buds!

Fat Cravings Basics

The only way to curb fat cravings is to work with them, not against them. Depending entirely on willpower to curb a craving seldom works and more likely will lead you hell-bent to a binge. Whether cravings are physical or psychological or both, they are real. The good news is that you can develop a strategy to plan for, avoid, or give in to (in moderation) a craving so it won't do *you* in.

The Feeling Good Diet (see chapter 13) is the basis for controlling your cravings. Follow this low-fat, nutrient-packed eating plan. Divide your food intake into four to six small meals and snacks throughout the day, and always eat something nutritious for breakfast. But it all takes time. Even if you follow the Feeling Good Diet to the letter, it may take several weeks before you notice a difference, especially if your eating habits have been erratic for some time.

Slowly make dietary changes by following the three-step approach outlined in this book. The secret to modifying your nerve-cell response and your fat metabolism is to introduce a gradual shift in sensitivity to these chemicals, including galanin and the endorphins. Small changes lead to big changes over time.

Slowly reduce your dietary fat. If your body is accustomed to a large serving of something sweet-and-creamy late at night, reduce the serving size and slowly substitute more nutritious foods so that eventually you either are not eating after dinner or are choosing only nutrient-packed snacks.

Focus on fiber. Fruits, vegetables, whole grains, and legumes are fiber-packed foods that are filling without being fattening. The soluble fibers found in these foods are especially effective in curbing erratic swings in blood-sugar levels, which ultimately helps reduce food cravings. In addition, unprocessed fiber-rich foods are usually low in fat, so you can eat larger quantities of food, chew more, and feel more satisfied. For example, a tablespoon of salad dressing or peanut butter has the same calories (100) as more than three cups of salad or air-popped popcorn. At every meal and snack, include at least one serving of fruit; vegetables; whole-grain breads and cereals; and legumes, such as kidney beans, chick-peas, or black beans.

Anticipate cravings and plan ahead. Most people know when a craving will hit, but to help identify these times keep a food record for a few weeks that records when, what, and how much you eat and how you felt before and after the meal or snack (see the worksheet on page 75).

If you feel overwhelmed whenever you pass by a doughnut shop or the bakery, you can:

1. Avoid the situation—take a different route to work.
2. Plan a new response—select a low-fat alternative such as a bagel rather than the higher-fat doughnut.

WORKSHEET 3.1 Cravings Control Record

Write down everything you eat and drink and how you felt before and after the meal or snack. At the end of two weeks, review your records to identify your craving-prone times of the day or situations, how you use food to improve your mood or energy level, and the types of foods you are most likely to crave. Then develop a plan to curb your cravings or schedule them into your eating plan. Use this sheet as a master copy.

DATE:____________________

				THOUGHTS/FEELINGS	
WHEN?	WHAT?	HOW MUCH?	WHERE?	BEFORE	AFTER

3. Eat beforehand to eliminate hunger and your vulnerability to the tempting food.

If your cravings come during your energy lull in the day, such as midmorning or midafternoon, you can:

1. Bring a nutritious and pleasurable food with you so you are not at the mercy of office vending machines or the snack cart.
2. Select nonfat foods that give similar satisfaction; if you crave something sweet-and-creamy, try a creamy nonfat yogurt, nonfat cream cheese and jam on crackers, or a small piece of a fat-free cake.

Late-night fat cravings are most common when a person skips meals or snacks during the day, avoids eating breakfast, or eats too many sugary foods throughout the day. These cravings are a conditioned response; the more often you snack at night, the stronger your body's cravings in the future. Often, just two weeks of the Feeling Good Diet will put an end to late-night cravings. Of course, there is nothing wrong with a small snack at night if it fits your eating plan and is a nutrient-packed food. You may even use this time for an indulgence, such as a small serving of ice cream. Use the worksheet on page 77 to chart your progress.

Exercise is essential to control cravings. Exercise curbs hunger, helps burn calories, and realigns the appetite-stimulating nerve chemicals and hormones. Try exercising during your vulnerable time of day. Go for a walk during your midmorning break, or ride an exercise bicycle while watching TV in the evening (see "Question Your Cravings," page 78).

Fake Fats: Savior or Menace?

Imagine eating French fries, doughnuts, double-dipped cones, and fudge without a worry about your heart or your waistline. Fat substitutes such as NutraSweet's Simplesse might make this dream come true. Simplesse, which duplicates the richness of fat, is made from egg and milk protein. Currently, it is used in frozen desserts such as Simple Pleasures, but soon it will be in nonfat salad dressings and mayonnaise products. So far no adverse effects from its use have been reported.

WORKSHEET 3.2 Your Cravings Control Plan

Use the following worksheet to plan and monitor your cravings control progress. Customize the form, using check marks, bar graphs, or written notes, to best suit your needs. Keep in mind you want to take small steps toward long-range goals. Use this worksheet as a master copy.

Long-term goal for managing my fat tooth: ______________________________

Short-term goal for this week is (include details, such as when, where, and how often): ____________

____

MONTH/DAY **WHAT PROGRESS DID I MAKE TOWARD MY GOAL?**

MONTH/DAY		NOTES
________		
________		
________		
________		
________		
________		
________		

Question Your Cravings

Before indulging in a snack attack, ask yourself, "Am I really hungry?" and "Is this food really what I want to eat?" If you answer yes to both questions, then give in to the craving. If it is a high-fat food, limit the serving and supplement it with more nutritious foods. If you answer no to either or both of those questions, then identify what you really want. It may be only a glass of water or to step outside for some fresh air. Simply being aware of your feelings and needs may be all it takes to curb a craving.

Some fat cravings are linked to powerful emotional rewards. Doughnuts and coffee, a chocolate croissant, or a box of candy may unconsciously be associated with friendship, security, good times, or other positive feelings. If this is the case, you can acknowledge the link and occasionally indulge yourself; you can find another food; or better yet, discover some activity that gives you the same positive feelings without the calories and fat.

Another fake fat, called Olestra, is still in development. Olestra is derived from edible oils and sugars, and it rolls off the tongue much like other fats, providing a similar rich taste, but it is calorie free because it is not absorbed by the body. If approved, Olestra could replace conventional fats in everything from home-baked desserts to fast-food fries and potato chips. Initial requests from its manufacturer, Procter & Gamble, for FDA approval were denied when laboratory animals developed cancer, liver damage, and other serious problems after ingestion of Olestra. However, subsequent testing supports the safety of this fake fat when consumed in moderate doses. Fat substitutes may be a promising breakthrough for those who have sweet-and-creamy cravings, since they mimic the feel of fat without the calories.

On the other hand, a study by the Monell Chemical Senses Center in Philadelphia reported that people accustomed to eating a high-fat diet who switch to creamy nonfat foods such as nonfat cream cheese and nonfat sour creams were less content or successful at their eating plan than were people who stopped eating all creamy foods regardless of fat content. Apparently the people who learned to like low-fat foods without a fake-fat "mouth feel" did not miss that creaminess. Since the jury is still out on this issue, you must decide for yourself whether to switch to a lower-fat, reduced-sweet diet or to use the new products that give a sweet-and-creamy taste without the fat and sugar.

If you can't lick 'em coming in, maybe you can help 'em going out. That is the theory, at least, behind another method for ferreting the fat from people's diets. Researchers are currently testing the safety and effectiveness of a compound called Orlistat, which appears to neutralize an important fat-processing enzyme in the digestive tract. This enzyme blocker might reduce fat absorption by as much as 30 percent. So even if you ate a high-fat food, only approximately two-thirds of the fat would be absorbed. Orlistat has side effects, however. It probably can't be consumed in doses large enough to have a significant effect on fat intake, since excessive unabsorbed fat in the digestive tract causes an unpleasant condition called steatorrhea, characterized by abdominal bloating, fatty diarrhea, and gas. Even at its best, Orlistat would be an add-on to a low-fat diet.

Chocolate: Can't Live with It, Can't Live without It

- It was touted as an aphrodisiac and drunk by Montezuma.
- It was guzzled by Casanova, who thought it improved his strength and endurance in amorous pursuits.
- It was once thought to have healing properties.
- It was called "the fighting food" by soldiers in World War II.
- It was consumed in excess of eleven pounds per person last year in the United States.

It's America's favorite flavor. Chocolate has been described as irresistible, wicked, naughty, essential, and divine. Some people can't get through the day without it. Others indulge their cravings in secret.

Apparently chocolate has always been a tantalizing item. The Aztec emperor Montezuma II drank fifty goblets a day, laced with honey and spices. By the 1660s, chocolate houses serving hot chocolate drinks were the rage in England. By the mid-1700s, English beer and ale establishments were so threatened by the popularity of chocolate that they petitioned for legislation to restrict its manufacture. That didn't stop chocolate lovers. By the 1840s, Fry & Sons chocolate factory in Bristol, England, created the first hard or "eating" chocolate, opening the floodgates for worldwide passions, cravings, and addictions.

Today chocolate is universally loved. Americans alone spend more than $5 billion each year on chocolate delights. In a study conducted at the University of

Pennsylvania, researchers found that chocolate was liked by almost everyone, but women were by far its greatest advocates. One in every two women reports having cravings for chocolate. The women in this study craved chocolate more than any other food and were most likely to crave chocolate when they were premenstrual. In fact, the more severe the PMS symptoms, the more likely a woman was to crave chocolate.

Our obsession with chocolate could be partly cultural. While a man receives a bottle of whiskey as a gift, a woman receives chocolates, possibly to sweeten her heart to love. Valentine's Day has become an annual tribute to chocolate and love. Chocolate also is closely associated with indulgence and pleasure. It is not a member of any food group, and is rarely part of the steak-and-potatoes main course, so it is not a component of our daily routine or of any of its obligations, responsibilities, or commitments. Consequently, chocolate symbolizes an escape from daily drudgery. Gourmet chocolates are touted as "sinfully delicious" and "wickedly rich." Most people can't resist a little legal "sin" now and again.

Chocolate's pleasantness might extend beyond indulgence to strike at the tip of your taste buds and the heart of your cravings. The cocoa butter in real chocolate gives it a rich texture. Cocoa butter is solid at room temperature but melts in your mouth at body temperature, providing what has been termed "a moment of ecstasy." While unsweetened chocolate is bitter, it becomes the queen of the sweet-and-creamy desserts when combined with sugar. Consequently, it can trigger a cravings-stimulating reaction involving the body's chemicals, from serotonin and galanin to the endorphins.

Cravings for sweets and chocolate are particularly related to depression. "It's no wonder people turn to chocolate when depressed or stressed," says Dr. Adam Drewnowski. "Chocolate is a combination of sugar, fat, and other compounds [including caffeine and a substance called phenylethylamine] that might stimulate endorphin release in the brain and produce an analgesic effect." The endorphins produce such a powerful pleasure sensation that anything that stimulates their production is likely to be habit forming.

Judith Wurtman, Ph.D., at the Massachusetts Institute of Technology speculates that people crave chocolate because it stimulates serotonin release and calms them. Chocolate also contains theobromine and caffeine, compounds that provide a mental lift. Finally, a compound found in chocolate called phenylethylamine, or PEA, stimulates the nervous system, increases blood pressure and heart rate, and is suspected to produce feelings similar to those experienced when a person is in love. PEA also is linked to the endorphins and thus to the pleasure response.

Not all of these connections between chocolate and body chemistry have been substantiated by well-designed research; consequently many questions remain. For example, cheese and salami are also sources of PEA, but they seldom evoke similar cravings. In fact, the amount of PEA in a candy bar is not likely to be enough to trigger romantic feelings. The endorphin-chocolate link is based on animal studies in which rats became chocolate junkies when given unlimited access to the tasty dessert, while they became indifferent to chocolate when researchers injected them with an endorphin-blocking drug. No such studies have been conducted on humans, so it is only speculation that people and rats share a similar endorphin rush when eating chocolate.

Others argue that a craving for chocolate is really the body's craving for its nutrients, such as magnesium. If this is the case, why don't people crave other magnesium-rich foods such as soybeans, peanuts, and beet greens? In fact, chocolate cravings usually can be satisfied only by chocolate or something that mimics its texture, taste, and smell.

In short, no one knows why we love chocolate, but few will deny the cravings are real. Since more than any other cravings, chocolate urges are not likely to "just go away," the best tactic is to include a small chocolate snack in your eating plan and give it a low-fat facelift (see "Some Chocolate Tricks," page 82, for low-fat chocolate ideas).

Fat Finale

Fat is the bane of many people's attempts to eat well. Affluent societies have become accustomed to having a wide array of sweet-and-creamy delectables at their fingertips. Our cave-dweller bodies—accustomed to crave these high-fuel foods—now must function in the twentieth century, where we are tempted to indulge at every street corner and even in the privacy of our own living rooms.

The Feeling Good Diet helps you appease and curb your cravings and to balance those cravings with nutritional good sense. Within a few weeks of following the guidelines in chapter 13, you should note a drop in cravings and improved feelings of well-being, energy, and general mental health. The longer you stick with this eating plan, the better you will feel.

Some Chocolate Tricks

The more you try to refrain from eating chocolate, the stronger the craving and the greater the likelihood of an all-out binge. Instead, if you put a small chocolate treat into your daily or weekly menu, you are not as likely to feel deprived or to overindulge later on. Here are a few ideas for chocolate snacks that fit the low-fat guidelines outlined in the Feeling Good Diet. Keep in mind that *low fat* does not mean *low calorie* and that many of these selections are still high in sugar.

1. Use cocoa powder instead of hard chocolate. Cocoa has only 30 percent fat calories compared to 50 percent in milk chocolate, 60 percent in some semisweet chocolate, and 76 percent in unsweetened chocolate. Use it in muffins, cookies, or blender drinks for a rich chocolate flavor with less fat. A fat-free chocolate glaze for desserts and fruits can be made by combining 2 tablespoons cold nonfat milk, 1 cup sifted confectioners' sugar, and 1 teaspoon unsweetened cocoa. An extra-rich chocolate angel food cake can be made with one package of angel food cake mix prepared according to directions, combined with 1/3 cup unsweetened cocoa; the cake has only 7 percent fat calories and less than 160 calories per serving.
2. Use chocolate-flavored syrups with 3 percent fat calories. Spoon them over nonfat vanilla yogurt, fresh strawberries, and orange slices, or use them as a dip for frozen grapes and bananas.
3. Eat chocolate with meals. At the end of a meal, you are less likely to overindulge and more likely to choose a small portion.
4. Buy chocolate in small quantities. Avoid the five-pound box of chocolates, the oversized candy bar, and the half-gallon of ice cream. Instead, buy one or two Hershey's Kisses, a Tootsie Roll, or miniature candy bars. A few pieces may satisfy the craving without your going overboard.
5. Warm low-fat fudge in the microwave and spread it thinly on graham crackers for a reduced-fat snack.
6. Look for low-fat, low-calorie versions of traditional desserts. Sara Lee light cakes—Double Chocolate Layer and other varieties—have less than 200 calories per serving. Pepperidge Farm also offers several varieties in their frozen dessert line that contain no more than 190 calories per serving. Low-fat Hostess cupcakes that are jam-filled rather than cream-filled have reduced the fat from 24 percent to 7 percent. Finally, Entenmann's Fat-Free Chocolate Cake is a low-fat version of the original.
7. If the smell of chocolate is your downfall, dab on a little perfume or aftershave under your nose.

Chapter Four

No Energy? It Could Be Your Diet

Do you grab for your coffee mug to jump-start your day? Does your energy level wane by midmorning? Do you have trouble concentrating after lunch or often skip your after-work exercise because you are too worn out? Are you frequently drowsy or wish you could just lie down? Do you yawn throughout the day or does your attention wander? If you blame your lack of energy on your busy schedule or assume you were born this way, think again. Fatigue is not normal, and you don't have to take it lying down. Often a few simple changes in what or how you eat is all it takes to put the spring back into your step. To begin, check your vital signs by taking the quiz on page 84.

Breaking the Fast

- "I'm not hungry in the morning."
- "If I eat breakfast, I'm hungry all day."
- "I don't have time to eat in the morning."
- "Breakfast is boring."

There are hundreds of excuses for not eating breakfast, but none of them is worth the cost to your energy level and general well-being. Breakfast is just that: it breaks the overnight fast and restocks your dwindling energy stores. Expecting your body to shift into full gear without stopping to refuel is like assuming your car will run on empty. You may initially feel energized, but waning blood-sugar levels eventually will do you in. In fact, even if you try to catch up by eating a

QUIZ 4.1 Reading Your Vital Signs

How do your energy boosters stack up to your energy busters? Rate how often you practice the following dietary habits, then total your score for a quick check of how your diet stacks up. Score as follows: 3—always; 2—often; 1—seldom; 0—never.

	SCORE
1. Do you eat four or more meals and snacks in a day?	______
2. Do you eat breakfast?	______
3. Do you limit your sugar intake?	______
4. Do you eat sugary foods alone?	______
5. Do you limit caffeinated beverages to three 5-ounce servings or fewer each day?	______
6. Do you consume at least 2,500 calories each day of fresh fruits and vegetables, whole grains, low-fat milk products, nuts, and protein-rich foods?	______
7. Do you take iron supplements when your iron intake is marginal?	______
8. Do you avoid severe calorie-restricted diets?	______
9. Do you snack lightly or not at all in the evening?	______
10. Do you avoid eating large meals?	______
11. Do you drink at least six glasses of water each day?	______
12. Do you avoid tobacco?	______
13. Do you limit alcohol intake to five drinks or fewer each week?	______
14. Do you get at least seven hours of restful sleep each night?	______
15. Do you take time each day to relax?	______
16. Do you practice some form of relaxation daily?	______
17. Do you exercise regularly?	______
Total	______

Scoring:

More than 40: Your diet and lifestyle support high energy. If you still suffer chronic fatigue, consult your physician and ask for a serum ferritin test to assess iron status.

30 to 39: Your diet and lifestyle might be contributing to fatigue. Select two changes from the above list that you will make to energize your diet.

Less than 30: Your diet and lifestyle are major contributors to waning energy levels. Select four or more changes, based on the above list, to get yourself back on track. After you have successfully implemented the dietary and/or lifestyle changes, expect it to take at least three weeks for your energy level to improve.

well-balanced lunch, you'll never regain the energy you would have had if you had taken ten minutes to eat a nutritious breakfast.

"It is well documented that children learn better and are more attentive when they eat breakfast," says C. Wayne Callaway, M.D., an associate clinical professor of medicine at George Washington University. Breakfast is just as important for adults.

Skipping breakfast because you're not hungry could be a conditioned response. "Your stomach knocks on the appetite door as if to say 'I'm hungry,' but if no one is listening, the hunger pangs eventually go away," says Evelyn Tribole, M.S., R.D., spokesperson for the American Dietetic Association. In short, your body needs the fuel, but you're ignoring the signals.

Ironically, people who skip breakfast in an effort to cut calories often do more snacking later in the day and overeat at evening meals; consequently, they struggle more with weight problems and chronic low energy, especially in the afternoon and evening. According to Dr. Callaway, "People who skip breakfast set up a night-eating syndrome whereby once they start nibbling, they can't stop." In contrast, breakfast helps boost your energy for the rest of the day, breaks the feast-and-famine cycle, and stimulates the metabolic rate, which helps maintain desirable weight and stabilize eating patterns.

Not being hungry in the morning could be a sign of overeating the night before. It's a vicious cycle: you skip breakfast; the night-eating syndrome begins in the late afternoon, often after work or while preparing dinner; this leads to a large dinner and/or late-night snack; and you wake up still full from yesterday.

Do you avoid breakfast because you think it causes you to eat more throughout the day? Again, the increased hunger is not caused by breakfast but by other irregular eating habits. Take a look at what foods you have chosen for breakfast. Sugary foods, even if they are natural sugars such as a fruit salad or toast and jam, trigger the insulin response and raise brain levels of serotonin, leaving you hungry (and sleepy) within two hours. This blood-sugar–brain-chemical roller coaster brings you back to the refrigerator for another snack.

Prolonged or frequent hunger attacks after breakfast could also be a response to food deprivation the day before. Your body's natural hunger cycle may be out of whack because of your feast-and-famine approach to eating. Irregular eating habits cause wide fluctuations in blood-sugar and insulin levels, which affect your energy level and the hunger cues you receive. Breakfast is one way to evenly distribute your day's calories and nutrients and help maintain a steady blood-sugar and energy level.

Breakfast Basics

The first step in feeling better is to eat breakfast, even if you're not hungry. It will take about two weeks to reprogram your hunger cycle before you begin waking up hungry or before the incessant hunger response to breakfast subsides. Eventually, however, you will stop overeating late at night, you will feel less hungry later in the day, and you will have more energy throughout the day.

The three rules for planning breakfast are:

1. Make it light.
2. Limit the fat.
3. Include a protein-rich food and a carbohydrate-rich food.

Large meals—that is, consisting of more than 1,000 calories—make you sleepy regardless of the time of day you eat them. Excessive fat intake slows digestion, interferes with the delivery of oxygen to the brain and other tissues, and causes lethargy. So skip the butter on toast, substitute low-fat milk for whole milk, and limit fat at breakfast to no more than 30 percent of total calories.

The balance of carbohydrates and protein is critical. If you eat too little protein, you're likely to feel hungry within a few hours, while too much carbohydrate is likely to make you sleepy by midmorning. Meals with a mix of protein and starch maintain blood sugar and energy levels for up to four hours or more.

Breakfast needn't be elaborate or traditional; it doesn't even have to be a sit-down meal. Avoid high-sugar breakfasts such as doughnuts and coffee, which trigger an initial energy boost but leave you drowsy within a few hours. Instead, choose an egg substitute and toast; a bagel with low-fat cheese and fruit; cereal and milk; a whole wheat English muffin with fat-free cream cheese and orange juice; or a bowl of oatmeal (mix in a little wheat germ) with low-fat milk and a banana. (For more on cereal for breakfast, see "Cereal Rules," page 88.) To avoid boring breakfasts, try nontraditional foods such as leftover pizza; whole wheat toast and tomato soup; or a sandwich (see "Breakfast Combos," page 87, for additional breakfast ideas).

If your home is more a zoo than a sanctuary in the morning, try a brown-bag breakfast. Pack low-fat yogurt, a muffin, and an orange. Or keep a stash of bagels or low-fat crackers, boxed orange juice, peanut butter, nuts, and dried or fresh fruit in your desk, glove compartment, or briefcase.

Breakfast Combos

The following are quick and easy low-fat breakfast ideas that offer a combination of protein and carbohydrates.

- Fill a crepe with low-fat ricotta cheese and fruit.
- Have ready-to-eat cereal with low-fat milk and fresh fruit.
- Fill a tortilla with shredded carrots, zucchini, low-fat cheese, and salsa.
- Have a cup of vegetable soup with cheese and bread.
- Mix fresh fruit into vanilla yogurt.
- Blend fresh fruit and low-fat milk to make a smoothie.
- Mix dried apricots with low-fat granola and milk.
- Fill a honeydew melon half with nonfat yogurt and sprinkle with sesame seeds.
- Fill a papaya half with cottage cheese and serve with a bran muffin.
- Fill a flour tortilla with cottage cheese and fresh fruit, and warm in the microwave.
- Top an English muffin with one ounce of nonfat cheese and broil until bubbly. Serve with a glass of orange juice.
- Toast a frozen whole wheat waffle and top it with fat-free sour cream and fresh blueberries.
- Warm a low-fat bran muffin and serve with applesauce and yogurt.
- The night before, mix oatmeal, raisins or chopped prunes, and hot water. Cover and let stand overnight. Serve with warm milk and fruit. Makes a delicious molded "breakfast pudding."
- Spread peanut butter on toast and add a sliced banana. Serve with orange juice.
- Spread fat-free cream cheese on a whole wheat bagel. Serve with orange juice and a bowl of sliced strawberries.
- Have a slice of cheese with a McDonald's Apple Bran Muffin or Dunkin' Donuts bran muffin. Serve with orange juice.
- Have a slice of vegetarian pizza. Serve with 100 percent fruit juice.

Cereal Rules

Cereal is the best alternative to the eggs and bacon breakfast. It's quick and nutritious, and it can maintain your energy level through the morning. Chosen carefully, cereal is an excellent source of vitamins, minerals, fiber, and energy-packed carbohydrates. Mixed with milk, it's a good source of protein as well. Look for ready-to-eat or hot cereals that are low in fat and sugar and high in fiber. Select ones that provide:

- At least 3 grams of protein per serving
- At least 2 grams of fiber per serving
- No more than 2 grams of fat per serving
- No more than 4 grams of sugar per serving

The last requirement may be difficult to determine, since sugar often is combined with starch for a total carbohydrate content. If this is the case, check the label and choose cereals that do not list sugar as one of the top three ingredients. Examples of cereals that meet most or all of these criteria are:

Shredded wheat
Grape-Nuts
Nutri-Grain
Mueslix
Wheat and Raisin Chex
Oatmeal or any other unflavored whole-grain hot cereal

Wake Up and Smell the Coffee

- "I can't imagine getting by without my coffee."
- "Coffee should be black as hell, strong as death, and sweet as love."—Turkish proverb
- "This little bean is the source of happiness and wit."—William Harvey, physician (1657)

Advertisements imply that people who drink coffee or colas are energetic and full of life. In reality, too much of these pick-me-ups is more likely to leave you yawning than get you going.

Coffee's welcoming aroma and promise of instant energy have made it the number one mind-altering drug and the second most popular beverage, just behind soft drinks. Americans consume half of the world's coffee, or 450 cups per person per year.

Caffeine is what makes coffee the morning cup of ambition. The caffeine blocks a nerve chemical called adenosine that otherwise blocks other energy-boosting brain chemicals. Thus, adenosine makes you sleepy or tired, while caffeine counters the effect of this energy blocker and helps the alertness chemicals do their job.

Virtually all of the caffeine in coffee is absorbed and is quickly distributed to all parts of the body. Within half an hour, the caffeine's stimulating effects can be felt. Caffeine has a direct influence on the brain and central nervous system. Thought processes and regulatory processes, such as heart rate, respiration, and muscle coordination, also are affected after drinking even one cup of coffee.

Coffee isn't all bad. Some people report that they think faster, work more efficiently, concentrate better, and are more alert after drinking one or two cups. Moderate coffee intake also might improve driving skills in rush-hour traffic, increase typing speed, elevate mood, and improve short-term memory.

However, coffee also can be a double-edged sword. When intake creeps above moderate, the initial high is followed by mild withdrawal symptoms, one of which is fatigue. A vicious cycle can result as a person drinks more coffee to prevent the inevitable let-down. The fatigue and reduced work performance associated with caffeine withdrawal can begin within hours of the last cup and can last up to a week or more. And people's tolerance to caffeine varies widely. Withdrawal symptoms are reported in some people even with small amounts, such as one to two cups daily, while other people can tolerate higher doses with no problems.

Caffeine also lingers in the body for three to four hours. As a consequence, coffee drinkers take longer to fall asleep, sleep less soundly, wake up more often, and wake up groggier than nondrinkers. A restless night is likely to leave you dragging the next day. Substituting a cup of tea or a diet cola for an evening cup of coffee will not prevent insomnia, however, since both the tea and the cola soda contain the same amount of caffeine as a cup of instant coffee. Finally, coffee acts as a diuretic, contributing to dehydration, which in turn causes fatigue. (See chapter 9 for more information on caffeine and sleep.)

Coffee Basics

Coffee goes hand in hand with some of our favorite memories and moments. There is no need to give it up—just cut back. One to three 5-ounce cups, or the equivalent of 300 mg of caffeine or less, in the morning or early afternoon appear to be safe and, except for the most sensitive people, should not contribute to fatigue.

Pay close attention to your serving size. Scientific studies use the 5-ounce cup, while a typical mug could contain twice that amount. Caffeine intake also should be compared to body weight, with short or young people scaling down caffeine intake to fewer than three servings. For example, one 12-ounce cola for a 30-pound child is equivalent to five cups of instant coffee for a 150-pound adult. Because coffee is a diuretic, it can contribute to dehydration and subsequently fatigue. Be sure to drink additional water and other fluids during the day to make up for fluids lost from drinking coffee (see Table 4.1).

People struggling with fatigue who drink a lot of coffee should gradually reduce their intake by one or two cups a day. They are most likely to feel tired or experience other symptoms of coffee withdrawal, such as headaches, if coffee intake is reduced too quickly. Other suggestions for reducing but not eliminating one of life's little pleasures is to switch to instant coffee or an instant coffee blended with chicory or grain. These coffees contain half the caffeine of regular brews. Or blend regular and decaffeinated coffee before brewing, or have your local coffee shop combine regular and decaf. Grain-based beverages such as Pero, Postum, and Cafix contain no caffeine and only 7 to 12 calories per serving. These are robust alternatives to the second or third cup of coffee.

Be aware that decaffeinated coffee is not free from suspicion. The solvent methylene chloride, used to extract the caffeine from the coffee bean, is a chlorinated hydrocarbon, a structure known to cause cancer. Although an analysis by Consumers Union showed no residue of methylene chloride in the finished coffee, other studies have found from two to ten parts per million (ppm) in decaffeinated beans. Many American decaffeinated brands use this solvent in processing.

Ethyl acetate is another solvent used in decaffeinating coffee. This substance is also used to flavor candies, and it breaks down in the body to alcohol and acetic acid, both relatively harmless compounds. Ethyl acetate appears to be safe and is used to a limited extent by Folgers, Hipoint, and other commercial brands. If you purchase coffee from a specialty store, ask what method is used for processing the decaffeinated beans.

Most people know there is caffeine in a cup of coffee or tea, but many don't realize that caffeine is also found in soft drinks, cocoa, coffee-flavored ice cream and yogurt, chocolate, and many over-the-counter medications, including headache remedies, diet pills, and sleep suppressants. For example, 1½ Dexatrim tablets contain the upper daily limit for caffeine of 300 mg.

A Sugar-Coated Sleeping Pill

Do you grab a candy bar when you feel tired? Do you soothe your weary mind with a doughnut? These quick fixes offer a temporary high that could actually be fueling your fatigue, sending you on a blood-sugar roller coaster. For example, researchers at Kansas State University measured mood in 120 college women who drank 12 ounces of water or beverages sweetened with either aspartame (NutraSweet) or sugar. Within thirty minutes the women who drank the sugar-sweetened beverage were the drowsiest. Some people are so sensitive to sugar or caffeine that they feel tired, irritable, or depressed within an hour of eating even two cookies or drinking one cup of coffee. Others can tolerate larger sugar doses before symptoms develop.

According to Larry Christensen, Ph.D., chairman of the department of psychology at the University of South Alabama, 50 percent of people suffering from depression report improvements in energy levels within a week of eliminating sugar and caffeine. "At first, we noted a link between depression and caffeine or sugar. However, we redirected our focus when we realized that mood changes were mediated by an energy component; people who stopped using sugar and caffeine first felt more energetic and then their mood improved."

Sugar is a good source of carbohydrate—the energy fuel—so why do sweets bring you down? For one thing, unlike starch, which slowly releases carbohydrate units called glucose into the blood, sugar dumps rapidly into the bloodstream, causing a rapid rise in blood sugar. To counteract this rise the pancreas quickly releases insulin, which shuttles excess sugar from the blood into the cells. Consequently blood sugar drops, often to levels lower than before the snack (see "Energy Bars," page 93).

TABLE 4.1 The Caffeine Scoreboard

ITEM	CAFFEINE CONTENT (MG)
Coffee (5-oz. cup)*	
Brewed, drip method	60–180
Instant	30–120
Decaffeinated	1–5
Tea*	
Brewed (5-oz. cup)	20–110
Instant (5-oz. cup)	25–50
Iced (12-oz. glass)	67–76
Cocoa drink (5-oz. cup)	2–20
Chocolate milk (8-oz. glass)	2–7
Chocolate, semisweet (1-oz. square)	5–35
Soft drinks (colas; 12-oz. glass)	
Sugar Free Mr Pibb	59
Mountain Dew	54
TAB	47
Coca-Cola, Diet Coke	46
Shasta Cherry Cola	44
Dr Pepper	40
Pepsi	38
Diet Pepsi, Pepsi Light	36
Canada Dry Diet Cola	1
Nonprescription drugs	
Dexatrim	200
Vivarin	200
Prolamine	140
Aqua-Ban diuretic	100
NōDōz, Appedrine	100
Excedrin	65
Anacin, Midol, Vanquish	33
Dristan	30
Prescription drugs	
Cafergot (migraine headaches)	100

Norgesic Forte (muscle relaxant)	60
Fiorinal (tension headache)	40
Darvon compound (pain relief)	32
Soma compound (pain relief)	32
Synalgos-DC (pain relief)	30

*Caffeine content will vary depending on the strength of the brew.

Sugar also increases tryptophan levels in the brain and triggers the release of the brain chemical serotonin, which in turn slows you down. Harris R. Lieberman, Ph.D., a research scientist, and Bonnie Spring, Ph.D., a professor of psychology, both at the Massachusetts Institute of Technology, report that people feel sleepier and have "less vigor" for up to three and half hours after eating a highly refined carbohydrate snack, as compared to a snack that contains more protein.

Finally, people who frequently snack on sweets are likely to consume inadequate amounts of the energizing nutrients. Researchers at the Division of Human Nutrition in Adelaide, Australia, report that the more sugar people consume, the higher their fat and calorie consumption and the lower their intake of vitamins and minerals—in particular, vitamin C, beta-carotene, the B vitamins, magnesium, potassium, and zinc.

Consuming sugar as a quick fix for dwindling energy merely results in a temporary high. In the long run, it can initiate a vicious cycle. "The person suffering

Energy Bars

Are energy bars really energy boosters or are they just high-tech candy bars? Most energy bars are low in fat and high in carbohydrates, but often the carbohydrates are sugar in the guise of fructose or high-fructose corn syrup. They pack an energy punch because they are high in calories—some contain as many or more calories than a candy bar—but they also may send your blood sugar into a tailspin. Some energy bars contain soluble fibers that help curb the blood-sugar rush and some are fortified with a smattering of vitamins and minerals. However, unless you just completed an hour of heavy-duty exercise, you're probably better off with a bagel or a handful of nuts, raisins, or Cheerios as a nutrient-packed snack.

from chronic tiredness and depression who turns to sugary foods may relieve the fatigue and feel better for a short while, but the depression and fatigue return," says Dr. Christensen. The person then must either reach for another sugar fix or seek help elsewhere. As opposed to the temporary sugar high, eliminating sugar and caffeine from the diet is a permanent solution. "Ninety percent of our patients went cold turkey [eliminated all sugar and caffeine from the diet]. They felt worse at first, but an overwhelming number of them felt better and had more energy within a week," says Dr. Christensen.

In short, snack defensively rather than feeding your fatigue. Choose nutrient-packed, time-released carbohydrates such as whole-grain bread sticks, fresh fruit, crunchy vegetables, low-fat granola, soft pretzels, or a fruit-filled crepe for between-meal snacks. Include at least two food groups at each snack and make at least one fresh fruit, a vegetable, or a grain (see "Snack Right," page 95, for healthful snack ideas).

Is Hypoglycemia to Blame?

Every condition from fatigue to personality disorders has been blamed on hypoglycemia, or low blood sugar. Hypoglycemia is not a disease but a symptom of abnormal blood-sugar regulation. It is common in diabetics and people with some other conditions, and it is typically characterized by blood-sugar levels below 50 mg/100 dl of blood. Documented symptoms of hypoglycemia include pallor, fatigue, irritability, inability to concentrate, headaches, palpitations, perspiration, anxiety, hunger, and shakiness or internal trembling. However, many more people believe they have hypoglycemia than actually test positive when given a blood-sugar test.

Dr. C. Wayne Callaway at George Washington University states that people can experience a pharmacological effect from sugar, even if blood-sugar levels remain within the normal range. People's responses to fluctuating blood-sugar levels vary greatly. Some people experience symptoms when the levels are well within the normal range, while others report no symptoms even when blood-sugar levels have dropped substantially. This makes it difficult to draw any direct links between sugar, hypoglycemia, and fatigue. It is likely that each person has a unique blood-sugar range, with fatigue or mood changes occurring when levels fluctuate above or below these levels.

Snack Right

For some energizing snacks, try the following:

- Fruit juice or fresh fruit, peanut butter, and crackers
- Whole wheat bread sticks and nonfat cheese
- Cheerios, raisins, and a cup of yogurt
- English muffin with all-fruit jam and fat-free cream cheese
- Fruit-filled crepe
- Low-fat granola
- Miniature raisin bagel with fat-free cream cheese
- Soft microwave pretzel
- Three-bean salad
- Hot or cold baked potato with nonfat sour cream or nonfat cottage cheese
- Pita bread stuffed with shredded jalapeño cheese and zucchini
- Rice cake with a slice of nonfat cheese
- Oven-baked, fat-free tortilla chips and/or potato chips
- Flavored rice cakes dipped in yogurt
- Graham crackers
- Whole wheat fig bars
- Oatmeal-raisin cookies, ginger snaps, or vanilla wafers and milk
- Frozen fruit-juice bars and crackers
- Water-packed canned fruit and cottage cheese
- Baked apple
- Whole wheat raisin bread dipped in nonfat apple-spice yogurt
- Bran muffin spread with apple butter
- Angel food cake with fresh berries
- Raw vegetables such as jicama, broccoli spears, cauliflower, green or red bell peppers, and Chinese snowpeas dipped in low-calorie dressing
- Baby carrots
- Pears, apples, cantaloupe, or watermelon dunked in honeyed yogurt
- Custard-style low-fat or nonfat yogurt

Drs. William Hudspeth and Linda Peterson at the University of Nevada at Reno report that the fatigue, depression, and hostility associated with hypoglycemia correspond to blood insulin levels, not blood-sugar levels, and also correlate with abnormal brain-wave activity. They theorize that high insulin levels cause the symptoms of hypoglycemia by allowing water and electrolytes such as sodium and potassium to enter brain cells.

The best dietary advice for sugar-sensitive people is to consume five or six small meals throughout the day, rather than the feast-and-famine scenario of a few large meals. In addition, they should consume some complex carbohydrate, protein, and fiber at each meal and snack. The soluble fibers found in oranges, apples, legumes, and oats are particularly effective in slowing the absorption of sugar. They allow a slow, steady release of sugar into the blood and help avoid the rapid rise in blood sugar associated with sugar or highly refined snacks.

Bypassing the Midday Doldrums

Does your motivation wane by midafternoon? Are you less able to concentrate as the day progresses? Are you drowsy on the drive home from work? Are you fit only to be a couch potato in the evening?

Even if you eat a nutritious breakfast and snack right during the morning, your energy could diminish as the day progresses if you don't stop to refuel. In short, what and how you eat for lunch could determine how you feel by midafternoon.

Keep lunch light. A low-fat midday meal that contains approximately 500 calories maintains afternoon alertness and boosts energy levels, while skipping lunch or indulging in a high-fat, high-calorie lunch of 1,000 calories or more can leave you yawning, unable to concentrate. A fatty meal also increases blood tryptophan levels (and, therefore, brain serotonin levels), thus lowering your fatigue threshold.

Carbohydrate-rich foods—from bread to dessert—can also elevate serotonin levels and make you drowsy in the afternoon and evening. In contrast, protein-rich foods increase the brain level of the amino acid tyrosine, a primary building block for the energizing chemicals dopamine and norepinephrine. In studies, tyrosine was found to boost alertness, vigilance, and concentration (see also chapter 1).

Women appear to be more susceptible than men to carbohydrate-induced drowsiness, but anyone will be less alert and make more mistakes after a carbohydrate-rich lunch of, say, pasta as compared to a turkey sandwich. Drs. Lieberman and Spring state that "the evidence that protein and carbohydrate meals have opposite behavioral effects continues to accumulate. It seems likely . . . that carbohydrate relative to protein decreases arousal level and impairs performance."

Consequently, plan your carbohydrates so they work with your energy levels, not against them. For example, you may feel relaxed after a carbohydrate-rich dinner of spaghetti, but the same meal at lunch could make you sluggish. Light lunches, such as a tuna sandwich, fruit, and low-fat milk or a salad, French bread, and yogurt, are more likely to keep you going throughout the afternoon. Other "brain power" foods include a small amount of fish, veal, skinless chicken, or legumes combined with grains and vegetables.

As discussed in chapter 2, people who crave carbohydrates are an exception to the rule. According to researchers at the Massachusetts Institute of Technology, people who crave sweet or starchy foods in the afternoon might have extra-low levels of serotonin. While others feel drowsy, carbohydrate cravers are energized and more alert after they eat carbohydrates, especially if they are complex carbohydrates such as cereals, breads, pasta, or starchy vegetables.

Midday Basics

If you are a carbohydrate craver, don't expect to "will away" those cravings. Make sure every lunch contains some complex carbohydrates, such as a bean and cheese tortilla or a baked potato topped with grated vegetables and low-fat cheese.

Plan to include a carbohydrate-rich snack for your low-energy times of the day or midday doldrums. For example, eat twenty to thirty of the new flavored miniature rice cakes or a handful of pretzels for the calorie cost of one candy bar or energy bar—and they're fat-free. A banana and a bagel also will do the trick; if carbohydrate cravings aren't your problem, you can add peanut butter, low-fat cheese, thin-sliced lean meats, or other protein-rich selections to the miniature rice cakes, bagels, or low-fat crackers to get a comparable energy boost.

Ironing Out Your Fatigue Problems

Does exercise wear you out? Are you tired even after completing only a few routine tasks? Does your fatigue interfere with your physical functioning? If so, your problem might be too little iron.

Iron deficiency is so widespread it might be considered epidemic. It certainly could be the leading cause of fatigue in women. While as few as 5 to 8 percent of all women are anemic, as many as 80 percent of exercising women and 39 percent of premenopausal women in general are iron deficient. Iron deficiency usually goes unnoticed, since routine blood tests for iron status, such as the hemoglobin and hematocrit tests, reflect only a woman's risk of anemia, the final stage of iron deficiency. Long before the onset of anemia, the tissue stores of iron have slowly drained, leaving a woman feeling tired and irritable. Her concentration and exercise ability are not up to par, and her immune system is affected, placing her at higher risk of developing colds and infections.

Iron-Poor Blood

Iron is a component of hemoglobin in the red blood cells and of myoglobin in the muscles and other tissues. These iron-dependent molecules are responsible for transporting oxygen from the lungs to and within the cells. When dietary intake of iron is inadequate or when iron absorption is poor, iron in the tissues is released to make up for deficits in the blood. The cells slowly suffocate from lack of oxygen and inefficiently burn carbohydrates for energy. Consequently, you feel sluggish, can't concentrate, or are exhausted after even minimal effort, such as walking up a flight of stairs. These symptoms occur as the tissue stores are drained, even when there are no signs of anemia. Symptoms worsen as the deficiency progresses to anemia.

Women—especially those who exercise, have been pregnant within the past two years, or consume fewer than 2,500 calories per day—are at particular risk for iron deficiency. For example, the elevated oxygen needs of exercise and increased urinary and sweat losses of iron place a greater demand on iron requirements in physically active people. The loss of blood during menstruation doubles a woman's requirement for iron, while her food and calorie intakes are low compared to men's.

A menstruating, moderately active woman should consume at least 18 mg of iron daily (more if her menstrual flow is heavy or she uses an intrauterine device for birth control). According to Fergus Clydesdale, Ph.D., head of the department of food science at the University of Massachusetts in Amherst, a well-balanced diet supplies approximately 6 mg of absorbed iron for every 1,000 calories. Based on this ratio, women must increase their average intake from 2,000 calories to at least 3,000 calories daily to meet their daily requirement of 15 to 18 mg.

Dr. Clydesdale points out that "this increased calorie intake equates to about a two-pound weight gain each week or 100 pounds a year." It's no wonder women opt for lower calories while typically consuming as little as 8 mg of iron daily.

Women also get most of their total day's iron from vegetables, fruits, and grains. Only 2 to 7 percent of this iron is actually absorbed, while 20 to 30 percent of the iron in red meat is absorbed. If a woman also drinks tea or coffee with her meals, iron absorption could fall even further.

Jan Johnson-Shane, Ph.D., R.D., an associate professor of nutrition at Illinois State University, has studied the beneficial effect of red meat on iron status. Her research found that small amounts—only 3 ounces a day—of red meat was all it took to improve iron status. The link between dietary fat and heart disease or cancer may have swung the pendulum too far, with many people now avoiding all red meat and consequently jeopardizing their nutritional status.

Dr. Johnson-Shane says, "It's important to look at the total fat intake, with red meat being only one source of fat in the diet. If the serving is small and extra-lean cuts are used as a side dish rather than the main course, then red meat is an excellent source of iron while still falling within the guidelines of a low-fat diet."

Iron Basics

Everyone, especially premenopausal women, should keep a close eye on personal iron status. Serum ferritin is the most sensitive indicator of iron status, but physicians don't routinely measure it, so be your own health advocate. Besides the routine iron tests—for hemoglobin and hematocrit—request more sensitive tests that reflect tissue iron levels, including serum ferritin and total iron-binding capacity (TIBC). A serum ferritin value below 20 mcg/L or a TIBC value greater than 450 mcg/L is a red flag for iron deficiency.

Also, increase your dietary intake of iron-rich foods as a first-line defense (see Table 4.2 below and "Iron-Clad Rules," page 101). In addition, a moderate dose of a daily iron supplement (18 mg) should improve iron status, mental function, and energy levels within three weeks. Severe iron deficiency may require a higher dose.

TABLE 4.2 Prime Sources of Iron

Select several servings daily of the following iron-rich foods.

FOOD	SERVING SIZE	IRON CONTENT (MG)
Oysters	3/4 cup	10.0
Liver, beef	3 ounces	8.0
Tofu	1/2 cup	7.0
Beef heart	3 ounces	6.4
Kidney beans	1 cup cooked	5.0
Swiss chard	1 cup cooked	4.0
Black beans	1 cup cooked	3.6
Beef, lean	3 ounces	3.0
Acorn squash	1 cup cooked	2.8
Hamburger, lean	3 ounces cooked	2.7
Prune juice	1/4 cup	2.6
Spinach	1/2 cup	2.4
Round steak, lean only	3 ounces cooked	2.3
Refried beans	1/2 cup	2.3
Lima beans	1/2 cup	2.2
Tuna, water-packed	3 ounces	1.6
Dandelion greens	1/2 cup cooked	1.6
Green peas	1/2 cup	1.5
Chicken, meat only	3 ounces	1.4
Mustard greens	1/2 cup cooked	1.3
Strawberries	3/4 cup	1.1
Tomato juice	1/2 cup	1.1

On the other hand, since excessive iron buildup in the body is possibly linked to an increased risk of heart disease and cancer, there is no reason for men or post-menopausal women to supplement with iron unless a serum ferritin test shows they are iron deficient, and then only with physician approval and monitoring.

Vitamins and Minerals in Short Supply

Does your fatigue interfere with your work, family, or social life? Are you more tired during times of stress, depression, or other emotional times? Is your current struggle with fatigue different in quality or severity from past bouts of tiredness? If so, take a good look at your diet.

Cutting corners on almost any vitamin or mineral will affect your well-being.

Iron-Clad Rules

There's more to consuming enough iron than just eating iron-rich foods or taking a supplement. Iron status, in fact, reflects a balance between iron inhibitors and iron enhancers in the diet. To tip the scale in your favor, do the following:

1. Consume small amounts of extra-lean meat—9 percent fat or less—with large amounts of iron-rich grains, vegetables, and beans—for example, spaghetti and meatballs.
2. Always eat a vitamin C–rich food with an iron-rich food, such as orange juice with a bowl of oatmeal.
3. Cook acidic foods, such as tomato-based sauces, in cast-iron cookware.
4. Take iron supplements on an empty stomach and avoid taking calcium or zinc at the same time as you take iron.
5. Drink tea and coffee between meals, since these beverages contain compounds called tannins that can reduce iron absorption by 80 percent or more.
6. Limit your consumption of unleavened whole grain breads, such as whole wheat biscuits or flour tortillas, since they contain a substance called phytate that inhibits iron absorption. This effect is reduced when vitamin C–rich foods are eaten with these foods—for example, a bean burrito made with a whole wheat tortilla, tomatoes, and cilantro.

For example, suboptimal intake of the B vitamins results in fatigue, poor concentration, apathy, and shortness of breath after minor physical effort. E. Cheraskin, M.D., and colleagues at the University of Alabama in Birmingham investigated the link between vitamin C intake and fatigue in a group of 411 dentists and their wives. Although their study is not conclusive, they did find that those people who consumed less than 100 mg of vitamin C each day were twice as likely to suffer from fatigue as people who consumed 400 mg or more.

A short supply of minerals also can drag you down, since many of these nutrients maintain and regulate the nervous system and energy metabolism. For example, a magnesium deficiency causes muscle weakness and fatigue, probably because of the mineral's role in converting carbohydrates, protein, and fat into energy. Magnesium also helps remove toxic substances such as ammonia from the body and regulates muscle contraction and relaxation.

Chronic Fatigue Syndrome: A Dietary Approach

Chronic fatigue syndrome (CFS) is characterized by debilitating fatigue that does not subside with bed rest and that reduces daily activity below 50 percent of normal for at least six months. Common symptoms include a mild fever, sore throat, painful and swollen lymph nodes, muscle aches and weakness, prolonged fatigue after exercising, headaches, mood swings, joint pain, and sleep disorders. People who suffer from CFS often feel their lives are being destroyed by fatigue and may also struggle with depression and poor concentration. At least eight symptoms that have progressed for at least six months must be present in order to clinically diagnose CFS.

While the cause of CFS is unknown, many researchers suspect that a viral infection at least initiates the disorder and leads to the prolonged fatigue state. If CFS starts as a viral infection, there is the possibility that it is contagious, especially for people with suppressed immune systems.

There is no foolproof test for CFS, which makes diagnosis difficult. Women are more likely than men to have it, although it is not clear why this is true. It could be that women report chronic fatigue more often, or that some hormonal link to the disorder has yet to be identified. The symptoms of CFS are vague, so patients are often misdiagnosed as having Lyme disease, lupus, or early multiple sclerosis.

The symptoms also resemble those of depression, panic disorder, anxiety, and hypochondria, which further muddies the diagnostic waters. Consequently, while as many as 70 percent of physicians acknowledge CFS as a real problem, only about 10 percent prescribe anything more than bed rest.

Unfortunately, there are no clear dietary guidelines for the prevention and treatment of CFS. The outdated theory of treating the illness by avoiding all funguslike foods such as mushrooms and yeast breads and using antifungal medications has been rejected, since there is absolutely no connection between CFS and yeast. Your best bet is to follow the Feeling Good Diet, which contains all the nutrients known to strengthen the immune system and maintain optimal health. In addition, the Feeling Good Diet limits fat to less than 30 percent of total calories, which helps stimulate immune function and improve resistance to infection.

One study from Great Britain's University of Southampton reported that patients suffering from CFS had low blood levels of magnesium and responded favorably within six weeks to magnesium supplements. Improvements in the patients' energy level and mood in this study were similar to improvements in insomnia, anxiety, and mood swings associated with magnesium supplementation noted in other studies. Unfortunately, not all studies have found a link between magnesium intake and risk of CFS, so the link remains controversial. Until more is known, it is wise to include several daily servings of magnesium-rich foods such as peanuts, bananas, low-fat milk, and wheat germ, or make sure your supplement contains magnesium.

The Energizing Lifestyle

Whether you are a lark and accomplish your best work in the morning or an owl who comes alive after dark, what and how much you eat can direct how energized you feel. The Feeling Good Diet forms the foundation for fighting fatigue. In addition, the following rules are important for boosting your energy level.

1. Eat a breakfast that includes some protein and some carbohydrates. Select at least one serving of protein-rich foods such as legumes, meats, or low-fat dairy and at least two to three servings of fruits, vegetables, and grains.

2. Limit caffeinated beverages to three servings or fewer and don't drink tea and coffee with meals.
3. Never eat sugar alone and limit your daily intake to 10 percent of total calories.
4. Eat several small meals and snacks throughout the day, so that you eat approximately every four hours. (This provides a steady supply of fuel to sustain a high energy level.)
5. Eat a moderate-size, low-fat lunch that contains a mixture of protein and carbohydrates. Select at least one serving of protein-rich foods such as legumes, meats, or low-fat dairy and at least three servings of fruits, vegetables, and grains. Those who crave carbohydrates may want to select even more grains and starchy vegetables.
6. If you crave carbohydrates, plan a carbohydrate-rich snack for your low-energy period of the day.
7. Do not overeat in the evening and avoid excessive snacking after dinner.
8. Consume ample amounts of iron-rich foods and take an iron supplement if your serum ferritin levels are below 20 mcg/L.
9. Avoid severe calorie-restricted diets. Too few calories means too little fuel and nutrients, which can leave you drowsy. People who repeatedly diet or consume very-low-calorie diets report that they have trouble concentrating, experience impaired judgment, and have poor memory. Long-term food restriction also results in lethargy, tiredness, depression, poor mental functioning, and greatly decreased feelings of energy.
10. Drink water. Chronic low fluid intake is a common but often overlooked cause of mild dehydration and fatigue. Thirst is a poor indicator of water needs. A general rule of thumb is to drink twice as much water as it takes to quench your thirst, or at least six to eight glasses a day.

11. Avoid alcohol consumption or limit your intake to no more than five drinks a week. Alcohol dehydrates the cells and suppresses the nervous system, causing poor attention, an inability to concentrate, and fatigue. Alcohol also interferes with a good night's sleep.

Exercise is one of the best antidotes for fatigue. The link is clear: people who exercise feel more energetic, while the sedentary get drowsier. Exercise increases blood flow to the muscles and brain, releases energizing hormones, and stimulates the nervous system to produce chemicals, called endorphins, that elevate mood and produce feelings of well-being. According to Dr. C. W. Smith at the University of Arkansas for Medical Sciences in Little Rock, "Exercise should be part of everyone's lifestyle, but may be a particularly important part of the treatment of patients with depression and chronic fatigue. It will reliably and consistently decrease feelings of tiredness and despondency."

In one study, eighteen people rated their energy levels after twelve days of either eating a candy bar or walking briskly for ten minutes. Results indicated that walking increases energy levels and lowers tension, while a sugary snack increases feelings of tension and only temporarily raises energy levels, followed by an increase in fatigue and reduced energy. So when you feel like lying down, get up and move instead. Of course, sometimes tiredness is simply a sign of too little sleep; in that case, a good night's rest is all you need. But if muscle or mental fatigue is caused by inactivity, exercise.

Lastly, you don't have to take fatigue lying down. Holly Atkinson, M.D., in her book *Women and Fatigue*, recommends keeping a journal to identify what times of day you are most energized, tired, or in the best and worst moods. Find out what precedes your periods of high and low energy, including sleep, stress, diet, or exercise. Once you have identified the source of your fatigue, you can develop a plan to combat the blahs and rev up your engine.

Chapter Five

PMS and SAD

- Do you crave chocolate and doughnuts during the winter months or the week before your period? At the same time, do you feel clumsy or puff up like Jabba the Hutt?
- Do you snap at your friends or hope you make it through the day without crying in public?
- Do you sleep too much, yet feel tired all day long?

Don't worry, you're not crazy. You probably have premenstrual syndrome (PMS), seasonal affective disorder (SAD), or both. PMS is the moodiness, anxiety, depression, food cravings, and bloated feeling many women experience the week to ten days before their period. The symptoms subside once the menstrual period begins and are followed by a symptom-free phase that lasts until after ovulation of the next cycle. People with SAD dread the autumn and winter, when their otherwise optimistic approach to life is replaced by depression, increased appetite and weight gain, lethargy, and an insatiable need to sleep.

PMS and SAD have more in common than meets the eye. For example, PMS symptoms worsen during the winter months for people with SAD. In addition, many of the symptoms once thought to be imagined are now suspected to be triggered by brain chemicals such as serotonin, which are regulated by what you eat. Thus, a few changes in diet might work wonders for people with either PMS or SAD.

Premenstrual Syndrome: The Period Before Your Period

A woman who is confident, clear-headed, and physically fit suddenly turns tearful, muddled, and uncoordinated the week before her period. While menstruation might be a slight inconvenience, the mild to severe mood shifts and physical changes that accompany PMS can be the true test of a woman's courage. Some women describe the shift in personality as a Jekyll and Hyde phenomenon: they feel and act fine for three weeks out of the month, then are "possessed" by a flood of emotional and physical feelings for the few days before their period.

Although 20 to 90 percent of all women are affected by PMS, the syndrome has been difficult to isolate and define. Consequently, PMS is a catchall for unexplained problems and is blamed for everything from murders to eating chocolate eclairs. What makes PMS so elusive is its complexity. Up to 150 different symptoms have been documented, from headaches, fatigue, forgetfulness, and mood swings to weight gain, breast tenderness, anxiety, and food cravings. A woman may have only one or a combination of symptoms, and the symptoms may vary each month (see "Do I Have PMS?" page 108).

For years, women were told their symptoms were "all in their head." Granted, many women say they felt better after taking a placebo they thought was medication, suggesting a psychological component. However, current research shows that PMS results from a complex range of factors, including fluctuations in hormones, hormonelike substances called protaglandins, and nerve chemicals such as serotonin; fluid and sodium retention; and low blood sugar. In addition, blood-fat levels such as cholesterol rise and fall in rhythm with the menstrual cycle. Many of these factors might be influenced by nutritional deficiencies or excesses, and they can be at least partly improved with changes in diet.

Keep in mind, however, that these hormonal shifts are part of a woman's natural monthly rhythm. They signal that something very important is happening: she is preparing for conception and motherhood. Therefore, PMS can be viewed either as a disorder or as a time of awareness and celebration. In cultures where people honor the female cycle, PMS symptoms often are nonexistent.

QUIZ 5.1 Do I Have PMS?

The only way you will know whether you have PMS is to keep a symptoms diary for three months and record your mood, health, and food intake every day. You probably have PMS if you notice changes for the worse—depression or irritability, breast tenderness or abdominal bloating, or poor eating habits—during the ten days prior to the onset of menstruation, for at least two of the three months recorded. Review your symptoms diary and answer the following questions to determine your PMS status. Answer these questions yes or no.

During the week to ten days prior to your period:

_______ **1.** Does your mood take a turn for the worse—do you feel more depressed, tearful, irritable, angry, hopeless, or insecure?

_______ **2.** Are you more uptight, on edge, tense, anxious, or stressed?

_______ **3.** Do you have trouble concentrating, solving problems, or remembering details?

_______ **4.** Are you less interested in hobbies, friends, work, or life?

_______ **5.** Are you easily fatigued or do you experience low energy?

_______ **6.** Do you notice an obvious change in your eating habits—overeating, food cravings, or food aversions?

_______ **7.** Do you have trouble sleeping?

_______ **8.** Do you notice any physical changes, such as breast tenderness, abdominal bloating, joint or muscle pain, weight gain, or headaches that do not occur during other times of the month?

If you answered yes to any of the above questions:

_______ **9.** Do these symptoms interfere with your work, social life, or family obligations?

_______ **10.** Are these symptoms independent of other health conditions, such as illness, stress, long-term medication use, or a diagnosed personality disorder?

_______ **11.** Have these symptoms been identified by keeping a symptoms diary for at least three months?

_______ **12.** Would you estimate that these symptoms are at least a third worse than any symptoms you experience during and for the two weeks following your period?

Scoring:

If you answered yes to three or more out of questions 1 through 8, 10, and 11, you probably experience some degree of PMS. The more yes answers, the more extensive your symptoms. If you answered yes to questions 9 and/or 12, you may be suffering from moderate to serious PMS problems and would benefit from diet and exercise changes; you should also discuss your symptoms with a physician.

The What and Why of PMS

Four PMS symptom categories have been identified. A woman might experience symptoms from one or more of these categories or the pattern of symptoms might change each month.

1. Tension symptoms include nervous tension, mood swings, irritability, and anxiety.
2. Hyperhydration symptoms include weight gain, swelling in the hands and feet, breast tenderness, and bloating.
3. Craving symptoms include increased hunger, cravings for sweet or salty foods, headaches, dizziness, and a pounding heart.
4. Depression symptoms include poor memory, frequent crying, insomnia, depression, and confusion.

An imbalance in the relationship between the female hormones—estrogen and progesterone—might be a contributing factor in PMS symptoms. For example, excess estrogen in proportion to progesterone remains in the bloodstream as a result of the liver's inability to break it down, possibly because of a shortage of B vitamins. One study found that nutritional supplementation optimized the ratio between these two hormones, with a reduction in or even elimination of PMS symptoms. Excess estrogen can also remain in the bloodstream when less estrogen is excreted. A high-fiber diet has been recommended for women troubled by PMS, because it enhances estrogen excretion. However, fluctuations in serotonin and other nerve chemicals also contribute to PMS.

Who Is a Candidate for PMS?

Since many PMS symptoms result from the natural and normal fluctuation in female hormones, it is safe to say that any menstruating woman is a likely candidate for PMS. Approximately one in every two women in their childbearing years experiences symptoms to a moderate or severe degree. There is no difference in the incidence of PMS between married and unmarried women or among women with one or more children. Women who work full time, who are between the ages of twenty-five and forty-four, or who have higher education have a slightly higher incidence of PMS. Exceptions always exist, however, including reports of PMS in young girls before menarche and in some women perimenopausally.

Often women in their thirties notice premenstrual difficulties for the first time. PMS might begin with a significant hormonal event such as pregnancy, after use of the birth control pill, or during a period of amenorrhea (failure to menstruate). Women with a history of toxemia during pregnancy have up to a 90 percent chance of developing PMS. Sterilization, especially tubal ligation, also might trigger the onset of premenstrual symptoms. A variety of lifestyle factors seem to aggravate symptoms; these include stress, an inadequate amount of outdoor physical activity, and a diet that is high in sugar and refined carbohydrates, salt, fat, alcohol, and caffeine.

While many women experience symptoms, they may not be aware they have PMS. Often women accept the effects of PMS as part of being a woman and silently cope with their symptoms. Keeping a diary of body and mood changes is the best way to determine if the symptoms you experience are related to PMS. You are a likely candidate for PMS if your symptoms cluster during the second half of your monthly cycle.

PMS Calories and Cravings

Both PMS and SAD trigger food cravings. One out of every three women experiences increased hunger and food cravings during the two weeks before her period and may consume as much as 87 percent more calories than at other times during the month. Theories abound on why women are hungrier during the premenstrual phase. Fluctuations in progesterone might at least partly explain the increase. Both progesterone and estrogen peak approximately one week after ovulation—at the beginning of the premenstrual phase—which is associated with increased calorie intake. Low blood sugar associated with PMS also has been blamed for increased hunger and food cravings.

PMS and sweets go hand in hand. Studies repeatedly show that women who are depressed and who battle food cravings during the premenstrual phase also are most likely to turn to chocolate and other sweets, with sugar intake increasing to as much as 20 teaspoons daily. Hormonal changes coincide with the increased appetite and might be partly responsible. For example, serotonin levels drop and estrogen and progesterone levels rise at about the same time as PMS symptoms and increased hunger develop. As discussed in chapters 1 and 2, serotonin is a brain chemical that helps regulate hunger, irritability, depression, aggression, pain, and sleep. As serotonin levels drop during the premenstrual phase, a woman understandably might experience increased cravings for foods that help elevate serotonin levels, such as sweet carbohydrates. Her craving for sweets is self-medication in an attempt to improve mood.

The link between serotonin and PMS is more than skin-deep. For example, Judith Wurtman, Ph.D., a research scientist at the Massachusetts Institute of Technology, reports that the most frequently reported symptoms of PMS, including cravings for carbohydrate-rich foods, sleep disturbances, and depression, coincide with dwindling serotonin levels. When comparing PMS sufferers with women who did not experience PMS symptoms, Dr. Wurtman found that the daily energy intake of PMS sufferers increased from 1,892 calories to 2,395 calories and carbohydrate intake increased 24 percent during meals and 43 percent from snacks. After eating a high-carbohydrate snack, the women showed some relief from depression, tension, anger, confusion, sadness, and fatigue, and they felt more alert and calm. Dr. Wurtman concludes that premenstrual women may overeat carbohydrates in an attempt to raise serotonin levels and improve their negative moods.

Endorphins, or more specifically a lack of endorphins, also might influence PMS risk. A surge in the pleasure-producing endorphins coincides with ovulation, but levels drop off during the premenstrual phase, possibly contributing to the depression, hunger, irritability, food cravings, and other mood changes. C. James Chuong, M.D., and colleagues at the Mayo Clinic in Rochester, Minnesota, report that endorphin levels are lower during the premenstrual phase (the two weeks before the onset of menstruation) in women with PMS than in the same women during the rest of the month or in PMS-free women. The researchers conclude that the endorphin deprivation might contribute to the onset of premenstrual symptoms. The low endorphin levels also might set off cravings for sweet-and-creamy foods that possibly elevate endorphin levels and mood.

The mood swings and depression that accompany PMS might be caused or aggravated by this high sugar intake. Research conducted at Texas A & M University shows that depression and fatigue often vanish when sugar and caffeine are removed from the diet. Some women are so sensitive to sugar that even one doughnut can affect their mood. This sugar sensitivity might be aggravated during PMS, intensifying the emotional highs and lows and escalating a minor food craving into a binge.

On the other hand, Dr. Wurtman suspects it is not the sugar but the fat in cookies, ice cream, and other sweet-and-creamy foods that poses a problem. "The fat in these foods slows down digestion and interferes with the serotonin effect," says Dr. Wurtman. To maximize serotonin levels and improve your mood, eat a low-fat, carbohydrate-rich snack, such as honey on an English muffin or all-fruit jam on toast, on an empty stomach.

As opposed to the temporary sugar high, eliminating sugar and caffeine from the diet and consuming more complex carbohydrates such as potatoes, pasta, rice, and whole grains might be a permanent solution. In a study conducted at MIT, PMS sufferers reported they were less tense, angry, confused, and tired when they ate a bowl of cornflakes rather than a candy bar. They also felt more alert.

Chocolate Cravings

Chocolate is many women's best friend during PMS. Some researchers suspect that chocolate cravings are unconscious desires for a compound called phenylethylamine (PEA), a substance in chocolate that stimulates the release of the neurotransmitter dopamine, which helps regulate mood. Another theory states that because PMS often involves alterations in blood sugar and magnesium levels, the increased cravings—especially for chocolate, since it supplies some magnesium—might reflect the body's attempt to restore normal blood sugar and magnesium levels. However, women do not crave other magnesium-rich foods such as soybeans or beet greens during the premenstrual phase (or during any phase, for that matter), so this theory remains controversial.

What is clear is that women usually cannot will away their chocolate cravings, especially during PMS. And since there is no evidence that small amounts of chocolate pose any harm to health or emotional well-being, satisfying a chocolate urge in moderation might be the best strategy. "Some Chocolate Tricks," page 82, in chapter 3, provides suggestions for having your chocolate and eating it, too, but with a low-fat facelift and in small amounts.

What Can You Do About PMS?

PMS may have come out of the closet, but its treatment is still in the dark ages. There is much more to be learned about this syndrome, so in the meantime, it is wise to err on the side of moderation.

The Facts and Fallacies About Fat

Limiting dietary fat—especially animal fats—and including a small amount of safflower oil in the daily diet might help reduce PMS symptoms. Although the connection is still poorly understood, a special compound in safflower oil called linoleic acid might help regulate prostaglandins, which are hormonelike compounds that cause some of the abdominal bloating and breast discomfort associated with PMS. One or two tablespoons of safflower oil in the daily diet supplies enough linoleic acid to meet the body's needs without jeopardizing any low-fat dietary goals.

Animal fat directly influences the blood levels of estrogen, which might be at the root of many PMS symptoms. Avoiding saturated animal fats or limiting red meat to 3 ounces a day might help curb dramatic fluctuations in estrogen and prevent monthly suffering.

One study on evening primrose oil, which contains vitamin E and a fat called gamma linolenic acid (GLA), reported that the oil might help regulate the production of prostaglandins. However, one study does not a conclusion make. In addition, most commercial primrose oil supplements contain mostly linoleic acid, not GLA. The U.S. Food and Drug Administration prohibits the sale of pure evening primrose oil, on the grounds that it is not considered safe and is not approved as a food additive.

Caffeine, Alcohol, and Other Drinks

Women drink more fluids during the premenstrual phase than at other times of the month, and some of these drinks could be aggravating their symptoms. Coffee and other caffeinated beverages are a case in point. Women who consume several caffeine-containing beverages each day, including coffee, tea, and colas, or even caffeine-containing medications, are more likely to have PMS and to suffer from severe mood and physical changes, such as tiredness, irritability, anxiety, headaches, breast tenderness, food cravings, constipation, and acne, than are women who consume less or no caffeine. The effect might be dose-dependent—that is, the more caffeine a woman consumes, the greater is her risk for PMS and the more severe are her symptoms. However, because PMS symptoms are unique to each woman, some women may tolerate caffeine while caffeine may aggravate symptoms in other women.

How caffeine aggravates PMS symptoms is unclear, although caffeine's effects on the nervous system are well known and probably contribute to PMS. Researchers at Oregon State University in Corvallis investigated caffeinated beverages versus fluid intake in general to see if the relationship to PMS was with fluids rather than coffee. Their findings, however, added further support for caffeine's effect.

Women with PMS should consider eliminating all caffeine from their diets to test whether or not the coffee, tea, chocolate, and colas are contributing to their symptoms. Changes should be evaluated after several months, since results may not show up immediately.

PMS sufferers are more likely than other women to drink more alcohol during the premenstrual phase. Although the increased alcohol intake might slightly reduce the pain and discomfort associated with PMS, it also aggravates antisocial behavior, hostility, anger, and other negative symptoms of PMS. Women who experience PMS symptoms are more likely than other women to drink too much and abuse alcohol, thus jeopardizing their overall health as well. In addition, alcohol intake during the premenstrual phase is associated with other harmful behaviors, such as increased tobacco use. Women with PMS, especially those with moderate to severe symptoms, should avoid alcohol or limit intake to no more than five drinks a week (one drink equals one 6-ounce glass of wine, one 12-ounce beer, or one shot of alcohol).

Will Supplements Do the Trick?

PMS sufferers consume more calories and fewer vitamins and minerals than do other women. PMS symptoms often improve when these women switch from their highly refined and processed diets to a nutrient-packed diet with or without supplements.

For example, researchers at USDA Human Nutrition Research Center in Grand Forks, North Dakota, report that many of the physiological, psychological, and behavioral symptoms related to the menstrual cycle might be associated with nutrition. In their study, menstrual symptoms were compared to blood levels of different vitamins and minerals. Results showed that low iron levels were most common in women suffering from depression and breast pain. Mood swings and poor concentration were associated with low intake of vitamins A, B2, and B6; folate; calcium; copper; and zinc. Despite this and other studies, controversy continues to rage over whether supplements are a universal therapy for PMS.

Vitamin B6: Some women respond favorably to vitamin B6 supplementation during the premenstrual phase, with significantly less depression, irritability, dizziness, vomiting, headaches, edema and bloating, weight gain, and fatigue. A study at St. Thomas's Hospital in London reported that vitamin B6 supplements reduced breast pain, or mastalgia, in women suffering from PMS who were unresponsive to hormonal therapy.

However, the vitamin B6–PMS link is not confirmed. In another study, 70 percent of the women taking a sugar pill they were told was vitamin B6 also reported improvements in symptoms, which suggests that at least some women respond to any therapy they believe will work.

How vitamin B6 might aid in the treatment of PMS is controversial. Some researchers theorize that pharmacological doses of this vitamin (200 to 800 mg) reduce blood estrogen levels and increase progesterone levels, thus improving the balance between these two female hormones. Other researchers speculate that the vitamin aids in the manufacture and release of serotonin, which in turn regulates appetite, pain, sleep, and mood. Another theory is that a suboptimal level of vitamin B6 produces a domino effect on the body's hormones—it decreases the release of dopamine, which increases levels of a hormone called prolactin, which triggers PMS symptoms. In short, disagreement prevails over if, why, or how vitamin B6 is useful in the treatment of PMS.

Even if vitamin B6 is effective, no one should self-medicate with this water-soluble vitamin in doses greater than 150 mg a day without physician supervision. Vitamin B6 can be toxic when consumed in large amounts for extended periods of time. In one study, twenty-three of fifty-eight women taking large supplemental doses of vitamin B6 for PMS developed numbness and tingling in their hands and feet, burning and shooting pains, clumsiness, and poor coordination.

These symptoms subsided when the women discontinued the supplements. Other researchers, however, question the accuracy of these reports, since numerous studies have found no harmful effects from taking vitamin B6 in doses up to 150 mg daily for short periods of time.

Vitamin E: Some women report less breast tenderness, bloating, and weight gain when they take large doses of supplemental vitamin E. However, other studies have found no significant improvements regardless of vitamin E intake, so supplementation with this vitamin is considered experimental.

Minerals: "The two most promising dietary links with PMS are calcium and magnesium," says James Penland, Ph.D., a research psychologist with USDA's Human Nutrition Research Center in Grand Forks, North Dakota. Women with PMS typically consume calcium-poor diets. In Dr. Penland's studies, increasing calcium intake to between 1,300 mg and 1,600 mg (the equivalent of four to five servings of milk or other calcium-rich foods) reduced PMS symptoms, such as mood and concentration problems, pain, and water retention. Increasing your intake of magnesium-rich foods such as nuts, wheat germ, bananas, and green leafy vegetables also might reduce the frequency and severity of headaches associated with PMS. "We're not talking about pharmacological doses of these minerals," says Dr. Penland. "Just increasing dietary intake up to recommended levels often is enough to see an improvement in symptoms."

Dr. Penland and his colleagues also have investigated other vitamins and minerals in relation to PMS sufferers, but the results are inconclusive. In their study, low blood levels of iron, the B vitamins, and zinc were most common in women suffering from depression, mood swings, poor concentration, and breast pain. "These findings indicate that there may be a relationship between diet and PMS, especially with iron, but it is too soon to make recommendations," says Dr. Penland.

Other Means of Relief

Step one in tackling PMS is to keep a symptoms diary that logs how you feel each day of the month. Any physical and emotional changes during the two weeks prior to menstruation could be a sign you have PMS. By defining your unique PMS profile, you can tailor your diet to prevent or lessen symptoms (see "Dietary Guidelines for PMS," page 117).

Dietary Guidelines for PMS

Follow the basic dietary guidelines outlined in the Feeling Good Diet (chapter 13). In addition:

- Limit all processed sugars to less than 3 teaspoons per day.
- Satisfy chocolate cravings with small amounts of low-fat chocolate foods, such as cocoa made with nonfat milk or chocolate angel food cake with no frosting.
- Include 1 to 2 tablespoons of safflower oil in your daily diet.
- Limit salt to minimize fluid retention and swelling.
- Make sure you consume at least eight servings daily of fiber-rich fruits, vegetables, whole grains, and/or legumes.
- Avoid caffeine, especially when anxiety and breast tenderness are problems.
- When calorie intake is below 2,500 calories, choose a well-balanced, moderate-dose vitamin and mineral supplement that contains 100 percent of the U.S. RDA for magnesium, zinc, iron, and the B-complex vitamins, and no more than 400 IU of vitamin E.
- Vitamin B6 supplementation (50 to 150 mg per day), started on day ten of the menstrual cycle and continued through day three of the next cycle, has produced positive results in some women.
- Include physical activity in the daily routine. Active women are less prone to severe PMS symptoms.
- Consult a physician if symptoms intensify or persist.

Step two is to take care of yourself. Treat yourself to a warm bath, a massage, a day off, or a walk in the country on the days when the PMS symptoms are raging. Read a good book or watch a favorite television show. Take time to be creative. Pay attention to your eating habits and nourish your body with wholesome, healthful foods and liquids.

Step three is to keep moving. Include some form of mild to moderately intense exercise in your daily routine. Choose an activity that is fun and consider this your playtime. Exercise helps reduce the tidal wave of hormones, increases pleasurable endorphins, curbs hunger, and calms you down. Even if you don't feel like moving, do it anyway.

Step four is to avoid stress. Choose calming activities and try to avoid deadlines and time demands during the premenstrual phase. Delegate assignments at work or at home, cut back on commitments, and let a few responsibilities lag.

This is not the time of the month to be superwoman. It is the time to take care of yourself and avoid stress.

Keep in mind that PMS is so common and so intertwined with normal fluctuations in a woman's hormones that the condition is more a natural biological and emotional experience than a disorder. Joyce Mills, Ph.D., emphasizes that in some cultures women's cycles are viewed as "a source of growth and empowerment" rather than a curse. However, for those women whose lives are seriously affected by PMS or whose symptoms are caused by unhealthful eating, inactivity, or stress, then diet, regular exercise, and effective coping skills can help curb suffering and improve overall health (see "Anti-PMS Foods," page 120). Remember to consult a physician if symptoms intensify or persist, since hormone and/or drug therapy might be indicated.

Are You SAD?

As the days shorten and the autumn leaves begin to fall, do you notice a change in your eating habits and mood? Would you rather doze in front of the television than visit friends and family? After the first of the year, do your cravings for sweets overpower all your New Year's resolutions to lose weight? Do you have to literally drag yourself out of bed in the morning to face another day? Do mundane chores at home or routine tasks at work seem monumental? Yet when the daffodils bloom in spring, do you feel a rush of energy and get a new lease on life? If you answered yes to most of these questions, you might be a candidate for seasonal affective disorder, or SAD.

What Is SAD?

SAD sufferers experience a wide array of personality and physical changes that are triggered by the onset of winter and that disappear in the spring. For example, during the winter months people with SAD are hungrier. They crave carbohydrate-rich foods, especially sweets. They are more susceptible to depression and irritability, anxiety and tension. They experience intensified PMS symptoms, are not interested in socializing, feel lethargic to the extent that it can interfere with work and daily duties, sleep more, and report a decreased sex drive. The increased food intake combined with the reduced activity results in weight gain, averaging nine to fourteen pounds or more. During the spring and summer months, the same person is enthusiastic, energetic (sometimes to the point of being hyperactive), less driven by food cravings, and loses weight. Do you suffer from SAD? Take the quiz on page 122.

Granted, feeling less ambitious and gaining a little weight during the winter is probably a natural response to the harshness of the season. In nature, this is the time when food is scarce, so animals sleep more and live off their bodies' fat stores, accumulated in the summer months when food was abundant. If people were badgers, they would hibernate during the winter and SAD would be a nonissue.

In fact, many people show seasonal variations in their eating and activity habits, food preferences, and weight. They may experience the "winter blues" or cabin fever. However, these changes are mild compared to those that occur in people with SAD, whose symptoms can make life miserable, ruin relationships, and destroy careers.

Lethargy and depression are two of the primary symptoms of SAD. Sufferers report that they feel hopeless, lack self-control, are anxiety-ridden, and experience heightened sensitivity to pain such as headaches and joint pain and plummeting self-esteem. However, the syndrome differs from classic depression. For example, people with SAD eat more carbohydrates, while most depressed people lose interest in food. SAD sufferers sleep too much, while depressed people are often insomniacs. Finally, with SAD the symptoms are cyclic; they appear in the autumn and disappear in the spring. Classic depression can strike at any time.

One in every ten people, including children and adults, develops SAD. Women are four times as likely as men to suffer from this disorder. SAD rates are also high in shift workers who sleep during the day, coal miners who work underground, and submarine crews who live without sunlight for long periods of time. People with a history of mood disorders or alcohol abuse or who have a close family member with SAD are also at high risk.

The farther from the equator a person lives, the greater is the likelihood he or she will experience some degree of SAD during the winter months. A person might be symptom-free while living in Florida, Southern California, or Italy and then experience SAD after relocating to Oregon, Minnesota, or northern Scotland. On the other hand, a person living in New Hampshire or Norway who has suffered from SAD for years may suddenly feel "cured" during a winter vacation in the Bahamas.

Anti-PMS Foods

This diet supplies 2,000 calories; protein, 20 percent of calories; carbohydrates, 59 percent of calories; refined sugar, 0; fat, 21 percent of calories; fiber, 35 grams. The diet provides 100 percent of the Recommended Dietary Allowances for all vitamins and minerals.

BREAKFAST	SERVING SIZE
Whole-grain cereal	1/2 cup cooked
Wheat germ	2 tablespoons
Nonfat milk	1 cup
Whole wheat toast	1 slice
All-fruit jam	2 teaspoons
Grapefruit juice	6-ounce glass
SNACK	
Whole wheat tortilla	1
Peanut butter	1 tablespoon
LUNCH	
Chicken sandwich:	
Chicken breast	2 ounces
Whole wheat bread	2 slices
Sprouts	1/4 cup
Honey mustard	1 teaspoon
Carrot-raisin-apple salad	1 cup
Nonfat milk	8-ounce glass
Melon balls	1/2 cup
Ice water with lemon	12-ounce glass
SNACK	
Whole wheat bagel	1/2
Nonfat cream cheese	1 ounce
Carrot juice	8-ounce glass

DINNER

Tofu and vegetable stir-fry:	
Tofu	1/2 cup
Mixed vegetables	1/2 cup
Safflower oil	1–2 tablespoons
Brown rice	3/4 cup
Low-fat (2%) milk	8-ounce glass

SAD and Light

SAD is not a new disorder, but it has experienced a resurgence in interest in the past ten to fifteen years as research has uncovered several pieces of the SAD puzzle. Although upsets in the body's biological clock, winter temperatures, and reduced availability of food were at first suspected to trigger seasonal rhythms associated with SAD, researchers at the National Institute of Mental Health changed all that when they linked SAD with light exposure. Interestingly, it is the eyes, not the skin, that are the critical factor.

Intense light hitting the retina of the eye triggers a cascade of events in the brain that culminate in a decrease in the level of a hormonelike substance called melatonin that otherwise makes people drowsy. In contrast, limited exposure to light, as is common during the shortened and cloudy days of winter, increases melatonin production. Under normal conditions people's wake-sleep times correspond with their melatonin levels; that is, melatonin levels begin rising in the evening and peak between midnight and 6 A.M. The morning's bright light hitting the eyes switches off melatonin production in the brain, which reduces a person's desire to sleep.

Researchers at the National Institute of Mental Health shined bright light into the eyes of laboratory animals and noted that their melatonin levels dropped. On the other hand, when melatonin is injected into animals, they overeat, oversleep, and are lethargic. When people are exposed to bright light, their melatonin levels also decrease. The results of this research have led scientists to suspect that the effect of light on melatonin levels might partly explain some of the symptoms of SAD.

In fact, light therapy (also called phototherapy) has been very successful in

QUIZ 5.2 Find Out If You're SAD

Are you unsure whether you suffer from SAD? If you live in the Northern Hemisphere, think back over the past several years. Do you usually feel your worst in December, January, and February? If you live in the Southern Hemisphere, do you usually feel your worst in June, July, and August? If you answer yes, you probably suffer from a seasonal disorder. The following will help you determine the severity of your symptoms. Tally your score to obtain a better idea whether you might be a candidate and how serious your symptoms are. This information should be part of a complete physical and diagnosis by a physician familiar with the symptoms and treatments for SAD.

Rate the following symptoms according to how dramatically they change for the worse during your winter months. Use the following scale: 0—not applicable; 1—mild change; 2—moderate change; 3—severe change.

PART A: SYMPTOMS

Mood:

Depression ________
Irritability ________
Feelings of hopelessness ________
Reduced self-concept ________

Stress:

Anxiety ________
Tension ________
Pain intolerance ________

Appetite:

Increased food cravings ________
Increased hunger ________
Weight gain* ________

Energy Level:

Reduced exercise ________
Limited energy to complete daily tasks ________

*A weight gain of two pounds or less is considered mild, while an increase in weight greater than ten pounds is considered severe.

Difficulty arising in morning ________

Increased hours spent sleeping ________

Socializing:

Reduced desire to be with friends ________

Avoidance of parties, dinners, and social gatherings, including holiday activities ________

Disinterest in church or community meetings ________

Total ________

Part B: Other Factors

Deduct one point from your total score for each yes answer to the following questions:

1. Is your mood unaffected by a winter vacation to a sunny location?
2. Do you have a personal or family history of depression or alcoholism?
3. Does your sex drive remain relatively constant throughout the year?

Scoring:

Total your score and compare to the following:

18 or less: You have mild physical and/or personality changes during the winter months, but they are not serious and do not affect the overall quality of your life or daily responsibilities.

19 to 35: You develop moderate physical and/or personality changes during the winter months that may interfere with your well-being or ability to function. Follow the dietary guidelines outlined in this chapter, exercise daily, and include some stress-management techniques in your daily routine. You might want to consult a physician, since light therapy may or may not be necessary.

36 or more: You are a likely candidate for SAD. You appear to suffer from marked physical or emotional changes during the winter that could seriously affect your work, relationships at home, and quality of life. However, you should confer with a physician for a more accurate diagnosis. Follow all the dietary guidelines outlined in this chapter, and include exercise and stress management in your daily routine. Light therapy may be useful, especially if you have experienced these symptoms during two or more consecutive winters.

curbing SAD symptoms. As many as 80 percent of SAD sufferers report significant improvement within four days when they are exposed to full-spectrum 2,500-lux (a measure of the light's intensity) light for one to two hours daily. (This light is five times brighter than the light in a well-lit office.) Some people show no improvement after a week of treatment but do respond when the duration or frequency of light therapy is increased. They report reduced appetite, slowed weight gain, reduced food cravings, elevation in mood, and improved sleep habits (they need up to three hours less sleep and sleep deeper during the night). Symptoms return within days when these people discontinue therapy; consequently, although the length of exposure usually can be reduced after the first few weeks, SAD sufferers usually must continue light therapy throughout the winter months.

SAD and PMS share some symptoms, including depression, fatigue, irritability, anxiety, carbohydrate cravings, sleep disorders, and personality changes. While light therapy has proved successful in the treatment of these symptoms for people with SAD, little or no research has been conducted to determine the effects of light on PMS. Let's hope future studies will investigate this possibility.

The Serotonin Connection

There is more to SAD than just melatonin. Approximately 20 percent of SAD patients do not respond to light therapy, and even those who do respond are not cured of all symptoms. In addition, people given a drug that suppresses melatonin production show lowered levels of the hormone but still experience SAD symptoms.

Serotonin might be the missing piece of the puzzle. The same area of the brain that releases melatonin also regulates serotonin production. In fact, melatonin is manufactured from serotonin. When melatonin levels increase, serotonin levels usually decrease, since more serotonin is converted to melatonin. On the other hand, exposure to light lowers melatonin levels and increases serotonin levels. Consequently, serotonin levels are lower while melatonin levels are higher in the winter as compared to the spring and summer, especially in people with SAD.

Serotonin is the nerve chemical that helps regulate hunger, carbohydrate intake, mood, pain, and sleep. As discussed in chapter 1, low levels of this nerve chemical are associated with increased carbohydrate cravings, depression, heightened sensitivity to pain, and troubled sleep patterns, while carbohydrate cravings subside, mood is elevated, pain tolerance improves, and sleep is more restful when serotonin levels are high. In fact, when people are given a drug called d-fenfluramine, which floods the brain with serotonin, they stop craving carbohydrates, lose weight, and feel less depressed.

The connection between serotonin and SAD is further supported by studies using the amino acid tryptophan, the building block for serotonin. Researchers at Fairleigh-Dickinson University in New Jersey compared the effects of tryptophan supplements combined with vitamin B6 and vitamin C, a placebo, or artificial evening light on SAD patients. The results showed that both tryptophan supplements and light therapy improved symptoms of depression, while the placebo had no effect.

Tryptophan supplements are no longer available in the United States because of a U.S. Food and Drug Administration ban enforced after a batch of contaminated supplements from Japan resulted in several cases of a rare disease. However, dietary starches and sweets, by stimulating the removal of other amino acids from the blood into the tissues, also raise blood and brain levels of tryptophan and can stimulate serotonin production.

Since carbohydrate-rich foods stimulate the production of serotonin, SAD sufferers who crave sweets, potatoes, pasta, rice, and bread during the winter months might be attempting to self-regulate their mood. They turn to starchy or sugary foods in an effort to feel better, calmer, and more relaxed. They snack on carbohydrate-rich snacks in the evening. They crave chocolate or ice cream. They eat more waffles, pancakes, and cereal at breakfast, and they add extra servings of potatoes and pasta at lunch and dinner. For some people, the carbohydrate snack makes them feel drowsy; for others, it allows them to concentrate better. Their bodies also may crave these foods in an effort to fight fatigue. Interestingly, SAD sufferers who eat a sweet snack at midday also respond better to light therapy than do people who do not cater to a sweet tooth, suggesting that the carbohydrate-induced increase in serotonin, combined with the light-induced reduction in melatonin levels, is more effective than either therapy alone.

Protein Power

To complicate the issue, tests show that SAD sufferers might be deficient in dopamine, a nerve chemical suspected to decrease with reduced exposure to light.

As discussed in chapter 1, dopamine is the brain activator; people are more alert and think more clearly when dopamine levels are high. Consequently, if cloudy winter months lower dopamine levels, this would contribute to the drowsiness, poor concentration, and other mood swings characteristic of SAD.

Fortunately, there is a dietary approach to combating low dopamine levels. Protein-rich foods such as extra-lean meat, chicken, fish, and low-fat milk products raise dopamine levels and thus might be the answer for SAD sufferers who do not respond to carbohydrate-rich foods.

SAD Basics

The SAD puzzle is far from complete. What is known, however, suggests that this disorder results from a complex imbalance of nerve chemicals, hormones, and the basic cycle of body chemicals called the biological clock. Fortunately, there is much a person can do to ease the symptoms and possibly even cure the disorder.

First, try light therapy. It has worked wonders for many SAD sufferers. SAD clinics are scattered around the United States, from San Diego to New York, and offer treatment with medical supervision. There also are clinics in Australia, Austria, Canada, England, France, Iceland, Ireland, Italy, Japan, the Netherlands, Switzerland, and other countries. Another option is to buy your own lighting equipment. There are several options, including the standard model, the window box, and the portable model. Make sure the light is of sufficient intensity and has been adequately tested, and that the bulbs are protected by a screen.

Second, take a good look at your diet. Keep a SAD Food and Symptoms Diary for at least a week (see Worksheet 5.1 on page 127). Write down everything you eat and drink and when, and note whether the meal or snack was high in either carbohydrate or protein. Also record your mood before and after eating (within thirty to sixty minutes). For example, were you tired, lethargic, depressed, enthusiastic, energetic, agitated, tearful, calm, relaxed, alert, refreshed, or optimistic? Also record any differences in what you craved versus what you actually ate. During this one-week trial, avoid drinking any caffeinated or alcoholic beverages, since the effects of these "drugs" might influence how you interpret the way food affects how you feel.

WORKSHEET 5.1 SAD Food and Symptoms Diary

For one week write down everything you eat and drink—whether the meal or snack was high in protein or carbohydrate, the time of day, your mood before and after, and any other notes, such as any differences between what you wanted to eat versus what you actually ate, who you ate with, what preceded the meal or snack, and what you were doing while you ate. Use this sheet as a master to make copies.

TIME	FOOD	AMOUNT	HIGH PROTEIN OR HIGH CARBOHYDRATE?	MOOD BEFORE	MOOD AFTER	NOTES

Next, analyze your diary. Look for patterns such as changes in mood that result from eating. For example,

1. How do you feel after a carbohydrate-rich snack?
2. Are you energized or dulled by a protein-rich meal?
3. What times of the day do you eat?
4. Do you eat at regular intervals or do your eating times vary?
5. Do you skip meals and, if so, which ones?
6. Is food intake evenly distributed throughout the day, or is it concentrated in a few big meals?
7. Is there a time of day when food cravings peak?
8. What foods do you crave?
9. Does the size of the meal affect your mood—for example, do heavy meals aggravate fatigue, and do light meals help you stay alert?
10. Are snacks and meals planned or impulsive?
11. How hungry are you at meal and snack time?
12. How fast do you eat? What happens when you eat too fast?
13. Are you taking any medications that might affect your mood or appetite?

Each person will find individual patterns and will be affected by what he or she eats in different ways. What is important is that you tailor your food intake to meet your specific needs. For example, if you note from your diary that protein-rich foods are invigorating, then plan a protein-rich meal for breakfast (for example, egg substitute, whole wheat toast, low-fat milk) and lunch (turkey sandwich, three-bean salad, and fruit; cheese or fish and lots of vegetables; chili with extra-lean meat and beans, corn bread, and yogurt). Leave the higher carbohydrate foods such as pasta, sweet potatoes, rice and vegetable dishes, and breads for dinner and evening snacks, where they may help you relax and prepare for sleep.

On the other hand, if carbohydrate-rich foods give you an energy boost, then include them in your breakfast (for example, pancakes, waffles, cereal) and lunch (bean burrito with rice, hot carrots, and vegetables) and leave the higher protein foods (seafood, chicken, and extra-lean meats) for dinner (see "Sample Menu for SAD," page 130).

Your diary can also provide information on when your body needs nutrients. For example, you may notice that food cravings are highest in the late afternoon and are usually for sweet-and-creamy selections such as doughnuts, a candy bar, or cookies. Knowing this, you can plan a carbohydrate-rich snack for this time of day. It can be a nutritious whole-grain bagel, or you can budget your calories to include a sweeter selection, such as a slice of angel food cake, a few cookies, or a brownie.

Third, do not ignore cravings! Attempts to rid the cupboards and refrigerator of all sweet temptations or to "will away" an urge are likely to do more harm than good, since you are denying your body the very nutrients it needs to regulate the nerve chemicals and hormones that affect mood. The need won't go away by removing the food; your cravings will increase. Instead, respond to those cravings, but do so in moderation and with planned, nutritious foods. Also, avoid combining eating with other activities. Do not read, watch television, or work while you nibble.

When you sit down to satisfy a craving, focus on the food. Take small bites and chew them slowly. This way you are likely to eat less yet feel more satisfied. It may take up to sixty minutes for a meal to affect your mood. So be patient, eat a moderate serving, and wait to see if your mood improves. If not, have another small serving. Including other calming activities during this vulnerable time of the day also can help. Listen to soothing music, take a warm bath, talk to a friend, or close your eyes and visualize the snack's improving your energy and mood.

Fourth, eat breakfast. Even if you aren't hungry, eat something. As mentioned in chapter 4, breakfast replenishes dwindling energy reserves and fuels the body during the morning hours. The protein and carbohydrates in a breakfast meal also help regulate the nerve chemicals and hormones that help curb the symptoms of SAD.

Fifth, avoid large meals. Meals of more than 1,000 calories, especially if they are high in fat, leave most people feeling drowsy. Lighter meals of approximately 500 calories for breakfast and lunch provide ample fuel without dragging you down. In addition, light meals in the evening are more likely to aid in a good night's sleep.

Sample Menu for SAD

Based on what you learned from keeping the SAD Food and Symptoms Diary, are you sensitive to protein or to carbohydrates? Does a protein-rich meal give you an energy boost? Do carbohydrates rev up your motor or leave you drowsy? Here are sample menus that will help fuel dwindling energy levels during the day yet leave you relaxed in the evening, regardless of whether you need protein or carbohydrates.

PROTEIN-RICH DIET	CARBOHYDRATE-RICH DIET
BREAKFAST	
Egg white, cheese, and spinach omelet	Oatmeal with wheat germ
Whole wheat toast	Whole wheat toast with jam
Fruit	Milk for cereal
Nonfat milk	Fruit and juice
SNACK	
Almonds and dried fruit	Almonds and dried fruit
Fruit juice	Nonfat milk
LUNCH	
Tuna salad sandwich	Curried vegetables and chicken (mostly vegetables and 2 ounces chicken)
Spinach salad with dressing	Rice
Nonfat milk	Fruit
Fruit	
SNACK	
Low-fat cheese	Cinnamon-raisin bagel
Crackers	Fat-free cream cheese
Fruit	Fruit

Dinner

Spaghetti with marinara sauce	Broiled salmon
Green beans	Baked potato
Garlic bread	Nonfat sour cream
Salad with dressing	Green beans
	Salad with dressing

Snack

Air-popped popcorn	Air-popped popcorn

Sixth, reprogram your body by following the Feeling Good Diet (see chapter 13) and developing a routine that includes several small snacks throughout the day and evening. Include some protein and some carbohydrates at each snack, such as peanuts and raisins, low-fat yogurt and fruit, low-fat cheese melted on an English muffin, or a bowl of cereal with milk. If you want to nibble in the evening, make it a carbohydrate-rich snack such as fruit, popcorn, or toast. Keep the snack light and plan it for approximately one hour before bedtime. Keep on hand a variety of low-fat, nutritious foods to soothe your sweet tooth or satisfy your food cravings. Plan your snacks so you will not fall prey to impulse eating.

Also, don't worry if you gain a little weight. Keep in mind that many people gain two to five extra pounds in the winter, probably as a natural means to increase body temperature and fuel the body during the cold months. Meals tailored to your body's needs, which include nutritious snacks during trouble-prone times of the day, will help curb or even halt the weight gain. Usually the few pounds gained will drop off come spring.

Seventh, avoid all alcoholic beverages and limit caffeinated beverages to no more than two servings per day. SAD sufferers consume more coffee, tea, and colas during the winter months than in other seasons, probably in an attempt to elevate mood and increase energy. However, caffeine's effects on the nervous system and the depression and irritability that many people experience during withdrawal from caffeine can aggravate SAD symptoms.

Beyond Diet

Light therapy and diet are the foundation for treating SAD; however, other lifestyle habits and treatments can help curb symptoms. For example, SAD sufferers should practice stress-management skills such as counseling, relaxation techniques, massage, and deep breathing. The benefits of exercise for SAD sufferers are similar to those for women with PMS: it helps balance the nerve chemicals and hormones, increases pleasurable endorphins, curbs hunger, relaxes the body, and improves sleep habits. Even moderate exercise such as a walk at lunchtime can have a noticeable effect on mood and energy levels.

SAD sufferers also might try installing UV sunlights in areas of the house where they spend the most time. They should also consider taking a winter vacation to a sunny climate, regulating their sleep patterns to avoid spending excessive time in bed, and taking positive action to reduce depression by replacing negative self-talk with positive thoughts, thereby regaining self-confidence. Several antidepressant medications—including the tricyclics; the monamine oxidase (MAO) inhibitors such as phenelzine; the serotonin-activating medications such as Prozac; and lithium carbonate, also known as Priadel—have been used with physician monitoring to treat SAD patients.

PMS, SAD, and Alcohol

Many mood-altering conditions such as PMS and SAD result from imbalances in the neurotransmitters and hormones that regulate behavior. Some of these chemicals—such as serotonin, dopamine, and the endorphins—can be mildly to dramatically altered by a single meal or a change in dietary habits. Cravings for sweets, starches, or caffeine—once thought to reflect a lack of willpower—are now recognized as stemming from fundamental biological drives to improve mood. This link between food and mood may also play a role in alcohol-addiction recovery and possibly many as yet unidentified emotional disorders.

For example, for recovering alcoholics, sweets provide a temporary elevation in energy level as well as a decrease in depression. These are symptoms that also improved when the person was drinking alcohol. Consequently, it may be that cravings for and increased consumption of sweets and caffeine-containing foods and beverages are a substitute for the alcohol in regulating mood during periods of abstinence, just as these foods help regulate mood in people with PMS and SAD. Acknowledging this food-mood connection, and working with it rather than against it, will help curb the discomfort of alcohol withdrawal and improve overall health and well-being.

CHAPTER SIX

Food and the Blues

Depression is no laughing matter. If you feel sad three out of every ten days, consider yourself lucky. One in every two people battles depression more often than this. In fact, depression is the most common psychiatric disorder in women in the United States. As many as one in twenty people has the blues four out of every five days, while more than 15 million Americans will suffer serious depression during their lifetime.

At one time or another, most people turn to food for solace, comfort, or relaxation. One person may snack from the refrigerator at the end of a stressful day. Another might find comfort in a pint of ice cream when alone on a Friday night. A friend says her midmorning doldrums are relieved by a cinnamon roll. A mother turns to food whenever she is blue.

In most cases the indulgence is harmless and comforting. However, in an effort to feel better, some people choose foods that unknowingly make them feel worse and that set up a vicious cycle of depression and overeating. If food is making you blue, there is something you can do about it.

Stop the Cycle, I Want to Get Off

The same carbohydrate-rich foods that trigger snack attacks (see chapters 2 and 3), make you feel drowsy (see chapter 4), and fuel your exercising muscles are also the foods you turn to when you are depressed. It is no coincidence that people want pasta, desserts, and other carbohydrate-rich foods when they feel down in the dumps. Carbohydrates have a profound effect on numerous body chemicals that regulate how a person feels and acts.

As mentioned in chapter 1, Drs. Richard and Judith Wurtman at the Massachusetts Institute of Technology propose that carbohydrates elevate brain levels of tryptophan and serotonin, which in turn alleviate irritability and elevate mood. A carbohydrate-rich snack of crackers and fruit, a candy bar, or even a whole wheat bagel alters brain chemistry and provides temporary relief from mild depression. In contrast, a high-protein snack such as a piece of barbecued chicken, a turkey sandwich, or a hamburger, by supplying more of the competing amino acids, reduces tryptophan and serotonin levels in the brain. Consequently, carbohydrate-sensitive people who eat a high-protein breakfast of eggs and bacon may experience mood swings and crave a doughnut by midmorning in an effort to raise brain serotonin levels and "feel better."

Interestingly, several conditions associated with depression, including premenstrual syndrome and seasonal affective disorder, are linked to increased cravings for carbohydrate-rich foods, suggesting that people unknowingly self-regulate their moods with the foods they eat. Despite the supporting evidence, the carbohydrate-serotonin-depression connection remains controversial. Several studies report no differences in mood resulting from eating a high-protein or a high-carbohydrate meal. Some studies show that carbohydrates elevate serotonin levels, but fail to show any connection with mood as a result. It may be that a certain degree of carbohydrate sensitivity is needed before symptoms are obvious enough to be measured in a scientific study. Or it could be that there is more to the food-mood link than just serotonin.

The Sugar Blues

Research conducted by Larry Christensen, Ph.D., chairman of the department of psychology at the University of South Alabama, shows that sugar and starches have different mood-altering effects, even though they both stimulate serotonin production. Dr. Christensen concludes that depression often vanishes when sugar (and caffeine) are removed from the diet. "We see improvements in mood when sugar is eliminated, even in people who are not depressed; however, these sugar-sensitive people probably would have become depressed in the future." Using sugar to self-regulate mood is a temporary fix. In the long run, it could start a vicious cycle. "The person suffering from depression who turns to sugary foods may relieve the depression and feel better for a short while, but the depression returns," says Dr. Christensen. The person then must either reach for another sugar fix or seek help elsewhere. As opposed to the temporary sugar high, eliminating sugar and caffeine from the diet is a permanent solution to depression for some people.

As with fatigue and food cravings, some people are so sensitive to sugar that even a small serving of something sweet, such as a cookie or doughnut, sends them on a mood-swing roller coaster. These supersensitive people should eliminate all sugar from their diet, including the hidden sugars in convenience foods such as catsup, canned fruit, fruit drinks, and fruited yogurt. Other people have a higher tolerance and experience symptoms only after eating a large amount of sugar, such as in a bag of cookies, or after days or weeks of grazing on sweets. They should cut back on concentrated sugars in candy, cakes, and other desserts but may tolerate the hidden sugars.

How sugar affects mood is poorly understood. "If you ask, 'Does removing sugar from the diet improve a person's mood and can it help treat depression?' the answer is yes. But the knowledge base is limited on how sugar exerts this effect," says Dr. Christensen. One theory is that concentrated sugars in the diet raise blood glucose above normal levels, which somehow interferes with glucose transport into the cells and tissues or triggers oversecretion of insulin from the pancreas, which drops blood sugar below normal levels. Since glucose is the primary energy source for most body processes, limiting its entry essentially would starve the cells. Low blood-sugar levels can also affect mood. In either case, a person feels depressed and lethargic.

A second theory is based on the connection between sugar and the endorphins—those naturally occurring morphinelike compounds in the brain responsible for euphoric feelings. If sugar does trigger a temporary release of these pleasure-producing chemicals, then turning to sweets is literally a form of unconscious self-medication. Again, however, the temporary high is usually followed by a more serious crash as blood sugar, endorphins, and other hormones and chemicals drop to lower-than-ever levels. The sugar-endorphin theory has not been tested in adults, but it does suggest interesting links between the cravings for sweets in women with premenstrual syndrome, people quitting alcohol or tobacco, and bulimics and the almost immediate relief from depression, tension, or fatigue.

These people describe the cravings as, "I need something to make me feel better and calm me down." The sugary snack provides a quick fix.

In addition, the more sugar you eat, the more likely your diet will be low in essential vitamins and minerals. It could be that marginal intake of one or more of these nutrients, such as magnesium or vitamin B6, could be contributing to low energy and depression.

Amino Acid Alchemy

One of the rationales for increasing intake of carbohydrates to improve mood is linked to how these foods increase blood and brain levels of the amino acid tryptophan. You can get the same effect by taking tryptophan pills with a carbohydrate-rich snack such as fruit, crackers, or a bagel. In fact, most of the research on tryptophan's effect on serotonin and mood used tryptophan supplements, not food, to get the effect. Numerous studies have shown that tryptophan supplements have an antidepressant effect and, in some people, may be as effective as antidepressant medications for improving mood.

For example, in a Scandinavian study, tryptophan was compared to the frequently prescribed antidepressant drug imipramine, which is sold under the brand name Tofranil. The amino acid was as effective as the medication and had fewer side effects. Other studies report similar results; sometimes the mood-elevating effects of tryptophan lasted longer than the pharmacological treatment.

But don't go looking for tryptophan tablets because you won't find them. A few years back, the U.S. Food and Drug Administration (FDA) pulled all tryptophan supplements from the shelf after an outbreak of a rare disorder called eosinophilia-myalgia syndrome was linked to the tryptophan pills. The condition, characterized by severe muscle pain and weakness, mouth ulcers, infection, abdominal pain, fever, and a skin rash, is potentially deadly. Later the disorder was more specifically linked to a contaminant in one brand of tryptophan supplements manufactured by a company in Japan called Showa Denko; however, the ban on over-the-counter tryptophan supplements remains. Until FDA lifts the ban, the only way a person can adjust tryptophan and serotonin levels is by increasing his or her intake of carbohydrate-rich foods.

The Role of Tyrosine

Another theory for the onset of depression is a decreased availability of or a deficiency in the function of the nerve chemical norepinephrine, a cousin to adrenalin. (See chapter 1 for a description of this neurotransmitter.) The amino acid tyrosine or phenylalanine (the latter of which is converted to tyrosine)—found in protein-rich foods such as turkey, chicken, or milk—is the building block for this nerve chemical, so increasing dietary intake of these amino acids should improve mood. However, the results of several studies have been contradictory.

Researchers at the University of Arizona at Tucson and at Boston University School of Medicine investigated the effects of tyrosine on a group of depressed patients and found no improvements in mood after four weeks of supplementing their diets with tyrosine. On the other hand, H. C. Sabelli, Ph.D., M.D., in the department of psychiatry at Rush-Presbyterian-St. Luke's Medical Center in Chicago, reported that a combination of vitamin B6 and phenylalanine improved mood in nine out of ten patients suffering from depression. Dr. Sabelli postulates that low levels of phenylalanine metabolites might be an indicator of depression. While other studies support a possible role of tyrosine in the management of depression, more research is needed before specific recommendations can be made.

No one should self-medicate with individual amino acids, since these building blocks for powerful nerve chemicals can have far-reaching effects on numerous body processes. However, tyrosine levels in the blood and brain can be raised naturally by eating a high-protein meal, such as a turkey sandwich with milk. If you are unresponsive to carbohydrate-rich meals and snacks, try a protein-rich diet. Monitor your mood closely to note any changes.

The Vitamin B6 Connection

Your mood is affected by more than just amino acids and carbohydrates. In fact, an equally likely reason for a blue day is inadequate intake of one or more vitamins.

Vitamin B6 is a case in point. Dietary intake of this B vitamin is often marginal in many segments of the population, including women of childbearing age, children, and seniors. Women typically consume half the Recommended Dietary

Allowance (RDA) for vitamin B6, and as many as 15 percent of women consume less than 25 percent of the RDA. Pregnant and breastfeeding women often consume only 60 percent of their RDA for vitamin B6. (Women are more likely to run short on vitamin B6 because they consume less food and fewer vitamin B6–rich foods such as meat.)

If your diet is short by even 1 mg of this vital nutrient, you could send your nervous system into a panic. Adequate intake of vitamin B6 is critical for the development and function of the central nervous system. But how vitamin B6 affects the nervous system and brain is only partly understood. Even marginal intake of the vitamin produces abnormal functioning of several enzymes responsible for the metabolism of a variety of nerve chemicals and nerve modulators, including serotonin, dopamine, and GABA, which regulate behavior. Too little vitamin B6 also leads to an accumulation of toxic breakdown products from nerve chemicals that irritate the nerves and are linked to many nerve disorders, from depression to seizures (see "Are You Getting Enough Vitamin B6?" page 140).

Confusion and depression are well documented and common yet vague symptoms of vitamin B6 deficiency. In one study conducted at Harvard Medical School and USDA Human Nutrition Research Center at Tufts University in Boston, more than one out of every four depressed patients was deficient in vitamins B6 and B12. In fact, vitamin B6 deficiency is reported in as many as 79 percent of patients with depression, compared to only 29 percent of other patients. In many cases, giving these patients vitamin B6 supplements (in doses as low as 10 mg a day) raises vitamin B6 levels in the blood and improves or even alleviates the depression, providing convincing evidence that the deficiency might be the cause, rather than the effect, of the depression.

Granted, overt vitamin B6 deficiency is rare in the United States; however, even a marginal intake—a person consumes enough of the vitamin to avoid classic symptoms, but not enough to sustain optimal health—could produce subtle changes in personality and mood. For example, low levels of vitamin B6 and serotonin are found in suicidal patients, in people with a low threshold for pain, and during depression, even though these people show no overt signs of malnutrition. In fact, the mood swings and depression that are considered side effects of medications, such as hormone replacement therapy, oral contraceptives, and antituberculous drugs, might be caused by drug-induced suppression of vitamin B6 metabolism and the consequent underproduction of serotonin.

QUIZ 6.1 Are You Getting Enough Vitamin B6?

Answer the following questions yes or no, then check your score at the end.

_______ **1.** Do you consume at least 2,500 calories daily of a variety of different minimally processed, wholesome foods?

_______ **2.** Do you consume at least 6 servings daily of whole-grain breads, cereals (especially oatmeal), pasta, or rice?

_______ **3.** Do you frequently eat bananas, avocados, baked potatoes (including the skin), acorn squash, or spinach?

_______ **4.** Do you frequently eat cooked dried beans and peas, such as lentils, lima beans, kidney beans, and white beans?

_______ **5.** Do you choose chicken rather than red meat, fish rather than lamb, and crab rather than luncheon meats?

Give yourself two points for every yes answer and deduct two points for every no answer to the above questions. Then continue to answer either yes or no to the following questions.

_______ **6.** Are you taking birth-control pills, hormone replacement therapy (HRT), an anti-Parkinson's drug such as levodopa, an antituberculous drug, or an anti-Wilson's drug such as D-penicillamine?

_______ **7.** Do you drink more than five alcoholic beverages each week?

_______ **8.** Do you eat a high-fat diet or consume several sweets and desserts daily?

Deduct one point for every yes answer and add one point for every no answer to questions 6 through 8. Then total your answers for a final score.

Scoring:

10 to 13: Your diet is probably adequate in vitamin B6. You should consider increasing your dietary intake of vitamin B6–rich foods or taking a supplement (with a physician's approval and monitoring) if you suspect larger-than-normal amounts of this vitamin might help alleviate PMS-related depression.

7 to 9: Your diet might be marginal in vitamin B6. Increase your intake of this vitamin by adding two or more of the following foods to the daily diet: banana, avocado, chicken without the skin, salmon, potato with the skin, collard greens, brown rice, wheat germ, oatmeal, and cornmeal. If you choose to supplement, find a multiple vitamin and mineral preparation that contains approximately 2 to 5 mg of vitamin B6.

Less than 7: Your diet is likely to be deficient in vitamin B6. Increase your intake of this vitamin by adding three or more of the vitamin B6–rich foods listed above to your daily diet. If you choose to supplement, find a multiple vitamin and mineral preparation that contains approximately 2 to 5 mg of vitamin B6.

B6 Basics

Marginal intake of vitamin B6 is compounded by medication, intense exercise, chronic dieting, alcohol consumption, and/or increased nutrient needs during times of illness or stress. To increase dietary intake of this B vitamin, include several servings daily of protein-rich foods, such as chicken, nuts, legumes, and fish, as well as bananas, avocados, and dark green leafy vegetables (see Table 6.1, page 153). Whole grains are preferable to refined grains, since more than 70 percent of the vitamin is lost during processing, and vitamin B6 is not one of the four nutrients added back when refined grains are "enriched" (see Graph 6.1, page 142).

Always consult a physician knowledgeable about nutrition before taking vitamin B6 supplements in doses greater than 150 mg for long periods of time.

Other Vitamins and Minerals: In the Pink or Feeling Blue?

Vitamin B6 is not the only deficiency that can bring you down. Marginal deficiencies of the other B vitamins, including vitamin B1, vitamin B2, niacin, folic acid, vitamin B12, vitamin C, and even large doses of vitamin A have been linked to depression.

Folic Acid: A deficiency of folic acid, a B vitamin essential for normal cell growth and maintenance, causes several personality changes, including depression. In addition, some people suffering from depression show improvements in mood when they increase intake of folic acid. A study at the Institute of Psychiatry in London found that 33 percent of patients suffering from depression-related psychological problems were borderline to clinically deficient in folic acid. Their mood improved with folic-acid supplementation.

GRAPH 6.1 What Processing Does to Vitamin B6

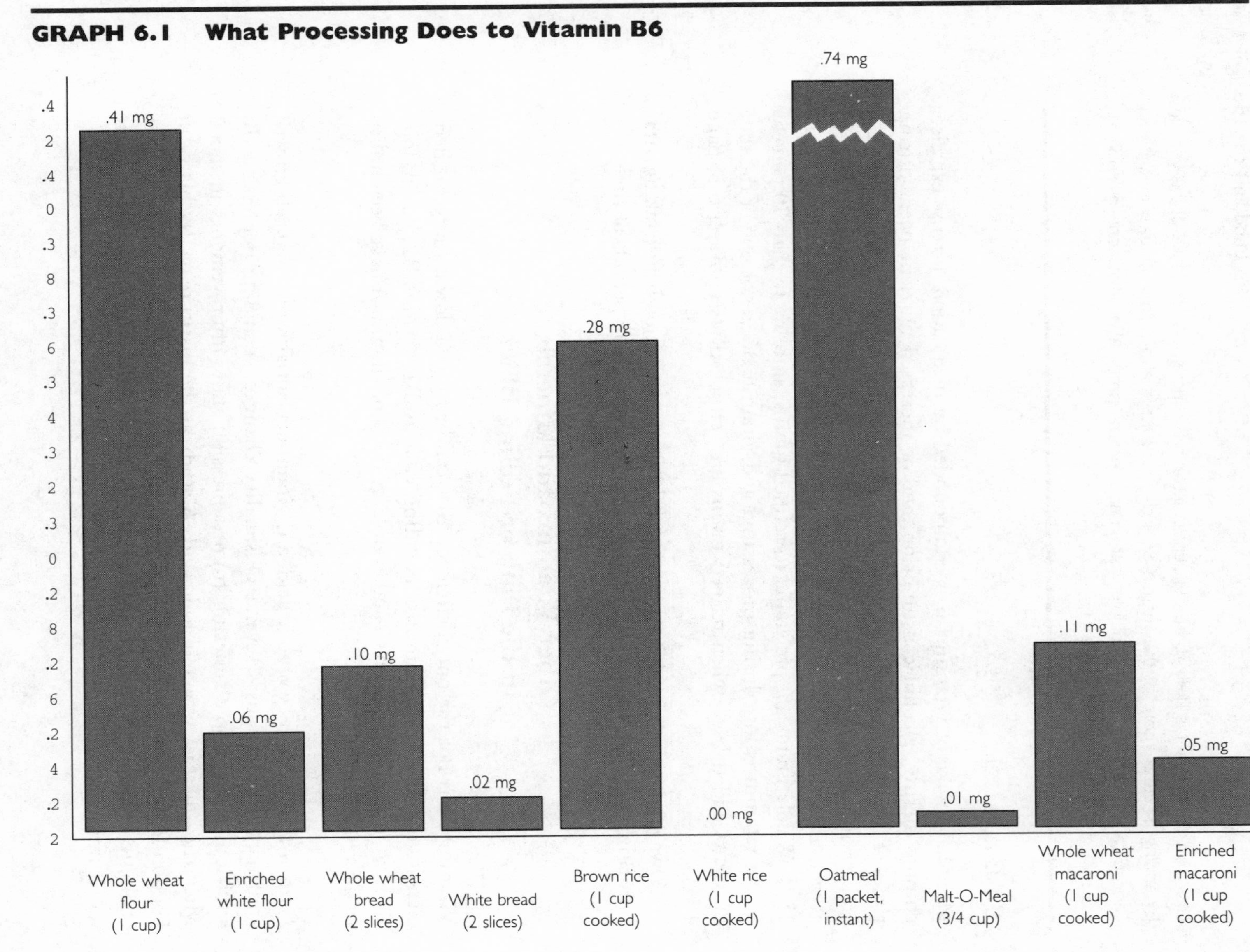

One study of healthy people between ages of twenty-five and eighty-three showed that those with the highest blood levels of folic acid also had the best mood, while those with "low-normal" blood folic-acid levels were more likely to suffer from depression. Giving these people either folic acid or a placebo improved mood in the depressed people who took the folic acid, but not in the placebo group, suggesting that the depression was caused by marginal folic-acid intake and was not psychosomatic. Some evidence suggests that folic acid raises serotonin levels, while a deficiency of the B vitamin results in lowered serotonin levels and increased risk of depression.

Folic-acid deficiency is considered the most common vitamin deficiency in the United States, and intake approaching half the 1980 RDA of 400 mcg is probably common. To compound the problem, folic acid is easily destroyed when foods are stored or cooked too long, reheated, or cooked in large amounts of water rather than steamed. Virtually all of the folic acid is gone when fresh broccoli is stored in the refrigerator for days, cooked until olive green, or allowed to sit under hot lights in a cafeteria. To judge your intake of folic acid, try the quiz on page 144.

Vitamin B12: People who consume marginal amounts of vitamin B12 are most likely to suffer from depression, have memory problems, and even experience paranoia. Increased dietary or supplemental intake of vitamin B12 in these deficient people raises blood levels of the vitamin and elevates mood. Even nondepressed people who have various mental disorders but no family history of psychiatric problems have low vitamin B12 levels. This suggests that in the absence of a genetic influence, diet may be a primary contributor to the depression and other emotional/mental problems.

Minerals: Low dietary intake of many of the minerals, including calcium, iron, magnesium, selenium, and zinc, is reported to cause depression, irritability, or mood swings. For example, at the University College in Swansea, Wales, researchers assessed the moods of fifty people, then gave them either a placebo or a 100 mcg supplement of selenium. After five weeks the selenium-supplemented people showed greater improvements in mood than did the people who took a placebo. The degree of mood change was directly related to the person's initial selenium status; that is, the people with the lowest initial selenium intake also reported the most depression and anxiety and showed the greatest mood improvement after taking the selenium supplements. Iron deficiency is common in active

QUIZ 6.2 What's Your Folic Acid IQ?

How much do you know about this essential B vitamin? Answers are at the end.

1. What form of cancer has been linked to folic acid levels?

a. liver cancer

b. breast cancer

c. cervical cancer

d. prostate cancer

2. Which one of the following foods is low in folic acid?

a. spinach (1 cup)

b. orange juice (1 cup)

c. carrots (2 whole)

d. black beans (1 cup)

3. Women should increase their folic acid intake to at least 400 mcg to prevent

a. premenstrual problems

b. birth defects

c. osteoporosis

d. insomnia

4. Large doses (800 mcg or more) of folic acid should not be taken without a physician's approval because folic acid at this level

a. can mask a possible underlying vitamin B12 deficiency

b. is toxic at these high doses

c. is fat-soluble and can accumulate in the tissues to dangerous levels

d. can cause nausea or headaches

5. Which of the following has the most folic acid?

a. avocado (1/2 medium)

b. beets (1/2 cup cooked)

c. iceberg lettuce (3 cups)

d. romaine lettuce (1 cup)

6. Half a cup of wheat germ has more folic acid than

a. 4 cups of cabbage

b. 18 stalks of celery

c. 5 cups of cooked corn

d. all of the above

7. If vegetables are stored at room temperature, either at home or at the grocery store, up to______percent of the folic acid will be gone in______ days.
   a. 50 percent in seven days
   b. 33 percent in five days
   c. 70 percent in three days
   d. 100 percent in two days
8. When you think of folic acid, think of______vegetables.
   a. dark leafy green
   b. dark orange
   c. fresh frozen
   d. crispy
9. When whole wheat flour is processed to make enriched white flour for breads and other bakery goods, approximately______of the folic acid is lost.
   a. none; folic acid is replaced in the enrichment process.
   b. 25 percent
   c. 40 percent
   d. 75 percent
10. One cup of kidney beans contains______percent of daily need (based on the 1980 U.S. RDA) for folic acid.
   a. 60 percent
   b. 50 percent
   c. 25 percent
   d. 10 percent

Answers: 1.c; 2.c; 3.b; 4.a; 5.d; 6.d; 7.c; 8.a; 9.c; 10.a.

---

women, children, and the elderly and can cause depression associated with fatigue. There is little or no evidence, however, that people already optimally nourished will benefit from additional amounts of minerals.

Fast-Food Blues

You're in a hurry and forget to pack a lunch, so once again you pull up to a drive-up window and grab a hamburger, French fries, and diet soda. The meal might soothe a grumbling stomach. It might even keep you going through the afternoon. But it just might be why you're fighting the blues. At best, you'll consume approximately 600 calories—43 percent or more of which are from fat. If the words *cheese*, *triple*, *pounder*, *whopper*, or *supreme* are in the hamburger's title, add another 300 calories and five additional teaspoons of fat.

Granted, there is no research linking a high-fat diet with depression. However, this fast-food meal is a loser when it comes to the vitamins and minerals that help boost spirits. For example, the meal supplies almost a third of an average woman's calorie requirement, but only 14 percent of her RDA for folic acid and less than 10 percent of her vitamin C needs. Other B vitamins also are in short supply compared to the large caloric debt. Men fare a little better, since their body size allows them to consume more calories. However, even a tall man must eat a lot of spinach salad to make up for the vitamin and mineral void left by a lunch like this. An occasional lunch of a hamburger and French fries has little or no effect on overall mood; however, if you frequently stop at drive-up windows, your fast-food choices might be doing you in.

If you are a fast-food junkie, you have several options. You can change your eating habits by gradually reducing the number of meals eaten away from home—say, from seven a week to six a week, then five a week, with the long-range goal of limiting weekly fast-food meals to no more than three.

Another option is to make better choices and supplement those choices with nutritious foods brought from home. For example, some fast-food restaurants now offer lower-fat alternatives to their high-fat hamburgers, which can be part of a nutritious meal if complemented with 1 percent low-fat milk, an orange, and a sackful of carrot and broccoli sticks brought from home. Or you can choose salad bars or packaged green salads (with low-fat dressing) rather than a taco salad with a fried tortilla shell and too much dressing, the latter of which can have more than 900 calories and more fat than three double cheeseburgers!

Beware of the wolf in sheep's clothing. Those battered-fried chicken bits have as much fat as five pats of butter, while some fish fillet sandwiches have up to 29 grams of fat, or more than 6 teaspoons. Even zucchini, when batter-coated and fried, has up to 23 grams of fat (5 teaspoons) and half a day's salt allotment.

Blues-Free Basics

If food is at the root of your blues, then the Feeling Good Diet (chapter 13) could be your cure. If followed closely and consistently, this eating plan provides all the vitamins and minerals in the right proportion and spaced evenly throughout the day to fuel your spirits and sidestep diet-related mood swings and depression.

As discussed in chapter 2, people who crave carbohydrates must work with, not against, their cravings. Make sure every meal contains some complex carbohydrate–rich foods. Breakfast can include French toast, waffles, pancakes, cereal, toast, or an English muffin. Lunch and dinner can feature pasta or rice dishes, bagels and cheese, Chinese food, or Italian food. Snacks should be fruits, crackers, bread, or starchy vegetables, along with other foods such as yogurt or slices of lean meat. In addition, plan a carbohydrate-rich snack, such as whole-grain breads and cereals or a starchy vegetable like a potato or a sweet potato, for that time of the day when you are most vulnerable.

Fortunately, even for sugar-sensitive people, a taste for sugar is often learned, which means it can be unlearned. "You see a doughnut, you eat one and your insulin levels jump to the occasion. Before long, you expect a doughnut at the morning break and your body learns to drive insulin levels up when pastries are around, much like Pavlov's dog learned to salivate when a bell was rung," reports Judith Rodin, Ph.D., a professor of psychology and psychiatry at Yale University. The sugar-depression cycle can be stopped by replacing sugary foods with nutrient-packed foods such as fruit, crunchy vegetables, whole-grain raisin bagels, or low-fat yogurt. Within a few weeks of following the Feeling Good Diet, you'll find these healthful eating habits will curb the insulin response and help stabilize your mood.

Sugar, caffeine, and depression don't mix. People who are fighting depression and who know they are sensitive to sugar should avoid all sugar-containing foods, including desserts, sugar-coated cereals, candy, sugar-sweetened beverages, and sugary snack foods such as granola bars. Read labels, since many unsuspected foods contain sugar, including muffins, canned and boxed fruit juices, frozen breakfast foods, and yogurt (see "Sweet Consciousness," page 148). Also, try eliminating coffee and other caffeinated beverages, foods, and medications (see "The Caffeine Scoreboard," page 92, for the caffeine content of selected beverages and medications). Keep in mind that it may take three weeks or more after you have eliminated sugar and caffeine from your diet before you notice an improvement in mood.

Pay attention to your intake of vitamin B6, folic acid, and vitamin B12. Take immediate action to improve your diet if you are falling short of your vitamin B6 needs (see "B6 Basics," page 141). Make sure you include at least two folic acid–rich foods in your diet plans—that is, mix spinach with scrambled eggs for breakfast, drink at least one glass of orange juice during the day, steam collard greens and mix them into mashed potatoes, or replace ice-

---

Sweet Consciousness

Most Americans consume 21 percent of their daily calories as sugar. Although exact recommendations have not been set, it is generally agreed that people should cut their intake of added sugar in half, to 10 percent of total calories or less. People who consume less than 2,000 calories have little room for extras in their diet, so they should consume even less added sugar. Here's how:

- First, cut back on sweets, such as doughnuts, candy, pies, cakes, cookies, and ice cream, since these foods are doubly harmful because of their high sugar and high fat contents.
- Second, limit soft drinks to no more than one serving a day, since they supply up to nine teaspoons of sugar per serving and are the biggest contributors of sugar in the diet. Colas also contain caffeine.
- Third, read labels. Although manufacturers are not required to list the percentage of sugar calories, you can get an idea of the sugar content by reading the ingredients list. A food may be too sweet if sugar is one of the first three ingredients or if the list includes several sources of sugar.
- Fourth, use more spices. Cinnamon, vanilla, spearmint, and anise give sweet tastes to foods without adding sugar or calories. Aspartame can also be used in moderation.

Regardless of the name, all added sugar is essentially calories with no redeemable nutrient qualities. A little sugar in the diet adds enjoyment and variety, especially when it comes from a natural source, such as fruit. Going overboard for sweets, however, could undermine your health.

---

berg lettuce with folic acid–rich romaine lettuce in salads. To maximize your intake of folic acid, purchase vegetables fresh, refrigerate them immediately, and use them within two days. Avoid overcooking dark green leafy vegetables and always cook them in a minimum of water; then add the cooking water to soups and stews. Finally, consume the recommended selections of vitamin B12–rich meat, chicken, fish, and/or milk outlined in the Feeling Good Diet.

Review your eating habits of the past few months. Have you made dramatic changes in your normal patterns? Are you dieting, frequently skipping breakfast, indulging in snacks in the evening, eating too many sweets, or limiting to less than three the times during the day when you eat snacks and meals? Do you have any food intolerances, allergies, or aversions? Any of these habits will alter your brain chemistry and possibly contribute to mood swings.

As you progress through the three steps of the Feeling Good Diet, make your changes gradually. Select two or three small changes and practice them until they feel comfortable. This will assure long-term success and allow your brain chemistry to adjust to the new eating style. For an idea of how much to reduce your sugar intake, see "What Is Your Sugar Quota?" (page 150).

A New Mother's Blues

Postpartum blues—it's that period right after the baby is born when a mother cries at the drop of a hat. She is confused and may leave pots to burn on the stove, forget to let in the dog, or even experience a blank when asked her phone number or address. Everyone knows about the postpartum blues, but no one knows what to do about them, and the doctor is likely to ignore the issue altogether. Consequently, one out of every two women finds herself home alone with a one-week-old child and a case of the blues. One in ten women suffers even worse or lingering symptoms.

The postpartum blues have been categorized as three distinct, overlapping degrees of depression: (1) the blues, which occur within the first few weeks after delivery, (2) postnatal depression, a more severe depression that usually sets in later and may last longer, and (3) postnatal psychosis.

The early blues are usually transitory and should not require specific treatment; time will heal them. Some researchers theorize that the prevalence of

What Is Your Sugar Quota?

Most people should reduce sugar intake to 10 percent of total calories or less. Sugar-sensitive people should cut it even further. To estimate sugar consumption, first identify your daily calorie intake. For people who consume 2,000 or more, the total calories are multiplied by .10 to obtain the total day's calories that should be supplied by sugar—200 calories. A 2,500-calorie intake means you have a 250-calorie quota for sugar.

Your calorie intake: ____________ × .10 = ____________ calories from sugar.

How many of the following foods would it take to break your quota?

FOOD	AMOUNT	CALORIES FROM SUGAR
Cola	12 ounces	144
Welch's Grape Juice Drink	8 ounces	84
Kellogg's Corn Pops cereal	1 cup	52
Kellogg's Smacks cereal	1/2 cup	128
Cranberry sauce	1/2 cup	180
Chocolate cake	1/12 cake	240
Ice cream	1/2 cup	100
Sherbet	1/2 cup	128
Cherry pie	1/6 medium pie	225
Jam	1 level tablespoon	48

postpartum blues in the United States is somewhat culturally based, since cultures that provide more support and assistance to new mothers also have lower or nonexistent rates of postpartum blues. Research on mothers in the United States also shows that women who are more satisfied with their care and with how they are handling the new baby are less likely to suffer from depression. (However, this may be a chicken-and-egg phenomenon, since it is difficult to determine whether the happy parents or the lack of depression came first.)

No one knows why some women experience maternity blues and others don't. Limited evidence shows a possible increased risk for women who bottle-feed or who deliver by cesarean section. Other studies show a possible association with increased levels of anxiety and depression prior to the pregnancy or even previous emotional problems. Still others theorize that people's expectations of delivery and parenting color the experience and influence the degree of depression. However, there is no conclusive proof for any of these suspicions. The good news is that almost half of all women who struggle with mood swings, memory loss, and depression in the first few weeks of motherhood recover by the sixth week.

How nutrition and other lifestyle factors might influence postpartum blues has not been studied. An interesting connection, however, might exist between diet and the endorphins. In one study, mood changes and endorphin levels in nineteen women were assessed throughout pregnancy, labor, and the postpartum period. Results showed that endorphin levels rose significantly during labor and remained high for a few days after delivery, while the onset of confusion and memory loss was significantly linked to a fall in endorphin levels on about the fourth day postpartum. The higher a woman felt during this endorphin rush, the more likely she was to experience depression several weeks later. The researchers conclude that while the endorphins might help see a woman through the pain of childbirth and promote mother-child bonding, their subsequent drop might contribute to postpartum depression some weeks later.

If endorphins fall in the weeks following delivery, then any dietary or lifestyle habit that increases endorphin levels might help buffer the drastically declining levels. For example, beginning a moderate exercise program such as walking as soon as possible (as well as renting funny videos, since laughter also triggers endorphin release) is a proven effective therapy for improving mood, possibly because it boosts endorphin levels.

Although chocolate, sugars, and possibly sweet-and-creamy concoctions are suspected to release endorphins (see chapters 2 and 3), the high is temporary and could have a rebound effect that would escalate depression. Consequently, a recent mother should avoid concentrated sweets, desserts, and other high-fat, high-sugar items until the mood improves naturally. She should also avoid all caffeinated beverages, foods, and medications for the first two months postpartum. Until more is known about how diet contributes to or helps prevent postpartum blues, the new mother should follow a nutrient-packed, low-fat eating plan such as the Feeling Good Diet. Fortunately, many food cravings and aversions experienced during pregnancy subside after delivery, which makes it easier to follow the dietary guidelines in the Feeling Good Diet.

Another interesting link between diet and postpartum blues involves vitamin

B6. Poor dietary intake of vitamin B6 during pregnancy and after delivery might influence the bonding between the mother and child and contribute to postpartum depression, according to a study conducted at Purdue University and the University of Tucson. Approximately one-third of breastfeeding women in the study consumed inadequate amounts of vitamin B6, which was linked to increased irritability in the infant and a decrease in responsiveness to the baby's cries by the mother. In fact, the vitamin B6–deficient mothers were more likely to ask older siblings to care for the newborn than were mothers whose vitamin B6 supplies were adequate. Since consuming enough vitamin B6 is a problem for many pregnant and breastfeeding women, new mothers should consume several servings daily of foods rich in this nutrient (see Table 6.1).

The Bottom Line

The consensus is that a multitude of factors are recognized as contributors to depression. Stressful events such as loss of a family member or friend, a difficult change in job or finances, and problems at home or at work naturally play a part. The medical conditions underlying depression may be detected in a routine medical checkup and include changes in blood sugar, low thyroid, or irregularities in blood or urine. Even a history of food sensitivities, physical problems related to foods—such as skin or respiratory problems—or a family history of allergies might contribute to the blues (see chapter 10).

In short, what you eat is only part of the battle against the blues. Regular exercise, effective coping skills, a strong social support system, and limiting or avoiding alcohol, cigarettes, and medications that compound an emotional problem also are important steps. Interestingly, exercise works best for couch potatoes. While avid exercisers are less likely to be blue, they are more likely to feel irritable if they stop exercising. Once you start exercising, both your health and your mood depend on sticking with it.

Depression can be a symptom of other problems, so always consult a physician if emotional problems persist or if they interfere in the long term with the quality of your life and health. In the meantime, keep in mind that what you choose to soothe your hunger will also be fueling your mood.

TABLE 6.1 Vitamin B6–Rich Foods

FOOD	SERVING SIZE	VITAMIN B6 CONTENT (MG)
Banana	1 medium	.480
Avocado	1/2 medium	.420
Chicken	3 ounces cooked	.340
Wheat germ	1/4 cup	.220
Collard greens	1/2 cup cooked	.170
Spinach	1/2 cup cooked	.161
Tomato	1 medium	.148
Brown rice	1/2 cup cooked	.127
Green peas	1/2 cup	.110
Broccoli	1/2 cup cooked	.107
Nonfat milk	8-ounce glass	.098
Orange	1 medium	.098
Peanut butter	1 tablespoon	.046
Apple	1 medium	.045
Whole wheat bread	1 slice	.041
White rice	1/2 cup cooked	.030
White bread	1 slice	.009

Chapter Seven

Stress and Diet

Everyone handles pressure differently. Some people eat less, others eat more. One person may exercise a lot during stressful times, while another turns to alcohol or coffee for solace. Although there is no way to avoid all stress and strain, there are ways to minimize the effects these pressures have on your mental and physical health. You can adjust your dietary habits to help you cope better.

Stress and Our Prehistoric Bodies

To be alive is to feel stress. Everything—from the ring of a doorbell to the loss of a loved one—can be stressful. Some things are stressful in a positive way. Starting a new job, running your first 10K race, or taking an art class are potentially stressful events that prompt us to reach our goals, become better people, or stretch our creative limits. Some stress is even fun, such as the thrill of a roller-coaster ride or a suspenseful movie. However, stress frequently comes cloaked as worry, anger, jealousy, and fear; and it is these stresses—called distress—that are most harmful to your health.

Stress is your body's knee-jerk reaction to a threat. It is one of those survival-of-the-fittest basic instincts that dates back to the beginning of human life. Stress to the cave dweller meant physical danger. In those days, a proper response to anything unusual or threatening was literally a matter of life or death. In Darwinian terms, those who responded quickly survived, while those who ignored the threat didn't.

The sight of a saber-toothed tiger triggered early people's nerves and glands to secrete hormones and chemicals; as a result, the cave dweller's pupils dilated, nostrils flared, and vision improved, all in an effort to better identify the nature of the threat. Muscles tensed and prepared the body to run, jump, or face the enemy. Breathing, pulse rate, and blood pressure increased, reflecting the body's increased demand for oxygen and blood to the muscles. At the same time, blood was routed to the muscles and away from the internal organs. The liver released large amounts of glucose (sugar) into the bloodstream, and fat particles (called free fatty acids) were released from fat cells to provide the fuel to fight or flee. Within a split second the body was transformed from a peaceful state to war mode.

Essentially we are cave-dweller bodies dressed in Calvin Klein jeans. We have traded the threat of a saber-toothed tiger for rush-hour traffic. We live distended lifestyles marked by overcrowding and other social ills. There is too much to do and too little time. More often than not, anger, unrealistic expectations, fears, self-doubts, and other internal conflicts reside inside our heads. Our heart still races, our blood pressure climbs, and our stress hormones adrenalin and corticosteroids flood our system in response to these modern-day threats.

Instead of expending our rallied defenses, as our ancestors did by running for cover or standing up to fight, we stew in our own juices. Stress hormones linger in the bloodstream, blood cholesterol and sugar levels stay high, and nerve chemicals soar in record numbers. It is this state of prolonged stress that is linked to conditions such as cardiovascular disease, peptic ulcers, asthma, and possibly even cancer. It puts a strain on the immune system, further reducing resistance to colds, infections, and disease. How well do you respond to stress? Tally your stress points using the quiz on page 156.

Stress in Relation to Nutrition

Stress and nutrition are closely intertwined. A nutritional deficiency is a stress in itself, since a suboptimal amount of one or more nutrients places a strain on all the metabolic processes dependent on that nutrient. For example, a marginal iron deficiency results in reduced oxygen supply to the tissues and brain; in turn the oxygen-starved tissues leave a person feeling tired, irritable, and unable to concentrate. Likewise, an inadequate intake of the B vitamins stresses the cells' ability to convert carbohydrates and fats into energy. Suboptimal amounts of

QUIZ 7.1 Tally Your Stress Points

Is your life balanced with some peace and an occasional bout of frenzy? Are you always calm, or usually nuts? Answer each of the following questions on a scale of 1 through 5, depending on whether the statement for you is always true (1), never true (5), or somewhere in between.

1. ________ I eat at least three nutritious meals or snacks a day.
2. ________ I am doing things I really like to do.
3. ________ I am full of energy.
4. ________ I get at least seven hours of sleep.
5. ________ I give and receive affection and attention regularly.
6. ________ I have a circle of close friends and relatives who live close by and on whom I can rely. I feel comfortable disclosing my feelings and beliefs to them.
7. ________ I believe most things will turn out all right and am optimistic about the future.
8. ________ I set aside at least thirty minutes a day for quiet time.
9. ________ I do something fun at least three times a week.
10. ________ I exercise at an intensity that causes me to perspire at least four times a week.
11. ________ I avoid tobacco smoke and drink fewer than five alcoholic drinks a week.
12. ________ I feel I can reach my goals.
13. ________ I am able to pay my bills.
14. ________ I worry only about things that really matter and usually handle daily stresses successfully and quickly.
15. ________ I am in good health.
16. ________ I usually feel calm and rested and seldom feel nervous, jittery, or high-strung.
17. ________ I enjoy life.
18. ________ I am happy with my work and/or community involvement.
19. ________ I seldom feel that too many demands are placed on me.
20. ________ I am a good time manager and may be busy, but I seldom feel overwhelmed by responsibilities.
21. ________ I do not take street drugs and use prescription medications only when necessary and only with a physician's approval and monitoring.
22. ________ I laugh or chuckle daily and belly laugh regularly. (The average person laughs 540,000 times in his or her life. That equates to a minimum of twenty-one laugh episodes each day!)

Scoring:

Under 36: Your stress level is relatively low.

37 to 46: You are moderately stressed and should take an inventory of your life to see what could be done to reduce stress.

47 to 57: You find your life to be very stressful and cannot support optimal health. Take action to reduce your stress load and increase your commitment to healthy habits and activities.

More than 57: You find life extremely stressful. Don't waste another minute before making several changes to reduce the pressure. Choose a plan that will give you the greatest relaxation payoff for the least amount of effort.

---

beta-carotene and vitamin C weaken the body's antioxidant defenses, exposing the tissues to increased risk of damage and disease.

In addition, how well your body is nourished prior to and during a stressful event affects how well you handle the stress. In short, a well-nourished person copes better than a poorly nourished one.

On the other hand, stress affects your nutrient needs by reducing absorption, increasing excretion, altering the use of, or stepping up the daily requirements for certain nutrients. Yet people's eating habits often are at their nutritional worst during high stress. Consequently, a person is more vulnerable to nutritional deficiencies when stressed than during almost any other time in life.

Any type of stress—from the physical stress of disease or surgery to the emotional stress of losing a loved one to the mental stresses at work—may upset the nutritional balance. If the stress is short-lived and you are well nourished, the stress is not likely to significantly affect nutritional status. However, if you are marginally nourished and/or the situation lasts for some time, nutritional status and overall health are bound to suffer unless immediate action is taken to improve diet and coping skills.

Most of the research linking nutrition with stress has focused on physical stress such as surgery, burns, or intense exercise. Emotional and mental stress is a more elusive target, since no two people respond to the same event in the same way. Nevertheless, emotional and mental stress theoretically should alter nutritional status in a similar way to physical stress, since emotional stress alters hormone levels, which in turn affect nutrition-related metabolism. One thing is certain: emotional and mental stress suppress the immune system just as strongly as physical stress, if not more so.

The Immune System Under Attack

There is considerable evidence that emotional and mental stress suppress the immune system, reducing the ability to fight off colds, infections, and disease. Let's first take a brief look at what makes the immune system tick, then discuss how stress and nutrition affect that process.

The War Zone

Your body is like a fortress under siege. Everything in the environment, from the food you eat to the people you greet, exposes you to viruses, bacteria, and other microorganisms (or "germs") that can cause infection and disease. Whether or not you succumb to these daily attacks depends in part on the strength of your immune system.

The immune system is the body's main defense against both foreign invaders and abnormal cell growth such as cancer. The armed forces of this system include organs, tissues, millions of cells, and numerous chemicals. For example, specialized white blood cells, called B-cells, circulate in the blood and other body fluids, where they neutralize the toxins produced by bacteria. B-cells secrete chemicals called antibodies, which are like long-range missiles tailored to destroy foreign invaders.

T-cells are the cornerstones of immunity within the cells. Among other things, T-cells produce chemicals called lymphokines such as interferon, a protein that defends cells from viruses and is suspected to be a natural defense against cancer. Other specialized cells in the immune system include natural killer cells (free agents that act independently of other immune forces to locate and destroy the enemy), macrophages and monocytes that surround and "neutralize" hostile substances, and other white blood cells.

This complex defense system provides constant feedback on the "state of the union." The result is a sensitive and intricate system of checks and balances that, in the presence of optimal nutrient intake and moderate to low stress, helps guarantee an armed response to germ warfare that is efficient, quick, and specific. On the other hand, a weakened immune system may not recognize an invader or may fail to mount a strong attack. The results can be chronic or repeated infections, or more serious illnesses such as cancer.

Immunity, however, is not a black-and-white issue. "Whether the attacking organism or the immune system prevails depends on many factors, including a person's nutritional status, general health, stress level, and sleep patterns, as well as the force of the onslaught," says Darshan Kelley, Ph.D., a research chemist at the Western Human Nutrition Research Center in San Francisco. It is the total picture that determines a person's resistance to disease.

The Stress Factor

Have you ever caught a cold after a big event? Have you had to call in sick the week after a big deadline at work? Did you ever come down with the flu after "burning the candle at both ends"? Have you partied all weekend and been sick all week? If so, you have experienced firsthand the direct line between stress and your immune system.

As your heart starts racing and the perspiration appears on your brow, the stress response suppresses your immune system. Antibody production decreases, T-lymphocytes retreat, and B-lymphocyte numbers decline. Even minor nuisances such as loud noise, bright lights, or a sleepless night can affect your body's natural defenses. Depression, loss of a loved one, and other major stresses also suppress the immune system by as much as 50 percent in some people. Consequently, the more a person is stressed, the greater the likelihood of developing a cold, infection, or more serious illness. In contrast, healthy, de-stressing habits include:

- Avoiding tobacco
- Limiting alcohol consumption
- Sleeping at least seven hours a night
- Working fewer than ten hours a day
- Exercising regularly
- Eating breakfast
- Eating a nutrient-packed, low-fat diet
- Coping effectively with stress

Positive beliefs, attitudes, and expectations, including hope, trust, love, faith, and laughter, turn otherwise stressful events into more pleasurable ones and greatly reduce the risk of suppressing the immune system. In fact, these positive emotions may actually enhance immunity! The body has an amazing ability to adapt, so that the immune system bounces back as the body becomes accustomed to the tension. However, repeated onslaughts coupled with poor nutrition will eventually wear down even the most tenacious defense system.

Stress-Fighting Nutrition Factors

Diet, immunity, and stress are so intertwined that it is difficult to know where one stops and the next begins. Both stress and suboptimal nutrition can suppress the immune system. In addition, stress can increase nutrient needs and decrease nutrient absorption, jeopardizing those aspects of immunity that depend on specific nutrients for optimal function. A compromised immune system in turn can place stress on the body that results in disease and infection. It's a vicious cycle.

The Minerals

Researchers at the U.S. Department of Agriculture studied the effects of work-related stress on mineral status and found that, despite adequate dietary intake, blood levels of several minerals dropped as much as 33 percent and tissue stores for certain nutrients were depleted during a five-day "Hell Week" at work where employees were given extra work and asked to meet difficult deadlines.

Depletion of minerals can jeopardize the immune system and aggravate the stress response. For example, stress triggers the release of the stress hormones, which increase magnesium loss from the cells (especially from the heart and other vital organs), increase the loss of magnesium in the urine, and increase dietary requirements for the mineral. On the other hand, a magnesium deficiency raises stress-hormone levels, escalates the stress response, and causes stress-related depression and irritability. In studies on laboratory animals, a magnesium deficiency increased sensitivity to noise and overcrowding, whereas the animals were better able to cope when their diets were high in magnesium.

In human studies, Type A personalities, who are more stressed, are also more prone to stress-related disease, have higher blood levels of the stress hormones, and have lower magnesium levels than their more relaxed Type B counterparts. The link between magnesium and stress is so strong that researchers at the American College of Nutrition recommend supplementing with magnesium during times of stress because of increased magnesium loss and elevated requirements.

Other immune-stimulating minerals such as chromium, copper, iron, and zinc also are jeopardized owing to elevated requirements or increased excretion during times of stress. This in turn jeopardizes the immune system. Even a marginal deficiency could increase the risk for stress-related illness or disease. For example, people with poorly functioning immune systems also have low blood levels of zinc. When they take zinc supplements or increase their intake of zinc-rich foods (such as oysters, whole grains, extra-lean meats, and turkey), their immune response improves.

The Antioxidants

The antioxidant nutrients, including vitamin C and vitamin E, are affected by stress and also help regulate the immune system. (See chapter 8 for a discussion of antioxidants.) Both emotional and physical stress increase the amount of dietary vitamin C needed to maintain normal vitamin C levels in the blood. In addition, the stress glands, including the adrenals and the pituitary, are major storage sites for vitamin C in the body. During times of stress, these stores are depleted. Since the immune system depends on a constant supply of vitamin C, a cycle develops whereby stress depletes vitamin C levels in the body, which in turn reduces the body's resistance to infection and disease and increases the likelihood of further stress. The harmful effects of the stress hormones are reduced and the body's ability to cope with stress improves when dietary intake of vitamin C improves.

At this time, only environmental stressors such as air pollution are clearly associated with an increased need for vitamin E. This vitamin protects immune and lung tissue from the highly reactive and damaging compounds in ozone called free radicals, thus potentially increasing resistance to lung disease and possibly cancer. In contrast, inadequate vitamin E levels are associated with increased tissue damage from ozone. Numerous studies show that supplementation with vitamin E above recommended dietary amounts might be necessary to provide a strong defense against ozone exposure, especially in people who exercise heavily or who live in large cities and inhale greater amounts of this damaging compound.

American diets are often low in vitamins C and E and possibly other antioxidants, such as beta-carotene. In addition, researchers disagree on whether diet alone is enough during times of stress. "Recent evidence shows that consuming between 100 IU and 400 IU of vitamin E daily can improve a person's risk for developing heart disease, strengthen immunity, and possibly lower the risk for some cancers," says William Pryor, Ph.D., Boyd Professor of Chemistry and Biochemistry at Louisiana State University in Baton Rouge. However, it is difficult to consume that much vitamin E in food. For example, it would take 1 1/4 cups of safflower oil, the equivalent of 2,400 calories in fat alone, or 23 cups of spinach to reach 100 IU in vitamin E. Consequently, some researchers speculate that supplements might be necessary.

Dr. Pryor and other researchers suspect that the amount of beta-carotene needed for optimum immune function, especially during times of stress, is also difficult to achieve from food alone. "Beta-carotene is the greatest hope we have because of its strong anticarcinogenic effects, but the inconvenience of eating enough vegetables to get ample beta-carotene makes meeting these standards through diet alone unlikely for many people," says Dr. Pryor.

Other researchers disagree. "A proper diet, which includes several servings of fruits and vegetables every day, provides all the vitamin C needed for optimal immune function of healthy people," says Robert Jacob, Ph.D., at the Western Human Nutrition Research Center in San Francisco. According to Dr. Jacob and other researchers, it takes approximately 200 mg of vitamin C (the amount obtained from six ounces of orange juice, 1/2 cup of cantaloupe, and 1 cup broccoli) to keep the immune system running smoothly and to meet the extra demands of stress. However, some stresses, such as cigarette smoking and certain chronic diseases, increase the body's need for vitamin C even more. In reality, 90 percent of Americans are not following the recommendations to eat at least five to nine servings of fresh fruits and vegetables, as outlined in the USDA Food Guide Pyramid; many people do not eat even 60 mg of vitamin C (the adult RDA) each day, let alone 200 mg.

The B Vitamins

Vitamin B requirements may go up slightly during times of stress. Most of the B vitamins function in the development or maintenance of the nervous system, which is in overdrive during stressful events. The requirements for vitamins B1, B2, and other B vitamins are based on calorie intake. Therefore, a marginal deficiency can result from either a vitamin-poor diet or excessive intake of high-calorie, nutrient-poor foods such as sweets and refined or highly processed foods. Even marginal vitamin deficiencies might further upset the nervous system and contribute to stress-related symptoms such as irritability, lethargy, and depression. In addition, these nutrients are needed for optimal immune-system function.

For example, studies conducted at Loma Linda University in California and at Oregon State University in Corvallis reported that increasing vitamin B6 intake in some people raises blood levels of the vitamin and enhances the immune response. Large supplemental doses of vitamin B6 can be toxic, so moderate supplements (less than 25 mg daily) and food are the best sources of this vitamin. During times of stress, people should consume at least three or more servings of vitamin B6–rich foods each day, such as bananas, avocados, fish, baked potatoes, and dark green leafy vegetables (see Table 6.1 on page 153 for a list of vitamin B6–rich foods).

Carbohydrate Needs During Stress

Calorie, protein, and carbohydrate needs may increase during severe stress. Severe physical traumas can increase the metabolic rate by as much as 55 percent, and fever can increase the metabolic rate by 13 percent for every 1 degree celsius rise in body temperature. This would increase the need for calories, protein, and the B vitamins required to effectively metabolize them. There is no evidence that calorie and protein needs are affected by moderate physical or emotional stress. However, stress does stimulate the breakdown of serotonin, suggesting that increased intake of complex carbohydrates such as whole-grain bagels, breads, cereals, and pastas would help replenish serotonin levels and aid in soothing the stress response.

Another interesting link between stress and food regards the nerve chemical neuropeptide Y, or NPY (see chapter 1 for a detailed description of NPY). Stress triggers the release of stress hormones, including cortisol, from the adrenal glands. Cortisol turns on production of NPY in the brain, and this nerve chemical increases cravings for carbohydrate-rich foods, especially sweets. A bout of stress in the morning when NPY levels already are high may keep NPY turned on all day. Breakfasting on carbohydrates not only appeases the NPY levels but also helps a person calm down and feel better, possibly because it increases serotonin levels. Consequently, weight gain during stressful times might be a result of this escalation in NPY, which prompts more eating, coupled with reinforcement of feeling better because of elevated serotonin levels.

From Mood to Food and Back to Mood
Stress→↑cortisol from the adrenal glands→↑NPY→↑cravings for and consumption of carbohydrate-rich foods→↑serotonin→↑feelings of calm.

The sweet-and-creamy taste found in chocolate and desserts and lactose and fat found in milk also might trigger the release of endorphins, the brain chemicals that calm and soothe. Milk fat, which may stimulate the release of endorphins, has a quieting effect on baby animals that persists even after the milk is taken away.

If these nerve chemicals are charting your course, then work with your chemicals rather than against them. Plan nutrient-packed carbohydrate snacks such as raisin toast with all-fruit jam or Cheerios and dried apricots for your craving-prone times of the day. In addition, keep moving. Exercise helps burn extra carbohydrates so they are not converted to fat. See "Breakfast Quick Fixes," page 165, for some sample menus.

Stress and Fat Don't Mix

A low-fat diet stimulates the immune system, while diets high in fat might increase a person's susceptibility to infection and disease. According to Dr. Darshan Kelley, dietary fat, especially the polyunsaturated fats found in vegetable oils, suppress the immune system while fish oils might stimulate immunity. However, the issue is far from resolved. "In some studies on animals, the immune system is stimulated when [fish oils] are added to the diet; however, other stud-

Breakfast Quick Fixes

Are you burning the candle at both ends, with no time left for breakfast? The following meals can be prepared in five to ten minutes, so there is no excuse for not eating breakfast. Remember, allow yourself a few minutes to sit down, relax, and enjoy the meal!

Breakfast 1

Piece of fresh fruit, such as a banana, peach, 1/2 cup of berries, or 1/4 cantaloupe
Whole wheat toast with peanut butter and honey
1 percent low-fat milk

Breakfast 2

Melted cheese on whole wheat toast, bagel, or tortilla
Sliced apples, raisins, and nuts in a bowl

Breakfast 3

Dried or fresh fruit with plain low-fat yogurt and almonds
Whole-grain muffin with apple butter

Breakfast 4

Peanut butter mixed with wheat germ and honey and spread on whole wheat bread
Fresh cherries
Nonfat milk

Breakfast 5

Low-fat cottage cheese with fresh fruit and a drizzle of honey
Toasted English muffin with all-fruit jam

Breakfast 6

Instant oatmeal with wheat germ, chopped nuts, and raisins
1 percent low-fat milk
Orange

Breakfast 7

Breakfast smoothie: puree 2 pieces of fresh fruit, 1/4 cup orange juice, 1 cup plain nonfat yogurt, 2 teaspoons honey, nonfat dry milk, 1/4 cup wheat germ (optional), and 2 ice cubes

ies show suppression of the immune system. We may find in the future that it is the ratio [of vegetable oils to fish oils] that is the determining factor," says Dr. Kelley.

Studies on animals show that limiting total fat in the diet is key, regardless of the ratio of different types of fat, and helps improve wound healing and immunity in stressed animals. Until more is known about how fat affects the stress response and immunity, following a low-fat diet as outlined in the Feeling Good Diet (see chapter 13) is the best bet.

Sugar and Caffeine Urges

Stress can bring out the nutritional worst in a person. At a time when nutritional needs are at an all-time high, people forget to eat or eat all the wrong things. They eat too fast or only sporadically. They choose a food because it sounds good, it is handy, or they are hoping for a quick pick-me-up.

The two worst stress offenders are caffeine and sugar. Although manufacturers would like you to believe that anything sweet will give you an energy lift, in reality these foods only add fuel to the stress fire. At a time when you need your mental, physical, and emotional reserves, sugar and caffeine can leave you with plummeting blood-sugar levels and brain chemistry in disarray. In short, sugar and caffeine only make stressed matters worse.

Caffeine Jitters, High Anxiety

Caffeine gives coffee and cola their punch. Virtually all the caffeine in these beverages is absorbed and is quickly distributed to all parts of the body. Within half an hour, its stimulating effects can be felt. Caffeine has a direct effect on the brain and central nervous system. Thought and regulatory processes such as heart rate, respiration, and muscle coordination are affected after drinking even one cup of coffee. Three or more cups can give you "coffee jitters." In addition, coffee consumed with food can reduce mineral absorption, especially iron, by as much as 90 percent and can rob the body of other minerals such as calcium and magnesium, needed especially during times of stress.

Caffeine lingers in the body for three to four hours to escalate the stress response. In fact, caffeine alone can cause anxiety symptoms. As a consequence, it aggravates the stress chemicals and interferes with sleep; coffee drinkers take longer to fall asleep, sleep less soundly, and wake up more often. Substituting a cup of tea or a can of diet cola for an evening cup of coffee is not the perfect solution, since both tea and cola contain the same amount of caffeine as a cup of instant coffee.

Drinking too much coffee when you're stressed also can affect your future health. Caffeine in doses greater than 900 mg (the equivalent of five cups of coffee a day) may increase total blood cholesterol and LDL-cholesterol levels, raise blood pressure, and induce heart arrhythmias—all factors that increase a person's risk of developing heart disease. However, it is not clear whether these effects are caused by caffeine or by one or more of the 300 other compounds in coffee. In addition, people who drink a large amount of coffee are more likely to have other stressful habits such as smoking, not exercising, drinking alcohol, or eating a high-fat diet—adding insult to injury.

Sweets Stress

Chronically stressed people, such as Type A personalities who are competitive, achievement-oriented, pressured for time, and highly involved in their jobs, also turn to sugar for solace more than their more relaxed counterparts, Type B. In addition, the more outgoing a person is, the more likely he or she is to grab a sweet treat, whereas more reserved individuals prefer less sweet desserts.

A candy bar may seem like a good idea when you're stressed, but if you're looking for a real stress fix, grab a bagel instead. If not a convicted felon, sugar is an accomplice in many health problems, since it either replaces nutritious foods or adds unwanted calories. When sugar intake increases above 9 percent of total calories, vitamin and mineral intakes decrease progressively, compromising the immune system and adding stress to a body already under pressure. A high-sugar diet also increases urinary loss of minerals, including magnesium and chromium.

Sugary foods added to an otherwise ample diet tip the calorie scale in favor of weight gain. Laboratory animals fed a high-sugar diet, even when fat intake was low, consumed more calories and gained more weight compared to animals who ate more starch and less sugar. In short, excessive sugar intake, with or without a low-fat diet, encourages overeating and obesity. Weight problems add stress by contributing to the development of cancer, cardiovascular disease, diabetes, and osteoporosis.

Cholesterol and Hostility: Is There a Connection?

For years people have been told to lower their blood cholesterol levels and to take it easy because aggressive and competitive Type A personalities are more prone to developing heart disease. Then, in the early 1990s, researchers switched gears and reported that people with low blood cholesterol levels might avoid heart disease but were more depressed and aggressive and likely to commit suicide or die a violent death.

The obvious but erroneous assumption is that there is a direct link between low cholesterol levels and hostility. Some people even jumped to the conclusion that low-fat diets make people angry enough to kill themselves. It is more likely that some other variable is linked to low cholesterol and hostility, or that the link is nonexistent and this was only a fluke in a few studies. For example, other health behaviors such as tobacco and alcohol use and high-calorie diets are linked to aggressive behaviors and might provide the missing link to cholesterol.

In fact, more recent studies have not established a connection between low blood cholesterol and hostility. A study from the University of Edinburgh, Scotland, found no association between low cholesterol levels and anger; however, researchers did find that hostility increased as blood triglyceride (another form of fat linked to heart-disease risk) increased. In addition, symptoms of depression decreased as blood triglyceride levels decreased. Studies from the State University of New York at Stony Brook and from the Oregon Health Sciences University in Portland concluded that mood improves, with less depression and aggressive hostility, when blood cholesterol levels drop.

The lesson to be learned is that one study does not a conclusion make. A single study, even when well designed, provides food for thought but must be replicated in other well-designed research studies before the results can be taken seriously enough to make general dietary and lifestyle recommendations.

Diet in general has been linked to hostility and criminal behavior; however, no well-designed studies have backed up these claims. One study did show that antisocial men with more aggressive personalities secreted more insulin after consuming a high-sugar snack than did less aggressive men. However, this does not establish a cause-and-effect relationship between hostility and candy or soda pop consumption.

Stress-Proof Basics

The bottom line is that too much stress isn't good for you, although sometimes it is unavoidable. So when you can't beat the stress, join it, but go into battle nutritionally well armed.

At the front lines of your nutritional defense should be a recognition that nutritional needs peak during stress. Every bite counts. That's why the Feeling Good Diet is the foundation of a solid defense strategy, with some modifications.

First, cut back on colas. Granted, most people don't drink enough fluids when under stress and would benefit by hydrating their high anxiety; however, soda pop should not be the fluid of choice. Americans consume more than 450 servings per person per year of soft drinks; at 5 to 9 teaspoons of sugar per serving, that equals 2,250 to 4,050 teaspoons of sugar from soft drinks alone. One 12-ounce cola drink has approximately the same amount of caffeine as one cup of instant coffee. So limit your intake to no more than one 12-ounce serving of soda per day, preferably a caffeine-free, diet variety.

Second, savor your one cup of coffee, but don't go back for a second. Too much caffeine will only amplify anxiety. Switch to decaffeinated or grain-based beverages, or mix regular coffee with decaffeinated. For every cup of coffee, drink two glasses of water.

Third, cut out sweets until the stress subsides. You don't have nutritional room for high-fat, high-sugar, low-nutrient foods. Plus, sweets fuel the stress response. Instead, turn to naturally sweet fruits, whole grains, and other nutritious foods recommended in the Feeling Good Diet (see Table 7.1).

TABLE 7.1 Calming Foods in the Feeling Good Diet

The following snacks contain 100 calories or less but are packed with vitamins and minerals that can help soothe a stressed body. Keep in mind that the total diet is what is important. No one food can transform an otherwise poor diet into a great eating plan.

SNACK	AMOUNT	GOOD SOURCE OF
Sweets		
Apricots, fresh	3 medium	Beta-carotene, potassium, iron
Baked apple with cinnamon	1 medium	Beta-carotene, potassium, iron
Banana	1 medium	Potassium, vitamin B6, magnesium
Banana Pop*	1	Potassium, vitamin B6, magnesium
Blueberries, frozen	1 1/4 cups	Beta-carotene, potassium, manganese
Figs, dried	2	Calcium, iron, magnesium, potassium, selenium
Fruit, mixed dried	2/3 cup	Vitamin B6, potassium, calcium, iron, copper, manganese
Fruit Pop*	1	Beta-carotene, vitamin C
Grapes, frozen	1 cup	Beta-carotene, potassium, manganese
Mango	1 medium	Beta-carotene, niacin, vitamin B6, folic acid, calcium, vitamin E, potassium
Orange	1 small	Vitamin C, folic acid, beta-carotene, calcium, potassium
Papaya	1 medium	Beta-carotene, vitamin C, potassium, calcium

*See "Recipes for Feeling Your Best" at the back of this book.

Peach, canned in own juice, with nonfat yogurt	1 small 1/2 cup	Beta-carotene, potassium, calcium, magnesium, vitamin B2, protein
Raisin bread dipped in nonfat apple spice yogurt	1 slice 1/4 cup	B vitamins, iron, calcium, magnesium, vitamin B2
Raspberries, fresh	2/3 cup	Beta-carotene, vitamin C, potassium, iron, magnesium, manganese
Strawberries, fresh	2 cups	Vitamin C, folic acid, potassium, iron, manganese
Crunchy		
Broccoli, raw, with nonfat sour-cream dip	1 cup 1/4 cup	B vitamins, folic acid, vitamin C, vitamin E, calcium, magnesium, potassium, selenium, zinc
Cantaloupe	1/2	Beta-carotene, folic acid, vitamin C, calcium, magnesium, potassium
Carrot sticks with nonfat cream cheese–garlic dip	1 1/3 cups 1/4 cup	Beta-carotene, calcium, iron, potassium
Celery sticks filled with nonfat ricotta cheese and unsweetened crushed pineapple	4 stalks 1/3 cup 1/3 cup	B vitamins, calcium, magnesium, potassium, zinc
Fat-free oven-baked tortilla chips	1 ounce	Iron, magnesium, zinc
Nonfat refried beans, chips with salsa	1/4 cup 1 ounce 1/4 cup	B vitamins, iron, folic acid, vitamin C, magnesium, potassium, zinc
Red bell peppers with curried nonfat yogurt dip	2 1/4 cup	Vitamin B6, folic acid, vitamin C, vitamin E, potassium

Shredded carrots and raisins mixed with nonfat poppyseed dressing	1 cup 1 tablespoon 1 tablespoon	Beta-carotene, B vitamins, calcium, iron, potassium, selenium, zinc
Savory		
Black beans with cilantro	1/2 cup	B vitamins, folic acid, calcium, iron, magnesium, potassium, selenium, zinc
Lentil soup	3/4 cup	Protein, folic acid, calcium, iron, magnesium, potassium, selenium, zinc
Nonfat milk with almond extract	1 cup	Protein, calcium, vitamin B2, vitamin D
Warm microwave pretzel	1	Iron, zinc
Wheat germ (sprinkled on anything)	1/4 cup	B vitamins, vitamin E, calcium, iron, magnesium, potassium, selenium, zinc

Fourth, keep fiber in mind. Often the digestive tract is hit hard by stress. To ensure normal bowel function, each day consume at least five servings of fiber-rich fresh fruits and vegetables, six servings of 100 percent whole-grain breads and cereals, and one serving of cooked dried beans and peas. A variety of fibers are important, so don't depend exclusively on a processed bran cereal for your daily fiber needs. Insoluble fibers such as cellulose, hemi-cellulose, and lignin are found in bran; whole-grain breads, cereals, pastas; fruits; and vegetables. Soluble fibers such as pectin, gums, and mucilages are found in apples; citrus fruits; nuts; oats; and cooked dried beans and peas.

Fifth, if you lose your appetite when you're under pressure, try to eat six to eight small snacks throughout the day rather than force yourself to eat a big meal. Listen to your body and eat foods that sound good as long as they are wholesome, such as vegetables, fruits, whole grains, low-fat milk products, extra-lean meats, nuts and seeds, and legumes. If you tend to overeat when stressed, snack on low-fat goodies and eliminate high-fat temptations until your willpower returns. Stash some nutritious foods in your car's glove compartment; your desk drawer, briefcase, or purse; or the employee kitchen so you won't be caught off guard by a craving. Increase your exercise to make up for the extra calories and to burn up some of the stress chemicals. Studies repeatedly show that exercise is one of our best stress relievers!

Sixth, eliminate alcohol or limit your intake to five drinks a week or fewer. Alcohol adds stress to the body rather than giving the calming, nurturing effect you need. It also contains empty calories, which you can't afford right now.

Seventh, take a moderate-dose multiple vitamin and mineral supplement. Find one that supplies between 100 and 300 percent of the U.S. RDA for all vitamins and minerals, including the B vitamins, calcium, magnesium, and the trace minerals chromium, copper, iron, manganese, molybdenum, selenium, and zinc. Vitamin E is safe in adult doses up to 400 IU. Vitamin C is safe up to 500 mg, unless you have a history of kidney stones, in which case you should consult a physician before taking a supplement.

A supplement taken in small, multiple doses will have higher absorption and usefulness compared to a one-a-day supplement. The multidose supplement also reduces the likelihood of secondary deficiencies brought about by consuming too much of one nutrient without enough of another.

Avoid supplements touted as "stress" or "therapeutic" formulations; they often contain large amounts of randomly formulated nutrients such as the B vitamins and little or no other nutrients. At best, these products are a waste of money; at worst, their imbalanced formulations can aggravate a preexisting nutrient deficiency, which further compromises your immune defenses and your ability to cope with stress. "Balance is the key with the minerals," says Adria Sherman, Ph.D., chairperson of the Department of Nutritional Sciences at Rutgers University. "Minerals interact with each other and a large dose of one mineral can offset absorption and use of other minerals. Therefore, making sure you consume the minerals in the proper ratio to each other is essential for optimizing their effects on the immune system." Dr. Sherman also emphasizes that this balance is best found in nutritious foods, not supplements.

Finally, take the diet quiz on page 174 to measure the wisdom of your food choices. Recheck yourself after having followed the Feeling Good Diet for a couple of weeks.

QUIZ 7.2 How Does Your Diet Measure Up Stress-wise?

Answer the following questions. There are no partial scores; you either score all of the points for the question if you answer yes, or you score no points for that question if you answer no. Retake the quiz periodically to monitor your progress.

During stressful times . . .	YES/NO	POINTS POSSIBLE
1. Are mealtimes relaxed, pleasant?	________	10
2. Do you eat breakfast daily?	________	5
3. Do you avoid overeating at night?	________	4
4. Do you limit coffee, tea, colas to two servings or fewer daily?	________	5
5. Do you limit or avoid sugar?	________	5
6. Do you eat several small meals and snacks, rather than one or two large meals or sporadically?	________	10
7. Do you plan ahead to avoid filling up on junk foods?	________	3
8. Do you limit alcohol intake to five drinks or fewer each week?	________	5
9. Does half of your protein come from legumes and half from meat, chicken, or fish?	________	3
10. Do you avoid high-fat foods such as luncheon meats, bacon, fatty meats, whole-fat dairy products, oils, margarine, chips and other fatty snacks, or fried foods?	________	5
11. Do your meals reflect an emphasis on grains, fruits, and vegetables?	________	7
12. Are at least 50 percent of your breads, cereals, and pastas from whole grains?	________	4
13. Do you eat at least five servings of fresh fruits and vegetables daily?	________	3
14. Do you include at least two servings of citrus or other vitamin C–rich foods in your daily diet?	________	5
15. Do you consume at least two dark green leafy vegetables such as broccoli, spinach, or kale?	________	5

16.	Do you select at least three servings of nonfat dairy products or other calcium-rich foods daily?	________	5
17.	Do you limit your intake of convenience and fast foods?	________	3
18.	Do you drink at least six glasses of water each day?	________	5
19.	Do you take a moderate-dose multiple vitamin and mineral supplement that includes at least 100 percent of the RDA for the B vitamins, calcium, magnesium, iron, selenium, and zinc?	________	5
20.	Do you take extra vitamin C and vitamin E, but keep the dose at no more than 500 mg and 400 IU, respectively?	________	3
	Total	________	

Scoring:

Possible total: 100 points. Your initial goal should be a passing grade of 75—not a perfect score—with a plan to keep getting better.

Below 75 points: Make changes now to improve your diet to better cope with stress. At least take a moderate-dose multivitamin and mineral supplement until your diet is back on track.

Between 75 and 90: You have a reasonably good diet that should help cushion the harmful effects of daily tension.

Greater than 90: Shows you take the time to care for yourself, even when the going gets rough! Congratulations!

CHAPTER EIGHT

Smart Foods

Diet folklore is richly woven with threads of food and mind. For example, the ancient Greeks believed that mental illness resulted from imbalances among the body's four "humors," which included heat, cold, moisture, and dryness. Since these qualities also were found in foods, the consumption of specific items was believed to restore balance to the body's humors and correct problems of temperament.

The belief that food contains intrinsic properties that affect thinking, intellect, behavior, and even spirituality has been passed down to the current health food movement. At the turn of the century, Sylvester Graham (who gave his name to the graham cracker) and John Harvey Kellogg (the breakfast-cereal king) both proposed that toxins produced during the digestion of meat affected mental functioning. Regardless of whether or not these and many other beliefs are accurate, they shaped the current natural-foods movement and are still influencing grassroots beliefs about how food affects the mind. The latest diet-mind fads are "smart drinks," made from mixtures of vitamins, minerals, and amino acids and touted as one-shot solutions to improve stamina, memory, and thinking.

Despite lingering misconceptions, we have come a long way in a short time when it comes to knowledge of food and the mind. Food may not affect body humors nor does the digestion of meat lower your IQ. And unfortunately the quick fix of a nutrient cocktail also is a simplistic approach to tackling the complexity of the mind. However, what you eat could have profound effects on how you think, on your intelligence level, and on your memory. For example, what you eat affects the following:

1. The level of nerve chemicals in the brain that regulate all mental processes.
2. The development and maintenance of brain cell function and structure.
3. The insulating sheath surrounding the nerve cells that speeds the transport of messages from one neuron to another.
4. The level of enzymes and their activity, which enhances brain functions.
5. The amount of oxygen that reaches the brain.
6. The rate of accumulation and removal of cellular debris.
7. The ability of brain cells to transmit electrical messages.

As a consequence, inadequate intake of one or more nutrients can result in the deterioration of brain cell function with resulting memory loss, reduced ability to think clearly and quickly, poor concentration, acceleration of the age-related changes in brain tissue, reduced ability to reason leading to lowered IQ, and a dwindling desire to learn. How's your mental health? To find out, take the quiz on page 179.

No one knows exactly how much of what dietary components are needed for optimal mental functioning. It is clear, however, that nutrition plays a vital role in intellect, memory, thinking, and personality, and that brain power fluctuates depending on what and when you eat. Ultimately, your brain is an organ just like your heart and liver, and it needs a constant and optimal supply of nutrients to function at its best. Research has clearly identified the profound and lifelong effects of malnutrition early in life (that is, from conception through the first two years of life), when the nervous system is developing. For example, an inadequate supply of iodine results in severe mental retardation, too little folic acid results in neural tube defects, and not enough protein and calories results in small head and brain size as well as reduced motivation and desire to learn, IQ, and intellect. A shortage of iron results in apathy and lowered IQ scores later in life, while not enough vitamin B6 results in seizures and irritability in newborns.

Since the cause-and-effect link between diet and the brain is clear-cut during this critical period, it is also likely that inadequate nutrition at other stages of life affects how we think, remember, learn, and concentrate. For example, lifelong poor dietary habits probably speed the progression of age-related memory loss and other cognitive functions. On a more positive note, many of the effects of poor nutrition are reversible if dietary habits are permanently changed. In essence, at most stages in your life you have the ability to improve your memory, intellect, concentration, and IQ by making a few simple changes in what and when you eat.

However, don't take feeling good as a sign of thinking good. The Recommended Dietary Allowances (RDAs)—the standard for assessing nutritional status—are based on physical symptoms of vitamin, mineral, and protein deficiencies. Yet the brain shows changes in thinking patterns, memory, personality, and intelligence long before symptoms appear in the body. You may have trouble remembering things, feel "under the weather," or just not be as sharp as you used to be. Consequently, vague yet profound changes in mental ability can progress undetected because you otherwise feel fine. In fact, impaired mental function always precedes physical problems, so look to your diet first before blaming age or heredity for lapses in memory, thinking, concentration, or other mental abilities.

Feeding the Mind

If you are having trouble concentrating, staying motivated, or just thinking clearly, take a look at your breakfast habits. The brain depends entirely on glucose to fuel its millions of daily thought processes. Skipping meals frequently will drain glucose reserves and essentially force the brain to "run on fumes." It is no wonder that people who skip breakfast often have difficulty staying alert later in the day.

On the other hand, breakfast restocks these dwindling glucose supplies and helps people think quickly and creatively throughout the day. Studies with children show that eating breakfast improves school attendance, reduces illnesses, increases motivation and interest in learning, and elevates mood—all of which improve learning. Adults also perform better at work if they have eaten a nutrient-packed breakfast. Granted, a well-nourished person can occasionally skip breakfast with minor negative effects on his or her ability to think. However, skipping meals frequently could be undermining your ability to mentally "stay on your feet."

What you eat also determines your brain power. Although carbohydrate-rich foods at breakfast, such as pancakes, toast, waffles, and cereal, help fuel your thinking during the morning hours, they may make you sleepy and less able to

QUIZ 8.1 How's Your Mental Health?

Answer yes or no to the following questions, then count the number of yes and/or no answers.

_______ **1.** Lately, I've had trouble naming things that are familiar to me.
_______ **2.** My memory isn't as good as it used to be.
_______ **3.** I often forget important meetings, appointments, or other planned responsibilities.
_______ **4.** I find it more difficult to concentrate than in the past.
_______ **5.** I frequently feel "fuzzy-headed."
_______ **6.** I sometimes get confused about what time it is or where I am.
_______ **7.** I rely on coffee to stay alert.
_______ **8.** I sometimes repeat the same story to the same people within a short time.
_______ **9.** I'm not as interested in learning and trying new things as I used to be.
_______ **10.** My attention span isn't what it used to be.
_______ **11.** I often walk into a room and can't remember what I came in to get.
_______ **12.** I have trouble listening to people because my mind wanders.
_______ **13.** I frequently find myself staring blankly out the window.
_______ **14.** My verbal skills and vocabulary are not as good as they used to be.
_______ **15.** I have trouble keeping up with conversations and often bluff my way through.
_______ **16.** My work performance has dropped recently.
_______ **17.** I put things away and then can't remember where I put them.

Scoring:

Few people can answer no to all of the above questions. However, the more times you answered yes, the more likely it is that you are suffering from mental fatigue. In most cases, memory loss, confusion, or other mental problems are temporary and only a minor irritant, easily corrected by changes in your diet or lifestyle. More serious problems always should be discussed with your physician.

concentrate after lunch. Bonnie Spring, Ph.D., a professor of psychology at Harvard University, reports that seniors are particularly susceptible to the effects of carbohydrates. Her studies show that mental alertness and ability to concentrate decrease after a midday meal of carbohydrate-rich foods. This effect is compounded if the carbohydrates come primarily from sugar-laden foods, because these foods supply few vitamins, minerals, or other brain-enhancing nutrients.

High-fat meals and "heavy" meals that contain more than 1,000 calories also may leave you more interested in a nap than in staying alert. In contrast, a light midday meal that supplies approximately 500 calories in a mixture of protein and carbohydrates with a little fat—such as a turkey sandwich on whole wheat bread (no mayonnaise) or spaghetti with meatballs (made with extra-lean meat) and fresh fruits and vegetables—fuels the body without making you groggy. The best way to enhance brain power is to follow the Feeling Good Diet (see chapter 13) and:

1. Always eat breakfast.
2. Keep your meals small and frequent.
3. Combine a little protein with a lot of carbohydrate-rich foods.

Low-calorie diets can temporarily affect your ability to think clearly. In a study conducted at the AFRC Institute of Food Research in Reading, England, fifty-five dieters between the ages of eighteen and forty scored poorly on a mental aptitude test compared to nondieting women. Short-term memory and the ability to quickly process information are impaired in dieters; mental ability continues to deteriorate the longer these people diet. Bulimics who swing from abstinence to binge eating show a marked reduction in mental ability, possibly because of altered nerve chemical function. In contrast to severe dieting—which is harmful to your health and is ineffective for permanent weight loss—cutting back on dietary fat and losing weight gradually (no more than two pounds a week) actually stimulates mental function and improves overall well-being.

Besides having overall nutritional effects, several specific nutrients have direct effects on brain function, thinking ability, and memory. These nutrients include the antioxidants (beta-carotene, vitamin C, and vitamin E), the B vitamins, iron, and choline.

The Antioxidant Theory of Aging

Although the underlying mechanisms of the aging process are poorly understood, a relatively new theory involving the antioxidants most accurately explains some mechanisms of aging.

The story of the antioxidants and aging begins with free radicals. These highly reactive substances, including oxygen particles, are found in air pollution, tobacco smoke, radiation, herbicides, and rancid fatty foods such as French fries, and they are also produced in the body during normal metabolic processes. Free radicals attack the body's cells, producing a new free radical and, if left unchecked, initiating a chain reaction.

When a free radical attaches to one of the fats in a cell membrane, the shape of the fat is changed, similar to what happens when a vegetable oil turns rancid. When a fat is altered in the body, the structure and function of the cell membrane is damaged and the membrane can no longer transport nutrients, oxygen, and water into the cell or regulate removal of waste products from the cell. Continued free-radical attack renders the cell useless, rupturing its membrane and releasing its cellular contents. The leakage of cellular chemicals out of the cell further damages the surrounding tissues.

The power center of the cell, called the mitochondria, where all energy is produced, is vulnerable to attack by free radicals. This damage shuts down energy and protein production and the cell dies, leaving only a cell remnant. The remnants accumulate around and in the nerve cells, inhibiting the nerve cell's ability to send messages. The age of a nerve cell is determined by the number of cell remnants—called "clinkers"—that have accumulated. The deterioration of brain cells is the hallmark of aging and memory loss. In essence, the garbage that accumulates from free-radical attacks on nerve cells is at least a contributing factor, if not the primary cause, of many of the chronic degenerative diseases associated with aging.

Free radicals also attach to a cell's genetic code, called DNA, which regulates cell reproduction and function. The cell may die when the genetic code is so altered that its messages can no longer be read by the cell. In addition, RNA, the essential messenger in the nerve cell that receives instructions from the DNA and makes sure that the message is carried out within the cell, is also susceptible to attack and destruction by free radicals. Excessive cell death means there are fewer nerve cells available to store, access, and transfer information, and fewer connections between nerve cells. Consequently, memory, thinking, and intelligence are affected.

One way to imagine the lifelong effects of free-radical damage is to picture a room filled with glowing lights that represent active brain cells. A wild golf ball is shot about the room randomly, knocking out lights. At first the few broken lights have little or no effect on the room's brightness. Eventually, however, enough lights have been broken that the room dims. Finally, so many lights have broken that you can no longer find your way out of the darkened room—the equivalent of years of unrestrained free-radical damage to the nervous system.

The Anti-Aging Antioxidants

Fortunately, the body has an antioxidant system comprising enzymes, vitamins, and minerals that deactivate free radicals so they cannot attach to membranes, nucleic acids, or cellular components.

The primary antioxidant nutrients are beta-carotene, vitamin C, vitamin E, and selenium. Beta-carotene prevents the formation of several highly reactive free radicals, while the fat-soluble vitamin E protects the cell membranes by scavenging free radicals before they attack fat molecules in the nerve cells. Since the brain consists of almost 60 percent fat, primarily found in the cell membranes and other critical structures, vitamin E's protective ability could have far-reaching effects on brain cell structure and function and, consequently, on mental ability. In fact, studies show that low vitamin E levels are associated with nerve damage.

Water-soluble vitamin C helps guard against harmful reactions occurring within and surrounding each cell. For example, laboratory animals whose diets were rich in antioxidants lived longer than animals whose diets were low in vitamin C. Vitamin C not only functions as a nervous system protector but also aids in the manufacture of several nerve chemicals and may act independently to regulate nerve function. Finally, selenium is an essential component of glutathione peroxidase, another antioxidant enzyme that converts free radicals to harmless compounds.

In these ways, antioxidant nutrients help protect against premature aging and possibly maintain a well-functioning nervous system and brain. These anti-aging nutrients might slow down or control the rate of aging (and ultimately, senility) by suppressing the rate of brain cell damage caused by free radicals. But this system is only as good as a person's diet. When antioxidant intake is optimal throughout life, free-radical damage is kept at bay, whereas a consistently poor diet, low in antioxidants, weakens the body's defenses and allows free radicals to proceed unchecked. Table 8.1 is a list of foods that are good sources of antioxidants.

B's on the Report Card

An inadequate intake of several B vitamins, including vitamin B1, vitamin B2, niacin, vitamin B6, vitamin B12, and folic acid, could be at the root of your brain drain. In some cases, such as for psychiatric patients, the deficiency is secondary to the mental illness. However, in many more cases poor intake of one or more of these nutrients initiates a vicious cycle of mild depression, apathy, and lowered mental function that further reduces food and nutrient intake.

Vitamin B1

It is difficult to believe anyone could consume inadequate amounts of vitamin B1, since this B vitamin is even added to highly refined white breads and cereals. However, marginal deficiencies are not uncommon, especially in adolescents, seniors, and people who abuse alcohol. The symptoms show up primarily in the nervous system, probably because vitamin B1 is essential for extracting energy from the brain's number one fuel source—glucose. Fatigue, loss of appetite, weakness, mental confusion, memory loss, emotional instability, reduced attention span and concentration, aggressive behavior, personality changes, and irritability are a few of the symptoms characteristic of poor vitamin B1 intake.

One study showed that B1-deficient children who supplemented their diets with the vitamin had quicker reaction times and scored better on memory and intelligence tests at the end of one year. If poor diet is the cause of these mental problems, then consuming more vitamin B1–rich foods, including wheat germ, brewer's yeast, green peas, collard greens, oranges, and cooked dried beans and peas, should quickly alleviate the symptoms.

Niacin

Attention to the link between niacin and mental health has swung from the ridiculous to the sublime. This B vitamin was once touted as the cure of the century for schizophrenia, yet later it proved at best only moderately effective as a therapy. Later research showed that niacin can cause liver damage when consumed in large doses. So even if niacin is somewhat effective for the treatment of serious mental illness, no one should self-medicate.

TABLE 8.1 Antioxidant-Rich Foods

FOOD	SERVING	AMOUNT OF ANTIOXIDANTS
Vitamin C[1]		
Green bell pepper	1 large	128 mg
Red bell pepper	1/2 cup diced	95 mg
Orange juice	6-ounce glass	90 mg
Grapefruit	1 medium	76 mg
Brussels sprouts	1/2 cup cooked	48 mg
Orange	1 medium	66 mg
Strawberries	1/2 cup	66 mg
Broccoli	1/2 cup cooked	52 mg
Collard greens	1/2 cup cooked	23 mg
Grapefruit juice	6-ounce glass	38 mg
Beet greens	1/2 cup cooked	18 mg
Tomato juice	6-ounce glass	30 mg
Cabbage	1/2 cup	24 mg
Asparagus	1/2 cup cooked	19 mg
Beta-carotene[2]		
Carrot juice	8-ounce glass	11,520 IU
Carrot	1 medium, raw	11,000 IU
Sweet potato	1 small	8,100 IU
Spinach	1/2 cup cooked	7,300 IU
Apricots	8 dried halves	5,500 IU
Collard greens	1/2 cup cooked	5,400 IU
Beet greens	1/2 cup cooked	5,100 IU
Cantaloupe	1/4 melon	3,400 IU
Peach	1 medium	2,170 IU
Romaine lettuce	3 1/2 cups chopped	1,900 IU
Asparagus	5 spears cooked	622 IU
Brussels sprouts	9 cooked	550 IU

[1]The RDA for vitamin C is 60 mg, but intakes of up to 250 mg or more are safe and possibly beneficial to health.

[2]There is no RDA for beta-carotene, but intakes of up to 15,000 IU are safe and possibly beneficial to health.

Vitamin E[3]		
Wheat germ oil	1/4 cup	63.6 IU
Wheat germ	1/2 cup	27 IU
Almonds	1/4 cup	25 IU
Safflower oil, preferably cold-pressed	1/4 cup	19.51 IU
Cottonseed oil	1/4 cup	13 IU
100% whole-grain cereal	1 cup	0.40 IU
100% whole wheat bread	1 slice	0.39 IU
Selenium[4]		
Organ meats	4 ounces cooked	149.6 mcg
Seafood	4 ounces cooked	37.9 mcg
Lean meat	4 ounces cooked	22.7 mcg
Chicken without the skin	4 ounces cooked	22.7 mcg
100% whole wheat bread	1 slice	12 mcg
100% whole-grain cereal	1/2 cup cooked	12 mcg
Nonfat milk	1 cup	3.6 mcg
Vegetables	1 serving	1.6 mcg (average)
Fruits	1 serving	0.9 mcg (average)

[3]The RDA for vitamin E is 12 to 15 IU, but intakes of up to 400 IU are safe and possibly beneficial to health.
[4]The RDA for selenium is 45 to 70 mcg, but intakes of up to 200 mcg are safe and possibly beneficial to health.

On the other hand, more than fifty body processes depend on niacin, including the release of energy from carbohydrates and the manufacture of many nerve chemicals and hormones that regulate thinking and memory. Consequently, it is no surprise that even a mild deficiency produces symptoms that include depression, confusion and disorientation, anxiety, irritability, and short-term memory loss. A severe deficiency results in dementia and psychosis. In contrast, consuming several servings daily of niacin-rich foods, such as chicken, salmon, peanut butter, green peas, and wheat germ, will correct these problems if they are caused by a deficiency.

Vitamin B6

Essential for normal development and maintenance of the nervous system, this B vitamin is needed from conception through adulthood. Pregnant women need to consume more vitamin B6 than is sufficient merely to support the mother's health; not doing so can have serious consequences for the developing infant, including irritability, seizures, and reduced learning ability. Even short-term poor intake of vitamin B6 can produce changes in brain waves in adults. In contrast, consuming several servings daily of vitamin B6–rich foods, such as bananas, chicken, fish, potatoes, collard greens, brown rice, and green peas, improves memory, especially long-term memory, and increases the brain's capacity to store information.

How vitamin B6 affects the nervous system is only partly understood. This B vitamin is essential for the normal breakdown of carbohydrates, protein, and fats for energy and aids in the conversion of amino acids (the building blocks of protein) into nerve chemicals that, in turn, regulate mental processes. The enzymes that regulate the manufacture and breakdown of nerve chemicals, including serotonin, dopamine, and GABA, are blocked when vitamin B6 levels are low, while the incomplete byproducts of these nerve chemicals accumulate and irritate the surrounding nerves. This latter effect may explain the seizures experienced by vitamin B6–deficient infants. The insulating sheath, called myelin, that surrounds nerve cells and speeds the transfer of messages through the brain is damaged when vitamin B6 is not available, thus affecting memory, reaction time, and thinking.

Even marginal dietary intake of vitamin B6 can affect thought, memory, and concentration, which poses a serious health concern since many people in the United States consume suboptimal amounts of this vitamin, including women of childbearing age, children, and seniors. In fact, women typically consume half the Recommended Dietary Allowance (RDA) for vitamin B6 and as many as 15 percent of women consume less than 25 percent of the RDA. Pregnant and breastfeeding women frequently consume only 60 percent of their recommended intake for vitamin B6. Although their poor intake may not produce obvious vitamin B6 deficiencies, their ability to think, remember, and reason could be cut short. Even more serious are the potential effects a marginal deficiency in the pregnant or breastfeeding mother could have on brain development in the infant.

Consuming at least 2,000 to 2,500 calories from foods in the Feeling Good

Diet will ensure optimal intake of vitamin B6. However, if your calorie intake falls below this amount, or you do not always eat well, a moderate-dose multiple vitamin and mineral supplement that contains approximately 2 to 10 mg of vitamin B6 provides safe nutritional insurance. Large doses of vitamin B6 (in excess of 150 to 250 mg for an adult) can be toxic if taken for long periods of time and should be used only with the supervision of a physician.

Vitamin B12

Claims that this B vitamin can cure everything from low energy, poor memory, and mental deterioration to aging, poor concentration, and irritability have obscured the truth about the link between vitamin B12 and mental function. Vitamin B12 might not be the powerful energizer or rejuvenator that food faddists claim it to be, but it does play an important role in maintaining a well-functioning brain. In addition, while there is no scientific evidence that any more than the RDA of 6 mcg a day is beneficial (some faddists claim that 6,000 mcg will improve memory), even this minute quantity, if absorbed properly, can work miracles.

Vitamin B12 is essential for the proper formation of the myelin sheath surrounding nerve cells. This insulated covering speeds nerve transmission much as an insulated wire transports electrical current faster than an uninsulated wire. A vitamin B12 deficiency, therefore, results in faulty formation of myelin, with symptoms including disorientation, numbness and tingling in the hands and feet, moodiness, confusion, reduced IQ, agitation, and dizziness. These mental problems often develop long before more obvious physical symptoms and can progress undetected to potentially irreversible stages.

Vitamin B12 along with folic acid is also essential for normal cell reproduction, including the manufacture of red blood cells. Consequently, inadequate intake or absorption of this B vitamin and/or folic acid results in poorly formed red blood cells that cannot carry oxygen to the brain. Fatigue, impaired mental function, decreased attention span, listlessness, and anemia result.

Vitamin B12 is abundant in foods of animal origin, including extra-lean meat, chicken, fish, milk and milk products, and eggs. Most Americans consume two to three times their daily need of these foods and so usually consume recommended levels of vitamin B12. (Strict vegetarians who avoid all foods of animal origin are an exception to this rule.)

Vitamin B12 status is more than just an issue of intake, however. The absorption of this B vitamin depends on a digestive substance in the stomach called intrinsic factor. Levels of this digestive aid often dwindle as a person ages. Consequently, the diet may be adequate in vitamin B12, but little may be absorbed, resulting in a deficiency that might contribute to the progression of age-related dementia and memory loss. In fact, seniors often have low blood levels of vitamin B12 even though they show no overt signs of a deficiency. Many of their problems of poor memory and concentration are improved when they either increase their intake of vitamin B12–rich foods or take a supplement. In severe cases where the body no longer makes any intrinsic factor, physician-supervised injections of vitamin B12 might be necessary.

Folic Acid

Folic acid is the most likely B vitamin to be low in the diet. In fact, typical American diets are sorely lacking in the folic acid–rich dark green leafy vegetables (such as broccoli, spinach, chard, collard greens, and romaine lettuce) and so contain approximately half the recommended daily amount of 400 mcg. In addition, folic acid in foods is easily destroyed by air and heat, so fresh produce that sits on the stand for days, is stored for days in your refrigerator, or is overcooked, reheated, or displayed on a cafeteria-style steam table may contain little or none of its original folic acid.

In addition to the growing evidence that suboptimal amounts of folic acid are directly linked to birth defects and possibly to cervical cancer, inadequate intake of this B vitamin also might affect brain power. Maintenance of the cells' genetic code and the manufacture of all new cells—from support cells in the brain to red blood cells—require folic acid. Having too little folic acid means cells do not replicate or new cells are made imperfectly. Tissue function is hampered because of the reduced number of cells and the possible increase in abnormal cell growth. The symptoms are widespread, since every cell in the body is affected by a folic acid deficiency. Anemia, irritability, behavior problems, and loss of appetite are only a few of the symptoms.

Folic acid deficiency also is linked to several serious psychiatric disorders, including clinical depression, organic brain syndromes, and schizophrenia. Some patients who supplement their diet with extra folic acid show greater improvements and have shorter hospital stays than do patients who do not supplement. In one study, eight out of nine folic acid–deficient patients who complied with supplementation guidelines for six months had excellent recovery successes compared to patients who did not supplement. Granted, not all psychological disorders are so easily treated; however, folic acid is relatively nontoxic, so increasing your dietary intake of this vitamin to 400 to 800 mcg in conjunction with optimal intake of vitamin B12 is safe and potentially helpful in the prevention and treatment of some mental disorders (see "Effects of the B Vitamins," page 190).

What Do Eggs, Wheat Germ, and Your Brain Have in Common?

Until recently, a vitamin B–like compound called choline was not considered an essential nutrient, since it could be made in the body and no deficiency symptoms had been identified. However, recent evidence shows that choline might be essential for brain development and function. In fact, it might be at the root of age-related memory loss.

Choline is a building block for a special category of fats called phospholipids (fats containing the mineral phosphorus), the essential components of the cell membrane. It also is a building block for the most important neurotransmitter for memory function—acetylcholine. Without optimal levels of acetylcholine, the brain cannot store or retrieve information, and a person experiences memory loss that can range from minor aggravation to total debilitation, as in the case of Alzheimer's disease. In contrast to the amino acids such as tryptophan, which must compete for entry into the brain before they are converted into nerve chemicals, choline enters unhindered. Consequently, the more choline you consume, the more gets into your brain.

Brain cells need choline to function properly. Although the body can manufacture some choline with the help of folic acid and vitamin B12, apparently it cannot produce enough to maintain normal brain function; consequently, blood choline levels drop when people consume a choline-poor diet, which could have far-reaching effects on their thought processes. For example, people flunk memory tests when they are given a drug that blocks acetylcholine function, but pass with flying colors when they are given a drug that raises acetylcholine levels.

On the other hand, choline supplementation during pre- and postnatal devel-

Effects of the B Vitamins on Thought, Memory, and Mood

Vitamin B1

Effects of Deficiency: Aggressiveness, anxiety, apathy, confusion, depression, fatigue, irritability, memory loss, nerve damage, poor concentration and attention span, psychosis.

Dietary Sources: Wheat germ, brewer's yeast, green peas, collard greens, oranges, legumes, asparagus.

Vitamin B2

Effects of Deficiency: EEG abnormalities, irritability.

Dietary Sources: Low-fat milk, yogurt, oysters, avocados, spinach, broccoli, Brussels sprouts.

Niacin

Effects of Deficiency: Nerve damage, apathy, anxiety, delirium, dementia, depression, irritability, mania, memory loss, mood swings.

Dietary Sources: Chicken, salmon, extra-lean beef, peanut butter, green peas, potatoes, brewer's yeast, low-fat milk, wheat germ.

Vitamin B6

Effects of Deficiency: Acute sensitivity to noise, EEG changes, fatigue, depression, irritability, reduced learning ability, seizures.

Dietary Sources: Bananas, avocados, extra-lean beef, chicken, fish, potatoes, collard greens.

Pantothenic Acid

Effects of Deficiency: Depression, fatigue, irritability, restlessness.

Dietary Sources: Oranges, collard greens, potatoes, broccoli, brown rice, cantaloupe, wheat germ.

Biotin

Effects of Deficiency: Depression, fatigue and lethargy, sleepiness.

Dietary Sources: Oatmeal, soybeans, peanut butter, salmon, low-fat milk, brown rice, chicken.

Vitamin B12

Effects of Deficiency: Abnormal EEG, confusion, delusions, depression, irritability, hallucinations, memory loss, paranoia.

Dietary Sources: Oysters, tuna, yogurt, low-fat milk, fish, chicken, cheese, extra-lean beef.

Folic Acid

Effects of Deficiency: Apathy, dementia, depression, delirium, forgetfulness, insomnia, irritability, psychosis, mental retardation in infants.

Dietary Sources: Brewer's yeast, spinach, orange juice, romaine lettuce, avocados, broccoli, wheat germ, legumes, bananas.

opment in animals produces marked improvements in memory that last into adulthood. Large supplemental doses of choline (500 mg to 20 g) also have improved learning performance in mature animals, while people suffering from memory loss who are given choline supplements often show improvements in short-term memory and abstract thinking.

The human body contains approximately 30 to 31 grams of choline. This compound is found in the diet as free choline or as a component of lecithin (phosphatidylcholine) in such foods as wheat germ and brewer's yeast. Average daily intake of choline is between 700 and 1,000 mg. Deficiency symptoms develop when intake falls below this amount, which may be common in recent years as more people have stopped eating cholesterol-rich foods such as eggs, which are also a primary source of choline. Richard Wurtman, Ph.D., a professor of neuroscience and the director of the Clinical Research Center at the Massachusetts Institute of Technology, believes that choline intake is probably low enough in some diets to cause memory problems.

Choline, Aluminum, and Alzheimer's Disease

Age-related memory loss, including Alzheimer's disease, might be associated with long-term marginal choline deficiency. Since levels of acetylcholine increase in proportion to dietary intake of choline, it is reasonable to assume that supplementation with or increased dietary intake of choline might improve memory function in older people. For example, some studies show that age-related memory loss is improved when laboratory animals are fed a choline-rich diet.

Studies have produced varying results, however. One study showed improvements in long-term memory when patients were given 35 grams (a little more than 1 ounce) of lecithin daily for four to six weeks. Other studies have shown that supplementation with choline or purified soya lecithin raises blood levels of choline but does not increase synthesis of acetylcholine or improve memory. If choline supplementation is effective, it probably is most useful in the early stages of memory loss, before pronounced structural changes in the brain produce irreversible damage. Until more research is conducted, there is no definitive evidence that commercial lecithin improves memory in the advanced stages of Alzheimer's disease. In addition, although the quality of lecithin supplements has improved in recent years, many products still contain as little as one-third choline, thus making their potency questionable.

Choline supplementation always should be discussed with a physician, since it can produce side effects such as diarrhea and is not advised for individuals with certain psychological conditions. For example, manic depressives should not supplement with choline, since the nutrient can aggravate the depressive phase of the illness.

The link between Alzheimer's and choline also might be related to the toxic metal aluminum. Transportation of choline into the nerve cells is an essential step in the formation of acetylcholine. Inhibition of this step, even when choline levels are adequate, interferes with nerve cell function and alters memory. One study showed that aluminum significantly inhibits the transportation of choline into certain cells. In addition, aluminum might affect acetylcholine metabolism by adversely affecting how much acetylcholine is made and how effective it is in transporting messages from one nerve cell to the next. This might explain why people with Alzheimer's disease also show abnormal accumulation of aluminum and low levels of acetylcholine in their brains. If this association between aluminum and choline is verified, then avoiding aluminum cookware, coffeepots, and all other aluminum products might help prevent the memory loss associated with senility. In addition, a calcium-rich diet (including at least three to four servings daily of calcium-rich, low-fat milk products) helps reduce aluminum absorption, and thus might have an indirect effect on maintaining brain function. (See also "Brain Drainers," page 194.)

Of course, senile dementia, including Alzheimer's disease, is related to more than just poor choline intake. Most older persons suffering from dementia consume nutrient-poor diets in general. For example, one study from the University of Wales College of Medicine reported that dementia patients consume diets low in calories, protein, vitamin C, niacin, and folic acid. Other studies report marginally to clinically low dietary intake of zinc, vitamin A, iron, vitamin E, and the B vitamins. Any or all of these deficiencies would aggravate memory loss. Often, small to dramatic changes in mental function are noted in elderly patients when nutrient intake is improved, with diet and/or supplements.

Iron Intelligence

As discussed in chapter 4, iron deficiency is the most common nutrient deficiency in the United States. As many as 80 percent of active women have low iron levels in their tissues, which can affect energy level, mental function, job performance, and even IQ.

Studies have repeatedly shown that both children and adults who consume iron-poor diets are more likely to have or develop learning disabilities, compared to people who consume enough iron. Symptoms of poor iron intake include:

- Shortened attention span
- Lowered IQ and intelligence
- Lack of motivation
- Poor hand-eye coordination
- Lowered scores on vocabulary tests
- Inability to concentrate
- Limited educational achievement
- Suboptimal work performance

Iron-deficient infants are more likely than well-nourished infants to be unhappy, irritable, tense, fearful, and withdrawn, and to show less interest in exploring their environment. Borderline iron deficiency also can impair the immune system, which increases a person's susceptibility to colds and other diseases. The good news is that people show marked improvements or, in most cases, complete reversal of symptoms when iron intake is increased.

For example, studies of university students conducted at the USDA Human Nutrition Research Center in Grand Forks, North Dakota, showed that as blood levels of iron increased, nerve activity in the left hemisphere of the brain—the region of the brain responsible for analytic thought—also increased. Higher iron levels also were linked to greater verbal skills and overall improved mental functioning.

Why do you have trouble concentrating or solving problems when your iron is low? Although not thoroughly understood, iron functions in at least two important ways to fuel your thought processes. First, it is essential for transporting oxygen to your brain and within each brain cell. Too little iron means your brain literally suffocates. Without adequate oxygen, the cells cannot convert glucose and other calorie-containing fuels into energy quick enough to meet cellular needs, so many of the cells' functions slow down or stop. By-products of cellular activity accumulate and further irritate cell function. As a result, you are tired, cannot think clearly, and are more irritable.

Brain Drainers

While many nutrients and substances in food enhance mental function, too much of other compounds such as aluminum, as well as some lifestyle habits, could interfere with thinking, concentration, and memory. Here are a few brain drainers:

1. *Mercury.* This toxic metal has an affinity for the brain, can alter the shape and function of nerve chemicals, and can cause a variety of psychological problems from irritability to inability to concentrate. Early symptoms of mercury toxicity include nausea, fatigue, headache, and forgetfulness, while advanced symptoms include memory loss and speech disorders.

2. *Lead.* This toxic metal damages brain and nervous tissue and is associated with a wide variety of symptoms, including reduced IQ and intelligence, behavioral problems, violent behavior, reduced attention span, learning disabilities, impulsiveness, inability to reason, and limited vocabulary. The metal can be inhaled or eaten, and people today average 500 times more lead in their bodies than did people who lived in preindustrial America. Lead is taken up by red blood cells and is gradually transferred to the bones, teeth, and other tissues. It is stored in and released from bone for up to ten years. If released during pregnancy, lead can affect the development of the growing infant, resulting in mental defects and later learning disabilities. A diet rich in calcium, iron, and zinc helps reduce lead absorption.

3. *Excess vitamin A.* Reduced concentration was traced to excessive intake of supplemental vitamin A (25,000 IU of vitamin A for two years) in a fifty-four-year-old woman with no other past history of mental or emotional disorders. Symptoms disappeared when she discontinued the supplements.

4. *Nicotine.* Tobacco smoke constricts blood vessels and interferes with circulation throughout the body. Oxygen supply to the brain is restricted, which causes reduced mental function. Chronic smokers have reduced numbers of brain cells and increased free radical damage to them from this oxygen deprivation.

5. *Alcohol.* Excessive exposure to alcohol is toxic to the brain and repeated exposures can produce personality changes, memory loss, reduced concentration, and other symptoms indicative of nerve damage.

6. *Stress.* People under chronic or acute stress, including insomnia, often show signs of attention deficit, inability to concentrate, and reduced short-term memory. High blood pressure also is linked to reduced attention span and memory loss.

7. *A sedentary lifestyle.* People who put their feet up rather than into a pair of walking shoes show reduced mental function. In contrast, daily physical exercise increases mental capacity and improves memory, concentration, and thinking ability.

8. *Obesity.* Research has consistently shown that laboratory animals that consumed a diet that included enough calories to maintain a lean body plus all the vitamins and minerals to sustain optimal health lived longer, acted younger, and showed enhanced mental functioning compared to animals that overate and gained weight.

Second, iron works directly with the nerve chemicals that regulate all mental processes. For example, iron is essential for normal functioning of the nerve chemical dopamine, which is important for numerous mental processes. Iron also is needed for manufacturing many essential brain proteins.

Recommended iron intakes are based on values that are known to prevent anemia. Unfortunately, anemia is the final stage in iron deficiency. For months or years prior to this advanced deficiency state, the iron slowly drains out of the tissues when dietary intake is not adequate to replace body losses. Anemia is generally perceived as an undesirable but tolerable disorder that poses no serious threat to general well-being. However, the profound yet often vague effects that even marginal iron deficiency can have on thinking, learning, and concentration can continue indefinitely, and can have a long-lasting influence on school and job performance, self-esteem, and even the achievement of life goals. In short, the matter of iron intake should not be taken lightly.

Not everyone is at risk of iron deficiency. Adult men and postmenopausal women have relatively low iron needs compared to their calorie intakes. Although it doesn't hurt to check blood iron levels (the most sensitive measurement is called a serum ferritin test), in the majority of cases these people can follow the Feeling Good Diet and rest assured they are consuming enough iron. Everyone else should be on the alert for iron deficiency, especially infants, children, teenagers, women during their childbearing years, pregnant and breastfeeding women, and seniors. For example, men generally consume more than 2,500 calories and almost twice their iron requirements and have about 1,000 mg of stored iron in their tissues. Women, on average, consume half that many calories, less than two-thirds their iron requirements, and are lucky if they store even 300 mg. Children's iron intakes and stores are typically even lower.

The iron epidemic is preventable. The most important tactic for preventing or reversing iron deficiency is to include several servings of iron-rich foods, including spinach, extra-lean red meat, legumes, dried apricots, raisins, and lima beans, in the daily diet. Always combine a vitamin C–rich food such as orange juice with an iron-rich food to maximize iron absorption and cook using cast-iron pots. If calorie intake falls below 2,000 to 2,500 calories, consider a moderate-dose supplement that contains iron and have a blood test done to make sure your serum ferritin levels are above 20 mcg/L. On the other hand, a high serum ferritin level—200 mcg/L or higher—which is most commonly found in men, is associated with an increased risk of developing heart disease or colon cancer. So supplements are only recommended for people with diagnosed low iron status. (See chapter 4 for more information on how to increase iron intake.)

Coffee, Tea, and Memory

Most morning wake-up rituals contain two well-worn practices: a grumble at the alarm clock followed by the stumble into the kitchen for a "cup of ambition." Not only does coffee provide the day's first jolt of reality, but it also is the brew that joins friends in talk, serves as a midmorning pick-me-up, is a companion during monotonous jobs or long-distance drives, and pumps up many people's motivation and energy level.

Coffee's welcoming aroma and its promise of fending off fatigue have made it this country's number one mind-altering drug and the second most popular beverage, just behind soft drinks. Americans consume half of the world's coffee, or 450 cups per person per year. But does coffee and its cousin, tea, really help you think better?

The caffeine in coffee and a related compound called theobromine in tea have a direct effect on the brain and central nervous system. Thought functions and regulatory processes, such as heart rate, respiration, and muscle coordination, are affected after drinking even one cup of coffee or tea. For the groggy morning employee, that cup of coffee improves driving skills in rush-hour traffic, increases typing speed, elevates mood, and improves short-term memory.

However, in the case of caffeine, more is not necessarily better. Three or more cups can give you the "coffee jitters" and actually muddle your concentration and thinking. While it does temporarily sharpen your reaction time and increase your alertness, caffeine also can contribute to a midmorning slump.

In addition, coffee consumed with food can reduce absorption of mind-enhancing minerals, especially iron, by as much as 90 percent and can rob your body of other minerals such as calcium. Women and athletes at risk for iron deficiency or osteoporosis might further compromise their health if they frequently consume coffee during their meals.

From café au lait, *café con leche, caffè solo,* and espresso to a "bottomless" cup of automatic drip, coffee is a social event worldwide. One or two cups of America's favorite brew appears to be harmless (except for pregnant or breastfeeding women and for children) and might give you a mental lift. However, some people who are particularly sensitive to the effects of caffeine might be better off without it, and most people should avoid more than three cups of coffee or tea daily.

Building a Better Brain

Your thinking isn't up to par? How do you start a new diet to get your brain back on track? If you think you can pop a pill or order a "smart drink" at a local juice stand and be smarter overnight, think again. It's not that simple. But most of the nutrients you need, including the B vitamins and iron, are supplied in the proper amounts and ratios in the Feeling Good Diet (see chapter 13). If you consume less than 2,500 calories, a moderate-dose multiple vitamin and mineral supplement will provide nutritional insurance for those nutrients that you might not be getting in their optimal amounts, especially iron, folic acid, and magnesium. In addition, the antioxidants appear most beneficial in amounts greater than are typically consumed in the diet; you might consider supplementing even the Feeling Good Diet with extra amounts of vitamin C, vitamin E, and beta-carotene. (See chapter 15 for guidelines on choosing vitamin and mineral supplements; also see "Smart Foods and Snacks," page 198, for nutritionally packed foods that stimulate brain function.)

Choline is a different matter. The best dietary sources of this B vitamin–like substance are liver and egg yolks. Unfortunately, these foods also are the richest sources of cholesterol, a fatlike substance strongly linked to an increased risk of developing heart disease. Other choline-rich foods include wheat germ and brewer's (not baker's) yeast. Wheat germ can be added to cereals, pancake and waffle batter, biscuit and bread recipes, meat loaves, and other homemade foods, while brewer's yeast can be mixed with orange juice. If you decide to take lecithin or choline supplements, look for a high-quality brand that lists the exact content of choline or phosphatidylcholine (in milligrams). Other supplements touted as memory enhancers—from the herbs ginkgo biloba and ginseng to the amino acid glutamine—are still considered experimental therapies.

Reprogramming your body's aging process and revving your brain's motor take time. Ideally, the body and mind should receive optimal levels of all the essential brain-building nutrients from conception and continue throughout life. The good news is, it is never too late to start building a better body. The body is constantly losing old cells and replacing them with new ones, so optimal nutrition that starts today can have a profound influence on these rejuvenating tissues, including the heart and arteries, digestive tract, skin and hair, and other organs. Optimal nutrition helps rebuild and regenerate these tissues gradually, so that within three months to a year, you can feel and look better than ever.

Unfortunately, brain cells do not regenerate and are not repaired as readily as are other body cells. So the sooner you adopt the Feeling Good Diet, and increase your intake of the antioxidant nutrients, choline-rich foods, iron, and other brain boosters, the better off you will be.

Smart Foods and Snacks

The following foods and snacks are packed with the nutrients that stimulate brain function (for each recipe, see "Recipes for Feeling Your Best," beginning on page 367).

Quick 'n' Easy Blueberry Waffles
Oatmeal Magic

Crunchy Peanut Butter Sandwich
Black Bean and Couscous Salad

Vegetable Garlic Soup
Grilled Salmon with Green Mashed Potatoes

Nutrient Cocktails
Crunchy Vegetables and Garlic Dip
Fresh Salsa and Chips
Hot and Spicy Refried Beans
Banana Pops

CHAPTER NINE

Can't Sleep?

- Do you have trouble getting to sleep, staying asleep, or waking up too early?
- Do you toss and turn rather than sleep through the night?
- Have you tried counting sheep or watching the clock, to no avail?

If you answered yes to any of these questions, you may suffer from insomnia. If it is any consolation, you are restless bedfellows with some very famous people who spent many a sleepless night, including Napoleon Bonaparte, Winston Churchill, Charles Dickens, Cary Grant, and Marilyn Monroe. The good news is that with a few diet and lifestyle changes, most people can improve their sleep habits—some may even start sleeping like a baby. So take the quiz on page 200 to help isolate the causes of your sleep problem.

You're Not Alone

The statistics on insomnia are eye-opening. Researchers estimate that 95 percent of adults experience some form of insomnia during their lives. Approximately 70 percent state that they routinely do not get enough sleep. One out of every three adults reports difficulties in falling asleep or in staying asleep; 17 percent of adults consider the problem serious enough to seek medical attention. Between midnight and 3:00 A.M. on any given night, approximately 20 million Americans are watching television; many are watching simply because they can't sleep. Each year, more people spend more money on over-the-counter

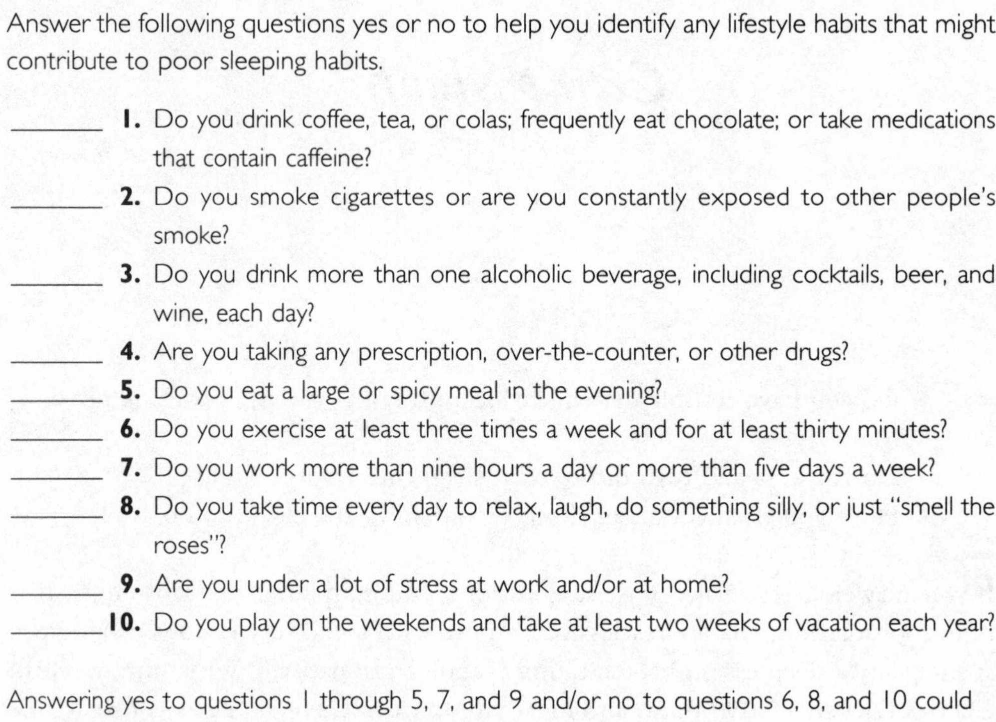

QUIZ 9.1 Sleep Busters

Answer the following questions yes or no to help you identify any lifestyle habits that might contribute to poor sleeping habits.

_______ **1.** Do you drink coffee, tea, or colas; frequently eat chocolate; or take medications that contain caffeine?

_______ **2.** Do you smoke cigarettes or are you constantly exposed to other people's smoke?

_______ **3.** Do you drink more than one alcoholic beverage, including cocktails, beer, and wine, each day?

_______ **4.** Are you taking any prescription, over-the-counter, or other drugs?

_______ **5.** Do you eat a large or spicy meal in the evening?

_______ **6.** Do you exercise at least three times a week and for at least thirty minutes?

_______ **7.** Do you work more than nine hours a day or more than five days a week?

_______ **8.** Do you take time every day to relax, laugh, do something silly, or just "smell the roses"?

_______ **9.** Are you under a lot of stress at work and/or at home?

_______ **10.** Do you play on the weekends and take at least two weeks of vacation each year?

Answering yes to questions 1 through 5, 7, and 9 and/or no to questions 6, 8, and 10 could be a contributing factor in your sleep problems.

and prescription sleep aids and pills, yet fewer people are sleeping through the night.

While insomniacs lie in bed wishing they could fall asleep, sleep-deprived individuals would gladly fall asleep if they could just get to bed. Since the late 1800s, the average night's sleep has gradually decreased in duration. Today, many people get less than seven hours of sleep each night, while our grandparents snoozed about nine hours a night. According to the National Commission on Sleep Disorders Research, millions of Americans suffer from a simple lack of sleep. Chronic grogginess, in turn, increases a person's risk for traffic and other accidents, reduces efficiency at work, and is a form of general stress. Are you sleep deprived? Take the quiz on page 201 to find out.

People who suffer from chronic insomnia are a different story. They not only have trouble sleeping at night but also are unproductive during the day. Insomniacs are more likely to be depressed, be short on tolerance, be more irritable and less attentive, and suffer temporary memory loss. Repeatedly missing a good night's sleep can affect your relationships at home and at work or can influence your job satisfaction, sanity, and general happiness. Insomniacs often give up hobbies, recreational activities, or socializing because they are too exhausted, and the quality of their lives deteriorates further.

Insomniacs are accident-prone. For example, one out of every five highway traffic accidents is the result of a driver having fallen asleep at the wheel. Insomniacs also recover more slowly from stress and are more prone to infections and illnesses than are more rested individuals. In short, insomnia is much more than a sleep disorder, since quality of life depends on quality of sleep.

QUIZ 9.2 Are You Sleep Deprived?

While occasionally not getting your full dose of restful Z's won't hurt, night after night of insufficient sleep can jeopardize your health. If you answer yes to more than three of the following questions, you might be a member of the sleep-deprived set.

_______ **1.** I fall asleep five minutes after my head hits the pillow at night.

_______ **2.** I drink caffeinated beverages, such as coffee, tea, or colas, during the day to stay alert and often have an alcoholic beverage at night to relax.

_______ **3.** Getting up in the morning is not easy. I sleep through my alarm or turn it off and go back to sleep.

_______ **4.** I am easily irritated by minor upsets or am grumpy with family members or coworkers because I am tired.

_______ **5.** I have trouble keeping my eyes open when I drive in the late afternoon or at night.

_______ **6.** I have trouble concentrating and even nod off occasionally during the late afternoon and evening.

_______ **7.** I would participate in more social activities or hobbies if I weren't so tired.

_______ **8.** I've had two or more bouts with the common cold, flu, and/or other minor health nuisances in the past six months.

One Bad Night Does Not an Insomniac Make

Insomnia is a blanket term for a variety of sleeping disorders. In general, insomnia has three groupings: (1) transient insomnia, which refers to a few sleepless nights; (2) short-term insomnia, which refers to more than two or three weeks of poor sleep; and (3) chronic insomnia, which can last months, years, or even a lifetime.

Transient or short-term insomnia often results from an event or situation, such as stress, the loss of a loved one, jet lag, or variable work shifts. Chronic insomnia is more likely to result from a medical or emotional condition, such as peptic ulcer or arthritis, that causes night pain or from the mental turmoil of depression and anxiety. For example, up to 74 percent of asthmatics and 90 percent of people suffering from depression report difficulties sleeping. Staying asleep or waking early is often a sign of depression and is also more common as people get older, while inability to fall asleep is common in people who are overstressed. Research indicates that more than half the time insomnia is caused by psychological and emotional stress. People often report that they can't sleep because they are "all wound up," have too much work to do, or have to juggle children, work, and home responsibilities, leaving little time for sleep.

What Is Your Sleep Quotient?

A common misconception is that everyone needs eight hours of sleep nightly. While this is the average required rest, it is by no means true of everyone. Some people need only four hours while others require a minimum of ten hours to feel refreshed and rested. The "short sleeper" is not overactive, just as the "long sleeper" is not lazy. Sleep needs differ just like fingerprints, shoe sizes, and personalities.

How much sleep do you need? That depends on you. If you wake up refreshed and ready for the day, then you probably are sleeping enough. If you feel tired and have trouble functioning during the day, you probably aren't getting enough sleep.

What Causes Insomnia?

We spend a third of our lives in bed, yet we have a very sketchy idea of what causes sleep disturbances. Peter Hauri, Ph.D., director of the Mayo Clinic Insomnia Research and Treatment Program, states in his book *No More Sleepless Nights* that sleep is a complex issue. There is no "sleep center" per se in the brain, but rather a series of satellite centers strung together like pearls from the lower brain stem to the higher centers in the forebrain. Dr. Hauri explains that some of these centers push arousal signals while others push sleep buttons. Both are on simultaneously, so your sleep-awake status depends on which system is dominant at any particular time.

A multitude of "sins" can tip the sleep scale in favor of insomnia. Muscle activity, stress, active thought, noise, light, and even certain dietary factors press the arousal buttons in the brain. Sometimes sleep disturbances result from sporadic sleeping habits, a disruption in normal sleeping patterns (such as being on vacation or sleeping in an unfamiliar bed), or afternoon naps. Women going through menopause and people suffering from chronic fatigue syndrome (CFS) also tend to sleep poorly. Sedentary people are more prone to insomnia than are physically active people; however, exercising or even meditating within four hours of bedtime can invigorate the body and interfere with getting to sleep. Ironically, sleeping pills disrupt normal sleep rhythms and can lead to insomnia if taken over the long term. Even snoring, grinding your teeth, or a condition called sleep apnea, where a person stops breathing for a few seconds, can interfere with a good night's sleep.

Hormones may influence sleep patterns. Some women report needing more sleep during the premenstrual phase of their cycle. A woman may sleep more during the first trimester of pregnancy and less during the last trimester. Sleep disorders increase as a person ages or experiences health problems such as seasonal affective disorder (SAD), a condition characterized by depression, fatigue, prolonged sleep, carbohydrate cravings, and overeating duing the winter months (see also chapter 5). What disturbs your sleep? See "Doze Disturbers," page 204.

Some Sleep-Stealing Foods

Your sleep problem might not be in the bedroom but at the table, since many dietary habits can interfere with getting to sleep, staying asleep, or even how

---

Doze Disturbers

You are entitled to at least 202,300 hours of sleep and 127,500 dreams in your lifetime, yet many people fall short of this quota. The delicate balance between sleep and wakefulness can be upset by a host of life events, emotional problems, or changes in your environment. Here are just a few doze disturbers:

- *Stressful life events:* Marriage, divorce, death of a loved one, birth of a child, relocation, excessive time demands, severe illness in a relative or close friend.
- *Emotional upsets:* Relationship problems, work-related problems, guilt, worries about health, problems with children, arguments, anticipation of an upcoming event such as hospitalization or medical examination.
- *Medical conditions:* Asthma, hypertension, peptic ulcer, panic disorders, anorexia nervosa, nasal congestion.
- *Dietary factors:* Caffeinated coffee, tea, or colas; chocolate; large or spicy meals in the evening; vitamin or mineral deficiencies; discomfort from indigestion or gas caused by eating habits; alcohol abuse.
- *Environmental factors:* Noise, light, extreme weather changes, a room that is too cold or too warm, sleep habits of bed partner.
- *A change in routine:* Being on vacation, sleeping in an unfamiliar bed, jet lag, a variable work shift.

---

peacefully you sleep. The link between diet and sleep is not a new discovery. Hippocrates, the father of medicine, as far back as 500 B.C. noted that some foods made people sleepy. In *Henry IV*, Shakespeare describes the sleeping Falstaff as "unbuttoning . . . after supper and sleeping upon benches after noon." Even Goldilocks, in the story "The Three Bears," takes a nap after eating porridge.

While research has uncovered some portions of the insomnia picture, there is little information about how diet affects sleep. Most of the hard, cold facts about diet and sleep come from studies on animals; basically, the more you feed a rat, the more he sleeps. In fact, increase the calories and a rat may sleep up to 60 percent more than usual. In contrast, restrict the calories and sleep patterns are disturbed. It takes only four days of starvation to reduce sleep time by as much as 60 percent, while dream time is cut by 75 percent.

The association between diet and sleep in humans is not as clear-cut. Researchers at San Jose State University in California and at Loyola University in New Orleans reported that diet has nothing to do with sleep. However, other researchers disagree. Several dietary habits—including consumption of coffee and alcohol, the size and spiciness of the evening meal, quick-weight-loss dieting, and even some food additives—could keep you tossing and turning.

I Dream of Caffeine

Coffee keeps you awake—which is usually why people drink it. A cup of coffee or tea in the morning, or even a glass of cola or a chocolate doughnut in the early afternoon, is a quick pick-me-up and probably won't affect your sleep. However, even one caffeinated cola, one cup of coffee or hot cocoa, or even one caffeine-containing medication later in the day can leave some caffeine-sensitive people wide-eyed for up to twenty hours. Even if you are not particularly sensitive, too much caffeine can cause shakiness, nervousness, irritability, and insomnia. Often, people either are unaware of how sensitive they are to caffeine or underestimate how many cups of caffeinated beverages they have consumed. They may not experience coffee jitters, but they are listening to the radio at 2:00 A.M. Coffee is a diuretic, and the increased need to urinate also can cause night awakenings.

Try eliminating caffeine from your diet if you suffer from insomnia and drink more than two cups of coffee during the day or any coffee after 1:00 P.M. If you feel and sleep better after two weeks of being caffeine-free, then avoid caffeine permanently. Some people experience withdrawal symptoms including depression, irritability, headaches, fatigue, or tearfulness within a few hours of going off caffeine. These symptoms may last up to four days, after which the energy level and mood should improve, leaving you feeling better than ever.

For some people, saying no to coffee is harder than it sounds. If you're convinced you really need a cup of coffee to keep you going, then allow yourself a cup here and there after the two-week trial, and monitor how each cup affects your mood, energy level, and sleep patterns. You are consuming too much when coffee addiction and insomnia reappear.

To cut back on caffeine:

- Drink decaffeinated or grain-based beverages as alternatives.
- Substitute carob for chocolate.
- Throw away the first cup of tea made from a tea bag, since it has the most caffeine.
- Replace caffeinated colas with sparkling water.

Children or pregnant women and caffeine don't mix. Insomnia in children often is a result of excess cola or chocolate consumption. Keep in mind that for a small body, a 12-ounce cola has the caffeine equivalent of several cups of coffee for an adult! Pregnant women should avoid all caffeinated beverages, since caffeine crosses the placenta, disturbs sleep patterns in the growing baby, and is associated with increased risk of birth defects and delayed growth.

Don't Drink and Doze

A nightcap may make you sleepy at first, but you'll sleep less soundly and wake up more tired as a result. Alcohol and other depressants suppress a phase of sleep called REM (rapid eye movement), during which most of your dreaming occurs. Less REM sleep is associated with more night awakenings and a more restless sleep.

For example, people who abuse alcohol have abnormal sleep patterns, with hundreds of mini-awakenings throughout the night. Their REM sleep is low and they spend little or no time in the deep phase called delta sleep. They may spend more time in bed, but they sleep poorly and are groggy throughout the day. Even during recovery, an alcoholic's sleep problems can linger for months or years. Babies born to women who drank alcohol during pregnancy show disturbed sleep patterns and increased irritability.

A glass of wine with dinner probably will not affect your sleep; however, it's best to avoid drinking any alcohol within two hours of bedtime. You should start sleeping better within two weeks of being alcohol-free, if alcohol has been a contributing factor in your sleep problems. It goes without saying that you should *never* mix alcohol with sleeping pills!

The Evening Meal May Be Doing You In

What and how much you ate for dinner could be at the root of your insomnia. Large, fat-laden dinners make you drowsy, but they won't help you sleep through the night. Heavy meals stimulate prolonged digestive action, which can keep you awake. Instead, try eating your biggest meals at breakfast and/or lunch and eat a light evening meal of 500 calories or less and a small low-fat snack before bedtime. Include some chicken, extra-lean meat, or fish at dinner to help curb middle-of-the-night snack attacks.

Spicy or gas-forming foods also might be contributing to your sleeping problems. Dishes seasoned with garlic, chilies, cayenne, or other hot spices can cause nagging heartburn or indigestion. Foods seasoned with MSG (monosodium glutamate), a taste enhancer often added to Chinese food, can cause sleep disturbances, vivid dreams, and restless sleep in some people; the higher the dose, the greater the likelihood of a reaction. Eating gas-forming foods or eating too fast and swallowing air also can leave you bloated and uncomfortable, which in turn interferes with sound sleep. Try avoiding spicy foods at dinnertime. Limit your intake of gas-forming foods to the morning hours and eat slowly, thoroughly chewing the food and avoiding gulping air (see "Gas Control," page 208).

The Anti-Slumber Diet

A strict diet or any other dramatic change in eating habits can leave you sleepless. In contrast to obese people who, in general, tend to sleep more than their leaner counterparts, people on diets of 1,000 calories or less a day are likely to wake up hungry in the middle of the night, sleep less soundly, and have trouble getting back to sleep. Including some protein-rich foods at dinner, such as chicken or fish, or eating a light snack just before bedtime may help curb hunger pangs. However, the best bet for long-term weight management and sound sleep is to make your dietary changes gradually and eat at least 2,000 to 2,500 calories a day of nutrient-packed, low-fat foods, as outlined in the Feeling Good Diet.

Gas Control

The following foods are possible gas-formers. Since people differ on which foods they can tolerate, try eliminating one of these foods at a time and observing the results. Avoid eating any foods that cause discomfort after noon.

Apples (raw)	Corn	Pimientos
Avocados	Cucumbers	Radishes
Beans—black, garbanzo, kidney, lima, navy	Green peppers	Rutabagas
	Honeydew melon	Sauerkraut
Broccoli	Kohlrabi	Scallions
Brussels sprouts	Leeks	Shallots
Cabbage	Lentils	Soybeans
Cantaloupe	Onions	Turnips
Cauliflower	Peas, split or black-eyed	Watermelon

Sleep problems escalate with increasing calorie and food restriction. People suffering from anorexia and bulimia—serious eating disorders where food intake is restricted either through self-imposed starvation or with purging techniques such as vomiting and excessive use of laxatives—are prone to sleep disturbances. They wake up more frequently, awake too early, and dream less than normal eaters. All of these symptoms are resolved with weight gain and resumption of normal eating habits.

Are You Allergic to Sleep?

Several other food-related habits can interfere with sleep. For example, food allergies (corn, wheat, and chocolate are some of the more common ones) can trigger reactions, and lactose intolerance can cause bloating and cramping that disturb sleep patterns. Termed food-allergy insomnia, these conditions interfere with getting to sleep and staying asleep, and are usually seen in infants who are intolerant to milk products. Usually the disorder spontaneously subsides between the ages of two and four. In adults, avoiding the offending food is the simplest and most successful method (see chapter 10).

Rare cases of medically diagnosed hypoglycemia (low blood sugar) can trigger discomfort and hunger, even in the middle of the night, and can lead to night awakenings. Hypoglycemics should not snack on cookies, ice cream, or other high-sugar foods before bedtime, since these foods only aggravate low blood sugar and sleep problems.

Night Awakenings

Some people suffer from night awakenings, whereby they wake up and cannot get back to sleep without having a snack. Although most common in small children, anyone can develop this sleep problem at any stage in life. The midnight snack attacks may be triggered by hunger or a medical condition such as an ulcer that requires food to soothe the pain, or they may be just habit. "Often these night-time eaters have eaten too few calories during the day," says Gary Zammit, Ph.D., director of the Sleep Disorders Institute at St. Luke's/Roosevelt Hospital in New York City. "Night eating is reduced by 50 percent or more in some people when they increase their daytime food intake." In some cases, your best bet is to break the cycle. Stop rewarding your stomach by feeding it every time it wakes you up. Instead, read a book, drink a glass of water, or ignore the craving. Or, according to Dr. Zammit, some people can wean themselves from midnight snack attacks by gradually eating less food, less frequently. It takes about one to two weeks to break the habit. (See "Sleep Eaters Anonymous," page 210.)

The Truth About Tryptophan

Tryptophan is nature's sleeping pill. As discussed in chapter 1, this amino acid is a building block for the neurotransmitter serotonin. The brain chemical relays messages from one nerve cell to another and aids in the regulation of emotions, behavior, pain, and sleep. In addition, tryptophan is linked to the metabolism of melatonin, a hormone associated with the regulation of mood and sleep.

Taking tryptophan supplements increases serotonin levels, reduces the time

Sleep Eaters Anonymous

Midnight snacking has taken on a new meaning. People with a rare eating disorder called sleep-related eating binge during the night without waking up and have no recollection of the episode the next morning. The eating attacks occur frequently, often nightly, and are characterized by gorging on sometimes unpalatable foods such as buttered cigarettes, raw bacon, or salted cat food. The excessive intake of calories (for example, one woman ate twice her total daytime calorie intake during these middle-of-the-night feedings) can result in weight gain and other health problems. Sleep-related eating is not a full-moon version of anorexia or bulimia, but rather it appears to be more related to sleepwalking and is amenable to treatment and medication. For more information, contact a local accredited sleep center or call the National Sleep Foundation (see the resources section at the back of this book).

necessary to fall asleep by as much as 50 percent, and enhances the quality and length of sleep in some people. Studies show that tryptophan supplements must be taken at night to be an effective sleep inducer. During the day, one of the body's enzymes counteracts the effects of serotonin on sleep; blood levels of this enzyme fall at night, however, which frees serotonin to influence sleep centers in the brain.

Tryptophan is short lasting and might have its greatest effect in inducing sleep rather than preventing night awakenings or sleepiness the next morning. The amino acid probably is ineffective in treating someone with chronic insomnia, but it might be helpful for those with transient and short-term insomnia. Tryptophan has many benefits compared to sleeping pills. Medications work by numbing the nervous system, whereas tryptophan alters the normal regulators of the sleep response. People with the greatest difficulty falling asleep are the ones who benefit most from tryptophan supplementation. The normal stages of sleep and monthly sleep cycles are not altered by this amino acid, as they often are by medications. Unfortunately, tryptophan supplements are not currently available in the United States. In the late 1980s, the Food and Drug Administration banned all tryptophan products because of a contaminated supply from Japan.

Snooze-Promoting Nutrients

The next-best thing to taking tryptophan supplements is to self-regulate your natural tryptophan level by eating a high-carbohydrate, low-protein snack one or two hours before bedtime. The amount of serotonin in the brain is dependent on the tryptophan level. As mentioned in chapter 1, a high-carbohydrate snack such as a bagel raises brain levels of tryptophan, which in turn increases brain levels of serotonin. Consequently, pain tolerance improves, insomnia is reduced, and mild depression is often alleviated.

Interestingly, in laboratory experiments both animals and people who have been deprived of sleep have shown increased preference for carbohydrate-rich foods. In one study, rats deprived of sleep for seventy-two hours ate more carbohydrates during the sleep-deprivation phase and even after recovery. The carbohydrate cravings might be an attempt to self-regulate the sleep cycle.

In contrast, a high-protein bedtime snack provides tryptophan but also includes large quantities of other amino acids that compete with tryptophan for absorption and entry into the brain. A high-protein snack—such as a piece of chicken, a glass of warm milk, or a handful of nuts—probably inhibits tryptophan absorption and causes a drop in the brain level of serotonin, which might upset sleep. (The warm milk still might help because the warm liquid soothes, relaxes, and provides a feeling of fullness.)

A high-carbohydrate snack maximizes the potential effects of tryptophan because it allows the amino acid to pass unhindered into the brain, where it stimulates the production of serotonin. "According to our preliminary studies," comments Dr. Zammit, "a light carbohydrate-rich snack [before bedtime] may not influence how fast you fall asleep, but it may help some people sleep longer and more soundly."

To maximize the tryptophan effect, the best bedtime snacks for someone suffering from sleep disturbances are high-carbohydrate, low-protein snacks such as a banana or apple, toast and jam, a baked potato seasoned with chives and nonfat sour cream, air-popped popcorn, or oven-roasted potato chips, eaten about one or two hours prior to bedtime. Keep the snack small, since large meals or volumes of liquid just before bed can disturb sleep, increase night awakenings, cause bad dreams, or increase the need to use the toilet. People who are not sugar sensitive might try a small dish of sherbet or sorbet, a small serving of a commercial fat-free dessert, or a low-fat oatmeal-raisin cookie.

An exception to this rule is narcoleptics, who suffer from excessive daytime sleepiness, sleep paralysis, and sudden sleep onset. Narcoleptics sometimes experience sleep attacks during or following meals, especially meals high in carbohydrates. They should avoid carbohydrate-rich meals and eat small, frequent meals rather than large, infrequent meals. Narcoleptics also should avoid skipping meals during the day.

B Vitamins, Minerals, and Your Snooze Control

A general disregard for nutritional needs can cause insomnia, fatigue, and other sleep disorders. Regardless of worries, tensions, and other factors, the bottom line is that well-nourished, healthy people sleep better than unhealthy people.

To be more specific, marginal intake or elevated requirements for several of the B vitamins has been linked directly to sleepless nights. In a study conducted at the National Center of Neurology and Psychiatry in Tokyo, chronic insomniacs began sleeping better within days of taking daily B12 supplements. Sleep problems returned when the vitamin B12 supplements were discontinued, suggesting that the improvements in sleeping were a direct result of the vitamin supplements.

Researchers at the National Institute of Mental Health replicated these findings when they supplemented the diet of insomniacs with vitamin B12 and found improvements in sleep. Blood levels of vitamin B12 were normal prior to and during the study, suggesting these patients rquired higher than usual vitamin B12 intakes to maintain a normal sleep pattern. However, the dosages used in these studies were very high—up to 3,000 mcg per day (the RDA is 2 mcg); any megadose vitamin therapy should always be under a physician's supervision.

Vitamin B6 also is suspect in insomnia. This B vitamin is essential for normal production of serotonin. A diet low in vitamin B6 is associated with increased risk of developing insomnia, irritability, and depression, whereas sleep patterns and mood improve when B6 intake is increased. Increased intake of other B vitamins, including folic acid and vitamin B1, also improves sleep in some people. Vitamin B1 supplementation, for example, reduced the need for daytime naps, improved sleep patterns, and increased activity in eighty healthy elderly women studied at the University of California at Davis. In some cases, vitamin B1 corrects a marginal deficiency and therefore is effective only for people who consume a vitamin-poor diet, while in other cases the vitamin appears to work in larger doses despite apparently adequate dietary intake. In all cases, you should discuss with a physician and dietitian the appropriateness of using pharmacological doses of vitamins before self-medicating. (For a list of vitamin B1–rich foods, see Table 9.1.)

Other nutrients are only indirectly linked to sleep and wake patterns. For example, calcium and magnesium work as a team to relax and contract muscles and to stimulate and subdue the nerves. Deficiencies of either mineral can cause muscle cramping and abnormal nerve function that, theoretically, might affect sleep; however, no research has been done to support or refute this connection. Sleep patterns also might be affected by low copper or iron intake. One study showed that low intake of copper (a trace mineral found in avocados, potatoes, soybeans, bananas, fish, chicken, and green vegetables) increased the risk of earlier bedtimes, longer latency to sleep, longer total sleep time, and a feeling of being less rested upon awakening. Low iron intake has also been linked to an earlier bedtime, more nighttime awakenings, and longer total sleep time. Increasing your daily intake of copper- and iron-rich foods certainly won't hurt and might help reduce your restless nights. (See "Eat to Sleep," page 215.)

Stress and Your Internal Clock

> "The lamb and the lion shall lie down together, but the lamb will not be very sleepy."
>
> —*Woody Allen*

Stress is the most common cause of insomnia. Often, by controlling the source of your stress, you can improve or completely eliminate your sleep problems. Ironically, sleep deprivation increases stress and also interferes with your ability to solve problems, thus speeding a downward spiral unless you can intercede to stop the process.

Besides practicing effective coping skills during the day, you must not allow stress into your bedroom. Set aside time during the day to deal with worries, then

TABLE 9.1 Vitamin B1–Rich Foods

Include at least three or four of the following foods in the diet each day for a total of at least 2 mg.

FOOD	AMOUNT	VITAMIN B1 CONTENT (MG)
Green peas	3/4 cup	0.33
Lima beans	3/4 cup cooked	0.28
Oysters	3/4 cup shucked	0.25
Orange juice	8-ounce glass	0.22
Collard greens	3/4 cup cooked	0.21
Dried beans	3/4 cup cooked	0.20
Dandelion greens	3/4 cup cooked	0.18
Asparagus	3/4 cup cooked	0.18
Orange	1 medium	0.13
Potato	1 medium, baked	0.12
Low-fat milk	8-ounce glass	0.10
Pasta, enriched	1/2 cup cooked	0.10
Brussels sprouts	3/4 cup cooked	0.09
Broccoli	3/4 cup cooked	0.09
Whole wheat bread	1 slice	0.06

turn to more relaxing thoughts in the evening. To help condition your body to relax, take a soothing hot bath or shower, read a nonsuspenseful book, or watch a television comedy before bedtime. Reserve bed for relaxation and sleep. Don't pay bills, argue with your spouse, or watch television in bed. Also, set a bedtime ritual that helps program your body to expect sleep. Have a high-carbohydrate snack or a glass of warm milk, then brush your teeth, close the curtains, get your clothes ready for the next day, set the alarm, and tuck yourself in. Follow the same ritual every night.

Don't program your body to toss and turn. If you are tired but can't fall asleep within thirty minutes, get up. Do something monotonous, such as reading a boring book, knitting, mending clothes, or listening to soft music. Stay up until you are sleepy again and then go to bed. Repeat this until you fall asleep. If you remain wide awake, use the time to do something fun—work on a hobby, write letters, or make something.

A major difference between good sleepers and poor sleepers is not what they do at bedtime but what they do all day. Good sleepers are more likely to be physically active. They exercise, walk to work rather than drive, park far from their destination and walk, take the stairs rather than the elevator—in short, they use every opportunity to move. The physical activity helps them cope with daily stress and tires the body so it is ready to sleep at night.

Eat to Sleep

The following twelve dietary guidelines for insomnia, when combined with effective stress-management skills, avoidance of tobacco, and sleep-enhancing habits, will help you make it through the night—asleep, that is.

1. Avoid all caffeinated beverages, foods, and medications.
2. Limit alcohol to two drinks or fewer each day and do not drink alcoholic beverages within two hours of bedtime.
3. Eat your biggest meal at breakfast or lunch and a light meal at dinner. Include some protein at the evening meal.
4. Avoid spicy foods at dinner.
5. Limit your intake of gas-forming foods to before noon.
6. Avoid MSG-containing foods, such as those served at some Chinese restaurants.
7. Eat slowly and chew your food thoroughly.
8. Avoid strict dieting or dramatic changes in dietary habits.
9. Consume a carbohydrate-rich, low-protein snack one or two hours before bedtime.
10. Drink a cup of warm milk at bedtime.
11. Make sure your dietary intake of the B vitamins, calcium, magnesium, copper, and iron is optimal. If not, take a moderate-dose supplement that contains 100 percent of the U.S. RDA for these nutrients.
12. Break the middle-of-the-night snack attack cycle by not rewarding your stomach with food.

Irregular sleep habits are a prime cause of insomnia. A person who slept poorly last night is likely to take a nap during the day or go to bed earlier the next night. However, the nap or early bedtime makes it harder to fall asleep at the normal time the following evening. So if you slept little or poorly, do not take a nap the next day (or if you must, limit the nap to less than thirty minutes). Try to go to bed at your normal time the next night, and do not take sleeping pills. Going to bed and getting up at the same time each day will help your body correct its internal clock.

Some people unconsciously set their sleep clock to a later and later hour. They can't fall asleep before midnight, but must get up at 6:00 A.M. They are tired all day, but seem to catch a second wind as the evening progresses. If you are one of these people, you can slowly reset your body's clock by going to bed fifteen minutes earlier each night, but getting up at the same time. Avoid coffee, eat a light evening meal and a carbohydrate-rich snack in the evening, and avoid overstimulating activities for the hour or two prior to bedtime. Be patient. It may take two weeks or more to adjust your body's clock.

The lark and owl syndromes can contribute to a person's sleep problems. Larks go to sleep and rise early, while owls excel when they go to bed and get up late. Differences in body rhythm may be biological or inherited, but they can't be ignored. Ask yourself whether you are a lark or an owl. Do you wake at sunrise or snooze until noon? Are you more productive in the morning or at night? Once you know your natural rhythm, you can work with it to achieve your best results with the least effort. You'll coordinate the demands of your life with your most productive times of the day and sleep when your energy level is at its lowest point.

The Sleep Journal

Many people have trouble sorting out the reasons why they can't sleep. Keeping a sleep journal for two weeks is a proven method for identifying your sleep-busters as well as your natural sleep-wake rhythms. The worksheet on page 218 is such a journal. Keeping a log will tell you when and how you sleep, your activity level, eating habits, the amount of daily stress, and other factors that might be contributing to your poor sleeping habits. The journal can be used alone or in conjunction with treatments such as biofeedback, hypnosis, and relaxation therapies. People with chronic insomnia may require the help of trained personnel at a sleep clinic. A list of accredited sleep disorders clinics in your area can be obtained from the American Sleep Disorders Association (see the resources section at the back of this book).

WORKSHEET 9.1 Your Sleep Journal

Answer the following questions each day for at least one week. Then look for patterns. On which days did you sleep the best? The worst? What happened during the day or at night that might have contributed to these sleep patterns? Also note any daily occurrences or habits that do not affect your sleep. Use this worksheet as a master to make additional copies.

Week of ____________

Daytime Habits	Mon.	Tues.	Wed.	Thurs.	Fri.	Sat.	Sun.
1. How much caffeine?							
2. How much alcohol?							
3. Any medications?							
4. How big/spicy was dinner?							
5. What was the evening snack?							
6. How would you rate your overall food intake?[1]							
7. What type and how much exercise?							
8. What was your stress level?[2]							
9. What was the source of your stress?							
10. Were you around tobacco smoke?							
11. Were you energetic or tired?							
12. What was your worry level?[3]							
13. What was funny or gave you pleasure?							
14. How happy and satisfied are you?[3]							

Week of ____________

	Mon.	Tues.	Wed.	Thurs.	Fri.	Sat.	Sun.
15. Did you take anything to help you sleep?							
16. Did you nap during the day?							
SLEEP HABITS							
17. When did you go to bed?							
18. When did you fall asleep?							
19. How often did you wake up during the night?							
20. What did you think about when you were in bed?							
21. How many minutes were you awake last night?							
22. What did you do when you woke up?							
23. When did you get up for the day?							
24. Compared to your typical sleep, how would you rate last night's sleep?[1]							
25. How refreshed and alert were you when you got up this morning?[1]							

For each of the indicated items, use the following scales, ranging from:

[1] 5 (excellent) to 1 (poor)

[2] 5 (low) to 1 (high)

[3] 5 (very happy and satisfied) to 1 (very unhappy and dissatisfied)

CHAPTER TEN

Not Feeling Up to Par? It Might Be What You're Eating

- A child develops sores in her mouth after eating fresh strawberries.
- A coworker says pineapple "doesn't agree with him."
- A neighbor states that she is allergic to milk, while someone else is irritable after eating mushrooms.
- A friend was rushed to the hospital with anaphylactic shock after eating chili that contained peanut oil.

There is no solid information on how many people experience adverse food reactions. Estimates range from as little as 0.2 percent of the population up to 50 percent. One source has reported that 20 percent of the population experiences food reactions at some time in their lives; yet only 1 to 2 percent have reactions that persist for long periods of time. The only widely accepted statistic is that food reactions are most common in infancy, are less common in childhood, and are even less likely to occur or persist into adulthood. Considering that there are thousands of substances in food, it is amazing that more people don't develop allergies, intolerances, and reactions to what they eat.

A primary reason why food reactions are so elusive is that they are so hard to replicate in scientific studies. Nine times out of ten, a person who reports an adverse reaction to a particular food does not show any symptoms after consuming the food in controlled situations—that is, in a double-blind situation where neither the scientist nor the person knows who consumes the suspect food and who consumes a placebo. Consequently, while many people say they are allergic or intolerant to a particular food, in reality very few people have a clinical food allergy.

Another stumbling block to identifying a food reaction is that no one agrees on the symptoms. Granted, clear-cut food allergies that trigger an immune response usually produce skin rashes and hives, digestive-tract problems, and respiratory disorders such as breathing difficulties. However, vague symptoms such as behavioral disorders, fatigue, anxiety, and headaches also have been attributed to food allergies—albeit with some controversy. The allergic tension fatigue syndrome (ATFS)—characterized by fatigue, lethargy, muscle and joint aches, and behavioral learning disabilities—is suspected to be caused by some food allergies.

Limited evidence suggests that food intolerances can affect mood. For example, people are more likely to experience fatigue when they consume a capsule of chocolate than when they take a placebo. Mental and emotional symptoms are more likely to develop in sensitive people when they consume a placebo. (The suspicion that a food craving is a symptom of a food allergy has not been supported by research.)

True Food Allergies

Not all food allergies are alike. In fact, most of the adverse reactions people experience from food are not allergies at all. More often than not, the food reaction is caused by an intolerance to a particular food, not an allergy.

A true food allergy is any negative reaction to a food or food component that involves an immune response. The reaction can be immediate or delayed. Immediate hypersensitivity-like allergies generate an immune-related response within minutes to several hours of eating the offending food; these are diagnosed in less than 1 percent of the population. The offending food is easy to identify, because the symptoms develop right after the meal or snack. In contrast, in delayed food allergies, symptoms do not appear for six to twenty-four hours after the offending food is ingested. By the time the person feels unwell, he or she has forgotten what might have been eaten. Consequently, this form of food allergy is much harder to recognize and the offending foods are more difficult to isolate.

In either immediate or delayed food allergies, the person is most likely to develop skin, respiratory, or digestive-tract problems, including hives, rashes, breathing difficulties, sores in the mouth, bloating, and diarrhea. The symptoms can range from mild to life-threatening, depending on a person's tolerance and the dose ingested. For example, some people can tolerate a tablespoon of peanut butter without showing symptoms, yet develop a mild rash after eating 2 tablespoons or more. Other people may die if they eat even half a peanut.

Usually the reaction is triggered by a protein in the food called an antigen. Foods contain many different proteins, yet only a few are associated with allergies. For example, cow's milk contains more than twenty proteins, but only four or five are likely to trigger a response. In addition, the digestive tract blocks absorption of approximately 98 percent of the allergy-inducing proteins, so the body confronts only the 2 percent that actually enters the bloodstream. The body must first become sensitized to the antigen, so the person does not experience problems the first time the particular food is consumed. It is the next time the food is eaten that the troubles begin. Even then, a person's response is somewhat influenced by heredity (if your parents were allergic to the food, you are at higher risk), how well your immune system is functioning (disorders of the immune system can aggravate an allergy), or stress.

Any food item can cause an allergic reaction. However, a few food categories are most commonly associated with the allergic response, including:

chocolate	fish	shellfish
corn	nuts	soybeans
cow's milk	oranges	strawberries
crustaceans	peanuts	tomatoes
eggs	peas	wheat

Sometimes a person is allergic to a raw food but can tolerate the same food cooked. For example, heated milk is less likely to cause a reaction than unheated milk. In addition, a situation called *cross reactivity* is common with allergies. That is, if you are allergic to one food, you are likely to be allergic to other foods in the same food family. So a person allergic to soybeans may also be allergic to peanuts, while a person allergic to walnuts may also be allergic to pecans. See "Food Families and Allergies," page 223, for a list of related foods.

How Do I Know If I Am Allergic?

The diagnosis of food allergies requires an array of medical procedures, including a patient history, physical examination, special immune-function tests, a trial "elim-

Food Families and Allergies

If you are intolerant or allergic to a food, you also may react to other foods in the same food family.

Plant Families

Apple: apple, crab apple, loquat, pear, quince
Citrus: quince, grapefruit, lemon, orange, tangerine
Cola nut: coffee, chocolate, cola drinks, tea
Goose foot: beet, spinach, Swiss chard
Gourd: cantaloupe, cucumber, melon, pumpkin, winter squash
Grass: barley, corn, oats, rice, rye, wheat
Heath: blueberry, cranberry, huckleberry, loganberry
Laurel: avocado, bay leaf, cinnamon
Lily: asparagus, garlic, leek, onion, sarsaparilla
Mint: basil, bergamot, marjoram, peppermint, oregano, sage, savory, thyme
Cruciferous: broccoli, cabbage, cauliflower, mustard, Brussels sprout, turnip
Pea: bean, soybean, lentil, pea, peanut, alfalfa, tamarind
Plum: almond, apricot, blackberry, cherry, peach, plum
Rose: blackberry, raspberry, strawberry
Sunflower: artichoke, chamomile, chicory, endive, lettuce, sunflower
Walnut: walnut, hickory nut, pecan

Animal Families

Birds: chicken, egg, duck, goose, pheasant, turkey
Crustaceans: crab, crayfish, lobster, prawn, shrimp
Fish: catfish, cod, flounder, halibut, mackerel, salmon, sardine, snapper, sole, trout, tuna
Mammals: cow (milk), goat, lamb, pork, rabbit, sheep
Mollusks: abalone, clam, cockle, oyster, scallop, mussel

ination" diet, and a "food challenge" in which suspected foods are systematically added to the person's diet with physician monitoring of symptoms. Never does the result of one test determine a conclusive diagnosis of a food allergy. (To judge your food allergy, see "Food Allergy Assessment," below. Also, allergy tests are discussed further in "Food Allergy Tests: Which Ones Are Best?" page 225.)

Food Allergy Assessment

Just because a food "doesn't agree with you" does not mean you have a true food allergy. The following tests and procedures are necessary to identify whether a person really has a food allergy and to what foods:

- *History.* A detailed description of symptoms, the time from ingestion of a suspected food to the onset of symptoms, the most recent reaction, the amount of the food needed to produce a reaction, and a family history of food allergies or intolerances.
- *Physical examination.* A complete physical assessment that includes height, weight, growth and development, nutritional status, existence of disease, and allergic conditions such as eczema and asthma.
- *Food and Symptoms Journal* (see page 227). A two-week diary of everything eaten and drunk, including when, where, how much, time of symptoms, and any medications taken.
- *Immune-function tests.* These include a skin test, RAST, or other assessments, and provide information on suspected foods. Results of these tests must be confirmed by an elimination diet.
- *Elimination diet.* A nutritionally adequate diet designed and monitored by a dietitian or physician that eliminates all suspected foods identified from the journal and immune-function tests and is followed for two to four weeks. All consumed items are recorded to determine if the trouble-prone food or a food family member is consumed unknowingly in other foods.
- *Food challenge.* After removing all suspected foods from the diet and experiencing a symptom-free period of two to four weeks, suspected foods are reintroduced one at a time in small doses—1/2 to 1 teaspoon. The amount is increased slowly until the typically consumed dose is obtained or until a reaction occurs. Positive reactions are repeated to eliminate the possibility of a chance occurrence.

You may want to do some sleuthing on your own to identify the foods you can and can't tolerate. For example, a home version of the elimination diet (see "Food Allergy Assessment," page 224) begins by eliminating the most common causes of food allergies, including cow's milk, chicken, eggs, and wheat. During this

---

Food Allergy Tests: Which Ones Are Best?

Food allergy testing is fertile ground for consumer fraud. Here's a brief list of some tests that work, and some that don't:

- *Skin test* (scratch, prick, or puncture). A small scratch or prick is made in the skin and a drop of the offending food substance (antigen) is applied. A red wheel indicates allergy. Although a sensitive test, the skin test can overdiagnose food allergies and always should be followed by a food challenge test.
- *RAST* (radioallergosorbent extract test) and *ELISA* (enzyme-linked immunosorbent assay). A sample of the person's blood is mixed with food on a paper disc and is then exposed to an immune-function test. These tests are as accurate as but more costly than the skin test.
- *Cytotoxic test.* A suspected allergy-producing substance is mixed with a sample of the person's blood and the number of broken white blood cells is counted. This test is unreliable and useless in diagnosing food allergy.
- *Provocative and neutralization tests.* Extracts of suspected offending substances are injected under the skin and any symptoms that develop are neutralized by a weaker or stronger injection. These tests are unreliable and useless in diagnosing food allergy.
- *Sublingual test.* Drops of an extract containing the suspected food component are placed under the person's tongue and symptoms are recorded. This test is unreliable and useless in diagnosing food allergy.
- *Pulse test.* The pulse rate is measured at specific intervals after eating a suspected food. This test is unreliable and useless in diagnosing food allergy.
- *Intestinal biopsy.* A test for inflammatory changes in the digestive tract lining that signal gluten enteropathy or celiac disease (inability to digest wheat or its protein gluten). This test is reliable but invasive and expensive.
- *T-cell evaluation.* Blood levels of special white blood cells are assessed and analyzed. This test is experimental and costly.

---

first phase, you can eat lamb, turkey, beef, pork, legumes, potatoes, rice and other nonwheat grains, all vegetables and fruits, and oils. If your symptoms improve on this diet, you may be sensitive to one of the foods eliminated. To identify which food or foods are the offending ones, start adding back one food at a time every two to three days, and watch for symptoms to reappear. If no symptoms occur after eating a food for at least three days, then cross that food off your "trouble-prone" list. (It helps to keep a journal during this process, such as the one presented in Worksheet 10.1 on page 227.)

In the second phase of the elimination diet, you can eat lamb, potatoes, rice, most vegetables and fruits, and safflower oil, but you should eliminate all other animal protein, including milk, eggs, meat, fish, and poultry; wheat, oats, corn, millet, tomatoes, and corn syrup; butter, margarine, and other oils; chocolate, coffee, and tea; and cornstarch and baking powder with cornstarch. Follow the same procedure here as you did in phase one. If symptoms persist, additional foods can be eliminated one by one.

To complicate matters even more, you may not be allergic to food per se, but to molds that grow on some foods. Mold allergies often produce subtle symptoms, such as headaches, fatigue, or nasal congestion. It is best to consult a physician to confirm a mold allergy. In addition, become aware of the foods that are most prone to mold growth and food storage methods that hinder the growth of food-borne molds. For example, the following foods are possible mold accumulators:

- beer
- buttermilk
- canned tomatoes and tomato products such as paste and catsup
- cheese
- dried fruits
- mushrooms
- sourdough, pumpernickel, and rye breads
- vinegar-containing foods such as mayonnaise and relishes
- wine
- yogurt

To reduce your exposure to molds, eat only freshly opened canned items and meats and fish cooked within the past two days; use only freshly ground extra-lean beef in cooking; and avoid making dishes from leftovers. Always refrigerate foods at 40 degrees F or colder and never allow raw or cooked foods to sit out for more than 30 minutes.

The results of an elimination diet and of a food challenge (see "Food Allergy

WORKSHEET 10.1 Food and Symptoms Journal

Record everything you eat and drink, how much, and when. Then record what type of symptoms you had and when you experienced them in the designated boxes. Use this sheet as a master to make copies.

	Day ____	Day ____	Day ____	Day ____	Day ____	Day ____	Day ____
BREAKFAST							
Symptoms							
SNACK							
Symptoms							
LUNCH							
Symptoms							
SNACK							
Symptoms							
DINNER							
Symptoms							
SNACK							
Symptoms							
Medications							

Assessment," page 224), as well as information obtained from keeping a food and symptoms journal, provide a clear idea of what foods you can eat and what ones you should avoid. Any food that may contain the offending item should be eliminated from your diet, so you must become an avid label reader. For example, the person who cannot tolerate corn must be careful to avoid any product that contains a corn-based ingredient, including corn oil, corn sweetener, baking powder (it contains cornstarch), and the corn-based starches and gums used in many processed foods.

A person who cannot tolerate wheat must avoid all commercial products that contain wheat, including:

- Cakes, cookies, and pies made with wheat flour
- Malted milk, Ovaltine, some commercial chocolate drinks, and nondairy creamers
- Prepared meats that contain wheat grains
- Regular noodles or packaged rice mixes
- Creamed vegetables, some canned baked beans, and commercially prepared vegetables
- All breads and cereals that contain wheat flour
- Wheat flour, wheat crackers, and wheat-based snack foods
- Most canned soups
- Any alcohol distilled from grain

Dealing with allergies to basic foods such as wheat, corn, or milk requires trained help from a dietitian to ensure that the diet remains nutritionally adequate. (For additional diet adjustments, see "The Allergy-Free Feeling Good Diet," page 229.)

As with any disorder, the best treatment for food allergies is prevention. Granted, many food allergies are inherited; however, some allergies may develop as a result of feeding infants formula rather than breast milk. Numerous studies have concluded that infants who are breastfed have a reduced risk of developing food allergies. Breastfeeding may increase an infant's tolerance to certain offending food ingredients, or it simply may reduce the exposure to offending items until the infant's digestive tract is more developed and able to handle these foods. In addition, breast milk contains immune factors that provide a passive resistance to food allergies.

The Allergy-Free Feeling Good Diet

Regardless of your food allergy, all of the guidelines for the Feeling Good Diet apply except for the following:

1. *Milk allergy.* Use fruit juice in dessert recipes, such as cakes, cookies, or puddings. Use soy or cashew milk in place of cow's milk. Include more servings of dark green leafy vegetables such as broccoli, spinach, chard, and kale to ensure adequate intake of calcium and vitamin B2. Take a vitamin D supplement if skin exposure to sunlight is limited.
2. *Corn allergy.* Use arrowroot or potato starch or double the amount of whole wheat, soy, or barley flour instead of using cornstarch in recipes.
3. *Egg allergy.* In baking, instead of one large egg, combine 2 tablespoons whole wheat flour, 1/2 teaspoon oil, 1/2 teaspoon baking powder, and 2 tablespoons milk, water, or fruit juice. Or use egg substitutes.
4. *Wheat allergy.* Substitute potatoes, sweet potatoes, yams, hominy, wild rice, special gluten-free noodles, specially prepared breads using nonwheat flours, cereals made from cornmeal or rice, oriental rice noodles, and bean noodles. Thicken dishes with cornstarch or tapioca. Select rice wafers, corn tortillas, popcorn, and rice or non-wheat-based crackers and chips. (A person allergic to wheat may also be allergic to oats, rye, and barley.)

Food Intolerances

More likely than not, a person's reaction to a food is caused by an intolerance, not an allergy. These reactions are brought about through a biological idiosyncrasy, a digestive-tract disorder, an enzyme deficiency, or even a psychological factor. The symptoms may mimic an allergic response—such as a rash or abdominal discomfort—but they also may include headaches, mood swings, fatigue, or even sleep problems. Almost any food or food ingredient can produce a reaction, including chocolate, wine, sardines, legumes, coffee, pork, peas, nuts, lemon candy, canned tuna, and food additives. However, the most well known intolerance is to milk products.

Milk has graced dining tables for more than 10,000 years, yet it continues to generate controversy. The dilemma is particularly pronounced for women and children, who have high requirements for the vitamins and minerals in milk but who may be concerned that they can't handle dairy products. Some women worry that milk will upset their stomach, slow them down, and interfere with their health. Others may steer clear of dairy products because of suspected allergies to milk and concerns that it may contribute to mood swings. Still others believe that if they can't tolerate milk, they probably also can't absorb its nutrients, like calcium.

Most of these concerns are unfounded. However, while a milk allergy is very rare (the 1 to 2 percent of children who are allergic to milk usually outgrow the problem by the time they are two years old), lactose intolerance is relatively common. Most people have heard of lactose intolerance, yet few understand what it is and many are misinformed about how it should be diagnosed and treated.

The Facts on Lactose Intolerance

The digestion of lactose, the main source of carbohydrates in milk, depends on an intestinal enzyme called lactase, which breaks down lactose into its sugar units—glucose and galactose. Once broken down, these simple sugars are absorbed into the bloodstream and are used for energy.

Most babies are born with an ample supply of lactase, so they easily digest lactose. However, lactase levels gradually decline after several months or years following weaning. Primary lactose intolerance develops when the lactase dwindles below levels necessary to handle the lactose consumed in the diet. Insufficient lactase means the undigested lactose travels to the large intestine and is partially broken down by bacteria to produce acids and gases such as hydrogen and carbon dioxide. Lactose also draws water from the surrounding tissues into the large intestine to dilute the concentrated sugar. This results in varying degrees of abdominal bloating, diarrhea, cramps, and gas within thirty minutes to a few hours of consuming a lactose-rich food. Less frequently, a person also develops bad breath, headaches, and/or fatigue. However, the lactose problem has no effect on the absorption of other milk nutrients, from calcium to vitamin D.

Any infectious or inflammatory disease that damages the lining of the digestive tract can produce a secondary lactose intolerance, which is temporary and subsides soon after the primary disease is successfully treated and the digestive tract has healed. However, in some serious digestive tract disorders the lactose intolerance persists. A third category—congenital lactose intolerance—is caused by an extremely rare metabolic defect present since birth.

Your ancestry might help determine your risk for lactose intolerance. Only an estimated 15 percent of people of Scandinavian and Western or Northern European descent develop lactose intolerance, while frequency is as high as 70 to 90 percent among African Americans, Asians, Jews, Native Americans, and Arabs. Are you lactose intolerant? Take the quiz below.

The prevalence of lactose intolerance has been greatly exaggerated, primarily because of studies in the 1960s that showed many people developed severe symptoms when they consumed 50 to 100 grams of lactose (the equivalent of one to two quarts of milk) on an empty stomach. The assumption was that if lactose could do this to you, so would milk.

QUIZ 10.1 Are You Lactose Intolerant?

Answer yes or no to the following questions.

_______ **1.** Do you frequently experience gas; digestive tract discomfort, bloating, and cramps; or diarrhea?

_______ **2.** Do uncomfortable symptoms develop within thirty minutes to two hours after consuming milk products, such as milk, cheese, or ice cream?

_______ **3.** Do these symptoms lessen or disappear when you avoid milk products for a week or more?

_______ **4.** Does anyone else in your family (grandparents, father or mother, brothers or sisters, or aunts or uncles) develop any of the above symptoms after eating milk products?

_______ **5.** Are you Asian, Jewish, American Indian, Hispanic, Arab, or African American?

_______ **6.** Did you first notice these symptoms during or immediately after a digestive tract disorder, such as the stomach flu or gastroenteritis?

Scoring:

There is no exact number of yes or no answers to the above self-assessment that will guarantee a diagnosis of lactose intolerance. However, the more yes answers, the more likely you are to be lactose intolerant. A yes answer to question 1 alone is no guarantee of lactose intolerance, since these are symptoms of many other disorders. A yes answer to question 6 suggests you may have developed a lactose intolerance secondary to some other digestive tract problem. If this is the case, the intolerance should gradually subside if you refrain from milk products while treating the underlying infection.

In the mid-1970s, this assumption was proved wrong. Research at Cornell University showed that most lactose-intolerant adults could consume at least 15 grams of lactose—the amount found in 1 1/4 cups of milk—on an empty stomach without developing symptoms. A study at Massachusetts Institute of Technology involving thirty white and sixty-nine black children found that more than half of the black children over the age of six were lactose intolerant, but all of them could drink a glass of milk with no problems. In short, they were lactose intolerant without being milk intolerant.

Today it is clear that lactose intolerance is not an all-or-nothing affair, and for most people it has little to do with milk tolerance. Some people can digest large quantities of both milk and lactose, other people can digest less, and a few can digest none at all. In addition, a lactose-intolerant person may develop a greater tolerance over time by consuming milk products in small doses throughout the day.

In all but the most severe cases, a person can consume small quantities of milk products. The smaller the serving size, the less likely a person will experience symptoms. Fat slows the transit of food through the digestive tract, thus making it easier for the bacteria to handle the lactose load. Therefore, whole or chocolate milk might be better tolerated than skim or unflavored milk. (For an idea of the lactose content of common foods, see Table 10.1.)

Fermented dairy products, including cheese and yogurt, are another solution for lactose intolerance. Half of the lactose is removed when milk is processed into cheese; aged hard cheeses such as Swiss and cheddar have the lowest lactose content. Bacteria called *Lactobacillus bulgarius*, and possibly another bacteria called *Lactobacillus acidophilus*, found in some commercial yogurts, digest lactose when milk is fermented to yogurt and stored. They continue to digest more lactose in the small intestine after a person eats the yogurt. Consequently, many people can handle yogurt even if they can't drink milk.

Unfortunately, not all fermented dairy products are created equal. Freezing destroys the digestive enzyme in these beneficial bacteria, so frozen yogurt—even when it contains "active cultures"—is not a good bet. Buttermilk is milk that is fermented with bacteria called *Streptococcus lactis*, which is not as efficient as *L. bulgarius* in digesting lactose.

For people with more severe cases of lactose intolerance, Lactaid, a milk product that has been treated with lactase and contains 70 percent less lactose than regular milk, can be consumed or used in recipes. Lactase drops can be added to milk twenty-four hours before consumption, and lactase caplets can be taken with a meal to essentially do for your body what it can't do for itself. These products can be purchased at most pharmacies or supermarkets.

Keep in mind that many foods—from broccoli and beans to watermelon—also cause gas and bloating. However, if you suspect you are lactose intolerant, avoid all dairy products for two weeks. (Watch for hidden sources of lactose, such as cream sauces and soups, breads, diet shakes, powdered eggs, puddings, hot dogs, and salad dressings.) If your symptoms vanish after the two-week test, experiment with milk products one at a time to see what you can tolerate. Start with small amounts of yogurt (1/4 cup) or cheese (1/2 ounce) with a meal. Space the trials, since symptoms may take from two hours to two days to develop. Keep a daily journal of what and how much you ate, when you ate it, and how you felt in the next few hours. From these trials, you can develop a personal repertoire of tolerated foods. You may find, for example, that you need to avoid dairy products for the two to

TABLE 10.1 How Much Lactose Is in That Food?

FOOD	AMOUNT	LACTOSE CONTENT (G)
Milk, protein-fortified	1 cup	13.6
Milk, skim or whole	1 cup	12.0
Buttermilk	1 cup	12.0
Milk, sweetened condensed	1/4 cup	11.0
Yogurt	1 cup	11.0
Ice milk	3/4 cup	8.0
Velveeta cheese	1 1/2 ounces	4.0
Lactaid, 1 percent milk	1 cup	3.0
Ice cream, 14.5 percent fat	1/2 cup	2.7
Feta cheese	1.5 ounces	2.2
Swiss cheese	1.5 ounces	1.5
Orange sherbet	3/4 cup	1–2
Half-and-half or sour cream	2 tablespoons	1.0
Cheddar cheese	1.5 ounces	0.5
Ricotta cheese, part-skim	1/2 cup	0–6
Cottage cheese	1/2 cup	0–4

three hours prior to a workout, but have no problems eating them at other times of the day.

Milk supplies up to 75 percent of an adult's calcium, 40 percent of most people's vitamin B2 needs, and almost all of their dietary vitamin D. If you are one of the few supersensitive lactose intolerants who cannot handle milk in any shape or form, you must take extra care to ensure optimal intake of these nutrients, plus magnesium and vitamin B12, either by increasing your intake of foods rich in these nutrients or by taking a supplement (see Table 10.2 below and "Where Will You Get Vitamin B2?" page 235).

Even if you suffer from all the symptoms linked to lactose intolerance, beware of the dangers of diagnosing yourself. Similar symptoms are signs of other, more serious conditions and should be assessed by a physician.

TABLE 10.2 Primary Sources of Calcium

Milk supplies up to 75 percent of an adult's calcium needs. Calcium is essential for maintaining optimal health and preventing osteoporosis and hypertension. Therefore, it requires careful planning to get enough if this food group is eliminated from the diet. The following foods are comparable in calcium content to a glass of milk. Most adults need 800 to 1,200 mg of calcium daily.

FOOD	AMOUNT	CALCIUM CONTENT (MG)
Soymilk*	30 cups	300
Nonfat milk	1 cup	296
Broccoli	3 cups cooked	294
Mustard greens	1 1/2 cups cooked	291
Collard greens	1 cup cooked	290
Oysters	1 1/2 cups raw	283
Canned salmon with bones	5 ounces	278
Orange	5 medium	270
Dried beans	3 cups cooked	270
Spinach	1 1/4 cups cooked	265
Dandelion greens	1 cup cooked	252

*Soymilk contains only 10 mg of calcium per cup, unless it is calcium-fortified.

Where Will You Get Vitamin B2?

Milk supplies approximately 40 percent of an adult's daily need for vitamin B2. If you don't drink milk, here are other sources of the vitamin B2 equivalent of a glass of milk—0.52 mg.

FOOD	AMOUNT
Asparagus, cooked	2 cups
Avocado	1 medium
Broccoli, cooked	2 cups
Chicken, meat only	9 ounces
Collard greens, cooked	1 1/4 cups
Dandelion greens, cooked	1 1/2 cups
Raw oysters	1 1/4 cups

Food Additives, Allergies, and Hyperactivity

In the past hundred years, more new compounds have been added to our food supply than had been introduced in all prior years combined. The human body has taken thousands, if not millions, of years to adapt to environmental changes, so it is no wonder that our modern human body cannot keep pace with the mass of new chemicals reaching it daily. Consequently, many people are suspicious of these man-made chemicals and are quick to blame food additives for everything from allergic reactions to personality changes. Are food additives at the root of food allergies, food intolerances, and personality disorders?

Yes and no. Most additives appear to be as safe as any naturally occurring chemicals in our foods, at least based on science's limited understanding of how these additives might affect health in the short and long term. However, some additives—such as monosodium glutamate (MSG)—produce mild discomfort in some people, while other additives, such as the sulfites used as a preservative in some wines, shrimp, and processed potatoes, have been deadly to a few highly sensitive people.

MSG: More Than Just a Flavor Enhancer

The food additive MSG produces symptoms that range from vague to severe. A person may experience numbness in the back of the neck, in the arms, or in the hands. Other reactions include mild to severe headaches, pressure around the cheeks or jaw, or even depression. The individual may feel weak, have heart palpitations, or have unusually vivid and bizarre dreams that night. Regardless of the symptoms and their severity, they always develop within minutes of eating food prepared with MSG and persist for several hours. Since MSG is used extensively in Chinese cooking, the disorder was labeled Chinese restaurant syndrome, or CRS.

MSG is a form of glutamic acid, one of the amino acids that help build proteins. This amino acid is found naturally in foods such as mushrooms and tomatoes, but it is bound to other compounds so it has no flavor-enhancing or health-harming effects. More than 80 million pounds of the purified additive are added to processed foods such as packaged soups, bouillon cubes, and TV dinners sold in the United States.

Some people can't handle MSG in this form and at this quantity. Studies in the 1970s showed that MSG caused brain and eye damage in newborn rats and mice, which stirred such a public outcry that the baby food industry stopped using MSG in its products. Throughout the 1980s and 1990s, studies have continued to find that MSG added to the diets of baby animals in the laboratory caused temporary and permanent damage to the brain that resulted in numerous mental defects such as reduced problem solving; it may be linked to cataract formation in the eyes; and it destroyed portions of the brain responsible for stimulation of certain immune functions.

John Olney, a psychiatrist and neuropathologist at Washington University School of Medicine in St. Louis, recommends that even pregnant and nursing mothers avoid the additive, just to be on the safe side. Researchers at the University Medical School in Szeged, Hungary, support this recommendation, having found that MSG crosses the placenta and might pose a risk for toxicity in human fetuses.

Some researchers suspect that MSG can influence mood and emotions in addition to the muscle and nerve symptoms just mentioned. For example, increased irritability, depression, and other mood changes have been noted when patients are fed MSG-laden foods as compared to patients who take a placebo. The dose needed to produce these symptoms may be as low as 5 grams, the amount in two bowls of wonton soup.

The widespread use of MSG and its subtle symptoms may explain the under-reporting of this food reaction. For example, researchers at the Royal North Shore Hospital in Sydney, Australia, removed all the MSG, preservatives, nitrites, and salicylates (an aspirinlike additive) from the diets of people who suffered from recurrent headaches. Within days, headache severity and frequency were reduced by half in 85 percent of the people. The headaches returned in 80 percent of the subjects when MSG and other additives were returned to their diet. Headache frequency and severity remained low as long as the subjects consumed the MSG- and additive-free diets. However, other studies have concluded that people who say they experience flushing and other adverse side effects whenever they eat MSG-laden foods show no symptoms under controlled conditions.

If you suspect you might react to MSG, check with an allergist or test yourself by eliminating all MSG-containing foods (MSG may be listed on a food label as monosodium glutamate, hydrolyzed vegetable protein [HVP], or flavoring) for at least two weeks. If symptoms disappear, then slowly put one food at a time back on your diet and monitor your mood, physical health, and emotions. Adverse reactions usually develop within minutes to an hour of ingesting MSG, which helps in the diagnosis.

The Hyperactivity Argument

In the early 1970s, Dr. Ben Feingold, from Kaiser Permanente Center in San Francisco, presented a report stating that hyperactivity in children was related to the amount of salicylates and food additives, especially colorings and flavorings, in their diet.

His information, obtained primarily from testimonials and case studies, led him to believe that an additive-free diet would cure or reduce the symptoms of hyperactivity in between 40 and 70 percent of children. Unfortunately, few studies were able to support Dr. Feingold's theory. For example, in one study the researchers selected groups of hyperactive children and placed them on two different diets. One diet followed Dr. Feingold's recommendations, while the other diet was disguised to look like Dr. Feingold's but actually contained salicylates and artificial colors and flavors. Results showed that children improved or their behaviors worsened on both the Feingold and the placebo diets.

In most studies that have attempted to prove the Feingold hypothesis, either the scientists, the families, or the children knew when their diets were changed. Consequently, they expected improvements. In other cases, the children received more attention because of the change in diet, and the increased attention—not the absence of food additives—was suspected of producing the improvements in behavior. In some cases, the children's inability to concentrate worsened as a result of following the additive-free Feingold diet. There is no proof that following a restrictive diet devoid of food additives will improve hyperactive behavior in children. Finally, megavitamin therapy—that is, using large doses of specific vitamins including niacin, vitamin C, or vitamin B6—for the treatment of hyperactivity has not proved successful.

"That Food Doesn't Agree with Me"

Since the dawn of civilization, food has been used to modify behavior. Certain foods have been assigned magical or mystical powers to heal, improve sexuality, cause illness, or bestow spiritual gifts. Every culture has its revered foods and its food taboos. For example, foods believed to be aphrodisiacs include garlic, dried frog, oysters, rhinoceros horn, grapes, and preserved dates. On the other hand, Hindus would rather starve than eat beef, Jains (members of one of India's oldest religions) do not eat seeded foods such as tomatoes or figs, and most Americans would not eat a cockroach if their life depended on it. Those customs are so well ingrained that even the mere mention of eating certain foods considered nonedible can generate nausea, vomiting, skin rashes, and other symptoms.

It is likely that individuals also develop personal food taboos based on their beliefs and experiences. In some cases, physical discomfort is linked to eating a particular food, even though the association is pure chance. In other cases, a physical or emotional reaction to a food cannot be explained by medicine's limited understanding of individual reactions. In either case, these unexplained food reactions are called pseudo food allergies.

In response to eating a particular food, people might report a wide array of emotional symptoms such as mood swings, irritability, irrational thinking, or depression; behavioral symptoms such as hyperactivity or nervousness; or physical symptoms such as headaches, digestive tract upsets, or itching skin. Once convinced that they have an "allergy," they avoid the food. In severe cases, a cycle develops whereby increasingly more foods are eliminated until the person jeopardizes his or her nutritional needs. Yet in most cases, no symptoms develop when the person undergoes a double-blind test in which he or she is unknowingly given either a placebo or the suspected troublesome food.

In a study conducted at the University of Toronto, people suspected to have adverse food reactions were tested. Those with confirmed food allergies were more likely to be men and to be younger—that is, less than forty-four years old. They also were more likely to be allergic to the foods most commonly recognized as potential food allergens, such as chocolate, milk, and shellfish, and they were more likely to experience symptoms from only a few foods. On the other hand, the people whose food allergies were not confirmed by tests were more likely to be older women with multiple food aversions to a wide array of foods not typically considered allergenic, such as bananas, cola, corn, and fried foods. Their symptoms also were less clearly defined and included dizziness, loss of concentration, difficulty in sleeping, depression, and weakness.

Pseudo food allergies are an unknown arena for science; consequently they are often passed off as being all in a person's head. Although this is a likely explanation, it is just as likely that individuals with unique metabolisms can experience unique reactions to particular foods or food constituents. In light of the current evidence that even one substance in a food, such as an amino acid or glucose, can set off a wide array of brain chemicals that, in turn, influence behavior, mood, pain sensation, hunger, and sleep, it is also possible that many food ingredients could influence the hormones and nerve chemicals that subtly regulate behavior. Regardless of whether an aversion to or a craving for a food fits the narrow mold so far identified by science, a person always should listen to his or her body and its signals, and then tailor the Feeling Good Diet to match optimal nutrition with that unique profile.

CHAPTER ELEVEN

Mood, Food, and Eating Disorders

They try to hide the clues, but the subtle signs of the anorexic and bulimic are all around us: the young woman hiding her frail figure with an oversized sweater and baggy jeans, who is buying only a pack of gum at the grocery store; the hollow-cheeked young girl with the grayish skin who boards the school bus each day; the girl who takes too long in the bathroom and comes out looking drawn and worn; the middle-aged woman whose overthinness makes her look older than her years and who is obsessed with her figure, exercise, and food; the young boy who is losing weight even though he appears to be eating normally. Sometimes you can see it in a person's poor complexion, dull hair, eroded teeth, or tired eyes. You can hear it in the sound of many toilets flushing in the college dormitories after lunch.

What you don't see is just as important as what you do. Anorexics often are missing from the dinner table, while in the case of bulimics, large quantities of food are missing from the cupboards. Gone also is the cheery, lighthearted girl or boy you once knew.

Eating disorders in westernized societies are on the rise. While plumpness is prestigious in societies where food is scarce, the same shape is often considered unattractive in areas where food is abundant, because fatness is considered a sign of weakness, not strength. So much safe and tasty food has never been so available to so many, while society's image of the perfect female has deteriorated from a voluptuous figure to a scrawny stick. Adolescent girls—and increasing numbers of women, boys, and young men—have turned to self-starvation, excessive exercise, or bizarre practices such as self-induced vomiting and the use of laxatives as ways to stop the inevitable weight gain. These self-destructive eating disorders are considered commonplace in some groups and almost trendy for adolescents and young women. Do you have an eating disorder? To find out take the quiz on page 242.

Early research on eating disorders characterized the victims as mainly white high achievers. Eating disorders are most frequent in groups such as cheerleaders, gymnasts, models, dancers, wrestlers, and straight-A female students. In addition, ten times more young girls than boys become anorexic, and girls from affluent, well-educated families are at highest risk. However, anyone can develop an eating disorder, at any stage in life, regardless of gender, economic and educational status, or religion. Anorexia and bulimia also are chronic disorders that can persist into adulthood.

Defining the Problem: Anorexia, Bulimia, and Binge Eating

Eating is a pleasure for most people, but for those preoccupied with food and thinness, it is a nightmare. Anorexia nervosa, bulimia, binge eating, and even obesity share many common causes, traits, and symptoms. For both the starver and the binger, the illness becomes the identity. These individuals are obsessed with food and weight. They characterize some foods as "healthy," such as fruit and vegetables, or as "forbidden," such as cake, chocolate, biscuits, chips, and ice cream. Tremendous guilt is tied to eating forbidden foods; at the same time, to give up this obsession with weight and food leaves the anorexic or bulimic feeling uprooted and uncentered, which fosters the underlying terror of weight gain.

Regardless of the eating disorder, it is accompanied by increased feelings of anxiety, depression, alienation, helplessness, fear of fat, and vulnerability to impulsive behaviors. In addition, abnormal eating habits are complex issues fueled by the availability of food, by a person's perceptions of food and of self, by social pressures and personality (a person with a history of depression is more likely to develop an eating disorder), and by a mix of appetite-control chemicals in the body.

Often these disorders are progressive, so that a person may start out dieting, occasionally binge eat, progress to bulimia, and end up anorexic, with or without bingeing. Or the eating disorders can coincide, so that an anorexic may practice bulimic behaviors, a condition called bulimarexia. However, each disorder has a distinct set of signs and sometimes a unique physical or emotional profile (see "The Eating Pattern Continuum," page 244).

QUIZ 11.1 Are You a Food Addict?

Answer yes or no to the following questions.

_______ **1.** Are you preoccupied with food?

_______ **2.** Are you concerned about your weight?

_______ **3.** Do you weigh yourself more than twice a week?

_______ **4.** Do you sneak food or eat in secret?

_______ **5.** Do you steal food or money to buy food?

_______ **6.** Are you uncomfortable in situations where there is no food available?

_______ **7.** Do you continue eating when other people have stopped?

_______ **8.** Have you ever lost control over how much food you intended to eat?

_______ **9.** Do you nibble at a party and gorge when you get home?

_______ **10.** Do you hide food wrappers?

_______ **11.** Do you arrange to be home alone so you can eat?

_______ **12.** Do you make extra batches of cookies, cake, or muffins while everyone is gone?

_______ **13.** Do you buy food for other people but eat it all yourself?

_______ **14.** Do you hide food in drawers, closets, the laundry hamper, the sewing machine, or other unusual places?

_______ **15.** Do you stay up late at night when everyone is in bed so you can eat?

_______ **16.** Do you spend time with other people who have eating problems?

_______ **17.** Do you make excuses for overeating?

_______ **18.** Do you feel more irritable, tired, and depressed than usual?

_______ **19.** Has life become increasingly more unmanageable?

_______ **20.** Has eating become more important than your family, friends, or work?

_______ **21.** Has food or eating interfered with any part of your life?

_______ **22.** Does eating a small dessert, such as a cookie or piece of pie, lead to intense cravings to eat more?

_______ **23.** Is food a primary source of security? Do you use it to feel better, calmer, less shy, or less anxious?

_______ **24.** Do you eat when you are depressed, tense, angry, or disappointed?

_______ **25.** Do you eat large amounts of food in a short amount of time—say, in less than two hours?

_______ **26.** Have you ever felt out of control when eating?

_______ **27.** Have you ever used vomiting, laxatives, diuretics, enemas, fasting, excessive exercise, or amphetamines as methods to control your weight?

_______ **28.** Have you ever felt ashamed of how much you eat?

_______ **29.** Has anyone ever said you have an eating problem or that you are too thin?

_______ **30.** Do you think you have a problem with food and eating?

Scoring:

Review your answers to these questions. They are meant only to provide feedback so you can assess your eating habits and attitudes toward food. Are there any patterns that you are concerned about? If so, seek help now from someone trained in eating disorders.

Anorexia: Starvation in the Face of Plenty

People with anorexia nervosa relentlessly pursue thinness and have a phobia, or exaggerated fear, of body fat and weight gain—even after they have lost 15 to 25 percent of their normal weight and are emaciated. For example, a girl who normally weighs 125 pounds and drops to 106 pounds would fit this description. They resort to strenuous exercise to lose weight and inches; an anorexic might do 200 sit-ups daily to flatten a stomach already sunken by starvation.

Anorexics are divided into two categories: the restrictive type who starves herself and the bulimic type who cycles between gorging and starvation. The long-term outcome is the same. Self-starvation results in a host of body and mood changes, the most evident being loss of menstruation and increasing thinness, which can lead to serious complications or even death if not treated. In fact, between 4 and 18 percent of anorexics die from complications resulting from starvation, the highest incidence of any psychiatric disorder.

Anorexics also have trouble sleeping, with increased night awakenings and shortened periods of dream sleep. These symptoms are common in people with depression, starvation, and malnutrition. But anorexics are more likely than people with other eating disorders to be obsessive-compulsive, stoic, perfectionist, introverted, and emotionally inhibited. Anorexics are at high risk of developing irregular heartbeats, bone fractures, and early-onset osteoporosis.

Anorexia nervosa is not new. Reports of self-starvation date back to the thirteenth century, although most early accounts reflected "holy anorexia," or a compulsive drive to seek spiritual perfection. Anorexia resurfaced in the 1800s and became a social problem in the 1920s, when the ideal feminine figure was the

The Eating Pattern Continuum

Eating disorders often progress from one disorder, such as binge eating, to another, such as bulimia. Even within bulimia, a person's eating habits may range from mild to severe. Or eating disorders may overlap; for example, up to 40 percent of anorexics also binge and purge. Consequently, eating disorders can be viewed as extending across a range from normal eating behaviors to life-threatening anorexia.

NORMAL ◄——————————————————————► **SEVERE**

Normal eating behaviors	Infrequent emotional overeating* and/or dieting	Binge eating	Bulimia nervosa	Anorexia nervosa

*Emotional eating often is associated with mood problems such as premenstrual syndrome (PMS) and seasonal affective disorder (SAD) and with alcohol recovery, depression, stress, and quitting smoking.

slinky, lithe flapper. Today anorexia is again on the rise, with estimates of up to 1 in every 100 adolescent girls between the ages of eleven and eighteen falling victim to the disorder.

Bulimia: The Myth of Having Your Cake and Eating It Too

Bulimia nervosa was first seen in the 1970s. Within twenty years it has become so prevalent that today it is estimated to affect 3 in every 100 girls and is considered the most common eating disorder. A bulimic typically is a girl or woman who, while extremely concerned about weight gain, goes on eating binges that can last from fifteen minutes to a few hours. During that time she will consume 2,000 to 15,000 calories or more, followed by self-induced vomiting or excessive use of laxatives, enemas, and/or diuretics to rid herself of the food. A bulimic may consume a gallon of ice cream, four bags of cookies, three pies, and a loaf of bread within two hours, or eat bowls of oatmeal at one sitting. However, eating even one forbidden food, such as a doughnut, can trigger vomiting in the bulimic.

The bulimic, like the anorexic, is preoccupied with food and body shape or weight. However, in contrast to the anorexic, who strictly controls her food intake, the bulimic feels out of control in regard to food and will binge at least twice a week (sometimes up to twenty times a day). She then feels the overwhelming need to negate the binge by vomiting or other purges. Since some of the calories consumed are absorbed before they can be expelled, bulimics tend to maintain average weight or may even be slightly overweight. In essence, the bulimic eats to feel better but chooses foods and amounts that actually make her feel worse.

Unlike anorexics, bulimics usually show no outward signs of their secret behavior; thus they are difficult to identify. Symptoms of excessive vomiting include eroded tooth enamel and decay, enlargement of the salivary glands in the neck, and skin irritations on the joints of the hands.

The bulimic, compared to the anorexic, is more likely to abuse drugs or alcohol and be more impulsive and sexually adventurous. Bulimics also may develop bowel problems such as constipation and diarrhea from laxative use, irregular menstruation, esophageal perforation (rips and tears in the esophagus) and pancreatitis, gastric atony, electrolyte imbalances from the excessive loss of fluids when vomiting, and metabolic acidosis.

Bulimics struggle with emotional problems. What began as pride in their ability to control their weight through purging turns to shame as they hide the secret food addiction. They are aware of their disordered eating habits but are afraid (even panicky) that they will not be able to stop the binge-and-purge cycle. The fear of losing control coupled with the isolation from keeping this secret brings depression, low self-esteem, and self-depreciating thoughts that only intensify the problem. The binge behavior initially brings relief, but as the condition continues, the binge no longer satisfies and actually makes the person feel even more guilty, disgusted, and helpless. In contrast, purging becomes increasingly more important for relieving anger and tension. Ironically, the bulimic starts out purging so she can binge and eventually binges so she can purge.

Binge Eating: Why Dieting Often Does You In

Binge eating is a less serious form of bulimia that is not usually accompanied by purging and is more common in overweight people. The binge is usually not triggered by hunger but rather by a negative emotion such as anger, stress, tension, irritability, or depression. A third of all dieters admit they binge eat at least twice a week and another 22 percent confess that they binge at least once a week. (The word *binge* is often used subjectively, with some people considering any quantity of a forbidden food, even three cookies, a binge.) Binge eaters might be less likely to lose weight and maintain weight loss compared to nonbingers, and are more likely to battle food cravings, especially cravings for carbohydrate-rich snacks. In fact, low-calorie diets often trigger binge eating in these people (see chapter 2).

Why Thinness Becomes an Obsession

Given the profound social pressure in our culture to maintain thinness, it is amazing that more women do not develop eating disorders. Almost 90 percent of women wish they were thinner. What causes some to resort to self-destructive eating behaviors, while others just diet a little and complain a lot about their weight?

No one knows exactly why some women progress to self-starvation or binge-and-purge habits. Anorexics and bulimics may have emotional struggles or problems stemming from childhood that underlie their eating disorders. Others may be genetically programmed to anorexia or bulimia. (If one identical twin has an eating disorder, the other twin has a 50-50 chance of developing an eating problem, while nontwin siblings have a 10 percent chance.) Social and family values, psychological issues (personality disorders, poor reasoning skills, and poor coping skills are common problems for people with eating disorders), hormone imbalances, and a history of physical or psychological trauma are possible contributors to the onset of eating disorders.

As time passes, without exception the food disorders get worse. In many cases seemingly harmless comments about a person's weight or the social pressure from dieting friends can fuel a determination to lose weight. Once a person has jumped onto the dieting bandwagon, it is very difficult to get off. In essence, if dieting weren't a trend, these susceptible people would not fall into the eating disorder trap.

Often, people with eating disorders report that they started to diet, but then found they couldn't do without the food that helped soothe both hunger and emotional pangs. Their next step was to binge and purge (in the case of the bulimic) or to control eating even further (in the case of the anorexic). Dieting spiraled into an eating disorder as the fear of fat became an obsession fueled by diet-induced imbalances in the body's appetite-control chemicals. Thus, even if psychological issues (a desire to lose weight) initiate the condition, physiological factors help perpetuate it. Hormones and nerve chemicals in the body are turned topsy-turvy as a result of eating disorders (see "Signs and Symptoms of Eating Disorders," below).

Signs and Symptoms of Eating Disorders

Preoccupation with food, dietary fat, and calorie counting
Constant weighing
Distorted self-image
Refusal to eat normally or at all
Frequent strenuous exercising
Loss of 15 percent of normal body weight
Menstruation stopped
Presence of downy hair on the arms and legs
Delayed puberty
Disturbed sleep and early awakenings
Restlessness and hyperactiveness
Isolation and desire to be alone
Rapid consumption of large amounts of food in a short period of time
Increased irritability and depression
Frequent vomiting
Frequent use of laxatives or diuretics
Secretive behavior
Difficulty in concentrating, a "spacey" mental state
Puffiness in the eyes and cheeks
Overachievement in school or work, pursuit of perfection, and fear of failure
Constant fatigue
Increased dental problems
Swollen parotid glands in the neck

When to Say When: CCK and Appetite

Erratic eating habits such as dieting, starvation, or bingeing send many of the appetite-control chemicals into a tailspin, starting a vicious cycle for an individual with an eating disorder. For example, cholecystokinin (CCK)—a hormonelike substance produced by the digestive tract that normally signals the brain when the stomach is full—does not kick in for bulimics. Consequently, their brains don't receive the signal to stop eating or else their system becomes desensitized to CCK so that they eat larger quantities of food at a faster pace before they feel satisfied. In contrast, semistarvation in anorexics oversensitizes their CCK system, so they feel full after eating even a few bites of food. Fortunately, the hunger-satiety system controlled by CCK normalizes when a person resumes healthful eating habits and, in the case of the self-starver, when she gains weight.

A Craving for Sweets: NPY and Serotonin

More than two-thirds of bulimics report that a binge is triggered by cravings for specific foods, sweets in particular. Since neuropeptide Y (NPY) and serotonin—the neurotransmitters that trigger cravings for carbohydrates—are disturbed in anorexics and bulimics, some researchers speculate that eating disorders might be fueled by neurotransmitters gone amok because of dieting. When laboratory animals are injected with NPY, they gorge on carbohydrate-rich foods until they become obese. NPY levels are elevated in anorexics who binge and are very high in bulimics, which might override normal signals of satiety and contribute to their compulsion to overeat sweet and starchy foods.

Serotonin might be related directly to binge eating in bulimics. Low serotonin levels are linked to depression and stimulate hunger, especially for sweets and starchy foods, while high serotonin levels increase feelings of satiety and calmness while reducing food intake. People who binge either have a deficit of serotonin or are insensitive to its satiating effects and so the mechanism for turning off the desire for carbohydrates isn't there. Bulimics are susceptible to seasonal variation in mood and eating, as are people with seasonal affective disorder (SAD) and premenstrual syndrome (PMS)—two conditions affected by low serotonin levels.

The carbohydrate-loaded binge increases serotonin levels and produces a calming effect, which is the object of the addiction. Increasing tryptophan levels by supplementing with this amino acid (the building block for serotonin), or by consuming moderate amounts of carbohydrate-rich foods throughout the day, might improve both mood and eating habits. For example, bulimics who have high tryptophan levels in the blood are more likely to stop the binge-and-purge cycle and suffer less depression than are bulimics who have low tryptophan levels, again suggesting a link between serotonin and risk of developing and maintaining an eating disorder (see "Feelings, Serotonin, and Overeating," page 250).

In a case study at the University of Ottawa, Canada, a patient with a five-year history of bulimia showed a marked reduction in binge eating within one week of supplementing her diet with tryptophan; her binge eating stopped by the third week. Other studies that used antidepressant medications, which enhance serotonin activity, also showed improvements in both mood and binge eating in bulimics. (See chapter 1 for more on serotonin, mood, and eating habits.)

In contrast, the physical and emotional stresses associated with anorexia might trigger other hormone and nerve chemical upsets that result in increased levels of serotonin. Elevated serotonin and another chemical called corticotrophic releasing hormone (CRH) might increase feelings of satiety and reduce hunger and appetite, thus overriding other appetite systems and perpetuating the self-starvation.

Understanding that much of the bizarre eating behaviors of self-starvers and binge eaters is perpetuated not by a personality defect but by fundamental nerve chemicals and hormones helps to remove the guilt, shame, and blame associated with these eating disorders. It also brings hope, because these appetite-control chemicals can be restored to balance when a more normal eating style and weight are resumed.

Starvaholics

Endorphins make us feel good. They also play a dual role in eating: they increase food intake to prevent starvation and they help a person adapt for the sake of survival in the face of starvation until food is available. Sarah Leibowitz, Ph.D., a professor of neurobiology at Rockefeller University, suspects that while endorphins help control food cravings in response to stress and starvation, imbalances are common in bulimics and anorexics and might contribute to the progression of these eating disorders. For example, endorphin levels are abnormal in bulimics, which might trigger an addiction to the endorphin drive to eat. Endorphins

Feelings, Serotonin, and Overeating

There are numerous situational, physical, and self-induced factors that can trigger overeating. Some of these are possibly related to levels of serotonin in the brain.

Triggers	In the brain			What can you do?
Situational: fatigue, stress, boredom, loneliness, lack of support Physical: PMS, SAD, carbohydrate cravings, puberty Self-induced: dieting, binge eating, smoking or alcohol withdrawal, medication withdrawal	Results in Emotional upsets (mood swings, depression, anxiety, self-doubt, irritability) →	Desire to raise serotonin levels higher than normal or to return depleted levels to normal	Results in Overeating	→Diet →Medication →Light therapy (SAD)

increase the pleasurable effects of overeating and are elevated after a purge, possibly adding to the feelings of euphoria bulimics may experience after vomiting.

Bulimic women who have low endorphin levels are more likely than people with higher endorphin levels to be depressed and to binge on sweet-and-creamy foods, such as ice cream, chocolate, and pie, possibly in an attempt to raise their endorphin levels and elevate their mood. Drugs that block endorphin levels in bulimics also reduce food intake and binge eating, possibly by preventing the wide fluctuations in endorphin levels that lead to binge eating.

In contrast, anorexics might become addicted to the elation and adaption to starvation. In the initial stages of dieting, endorphin levels are high, the dieter feels great, and she becomes addicted to the endorphin-induced rush. The starvation further elevates endorphin levels and a vicious cycle develops. The anorexic is so strongly addicted to the endorphin rush of starvation that she will sabotage treatment and later report that she felt an overwhelming force to avoid food that was beyond her control. The good news is that endorphin levels eventually return to normal in both bulimics and anorexics when they resume normal eating habits.

What's Wrong with Me?

Whatever begins the dieting spiral, it is likely that resulting imbalances in the body's chemistry are the major reasons why the eating disorders progress. Anorexics and bulimics aren't crazy. There is a natural nerve-chemical basis for the eating pattern that can eventually become all-consuming. A person may start out with a normal balance of chemicals, but the starvation or binge-and-purge cycle upsets the appetite-control chemicals.

Or some people may have an imbalance in one or more nerve chemicals that genetically programs them to gain weight. They adopt bizarre eating habits in a desperate attempt to avoid an inevitable obesity and to remain fashionably thin. Other people may have imbalances in their appetite-control chemicals that affect the hunger and satiety signals they receive and make them more likely to develop eating disorders.

Finally, some binge eaters may have imbalances in neurotransmitters that lead to emotional problems such as substance abuse or depression, and the eating disorder is secondary to these psychological problems. These links among mood, eating patterns, and nerve chemicals are potentially strong, since many of the chemicals that influence eating disorders—such as serotonin and the endorphins—also are powerful shapers of personality and mood, and have been associated with other food-mood problems, from food cravings to PMS and SAD.

Knowing that self-starvation and binge eating are fueled by powerful internal chemicals has helped steer research toward developing medications that can restore that balance. However, treatment of eating disorders continues to include counseling, nutrition, and behavior changes. As mentioned here, if attitudes and eating habits are changed—and in the case of anorexics, weight is normalized—the appetite-control chemicals also return to normal. In short, there is hope of recovery if a person can clear the initial hurdles in the treatment of an eating disorder.

Vitamin and Mineral Deficiencies

Anorexics and bulimics have a love-hate relationship with fat, sugar, and calories. They have the equivalent of a Ph.D. in dietary fat and know how much oil and grease are in just about any food. Anorexics have an aversion to eating anything that contains fat or that they think has fat in it, while bulimics gorge on the sweet-and-creamy foods on their "forbidden foods" lists. In fact, bulimics are more likely to binge after indulging in a small amount of forbidden food than they are after eating a safe food such as an orange or a carrot. It is as if the taste of the forbidden food sets off the appetite-control chemicals and sends the person headfirst into a binge. In addition, their satiety and taste signals are so confused they no longer know when they are full or hungry. Either way, the obsession with fat may result in vitamin and mineral deficiencies.

It comes as no surprise that both anorexics and bulimics consume diets low in vitamins and minerals. Even though some self-starvers eat nutrient-packed foods such as fresh fruits and vegetables, they don't eat or retain enough of them to reach even minimal standards for nutrition. Low calorie intake means insufficient amounts of protein, calcium, iron, magnesium, the B vitamins, and vitamin C, along with trace minerals and the fat-soluble vitamins, vitamins A, E, and D. General malnutrition, in turn, reduces the absorption of other nutrients, which further aggravates a person's nutritional status.

Vitamin deficiencies might contribute to the depression and mood swings common in eating disorders. Researchers at the University of Liverpool and the University of Surrey in Great Britain examined the associations among folic acid and vitamin B12, depression, and weight loss in forty-five anorexic girls. They compared the vitamin status of this group with vitamin levels in normal-weight bulimics and normal-weight girls without eating disorders. They found that 37 percent of the anorexics and 14 percent of the bulimics but only 11 percent of the healthy controls were deficient in folic acid. The anorexics also were more likely to be vitamin B12 deficient. Anorexics who were depressed were the most likely to be deficient in folic acid, and supplementing with this B vitamin improved their moods. Thus, folic acid might help regulate mood in people with eating disorders, while even a mild deficiency of the vitamin could contribute to the depression common in these disorders. (See chapter 6 for more information on vitamins, minerals, and mood.)

Poor dietary intake of calcium, vitamin D, and magnesium might undermine health later in life. Calcium- and vitamin D–rich milk products are mistakenly viewed as high in fat, and even if nonfat milk and yogurt are considered safe foods, the limited quantities often consumed result in a low intake of these nutrients. The same holds true for magnesium-rich foods such as peanuts, bananas, beet greens, avocados, and wheat germ. Consequently, bulimics and anorexics have lowered bone mineral density and are at increased risk of developing osteoporosis. Even a brief history of anorexia (two years) can reduce bone mineral content, thus weakening the bones and increasing susceptibility to fractures. Magnesium deficiency also increases the risk of muscle weakness, leg cramps, an inability to cope with stress, restlessness, irregular heartbeat, and poor concentration and memory.

Up to 40 percent of anorexics and bulimics have lost so much calcium from their bones that they are at considerable risk of fractures. Poor diet is a major cause, but starvation-induced low levels of the female hormone estrogen also contribute to this condition. Low estrogen is partly to blame for the loss of menstruation common in anorexics and in some bulimics. Since estrogen encourages calcium absorption and protects the bones from loss of calcium, depletion of this hormone leaves the bones defenseless. Weight-bearing exercises such as jogging help to offset this bone loss, but exercise alone is not a satisfactory solution. People with eating disorders need a higher amount of calcium than is typically required, yet they do not consume even recommended levels.

Since recovery is prolonged and patients often continue to eat sporadically for years after treatment, a physician should be consulted about possible estrogen replacement therapy and calcium supplements in the treatment of eating disorders. Because the nutritional status of anorexics and bulimics is so delicate, a physician always should be consulted before beginning any supplement program.

Zinc Deficiency and Eating Disorders

Zinc has a strong connection to eating disorders. The symptoms of zinc deficiency mirror many of the side effects of anorexia and bulimia, including loss of appetite and taste, decreased sexual desire and delayed sexual maturity, fatigue, increased susceptibility to colds and infections, mood disturbances, skin changes, and hair loss. People who are zinc deficient lose their desire for food, have poor appetites, and say that food doesn't taste good.

People with eating disorders typically consume suboptimal amounts of zinc-rich foods such as extra-lean meat, fish, oysters, lima beans, and wheat germ. Consequently, their daily intake of zinc averages one-half to two-thirds the recommended amount of 12 to 15 mg. One study reported that 54 percent of anorexics and bulimics were zinc deficient. Urinary excretion of zinc also is decreased, reflecting low zinc levels in the blood and tissues. In addition, anorexics do not absorb zinc well, which can aggravate an already compromised zinc status.

Although it is unclear whether zinc deficiency contributes to the onset of eating disorders, there is mounting evidence that low zinc intake helps perpetuate the problem. When some anorexics and bulimics start taking zinc supplements (such as zinc sulfate), they show improved sense of taste and appetite, increased body weight, improvements in mood and ability to cope, and even a return of menstruation within three to seven months. Likewise, anorexic symptoms return when these patients are taken off the supplements. Researchers at the University of Kentucky Medical Center in Lexington speculate that zinc deficiency "may act as a sustaining factor for abnormal eating behavior in certain eating disorder patients."

Restoring Good Eating Habits

"Act now" is the best advice when dealing with an eating disorder. Treatment and recovery become progressively more difficult the longer the disorder continues, and advanced cases often require hospitalization. The causes and perpetuating circumstances of eating disorders are varied and complex. In all cases, treatment must include a mixture of social, psychological, and biological factors, plus a dietitian-supervised eating plan that progressively reinstates normal eating habits. Antidepressant medication or other drugs may help realign the mental and physical systems that otherwise perpetuate these disorders.

The anorexic or bulimic first needs to begin changing his or her ideas and expectations about food, about eating, and about body weight and shape before making dietary changes. A realistic body image is essential for recovery. Here are some examples of perfectionist or unrealistic beliefs:

- "I must be thin because to be thin is to be successful and happy."
- "Self-indulgence is bad since it is a sign of weakness."
- "Self-control is good because it is a sign of strength and discipline."
- "Anything less than complete success is total failure."

These unrealistic beliefs must be replaced with realistic ones. This may be especially difficult for the anorexic who denies there is a problem, is proud of her self-control and emaciated shape, and distrusts anyone who tries to help. Gaining the anorexic's trust is essential for treatment.

Although the ultimate goal is to follow the guidelines of the Feeling Good Diet (see chapter 13), the first stage may be to find foods that are acceptable and are also moderate in protein, carbohydrates, and fat and do not trigger a binge. Bulimics cannot use food to feed their emotions. They must address their emotions and problems in constructive, nurturing, non-food-related ways. Bulimics usually binge on sugar-loaded foods or on highly refined carbohydrates. They therefore experience a withdrawal period that includes headaches, increased irritability, and even sleep problems when they try to break the eating cycle, often prompting them to return to their binge-prone food. These and any other addictive foods—as well as weight-loss diets and mood-altering drugs including alcohol—must be eliminated from the eating plan, while healthful ways to find physical and emotional gratification are identified and practiced.

Caffeine should be eliminated from the diets of people with eating disorders. Bulimics are especially likely to consume too much coffee (up to fourteen cups a day), colas, chocolates, and other caffeine-containing drinks. Even when they are sweetened with nonnutritive sweeteners such as aspartame (NutraSweet), they can aggravate feelings of anxiety and depression, wreak havoc with endorphin levels, and possibly increase the risk of binge eating.

Gradually, food intake is increased for the anorexic, or binge eating episodes are reduced as food intake is divided into several small meals and snacks for the bulimic. The initial diet for the anorexic should contain at least 1,500 to 2,000 calories, increased to 2,500 to 3,000 calories over the next one to two weeks to produce a gradual and controlled increase in weight.

Since eating disorders are chronic conditions, the person with the eating disorder—who often is a perfectionist and can be emotionally shattered when she fails on an eating plan—must develop strategies for handling slipups so that they do not progress into a relapse. Most people need professional help to accomplish this, although some bulimics can help themselves. Keeping a daily food diary that notes food intake, vomiting and other purge behaviors, and mood before and after eating can help identify mood-food patterns, eating progress, and food behaviors that still need work. In addition, removing or having a plan to counter the cues that bring on binges (being alone, keeping binge-prone foods in the house, tension, midafternoon cravings) and planning meals and snacks can help curb erratic eating habits.

Long-term poor eating habits, chronic malnutrition, poor food choices, and fluctuating blood-sugar levels upset the body's appetite-control chemicals and perpetuate eating disorders. Limited evidence shows that following a nutrient-packed, low-fat diet such as the Feeling Good Diet can help some bulimics break the cycle and reprogram their eating habits for health.

In one study, bulimic girls consumed either a nutrient-packed sugar-free diet that contained no binge-prone foods or a control diet resembling the girls' typical food intake. At the end of three weeks, the girls who had switched their eating habits to the nutrient-packed diet had stopped binge eating, while the control group continued their bulimic behavior. When the control group switched to the nutrient-packed diet, they also stopped binge eating. Normal eating habits were maintained as long as the girls stuck with the new eating plan.

Frequent, small meals—as outlined in the Feeling Good Diet—are the best approach to restoring balance to the body's appetite-control chemicals. Each meal should include some complex carbohydrate—such as half a bagel, cereal, or toast—to help maintain a constant level of serotonin, NPY, insulin and blood sugar, and other chemicals. Fruit is not a good source of carbohydrate because its main sugar is fructose, which is slow acting when it comes to raising serotonin levels. Always combine fruit with another food such as nonfat yogurt, crackers, or cereal. The diet also should supply optimal amounts of zinc- and calcium-rich foods and, if this is not possible, then zinc and/or calcium supplements with physician supervision should be considered. Improving zinc intake should begin immediately.

A moderate exercise program can help raise brain endorphin levels formerly raised by starvation or food. Prolonged, rhythmic exercise such as brisk walking, jogging, aerobic dancing, or bicycling naturally increases endorphin levels, elevates mood, and decreases pain. However, excessive exercise should be avoided, since it perpetuates the obsession with fitness and weight.

People who have struggled with an eating disorder for years, who have lost considerable weight, or who have other symptoms of an advanced eating disorder always should begin the recovery process with the help of a physician. Often, health complications go unnoticed until these people begin a "refeeding" program, which can upset the person's precarious equilibrium. Close physician supervision during the initial stages can help prevent problems.

Finding a new source of inner strength is critical to long-term recovery. The emotional battle raging within a person with an eating disorder undermines his or her self-confidence and self-trust. At the same time, the disease becomes that person's life, identity, and source of both pride and disgust. Assuming that changing only one's eating habits is all it takes is like treating a serious illness with a Band-Aid or an addiction to drugs by urging "just say no." Along with strong family and social support, professional counseling, nutrition, and medical attention, self-starvers and binge eaters must learn to trust, love, and respect themselves for their unique characteristics, not their weight, shape, or figure.

CHAPTER TWELVE

Food Abuse: Eating for All the Wrong Reasons

- "When the pace slows down and boredom sets in, I eat."
- "My friend and I had a big fight last week. I went home, stormed in the front door, and went straight for the refrigerator."
- "I turn to food when I'm facing a big project that I don't want to start. I guess eating is my way of procrastinating."
- "My eating is pretty normal while I'm at the office. But when I'm home alone at night I seem to lose all willpower to resist the chips."
- "My best friend can't eat when she's nervous. With me it is just the opposite; the bigger the worry, the more I eat."
- "My eating and my weight are a constant battle. I hate the way I look, but at the same time (and this may sound crazy) I feel safer when I'm heavy. It's a no-win situation."

One of the main themes of this book is that many of our food cravings, desires, preferences, and compulsions are fueled by a mixture of nerve chemicals. These neurotransmitters are intrinsically linked to the body's basic drive to survive and are as basic and instinctive as breathing. Most attempts to "will" them away only make them worse, so individuals must learn to work with—not against—their cravings. But neurotransmitters and hormones aside, people also eat to nourish more than their body—and sometimes for all the wrong reasons.

The Psychology of Food Choices and Eating Habits

Most people at one time or another turn to food to soothe their feelings. In fact, emotional eating is so common that many people consider it unavoidable and normal. The red flag for emotional eating is when you eat in response to a mood rather than in response to hunger. The former fuels the feelings; the latter fuels the body.

There is nothing wrong with an occasional snack to calm you down or make you feel better. However, emotional eating becomes a problem when it leads to compulsive eating, obesity, malnutrition, or other health issues. It is also a problem if it is used as a way to deal with emotions or to escape negative feelings, covering up underlying problems that should be addressed.

Anxiety, worries, tension, upset feelings, stress, and fear are common causes of emotional eating. Food becomes the tranquilizer that calms the nerves and soothes the anxiety. The anxiety is caused by anticipation of an event, such as having to give a presentation, or a thought, such as "I can't do this." In either case, the result is that you turn to food to soothe yourself. Or it may be that turning to food during times of stress is a learned response: whenever you were anxious in the past, you reached for the symbol of caregiving—food—to help you through the tough times. If those associations date back to childhood, when you were given food whenever you were upset or cried, then your adult eating habits become an unconscious way to deal with your tension.

The bigger the assignment, the higher the demands, the tighter the deadline, the more likely you are to eat. Women may be more vulnerable to this stress-eating scenario than are men. Researchers at the University of Michigan in Dearborn sat women and men at tables loaded with munchies, and had them watch either a bland film about travel or a high-anxiety film about gruesome accidents on the job. The women who watched the gory film ate twice as many cookies, candy, and crackers as the people who watched the travel film, while the men who viewed the gory film actually ate less food. As mentioned in chapter 7, this food-mood link may be reinforced by the calming effect of endorphins and serotonin released as a result of eating.

Boredom is a common trigger for emotional eating. Being bored is a state of minimal arousal and mental stimulation; it is just the opposite of anxiety, which is a high-arousal emotion. Thus, preparing food and eating effectively relieves that boredom, since it gives you something to do. Researchers in the department of psychology at Vanderbilt University in Nashville, Tennessee, reported that people who struggle with strong food cravings also are more susceptible to boredom, especially in the afternoon and evening hours, than are noncravers. Eating becomes a way to relieve boredom in the absence of emotional arousal.

Loneliness can lead a person to eat. The loneliness can stem from a lack of social contact or an absence of emotional depth in relationships. Food serves as a companion, offering comfort and reassurance in a pinch. It also numbs the unpleasantness and the inner ache of loneliness. The downside is that eating ultimately makes you feel worse because it leads to weight gain and guilt, and may even contribute to wavering self-esteem. These side effects, in turn, can interfere with building and maintaining satisfying relationships with others.

In situations such as boredom and loneliness, eating becomes a way to fill the emotional void. It is the interesting activity to curb boredom or the satisfying relationship to cure loneliness. While preventing boredom and developing meaningful relationships take time and effort, eating is easy and relatively effortless. Unfortunately, it is a quick fix that only adds to the problem in the long run. Boredom, anxiety, anger, depression, jealousy, and other emotions are a normal part of life, but using food to treat them or to avoid resolving them is not a long-term solution for feeling better.

Confusing Food with Love

Food is the most common tangible symbol of love and nurturing. At birth a baby learns to rely on someone else for food, and finds that feeding time is also a time for nurturing from and bonding with the caregiver. Our strong emotional link between food and love continues throughout life. Our culture's major events revolve around food, from birthdays and weddings to secular holidays and major religious celebrations. Socializing and celebrating are synonymous with eating.

We learn to confuse our emotions, rewards, and consequences with food. A child is told to eat his spinach before he can have dessert. Another child is instructed that unless she eats her sandwich she cannot go outside and play. Another child is told to "eat something; it will make you feel better." These and other messages during childhood help strengthen the links between food, reward, punishment, and love. Chocolates are a gift on Valentine's Day that say "I love you." Overeating on Thanksgiving is expected; indeed, you may be suspected of not liking the dinner (and therefore the cook) if you don't overindulge.

Food also is a source of self-nurturance, self-love, and self-protection for someone who silently deals with a past trauma. According to researchers at the University of California at San Diego, childhood abuse (including sexual and physical abuse), losing a parent to death or divorce during childhood, or experiencing a sad or violent childhood can cause an adult to be fearful and to unconsciously use food to gain weight. In their study, 40 percent of obese subjects reported having had one or more alcoholic parents compared to only 17 percent of the slender subjects. The obese subjects also were twice as likely to have grown up in families where beatings, verbal abuse, and other violence were common.

Weight gain creates a protective shell that allows such people to feel less vulnerable and to keep other people at a distance. For them, eating is also a way to cope with and numb the pain, and to nurture themselves. Or people may be so overcome with rage resulting from the trauma that they turn the anger inward. The self-hatred then leads to overeating, substance abuse, or other self-destructive behaviors. It is increasingly difficult to distinguish body needs from emotional needs when eating becomes a way to satisfy both physical hunger and emotional pain.

The irrational thoughts and beliefs that develop as a result of a trauma further confuse emotions with eating. For example, thoughts that you are unlovable, flawed, or unworthy fuel feelings of loneliness and erode self-confidence, self-esteem, and self-acceptance. Rather than identify what caused the bad experience in a relationship or a childhood trauma, people internalize the trauma and label themselves as inadequate. In all cases, the origin of the emotion must be identified and dealt with in a supportive, trusting way. Once that pain has been treated, the emotional eating can be addressed or may stop on its own.

Beyond Fad Diets

Not only does fad dieting not work, it is harmful to health and can lead to food abuse. Dieters train themselves to ignore their body signals, such as hunger, and to listen instead to what a weight-loss diet tells them to do. Hunger becomes an unacceptable reason to eat. In their attempt to substitute willpower for normal physical drives, they lose the ability to listen to their body's cues. Their faulty hunger awareness means they have trouble regulating their food intake once the diet is over. They may mistakenly associate feeling anxiety, loneliness, or other physical or emotional sensations with being hungry.

As emphasized throughout this book, restrictive diets almost always send the appetite-control chemicals into a tailspin. The eating pendulum swings from restraint to binge, sometimes resulting in obsessive eating, fear of food, desperation, and anger. The more dieters fail at dieting, the more likely they are to struggle with emotional eating and to be fearful about weight management and eating in general. They may even become paralyzed by the fear that they will lose all restraint and eat compulsively—a fear not unlike that in eating disorders such as anorexia and bulimia. Consequently, these people may develop a diet-induced fear of food.

The first step in undoing the harm done by fad dieting is to just say no forever to any restrictive diet that reduces daily energy intake below 1,500 calories. The second step is to regain a sensitivity to body signals, especially hunger. Ask yourself:

- Do I try to ignore hunger? If so, why? What happens when I ignore my hunger?
- Is hunger an enemy or a friend? Why?

Whenever you have the desire to eat, ask yourself whether or not you are hungry and to what extent. If you are not hungry or are only moderately hungry, think about what other factors might be influencing your desire to eat. Also, pay attention to the taste, texture, and aroma of food when you are eating. Eat slowly and listen for your body's signal that it is full. Then:

1. Follow the low-fat, low-sugar eating plan outlined in the Feeling Good Diet.

2. Develop strategies for overcoming triggers to binge or eat emotionally.

3. Develop a healthier relationship with food.

4. Find other ways to feel successful that go beyond the bathroom scale.

5. Exercise daily.
6. Focus on health, not weight.
7. Identify other health issues that might be underlying your emotional eating.

The ABCs of Food Abuse

People often believe that events just happen. They find themselves snacking from the refrigerator after work or eating while watching television in the evening—for no apparent reason. But a behavior doesn't just happen. There always is a reason—something that preceded the eating, that caused the behavior to occur. More important, a person always has a choice; no one is ever a victim of food abuse.

Food abuse follows a decided pattern—the ABCs—as shown on page 264. The reason for emotional eating is called the *antecedent*—something that precedes the eating. The antecedent can be an event, such as being criticized at work; a negative thought, such as "I can't do anything right"; or a feeling, such as depression, anger, or irritation. The antecedent is followed by a *behavior*, such as eating a bag of chips. The behavior is always followed by a *consequence*—the chips taste good and you momentarily forget about the scuffle at work, but you have eaten a food that does not fuel your best mood and you may feel guilty later. These are the ABCs of food abuse.

Learning Your ABCs

The best way to tone down your emotional eating is to identify the ABCs of why you eat: what causes you to start eating and what happens as a result. To do this, you need to keep a journal, such as the one found at the end of this chapter (see Worksheet 12.1, page 268), for at least one week. Record everything you eat and drink, or only those items you think are related to emotional eating. Also record when you ate, how you felt before and how you felt afterward, and anything else

ILLUSTRATION 12.1 The ABCs of Food Abuse

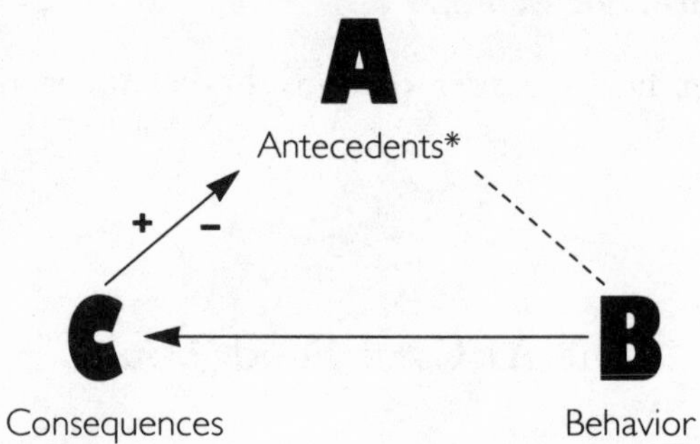

*Antecedents can be external cues, such as the smell, sight, or sound of food; people; places; or events. Or they can be internal cues, such as thoughts, attitudes, beliefs, or feelings.

that might be related to the experience (any other consequences or thoughts). Always record the information at the time of eating, since memory fades and is inaccurate even an hour after eating.

At first it may be difficult to target your feelings associated with eating, so at least write down any related thoughts. Try to recall what you were thinking just before you had the urge to eat. What brought on the thought? Keep in mind that these thoughts are always in response to something—an antecedent. For example, do you often feel sad or depressed just before a food craving? What triggered the depression? What negative or irrational thoughts contributed to the experience? Is the emotional column in your journal empty? This could be a sign that you are eating to avoid boredom. Do you eat chips when angry? Mushy foods when depressed? Caffeinated beverages or chocolate when sad? When you are feeling lonely, guilty, or in need of nurturing, do you crave foods that your mother served when you were a child?

Negative thoughts, beliefs, and emotions fuel food-abusive behaviors, so identify them and nip them in the bud. Listen to your self-talk, that internal dialogue that precedes emotional eating. Write down these thoughts in your journal to help you see them objectively. Are they rational or irrational? Once you have identified the thoughts and beliefs, you can begin replacing irrational ones with positive thoughts, using a technique called thought stopping. Thought stopping is a way to stop negative thoughts. You yell "Stop!" in your head at the first recognition of a negative thought. (Some people even picture a stop sign in their minds.) For example, a negative thought such as "This is too hard. I can't do it" can be stopped before it gains strength by silently saying "Stop!" (See also "Some Irrational Beliefs," page 266.) The technique works best when the negative thought is replaced with a positive one, such as "This is challenging, but I can do it." Once you identify the negative thoughts that precede emotional eating, you can develop a repertoire of positive thoughts to use when the need arises.

Note the time of day you are most likely to eat inappropriately. Do you crave foods in midafternoon? Is this a low-energy time of day, when you are likely to be bored? Do the foods you eat require preparation or some ritual? If so, this could be your way of relieving boredom. Plan even a short activity for this time of day to change the pace—make a phone call, take a walk, play music, or stretch. You'll relieve the boredom without turning to food. Do you eat in front of the television at night? Again, this could be a sign of boredom or tension. Try some nonfood activity such as riding a stationary bicycle, taking a hot bath, or writing letters. Even just increasing your awareness of why you are eating may help. (See also "Food Is Love, and Other Misconceptions," page 267.)

Slip Management

The more aware you are of when and why you eat, the more capable you will be of developing an eating plan tailored to your moods, your food preferences, and your lifestyle. However, even the best-laid plans can go awry. The secret is not to let a minor slip progress to a major relapse.

A slip is any time you get sidetracked from efforts to reach your goals. It may be a day when you do not follow the Feeling Good Diet or a week when you don't exercise. It may even be something as simple as eating a forbidden food.

A slip is not bad. In fact, it is normal and expected whenever a person is changing habits. How that slip is managed, however, could make or break the best intentions. If not addressed immediately and effectively, a series of slips will lead to discouragement, irrational thinking, and eventually a major relapse dur-

Some Irrational Beliefs

Many times emotional eating stems from irrational beliefs. Here are a few:

1. *The "all-or-nothing" belief.* If you are a perfectionist, this may apply to you. It is the "If you are going to do it, do it right" motto. For example, a person mistakenly believes he must follow an eating plan exactly or not at all, everyone must like him, or he should be good at everything. In reality, many things worth doing are not necessarily worth doing perfectly and even small changes may be better than none.
2. *The overgeneralization belief.* If you tend to take one event and generalize it to apply to everything, then this may apply to you. For example, one slip from following the Feeling Good Diet is viewed as proof you will never succeed, rather than just one small experience in an otherwise successful venture.
3. *The "too big/very insignificant" belief.* If you exaggerate your flaws and underestimate your strong points, this may apply to you. In this case, a minor slip—such as not exercising for one day—overshadows all the days you did exercise.
4. *The "should/have to" belief.* If you often find yourself saying *should, must, have to,* then this may apply to you. Irrational beliefs about what a person "should" do can cause unrealistic standards for performance that often lead to guilt and resentment. Examples include "Life should be fair," "I should follow my plan," or "I should be able to do this."
5. *The "I feel, therefore I know" belief.* If you justify your thoughts based on your feelings, this may apply to you. For example, the thought that "I feel guilty, therefore I must have done something wrong" is an irrational thought often used to justify a feeling. Feelings are not proof that a thought is correct, since feelings are created by thoughts and those thoughts may be irrational.
6. *The labeling belief.* If you categorize, label, or stereotype people or yourself, this may apply to you. Often using labels such as "loser" or "failure" results in redefining all your actions based on these stereotypes. For example, labeling yourself as weak might result in not making decisions or taking charge of your life.
7. *The entertainment committee belief.* If you feel responsible or blame yourself for everything that happens, this may apply to you. For example, a friend doesn't call when he said he would, so you mistakenly assume you did something wrong. This belief results in needless guilt and erodes self-esteem.

ing which you return to previous bad habits. In short, a slip does not inevitably result in a relapse, but every relapse begins with a slip.

To effectively manage a slip and fend off a relapse, identify those situations when you are most vulnerable, such as when you have certain thoughts or emotions, are ill, have an upset in routine including travel or a change in sleep habits, or feel a lack of support. Plan ahead how you will handle these situations. Weigh the short-term benefits of emotional eating (it temporarily makes you feel good) against the long-term consequences (mood swings, depression, poor sleep habits, poor physical health). Determine how to avoid the triggers of emotional eating or learn new ways to respond to them.

If a slipup just sneaks up on you, then learn from it. Treat the situation as an opportunity to grow. What caused the slip? How can it be avoided in the future? What will you do next time? Focus on the long term. How does this slip compare to your overall efforts? Avoid indulging in negative thoughts, such as the "all-or-nothing" belief (see "Some Irrational Beliefs," page 266).

Food Is Love, and Other Misconceptions

People often unconsciously respond to life based on outdated or incorrect beliefs. Here are a few:

1. *Food is love.* "The best way I can show someone that I care is by feeding them." There are many ways to show affection without using food, including spending time with a person, listening, sending flowers, remembering special occasions, or a smile and a hug.
2. *Food is responsibility.* "I should eat everything on my plate because there are starving people in the world." Eating when it is not physically needed is just as wasteful as throwing the food away.
3. *Food is a reward.* "The best way to reward myself and those people I love is with a favorite food." Life is filled with nonfood rewards, including going to a movie, a blue ribbon, a trophy, a present, or an afternoon at the museum.
4. *Food is fun.* "All social events should revolve around food." Spending time with friends and family is the main focus of a social event. Rather than get together to eat, get together to walk, fly a kite, watch old movies, or go for a drive in the country.

WORKSHEET 12.1 The Emotional-Eating Journal

Make copies of this worksheet and fill one in each day. Write down when and what you ate, how you felt and what you were thinking before and after eating, and any other related events, feelings, or factors (such as, do certain people or things trigger emotional eating?). Write down information immediately; do not rely on memory. Use the Comments section to list any other pertinent events or feelings during the day that may have affected your eating.

Day: ______________________________

TIME	EMOTIONS/THOUGHTS BEFORE	FOOD EATEN	EMOTIONS/THOUGHTS AFTER	OTHER

Comments: ____

____

____

____

Eating for All the Right Reasons

Just as every face, every nose, every smile is different, so are every person's food preferences. Sometimes those preferences are fueled by neurotransmitters programmed to keep the body well stocked with fuel. Sometimes they are guided by a need to soothe a feeling or dull an emotional pain. Or those preferences are just part of the person you are. For example, outgoing people tend to like sweetened foods more than do shy people.

Drawing a distinct line between neurotransmitter-triggered eating and emotional eating is difficult, and it is likely that the two go hand-in-hand. People's food preferences tend to mimic those of their parents. Our taste and smell sensitivities also vary greatly, and they have a strong influence on our food preferences and consumption habits. Even people's beliefs about food influence what they eat. For example, one study showed that people ate more food when they thought the meal was low in fat, compared to when they were told the meal was high in fat, even though the meals were identical in fat content. People eat for pleasure, health, tradition, and convenience.

Curbing your emotional eating is more than just a food issue, however. A healthful lifestyle is essential for healthy emotions and healthful eating. For example, daily exercise helps prevent (and lessen the symptoms of) depression, anxiety, and other feelings associated with emotional eating. Developing a personal community of supportive and loving family members, friends, and co-workers also is essential to a healthful lifestyle. Learning effective ways to cope with emotions that do not include food is a necessity. Finally, remember to keep eating and food in perspective. Food should taste good, look and smell appealing, and be good for you. It should nourish your body, your moods, and your mind.

II.

NUTRITION KNOW-HOW FOR FEELING YOUR BEST

Chapter Thirteen

The Feeling Good Diet

What you eat is often at the root of how you feel. Granted, there are no magic diet pills, nutritional potions, or herbal remedies to painlessly, effortlessly, and immediately make a troublesome mood go away. However, a few simple changes in your diet may be all it takes to improve your mood, boost your energy level, or help you sleep through the night. In some cases, the problem is too little of one or more nutrients; in other cases it is too much of something, such as sugar or caffeine. It may not be what, but when, you eat that has contributed to an emotional downhill ride.

The good news is it may take only minor adjustments in your eating patterns to produce a dramatic improvement in your mood. Even if your diet requires a major facelift, the process can be relatively painless if you make small progressive changes in your diet. The Feeling Good Diet helps you put your diet and your mood back on track. It is not a diet in the true sense of the word, but rather an eating plan that helps you slowly adapt your food preferences to help you feel your best (see "The Feeling Good Diet Philosophy," page 274).

The Un-Diet

Diets don't work. Quick-weight-loss diets produce temporary results, but the weight inevitably is regained; often, people gain back even more weight as a result. On the other hand, low-fat diets are difficult for people to stick with, so they abandon them in despair and return to familiar foods. Even the best low-fat or weight-loss diet was not designed to help you feel your emotional best or to improve your mental health. In fact, most strict diets aggravate mood and behavior problems.

The Feeling Good Diet Philosophy

The goals of the Feeling Good Diet are as follows:

1. Slowly reduce dietary fat to 25 percent of total calories, refined and added sugars to 10 percent or less of total calories, and caffeine to no more than two servings of caffeinated beverages each day.
2. Gradually increase intake of naturally occurring carbohydrates such as fruits, vegetables, grains and breads, and legumes, so that you consume at least three servings of fruit, four servings of vegetables, seven servings of breads and grains, and one serving of legumes each day.
3. Evenly disperse calories and nutrients into five or six mini-meals during the day.
4. Ensure optimal nutrient intake by consuming at least 2,500 calories from a variety of nutrient-packed foods each day and choosing a moderate-dose multiple vitamin and mineral supplement when calorie intake falls below this level.

For all people—from those struggling with mood, sleep, or energy problems to those who just want to feel a little better—the Feeling Good Diet is a breath of fresh air. It promotes mental, emotional, and physical health rather than counting calories, measuring fat grams, or calculating spoonfuls of sugar. It provides commonsense dietary guidelines to help you feel your best. And it promises results from realistic efforts.

A Way to Feel Better, Feel Younger, Think Faster

The Feeling Good Diet is a stepping stone to healthful eating. First, you keep track of what you eat, how much, and when by maintaining a food diary for one week. Next, from the eating patterns and food choices noted in the diary, you gradually adapt your current eating habits to meet the nutrition goals of Step 1 in the Feeling Good Diet. When the Step 1 dietary guidelines have become habit, you move to Step 2 and finally to Step 3 (see "The Three Steps of the Feeling Good Diet," page 276).

These dietary guidelines help you to make the transition from an eating plan that interferes with feeling your best to an eating style that helps you maximize your energy and good mood. When used with the specific dietary advice in the chapters on food cravings, fatigue, PMS, depression, stress, and sleep, the Feeling Good Diet combines the latest research and dietary advice into an eating plan that helps you feel your best.

The Rationale

As you read this and the following chapter, the rationale underlying the Feeling Good Diet guidelines will become clear. A brief explanation is provided here to summarize the basic components of this nutrition plan.

1. *Eat several small meals and snacks.* Research has repeatedly shown that people who divide their total daily food intake into mini-meals and snacks evenly distributed throughout the day maintain a more even temperament; are less prone to fatigue, insomnia, and depression; maintain a more desirable weight; and are less susceptible to disease, as compared to people who have most of their daily food intake in a few large meals. The body is also better able to absorb and use nutrients and maintain stable levels of blood sugar and nerve chemicals when supplied with frequent, moderate-size meals than when confronted with the feast-and-famine scenario characteristic of the traditional three square meals.

   On the other hand, nibbling can lead to cravings and gorging if a person uses mini-meals as an excuse to eat continuously all day. Ideally, most people should eat a moderate meal or snack approximately every four hours. The Feeling Good Diet gradually increases the number of meals and snacks from three to at least five. If you are already eating too often, you may want to set a personal goal to reduce the number of times you eat to no more than six each day.

2. *Eat breakfast.* Approximately one out of every two people skips breakfast, which is a big mistake. After an overnight fast, asking your body to shift into full gear without stopping to refuel is like expecting your car to run on fumes alone. People who skip breakfast

The Three Steps of the Feeling Good Diet

Step 1

1. Eat three to four times a day.
2. Follow the Step 1 Food Families eating plan, which will lower sugar intake to no more than three selections and limit fat intake to approximately 35 percent of total calories.
3. Limit caffeine from coffee, tea, and colas to no more than three servings daily.
4. Increase your water intake to two glasses a day.
5. If you consume less than 2,500 calories, take a moderate-dose multiple vitamin and mineral supplement.

Step 2

1. Eat something for breakfast.
2. Eat four to five times a day.
3. Follow the Step 2 Food Families eating plan, which will lower sugar intake to no more than two selections daily and will limit fat intake to no more than 30 percent of total calories.
4. Limit caffeine from coffee, tea, and colas to no more than two servings a day.
5. Increase your water intake to four glasses a day.
6. If you consume less than 2,500 calories, take a moderate-dose multiple vitamin and mineral supplement.

Step 3

1. Eat a breakfast that includes at least one selection of grains, one of fresh fruit, and one of low-fat dairy food.
2. Eat five to six times a day.
3. Follow the Step 3 Food Families eating plan, which will reduce sugar intake to no more than one selection daily and will limit fat intake to approximately 25 percent of total calories.
4. Limit caffeine from coffee, tea, and colas to no more than two servings a day.
5. Increase your water intake to six glasses a day.
6. If you consume less than 2,500 calories, take a moderate-dose multiple vitamin and mineral supplement.

struggle more with weight problems and low energy later in the day. As discussed in chapter 4, eating breakfast boosts your energy for the rest of the day, breaks the fast-and-feast cycle, prevents fatigue, and helps improve mood.

3. *Follow the three-step plan.* These progressive stages slowly wean you off of sugar and fat and reprogram your taste buds to enjoy nutrient-packed vegetables, fruits, grains, and other nutritious foods that boost your energy and help you feel your best. Use the Food-Family Eating Plans on pages 278–79 and Table 13.1, the Food-Family List, beginning on page 282, to select foods from each of the nine groups to design your daily menus.

4. *Limit caffeine.* Although caffeine provides a quick boost when we are lacking energy, it may contribute to fatigue and sleep or mood problems. Strictly limit coffee, tea, and cola.

5. *Limit sweet-and-creamy or sugary foods.* Reducing, or even eliminating, sugar from your diet is one of the most important factors in achieving mood and energy control.

6. *Increase your water intake.* Water is the most important contributor to general health and emotional well-being, yet it often is ignored or forgotten. Water is essential for all body processes. The chronic low-grade dehydration that results from drinking a little—but not enough—water is one of the most common causes of fatigue.

7. *Consider taking necessary supplements.* If you consume less than 2,500 calories, take a moderate-dose multiple vitamin and mineral supplement. Numerous national nutrition surveys report that Americans do not consume even adequate—let alone optimal—amounts of the vitamins and minerals important for optimal mood, energy, and mental function. Even the best diet is likely to fall short of one or more nutrients when energy intake is less than 2,500 calories. Therefore, a responsible supplementation program offers safe and potentially beneficial nutritional insurance. (See chapter 15 for guidelines on how to select a supplement.)

The Food-Family Eating Plans

The following eating plans are designed to meet your nutritional needs for each step in the Feeling Good Diet. With each progressive step, your intake of fat and sugar decreases while your intake of complex carbohydrates, fiber, vitamins, and minerals increases.

Step 1

Each day consume at least:

- Two selections from the Fruit Family (at least one selection should be a high–vitamin C item)
- Two selections from the Vegetable Family (at least one selection should be a high–beta-carotene item)
- Four selections from the Grains and Starchy Vegetables Family (at least two selections should be whole-grain items)
- Two nonfat or low-fat selections from the Milk Products Family (if you choose a fattier selection, then deduct the extra fat from the Fats and Oils Family allotment below)

Consume no more than:

- Two selections from the Meat and Legumes Family
- Two selections from the Nutritious Fatty Foods Family
- Five selections from the Fats and Oils Family
- Three selections from the Guiltless Desserts Family

Step 2

Each day consume at least:

- Three selections from the Fruit Family (at least one selection should be a high–vitamin C item)
- Three selections from the Vegetable Family (at least one selection should be a high–beta-carotene item)
- Six selections from the Grains and Starchy Vegetables Family (at least three selections should be whole-grain items)
- Two nonfat or low-fat selections from the Milk Products Family (if you choose a fattier selection, then deduct the extra fat from the Fats and Oils Family allotment below)

Consume no more than:

- Two selections from the Meat and Legumes Family
- Two selections from the Nutritious Fatty Foods Family

- Three selections from the Fats and Oils Family
- Two selections from the Guiltless Desserts Family

Step 3

Each day consume at least:

- Three selections from the Fruit Family (at least one selection should be a high–vitamin C item)
- Four selections from the Vegetable Family (at least two selections should be a high–beta-carotene item)
- Seven selections from the Grains and Starchy Vegetables Family (at least four selections should be whole-grain items)
- Three nonfat or low-fat selections from the Milk Products Family (if you choose a fattier selection, then deduct the extra fat from the Fats and Oils Family allotment below)

Consume no more than:

- Two selections from the Meat and Legumes Family
- One selection from the Nutritious Fatty Foods Family
- Two selections from the Fats and Oils Family
- One selection from the Guiltless Desserts Family

The Tortoise and the Hare

"But I want to feel good right now! Why can't I just move ahead to Step 3 and skip all the in-between dietary advice?" As mentioned in the introduction to this book, it is not dieting per se but how you adopt new eating habits that determines how successfully you will stick with your new eating plan. Rapid weight loss, radical changes in food intake or dietary habits, and other dramatic alterations in lifelong eating patterns wreak havoc with the brain chemicals that regulate appetite, body weight, and even basic survival instincts. The stricter the diet and the more rapid the changes, the more aggressive your brain chemicals are in trying to reestablish the old order.

On a more practical note, remember that it took years for you to develop your current eating habits. You have become accustomed to extra cheese in your lasagna and expect creamy gravy on your pot roast. To assume you can reprogram your taste buds overnight so they delight in a black bean and couscous casserole is asking more than the typical taste bud can deliver. Without the cooking skills or the taste for lower fat and less sweet fare, it is easy to feel overwhelmed, unhappy, deprived, or resentful of a new eating plan. Already burdened by depression, a sleep disorder, low energy, or other mood problems, you will soon begin wondering why you are bothering with this—yet another—diet.

By taking the Feeling Good Diet gradually, you'll gently reprogram your taste buds while you learn new cooking skills. This step-by-step approach works with, rather than against, your appetite-control and mood-altering brain chemicals, so you are more likely to feel and be successful.

In most cases, even only minor changes in fat, sugar, and caffeine intake can make dramatic differences in how you feel (see "A Word of Caution," page 281). For example:

- Eating something for breakfast, when typically you have skipped this meal, may be all it takes to boost your otherwise dwindling midmorning energy level.
- Replacing a sugary snack, such as a granola bar or piece of pie, with a bagel and nonfat cream cheese may soothe afternoon doldrums that might otherwise result in uncontrollable food cravings.
- Reducing the butter on your morning toast from 1 tablespoon to 2 teaspoons (a difference of only 1 teaspoon) can decrease the meal's fat calories by as much as 10 percent and help overcome cravings for fat.
- Replacing two beef tacos with two chicken tacos for lunch may decrease the fat from 46 percent to 33 percent of calories and keep you more alert after lunch.
- Switching from oil-packed to water-packed tuna can reduce the fat content of a meal by almost 20 percent, thus leaving more room for nutrient-packed foods.
- Replacing a soda pop with a glass of orange juice decreases your intake of refined sugar by nine teaspoons and helps avoid the blood-sugar roller coaster that can undermine mood.

Keep in mind that as you wean yourself from fat and sugar, the quantity and nutritional quality of your diet increases to make up for the lost calories. In short,

A Word of Caution

A note to the overzealous: While fat and sugar should be reduced, they shouldn't be eliminated. Fat is needed to help absorb the fat-soluble vitamins (A, D, E, and K), supply the essential fat called linoleic acid, and add variety to the diet. The body needs some salt (sodium) to regulate muscle and nerve function and maintain its natural fluid balance. Sugar adds taste and pleasure to a meal or snack. This dynamic trio is reduced, but you still can eat margarine, maple syrup, and turkey sausage in Step 3 of the Feeling Good Diet.

you eat more food for less calories! For those concerned about weight or figure, a bonus of the Feeling Good Diet is that you may lose excess body fat without really trying.

Reprogramming Your Taste Buds

If you are used to meals planned around meat; foods cooked or served with gravies, cream sauces, or butter; generous servings of dessert; fast-food lunches; or meals of only a bag of potato chips, then a light meal of pasta and salad can sound like a death penalty. The good news is that you can reprogram your taste buds to enjoy low-fat, high-carbohydrate fare.

Researchers at the Cancer Prevention Research Center in Seattle surveyed 448 women who had participated in nutrition classes to lower their fat intake. More than half of the participants reported that their love for fatty foods changed to a growing dislike for that creamy, greasy taste the longer they remained on a low-fat diet. More than 60 percent said they actually felt physical discomfort after eating high-fat foods. "The women had been consuming very high-fat diets—as high as 60 percent fat calories," says Elizabeth Burrows, M.S., R.D., researcher at the Cancer Prevention Research Center. Over the course of three to six months, the women lowered that fat intake to 20 percent. "They would go out to eat at a restaurant or friend's house, eat two or three fatty foods, and find they not only did not like the taste but had difficulty digesting the food," says Ms. Burrows. The secret is to make the adjustment gradually and avoid feeling deprived.

The Feeling Good Diet does just that. It slowly reduces the day's fat intake

TABLE 13.1 Food-Family List

The following are lists of foods grouped together based on their calorie and nutrient contents. This is only a sampling of foods, but it provides structure and specific examples when you begin adopting the Feeling Good Diet. As you become more comfortable with the dietary guidelines, you can branch out from these food families to include other low-fat, low-sugar foods.

Keep in mind that you can mix and match when and how you meet your quota of selections from each food family. For example, you may choose a hamburger bun or 2/3 cup of brown rice—each provides two selections from the Grains and Starchy Vegetables Family. Or you might choose to include 1 kiwi fruit at a meal, which is 1/2 selection from the Fruit category. In other words, do not mistake the words *selection size* to mean that you are allowed only the amount specified in these lists at any one meal.

FRUIT FAMILY (Step 1: 2 selections, Steps 2 and 3: 3 selections)

Each fruit and the amount stated here is equivalent to one selection of Fruit in the Feeling Good Diet. Each selection provides approximately 100 calories and 25 grams of carbohydrates. In general, these foods are also excellent sources of vitamin C, beta-carotene, trace minerals, and fiber. The dark orange varieties are especially good sources of beta-carotene, while orange juice is a good source of folic acid.

Consume at least 1 selection daily of the vitamin C–rich fruits marked with an asterisk (*).

ITEM	SELECTION SIZE
Apple	1 medium
Applesauce	3/4 cup
Apricots:	
fresh	6 small
canned without syrup	6 halves
Banana	1 medium
Berries:	
blackberries	1 1/4 cups
blueberries	1 1/4 cups
boysenberries	1 1/2 cups
raspberries	1 1/2 cups
strawberries*	2 cups

Cantaloupe*	2 cups cubed
Casaba melon	2 cups cubed
Cherries	20 large
Dates	4 medium
Figs, dried	2 medium
Fruit cocktail, canned without syrup	3/4 cup
Fruit Roll-Ups	2 rolls
Fruit salad, fresh	3/4 cup
Grapefruit*	1 medium
Grapes	1 cup
Honeydew melon*	1/2 medium
Juices:	
apple cider	6-ounce glass
apple juice	8-ounce glass
apricot nectar	6-ounce glass
grape	6-ounce glass
grapefruit*	8-ounce glass
orange*	8-ounce glass
papaya nectar	6-ounce glass
peach nectar	6-ounce glass
pear nectar	5-ounce glass
pineapple	8-ounce glass
prune	4-ounce glass
Kiwifruit*	2 small
Kumquats, raw	8 medium
Mandarin oranges, juice packed*	1 cup
Nectarine	1 large
Orange*	1 large
Papaya*	1 medium
Peaches:	
fresh	2 medium
canned without syrup	3/4 cup
Pear:	
fresh	1 large
canned without syrup	3 halves

Pineapple:	
fresh	1 cup
canned chunks	3/4 cup
Plums	3 medium
Pomegranate, raw	1 medium
Prunes	5 medium
Quince, raw	2 medium
Raisins	3 tablespoons
Tangerines*	2 large
Watermelon	2 cups cubed

VEGETABLE FAMILY (Step 1: 2 selections, Step 2: 3 selections, Step 3: 4 selections)

Each vegetable and its amount listed here is equivalent to one selection in the Feeling Good Diet. One selection provides approximately 50 calories, 10 grams of carbohydrates, and 4 grams of protein. These foods also are excellent sources of the antioxidant nutrients (beta-carotene and vitamin C), other vitamins, minerals, and fiber. Dark green leafy vegetables are particularly rich sources of beta-carotene and folic acid.

A selection is equivalent to 1 cup cooked, 2 cups raw, or the amount listed. Consume at least one selection (preferably two) of the beta-carotene–rich vegetables marked with an asterisk (*).

ITEM	SELECTION SIZE
Artichoke	1 medium
Artichoke hearts, canned, water-packed	
Asparagus*	
Bean sprouts	1 1/2 cups
Beans, green	
Beets	
Broccoli*	
Brussels sprouts	
Cabbage	
raw	3 cups shredded
cooked	1 1/2 cups
Carrots*	1 1/2 large or 2 medium
Carrot juice*	4-ounce glass
Cauliflower, cooked	1 1/2 cups

Chard,* cooked	$1\frac{1}{2}$ cups
Collards,* cooked	$1\frac{1}{2}$ cups
Dandelion greens,* cooked	$1\frac{1}{2}$ cups
Eggplant	
Kale*	
Leeks	
Mustard greens*	$1\frac{1}{2}$ cups
Okra	$\frac{3}{4}$ cup
Onions:	
raw	$\frac{3}{4}$ cup
cooked	$\frac{2}{3}$ cup
Parsnips	$\frac{1}{3}$ cup
Peas, green, cooked	$\frac{1}{2}$ cup
Rhubarb, frozen, raw	2 cups
Rutabaga	
Snow peas	$\frac{3}{4}$ cup
Tomatoes	2 medium
Tomato juice	8-ounce glass
Tomato paste	4 tablespoons
Tomato sauce	$\frac{2}{3}$ cup
Turnip greens,* cooked	2 cups
V8 Juice	8-ounce glass

GRAINS AND STARCHY VEGETABLES FAMILY (Step 1: 4 selections, Step 2: 6 selections, Step 3: 7 selections)

Each bread, cereal, starchy vegetable, rice, and pasta and its amount stated here is equal to one selection in the Feeling Good Diet and provides approximately 75 calories, 15 grams of carbohydrates, and 3 grams of protein. The whole-grain selections are also good sources of trace minerals, vitamins, and fiber, while the starchy vegetables, such as sweet potato or baked potato, are sources of either beta-carotene or vitamin C.

ITEM	SELECTION SIZE
Bagel	$\frac{1}{2}$ medium
Bread, whole wheat, rye, or white	1 slice
Cereal, cooked:	
oatmeal	$\frac{1}{2}$ cup

barley	1/2 cup
farina	1/2 cup
Cereal, cold:	
Grape-Nuts	1/3 cup
shredded wheat	1 large biscuit or 1/2 cup bite-size
puffed	1/2 cup
Cheerios	3/4 cup
cornflakes	3/4 cup
Corn kernels	1/2 cup
Corn-on-the-cob	1/2 8-inch ear
Crackers:	
Ry-Krisp	4
graham	3 2 1/2-inch squares
saltines	6
Dinner roll	1 small
English muffin	1/2
Flour	2 1/2 tablespoons
Hamburger bun	1/2
Hot dog bun	1/2
Noodles or pasta	1/2 cup
Lima beans	1/2 cup
Pita bread	1/2 pocket
Popcorn, plain, air-popped	2 cups
Potato:	
boiled or baked	1 small
mashed, plain	1/3 cup
Pumpkin	1 1/2 cups
Pretzels:	
thin sticks	55
three-ring	3
Rice	1/3 cup
Rice cake	2
Squash:	
acorn	3/4 cup

butternut	3/4 cup
hubbard	3/4 cup
Succotash	1/3 cup
Sweet potato, plain	1/2 cup
Tortilla, corn (not fried)	6-inch
Wheat germ	3 tablespoons
Yams, plain	1/2 cup

The following breads and cereals contain some fat. Reduce your intake of fat from other sources if one or more of these foods are included in your Feeling Good Diet. (Each selection contains approximately 1 teaspoon of fat.)

ITEM	**SELECTION SIZE**
Bread stuffing	1/4 cup
Corn bread	2-inch square
Crackers, Wheat Thins	15
Pancake	2
Taco shell	2
Tortilla, flour	8-inch
Waffle	4 1/2-inch square

Milk Products Family (Steps 1 and 2: 2 selections, Step 3: 3 selections)

Each food listed here is equal to one selection of a calcium-rich milk product in the Feeling Good Diet and provides approximately 100 calories, 15 grams of carbohydrates, and 9 grams of protein. In general, these foods also are excellent sources of magnesium, vitamin B2, and other vitamins and minerals. Fortified milk is the only dietary source of vitamin D.

ITEM	**SELECTION SIZE**
Buttermilk:	
fresh	1 cup
dried	4 tablespoons
Evaporated nonfat milk	1/2 cup
Nonfat milk	1 cup
Nonfat yogurt	3/4 cup
Powdered nonfat milk	1/3 cup

The following milk products also contain approximately 1 teaspoon of fat and an additional 45 calories per selection. Cut back on fatty foods if you choose one of these selections.

ITEM	SELECTION SIZE
Calcimilk (lactose-reduced low-fat milk)	1 cup
Cottage cheese, low-fat (2%)	3/4 cup
Lactaid (lactose-reduced low-fat milk)	1 cup
Low-fat milk (2%)	1 cup
Low-fat yogurt (2%)	1 cup
Soymilk (calcium-fortified)	1 cup

The following milk products contain just shy of 2 teaspoons of fat and an additional 60 calories, for a total of 160 calories per selection. Cut back even further on fatty foods if you choose one of these selections.

ITEM	SELECTION SIZE
Canned or evaporated milk	1/2 cup
Cheese:	
cottage cheese, creamed	3/4 cup
grated Parmesan	1/3 cup
low-fat cheeses with less than 150 calories per 2-ounce serving	1/3 cup
Goat's milk	1 cup
Whole milk	1 cup
Yogurt, plain	1 cup

Meat and Legumes Family (Steps 1, 2, and 3: 2 selections)

The following meats (or the equivalent in legumes or eggs) cooked without fat or oil are equal to one selection in the Feeling Good Diet and provide approximately 150 calories, 21 grams of protein, and 2 teaspoons or less of fat. These foods also are excellent sources of trace minerals such as iron and zinc as well as the B vitamins.

ITEM	SELECTION SIZE
Dried beans and peas	1 1/2 cups
Beef—chipped, flank steak, London broil, round steak, stew meat, tenderloin, filet mignon, top round roast	3 ounces

Veal—chop, steak, roast	3 ounces
Pork—boiled ham, Canadian bacon (high in salt), tenderloin	3 ounces
Poultry—chicken without skin, Cornish game hen, pheasant, quail, turkey without skin	3 ounces
Fish—bass, catfish, flounder, halibut, red snapper, sole, turbot	4 ounces
Cod	5 ounces
Shellfish—clams, crabs, shrimp	4 ounces
Scallops	5 ounces
Tuna, canned in water	4 ounces
Turkey luncheon meat (95% fat-free)	5 slices
Eggs (high in fat)	2
Egg substitute	1/3 cup

NUTRITIOUS FATTY FOODS FAMILY (Steps 1 and 2: 2 selections, Step 3: 1 selection)

Each of the following foods is a good source of two or more nutrients, but comes with a high-fat price tag. Each selection provides approximately 100 calories and between 1 1/2 and 2 teaspoons of fat. Ideally, these foods should be limited to no more than two selections per day.

ITEM	SELECTION SIZE
Avocado	1/4 medium
Beef—ground, sirloin steak, porterhouse, rib roast, ribs, T-bone steak	1 ounce
Cheese—full-fat hard cheeses including American, Cheddar, Brie, feta, gouda, Swiss	1 ounce
Ice cream	1/3 cup
Lamb—breast, crown roast, chop, shoulder, rib roast	1 ounce
Luncheon meats—bologna, hot dogs, turkey hot dogs, Italian sausage, salami, Spam	1 ounce
Nuts:	
almonds	2 tablespoons
Brazil	5 teaspoons medium
cashews	2 tablespoons medium
hazelnuts	2 tablespoons

macadamia	6 medium
peanuts	2 tablespoons large
peanuts, Spanish	2 tablespoons
pecans	8 large halves
pistachios	2 tablespoons
walnuts	8 halves
Peanut butter	1 level tablespoon
Pork—ribs, spareribs, drained sausage, steak	1 ounce
Seeds:	
pumpkin	1/3 cup
sesame	2 tablespoons
sunflower	2 tablespoons

Fats and Oils Family (Step 1: 5 selections, Step 2: 3 selections, Step 3: 2 selections)

The following selections of fats in the Feeling Good Diet provide approximately 100 calories and 2 or more teaspoons (10+ grams) of fat. These foods should be kept to a minimum when planning menus, preparing food, and ordering in a restaurant.

ITEM	SELECTION SIZE
Bacon	2 strips
Butter	1 tablespoon
Chocolate, unsweetened	2/3 square or 2/3 ounce
Coconut	1/2 ounce
Coffee whitener:	
liquid	1/2 cup
powder	8 teaspoons
Cream cheese	2 tablespoons
Cream, heavy	2 tablespoons
Cream, sour	3 tablespoons
Margarine:	
regular	1 tablespoon
diet	4 teaspoons
Mayonnaise	1 tablespoon

Oil	2 teaspoons
Olives, black	20
Salad dressing:	
low-calorie	Varies—check label
regular	2 tablespoons
Tartar sauce	4 tablespoons

GUILTLESS DESSERTS FAMILY (Step 1: 3 selections, Step 2: 2 selections, Step 3: 1 selection)

Desserts add pleasure and fun to the day's menu, and when chosen from the following selections, can be low in fat and nutritious. Each of the following guiltless desserts and "sweets" provides approximately 100 calories with no fat. Serving sizes are moderate to limit sugar intake. Remember, fresh fruits also make excellent desserts and contain no fat or refined sugar.

ITEM	SELECTION SIZE
Cake (no frosting):	
angel food	2-inch slice
sponge	2-inch slice
Cookies:	
animal crackers	20
vanilla wafers	5
Fruit ice	$1/2$ cup
Gelatin, fruit-flavored	$2/3$ cup
Honey	$1\,1/2$ tablespoons
Jam or jelly	2 tablespoons
Molasses	2 tablespoons
Sherbet	$1/3$ cup
Sugar, brown or table	2 tablespoons
Syrup, corn or maple	2 tablespoons

FREEBIES FAMILY

The following foods contain negligible calories and can be included in the diet without affecting the calorie content, while still providing small amounts of vitamins, minerals, and fiber.

Celery
Cucumbers
Endive
Green onions
Lettuce
Mushrooms
Parsley
Peppers—green, red, or chili
Radishes
Spinach
Summer squash
Zucchini

Catsup (limit to 1 tablespoon a day)
Club soda
Decaffeinated coffee
Gelatin, unflavored, plain
Herbs and spices
Lemon juice
Mustard

---

from the typical 37 percent of total calories to approximately 25 percent. It also gradually lowers sugar and caffeine intake, two dietary ingredients that contribute to mood swings, sleep problems, and fatigue. In addition, numerous tricks-of-the-trade incorporated into the Feeling Good Diet help satisfy your taste needs without fat and sugar (see Table 13.2). These and other meal-planning tips are discussed in detail in chapter 14.

Tailor Made for Good Health

The Feeling Good Diet avoids the "canned menu" plans of many other dieting methods—guidelines that left many people feeling defeated before they even began. Restrictive fad diets are a temporary fix for the lifelong challenge of attaining and maintaining emotional well-being. Granted, very low-fat diets (ones in which 20 percent of calories come from fat) help prevent, and possibly even regress, heart disease; but most people who switch overnight to low-fat fare have trouble sticking with the program. A healthful eating style, gradually tailored to your preferences, tastes, and time demands, can do wonders for your mental, emotional, and physical well-being, while providing a plan you can stick with.

You have two options with the Feeling Good Diet. If you need structure, at least when starting out, then follow Steps 1, 2, and 3 and the Food-Family Eating Plans (see pages 276 and 278–79). Menus based on these guidelines can be found in chapter 14. Follow these guidelines until they are habits and remember to take it slow. Even tailoring your diet for Step 1 may take weeks or months, depending on how much these recommendations differ from your customary diet and your level of commitment. The pace is up to you. When the Step 1 guidelines are habit, move in a similar fashion to Step 2, and then Step 3.

A less-structured option is to design your own three-step program based on the goals of the Feeling Good Diet outlined on page 274. You may want to use some of the Food-Family Eating Plan but personalize the guidelines to meet your specific needs. For example, you may have already reduced your dietary intake of fats from meats and added oils, and your main goal is to reduce the cravings for chocolate and ice cream that are contributing to your mood swings. You may already be following Step 3 of the Food-Family Eating Plan when it comes to fats and oils, meat and legumes, and low-fat milk products, but need a program for reaching the goals of Step 1 for desserts. After reading about insomnia in chapter 9, you may decide that caffeine is a primary concern. You may therefore choose to focus your

TABLE 13.2 Plan for Reprogramming Your Taste Buds

By following the three-step program outlined in the Feeling Good Diet, you slowly reduce your intake of fat and sugar and increase the fiber, vitamins, and minerals. And you eat more food for the same calories! In general, the steps in this eating plan provide nutritional values as follows. Add more selections from the Fruit, Vegetable, Grains and Starchy Vegetables Families or a nonfat selection from the Milk Products Family to increase your calorie intake.

	CALORIES	FAT (% OF CALORIES)	SUGAR (% OF CALORIES)
Step 1	2,000	37	20
Step 2	2,000	30	15
Step 3	2,000	25*	10

*Except in the cases of breast-cancer prevention and regression of heart disease, there appear to be no added benefits to reducing fat intake below 25 percent of total calories.

dietary goals on Step 3 for caffeine and tackle other dietary goals at a later date.

The less structured option requires more time and organization, but gives you the opportunity to tailor a plan specifically to your dietary needs. Read the portions of this book that pertain to your health concerns, and use that dietary information to target the dietary changes that will produce the results you want.

Before You Begin

The first step to feeling better is to assess whether you are willing to do what it takes to get where you want to be. The secret to establishing new habits is to have a plan, to make changes gradually, to see the new habits as fun, and to congratulate yourself for every small step made toward your ultimate goal. Make sure you are ready and willing to take the time and make the effort to change. The self-assessment quiz on page 295 is one way to measure your motivation and commitment to feeling your best.

Making Changes in Your Life

Next to the genes you were born with, lifestyle habits are the most powerful shapers of your mood. Those habits didn't begin yesterday; day in and day out, year in and year out, you have repeated those patterns and routines. So telling yourself to "eat right" or "exercise more" won't make those lifelong habits go away. You need a realistic plan, a few basic skills in changing behavior, and a way to stay motivated through the tough times. You must identify the habits that have contributed to your mood problems, set realistic goals, and practice effective tactics for developing new habits.

The Feeling Good Diet has taken some of the guesswork out of setting goals and designing strategies. If you move gradually through the three-step plan, you will slowly reprogram your taste buds without feeling deprived or overwhelmed. Your goals will be realistic, achievable, and specific. However, you may choose to subdivide these goals into weekly mini-goals, such as planning to replace your high-sugar midmorning snack with a piece of fruit. These mini-goals work well within the framework of the Feeling Good Diet and increase your chances for success in making dietary changes.

The Food and Mood Journal (see page 297) and other record-keeping forms in

QUIZ 13.1 Are You Ready and Willing to Make a Change?

Changing dietary habits, even when the steps are small, requires a commitment to stick with it. Before you take the plunge, be sure you are ready and willing to do what it takes to feel your best. In short, is this the best time for you to take charge of your diet?

Using a scale of 1 to 5 (1 = not at all, 5 = more so than ever), answer the following questions:

_______ **1.** Compared to attempts in the past to change your eating habits, how motivated are you to stick with it this time?

_______ **2.** How determined are you to stick with the Feeling Good Diet until you reach your dietary goals?

_______ **3.** Eating right when you're feeling down requires effort. How willing are you to take the time and make the effort to reach your goals?

_______ **4.** Dietary changes should be made gradually. If you tackle too many dietary changes too fast, you are likely to fail. Are you willing to take it slowly, possibly taking a year or more to reprogram your taste buds and redesign your diet, if the end result is having more energy and feeling your best?

_______ **5.** How much support for your dieting efforts can you expect from friends, family, coworkers, and other people around you?

_______ **6.** Learning new eating habits is like developing any new skill—it requires time. How much time do you have to make permanent changes in your life?

Scoring:

6 to 16: Reflects a low commitment to making dietary changes and a high likelihood of failure. Wait and try another time.

17 to 23: Reflects a moderate commitment to make dietary changes that will help you feel, think, and sleep better. However, you still need to work on motivation.

24 or higher: Reflects high motivation. This may be the best time to venture down the dietary road to feeling your best.

this book are essential for making those dietary changes. You can't change behavior until you know what behaviors you need to change. Keeping a journal or written record of your eating habits is the only way to identify which behaviors are contributing to your mood problems. Since memory is inaccurate and often biased, writing down information on when, what, and why you eat and how you feel before and after eating provides accurate feedback.

Keep these detailed records for one to two weeks, and you will note patterns. Everything you do is triggered by something, so watch for the thoughts, moods, events, and circumstances that begin an eating episode. Note the foods you've eaten just before a change in mood. These patterns are clues about the conditions, thoughts, and feelings that cause you to eat inappropriately, and can help you identify how foods affect the way you feel. You'll be able then to develop strategies for making changes in your habits. Granted, keeping records takes time and commitment; however, it is one of the most important skills you will learn!

Look for high-risk situations when you are likely to overeat, eat sugary or sweet-and-creamy foods, or experience low energy and undesirable moods. A high-risk situation is any time you are tempted to waver from the Feeling Good Diet. It might be a depressing moment, another person, a particular place, a specific event, a time of the day or season of the year, a high-stress period, or easy availability of specific foods such as coffee or dessert. High-risk situations can include discouraging thoughts or excuses we find for why it is all right to slip from the Feeling Good Diet. Feelings such as fatigue, happiness, loneliness, or anxiety do trigger emotional eating, but remember that your nutritional needs are greatest during these emotionally stressful times and poor eating habits will only make the situation worse.

Once you have set realistic goals, identified the behaviors you want to change, and learned what triggers those inappropriate habits, the next step is to develop tactics that will encourage new habits. These tactics are as varied as the people who use them and include:

- Shopping from a shopping list
- Discarding problem foods currently in the kitchen
- Eating at regular times
- Planning snacks
- Sending leftover desserts home with guests
- Avoiding the person, situation, or event that upsets you

WORKSHEET 13.1 The Food and Mood Journal

This worksheet will help you develop a clear picture of your eating habits and daily fluctuations in mood. It is essential that the information in this journal be specific, filled out promptly and honestly, and complete. Fill in the time and complete each column whenever you eat or drink, including meals, snacks, a glass of water—even a stick of gum.

Use a scale from 0 to 5 for the Hunger column: 0 = not hungry, 5 = very hungry. Use a different color pen to mark all foods and beverages that contain sugar or caffeine. Use this sheet as a master for making additional copies.

DATE:____________________

TIME	FOOD/ BEVERAGE	AMOUNT	HUNGER	WHERE?	WITH WHOM?	DOING WHAT ELSE?	FEELINGS BEFORE/AFTER

- Taking a walk to calm yourself when you can't avoid a stressful situation
- Substituting negative thoughts, beliefs, and attitudes with positive, encouraging ones

Refer to chapter 14 for more information on tactics useful in applying the Feeling Good Diet to shopping, preparing foods at home, and ordering foods in restaurants. For further tips on how to begin your new regime, see "Getting Started," page 299.

How you think and feel about making the dietary changes influences how much you eat or whether you stick with a new eating plan. It is important to understand and untangle the connections between eating and feelings. Certain beliefs or attitudes can cause problems. For example, an "all-or-nothing" belief that you must never eat a forbidden food can lead to feelings of failure. This type of thinking—not the cheating—weakens your control. Examine your beliefs, attitudes, and thoughts and counteract negative ones with realistic and positive ones.

Constantly remind yourself that it took a long time to develop the habits you have. Be patient with yourself as you take the steps to identify and replace old patterns with new eating habits that help you feel your best. Set realistic goals, keep records, plan and practice your new behaviors until they become habit, and develop a reward system that keeps you motivated. It doesn't matter if you slip off your regime every now and then. What matters is that you plan to do something about it to prevent the slip in the future.

You're Worth It!

There may be a simple answer to your lack of energy, depression, sleep disturbances, stress-related problems, or inability to concentrate. But even if these problems stem from factors other than your nutrition, eating well is the foundation for getting well. You don't have to feel this way. There is hope. That hope lies in making a lifelong commitment to be the best and healthiest you. Set a realistic image in your mind's eye of how you want to feel and look, and then make small daily adjustments to reach those goals, based on the Feeling Good Diet. This plan requires commitment to modifying your eating habits—but you're worth it, don't you think?

Getting Started

Here is a step-by-step guide for beginning the Feeling Good Diet.

1. Copy one week's worth of the worksheet on page 297, the Food and Mood Journal. Keep an accurate record of what foods, how much, when, and where you ate, how you felt before eating and during the one hour following eating, and any other related information that will help you recognize food-mood patterns, high-risk situations where you are likely to overeat or eat the wrong foods, situations that trigger snack attacks, or even how much you are eating. Be specific, accurate, and thorough in your record keeping. Remember, keeping records is not a test; there are no right or wrong answers, just feedback on how what you eat could be affecting how you feel. Be honest!
2. Review your Food and Mood Journal and complete the worksheet on page 300.
3. Familiarize yourself with the Feeling Good Diet, its philosophy, the Food-Family Eating Plans, and the Food-Family List.
4. Compare your eating style, based on information obtained from your journal and the self-assessment, to the Feeling Good Diet and the specific dietary information in the chapters pertinent to your mood problems. Choose the dietary changes you want to make in order for you to feel better. This may be as simple as adopting the dietary guidelines in Step 1 of the diet or choosing to mix and match these recommendations to better suit your food and mood needs.
5. Refer to chapter 14 for sample menus and tips on shopping, food preparation, and ordering meals in restaurants.
6. Practice new eating habits until they become automatic. (This step can take one week to one year or longer. If you adhere to the Feeling Good Diet guidelines, you should begin feeling better within a few weeks. It may take 12 weeks or more to reprogram your taste buds.)
7. Graduate to Step 2 in the diet and practice these new eating habits until they become automatic.
8. Graduate to Step 3 in the diet and practice these new eating habits until they become automatic.

WORKSHEET 13.2 A Look at Your Food and Mood Journal

Complete this self-assessment after keeping your Food and Mood Journal for at least one week. Look for patterns and trends that will help you design a personalized diet.

1. What times of the day and night did you most frequently eat? What patterns do you see? ______________________________

____

2. What patterns do you see in your food and beverage intake? How did snacks, skipping a meal, or unplanned eating affect your caloric intake? How did portion sizes affect your intake? Does caffeine or sugar affect your food intake? ______________________________

____

3. How did you feel before eating and during the first hour after eating? Do you see any patterns? ______________________________

____

4. What moods and feelings are associated with eating? Do you eat more or less when you are calm, relaxed, agitated, stressed, tired, or angry? ______________________________

____

5. What was your most frequent reason for eating? What patterns do you notice between foods eaten and feelings before and after you ate? ______________________________

____

6. Where did you eat most frequently? What connections do you see between the locations and your food intake? ______________________________

____

7. Who did you eat with? Did you tend to eat more or less with certain people? ______________________________

____

8. What activities were most strongly linked with eating? ______________________________

____

9. Describe the consequences linked with your eating. Do you see any patterns? ________

____

10. If you kept the journal for more than two weeks, did you notice any cyclical changes in your food intake or mood—for example, did you crave foods more during certain times of the month?____

____

CHAPTER FOURTEEN

Putting the Feeling Good Diet into Practice

The Shopping Tour

The healthful meals and snacks in the Feeling Good Diet begin with healthful ingredients. Following the diet will help you foster the skills needed to ferret out the fat and sugar when you shop, to choose wholesome foods, and to select foods that give the greatest nutritional yield for the lowest fat and sugar cost. In general, most of the nutritious foods are found on the periphery of the store, including the produce section, the bakery, the dairy case, and the meat department. The aisles in the middle stock the highly processed nutritional losers, such as chips, cookies, overly salted soups, and sugary breakfast bars, although some nutritious beans, grains, and low-fat canned goods can be found there too. Here are three easy rules for shopping:

1. Check the percentage of fat indicated on the label and purchase only products that contain 30 percent or less fat calories. This is the equivalent of no more than 3 grams of fat for every 100 calories. To check a product's fat content, multiply the grams of fat in a serving by 9, divide by the total number of calories, and multiply by 100. For example, suppose a label states that a serving supplies 4 grams of fat and 150 calories. So, 4 grams x 9 calories/gram = 36 calories divided by 150 calories = .24 x 100 = 24 percent fat calories.

2. Check the sugar content. Since many products do not list refined sugar directly, read the ingredients list and avoid any product that

lists sugar as one of the first three ingredients or that lists sugar (or any related sweeteners, including fructose, corn syrup, and honey) more than once for every five ingredients.

3. Keep it simple—purchase foods that are minimally processed. For example, choose 100 percent whole wheat bread rather than white bread; 100 percent fruit juice rather than a fruit juice blend; plain brown rice rather than seasoned rice mixes; fresh fish or chicken rather than processed meats; plain fresh or frozen vegetables rather than vegetables frozen in sauces; low-fat or nonfat plain yogurt rather than fruited yogurt; and whole fresh potatoes rather than scalloped or French-fried potatoes.

Now, let's take a shopping tour for more nutritious food purchases.

Produce Potpourri

What would you think if someone told you there are foods that are delicious, fat- and cholesterol-free, high in nutrients, and can help protect you from cancer, heart disease, premature aging, fatigue, and possibly memory loss? These miracle foods are nothing more than the fruits and vegetables you've been told to eat ever since you were young. They include luscious strawberries, juicy cherries, dribble-down-your-chin papaya, sweet watermelon, mouth-watering zucchini with garlic, refreshing cucumbers and tomatoes, and scrumptious cantaloupe.

It is easy to complain about all the foods you have to give up in order to eat better. But do you realize how many delicious foods you'll be eating more often? Fruits and vegetables supply hefty doses of vitamins, minerals, and fiber for very few calories and no fat (with the exception of avocados and olives). Yet nine out of ten people consume less than the minimum recommended servings of five fruits and vegetables a day (a better goal is seven to nine servings daily). Researchers from the National Cancer Institute in Bethesda, Maryland, reported that 45 percent of Americans consume no fruit in a day and 22 percent don't eat vegetables. Indeed, the average American consumes only about three servings of fruits and vegetables daily. Just about everyone should be spending more time in the produce department.

Left untouched by food manufacturers, there is no such thing as a bad vegetable or fruit. However, some are better than others. For example, iceberg lettuce is the nutritional equivalent of water, while romaine lettuce is packed with nutrients at the same calorie cost. Celery sticks, cucumbers, and bean sprouts add fat-free crunch to the diet, but nutrients are not their strength. On the other hand, dark green leafy vegetables and orange fruits and vegetables are superheroes when it comes to vitamin and mineral content. So purchase enough dark green and orange vegetables to supply at least two servings per person daily (see "Your Best Fruits and Vegetables," page 305). If time is your excuse for not eating more vegetables and fruits, look for prewashed and chopped vegetables, shredded cabbage, bags of bite-size carrots for snacking, peeled and cored pineapple, jars of minced garlic, and prepared fresh fruit salads in the produce department. Frozen berries and melons also add variety without adding time to meal preparation.

Which Is Best—Fresh, Frozen, or Canned?

If you are fortunate enough to have access to produce straight from the farm, then fresh is best. However, the longer that fruits and vegetables sit in a warehouse or grocery store, the more vitamins they lose. When selecting fresh produce, always choose crisp, plump, firm, and unbruised items. (To tell whether a fruit is ripe, smell it at room temperature. If it smells the way you want it to taste, then it probably is ripe.) Buying produce in season is one way to ensure freshness and reduce cost. Remember to purchase only quantities that you can eat within a few days.

If superfresh produce is not available, then your next best bet is frozen vegetables. Frozen vegetables have been processed immediately after harvest and are a better choice for people who cannot buy very fresh produce. Avoid purchasing packages of frozen vegetables that have ice crystals on the outside, since the frost is a sign that the packages have thawed and refrozen. To avoid losing nutrients and overall quality, immediately transfer frozen vegetables to your freezer at home; do not allow them to thaw in transit.

Canned vegetables are the last resort. The heating process used in canning destroys much of the vitamin C and folic acid, as well as some other vitamins, while salt and sugar often are added to canned fruits and vegetables. If you choose canned vegetables, never purchase cans that have been dented or that are rusting or bulging, and always use them within a year of purchase.

Your Best Fruits and Vegetables

All fresh fruits and vegetables (except olives and avocados) are low in fat, salt, added sugar, and calories and are high in fiber, vitamins, and minerals. However, some fruits and vegetables receive gold stars even among this prestigious group. (See "Recipes for Feeling Your Best," page 367), for more fruit and vegetable snack ideas.) The following fruits supply an extra dose of vitamin C, beta-carotene, and potassium, for approximately 50 to 75 calories per serving.

Apricots (4)
Cantaloupe (1/4)
Grapefruit (1/2)
Kiwifruit (1)
Mango (1/2)
Nectarine (1)
Orange (1)
Papaya (1/2)
Peaches (2)
Persimmon (1)
Raspberries (1 cup)
Strawberries (1 cup)
Tangerines (2)
Watermelon (2 cups)

The following vegetables supply ample amounts of beta-carotene, vitamin C, and/or folic acid, as well as fiber, iron, or calcium in each serving.

Asparagus (1/2 cup cooked)
Broccoli (1/2 cup cooked)
Brussels sprouts (1/2 cup cooked)
Carrot (1)
Collard greens (1/2 cup frozen)
Green peas (1/2 cup cooked)
Kale (1/2 cup cooked)
Mustard greens (1/2 cup cooked)
Red or green bell pepper, raw (1/2)
Romaine lettuce (1 cup)
Spinach (1/2 cup cooked, or 1 cup raw)
Sweet potato (1)
Swiss chard (1/2 cup cooked)

Your best bets for canned fruits and vegetables are those very difficult or impossible to obtain fresh, such as water chestnuts, bamboo shoots, and baby corn. Artichoke hearts (canned in water) and hearts of palm add variety and taste to salads. Canned corn, beets, tomato paste and sauce, and pumpkin are also nutritious selections that add quick vegetables to a meal. Fruits canned in their own juice, such as pineapple, cherries, mandarin oranges, pears, and peaches, or pureed fruit, such as applesauce, are nutritious foods to keep on hand for quick meals and snacks.

What About the Wax Coating on Produce?

Waxes formulated from plants and petroleum sources are used to replace the natural waxes of some vegetables that are removed during washing and to retain moisture during shipping. They also improve the appearance of these vegetables and fruits by reducing bruising during shipping and help prevent the growth of molds and other pathogens. Waxes are used on a variety of produce, including apples, peppers, cucumbers, eggplants, lemons, melons, oranges, peaches, pineapples, sweet potatoes, and tomatoes; however, not all fruits and vegetables are always treated with wax.

Wax coatings have been approved by the U.S. Food and Drug Administration as a safe addition to foods. However, a few wax coatings are made from animal products and are not suitable for people following a vegetarian or kosher diet. Another concern is not the wax but the pesticides and fungicides that often are sealed in with the wax. Since federal law requires wax labeling by shippers and retailers, you can ask your grocer for information on which fruits and vegetables at your store have been treated with wax.

What About Pesticides?

Although the evidence is not conclusive, you probably are better off avoiding pesticides on your fruits and vegetables if possible. The Environmental Protection Agency (EPA) reports that approximately seventy pesticides now in use are "probable" or "possible" cancer-causing agents. Several studies suggest—but do not prove—that exposure to low levels of pesticides for long periods of time can be harmful. For example, researchers at Mount Sinai School of Medicine and New York University Medical Center analyzed blood samples of women with and without breast cancer. They found that women who had the highest levels of DDE in their blood (a breakdown product of the pesticide DDT, banned from use more than a decade ago) were four times as likely to develop breast cancer as women with low levels of the pesticide residue.

While regulations on pesticide use are enforced somewhat in the United States, in other countries, regulations (if there are any) may not be enforced. Consequently, produce coming into the United States from other countries may contain illegal residues or levels of pesticides not allowed in this country. These foods are the ones to limit or avoid, if possible.

Despite the unanswered questions about pesticides, people should be eating more fruits and vegetables. For one thing, the permissible residue levels already include hefty margins of safety, so they are likely to be protective even if studies show some produce might contain too much. To limit your pesticide exposure, purchase certified organic produce or locally grown produce when possible, peel all waxed produce, and thoroughly wash all other produce (see "How to Reduce Your Exposure to Pesticides," below).

Keep in mind that pesticide residues also are found in meat, poultry, fish, butter, grains, and other foods. You can cut down on your risk by removing the fat, since that's where some pesticides are concentrated. The bottom line is that regardless of the pesticide controversy, fresh fruits and vegetables are the most nutritious foods in the diet and should be consumed in greater quantities.

The Grain Exchange

Along with fresh fruits and vegetables, grains have top billing in the Feeling Good Diet. In essence, there are no bad grains, as long as they are wholesome and

---

How to Reduce Your Exposure to Pesticides

1. Wash all produce. Add a drop or two of soap to the water to help remove pesticides and rinse thoroughly.
2. Use a vegetable scrub brush for potatoes, sweet potatoes, carrots, and other hard-surface produce whose skin you plan to eat.
3. Chop spinach, cauliflower, broccoli, and other produce with irregular surfaces before you wash it.
4. Peel nonorganic produce that has been treated with a wax coating, including cucumbers, apples, and eggplant.
5. Discard the outer leaves of iceberg and other head lettuce and cabbage. Trim the leaves and top from celery.
6. Purchase organically grown produce (labeled "Certified Organic") or produce grown locally with no pesticides.

---

minimally processed. Although the whole-grain varieties are more nutrient-packed, even white bread, rice, and "enriched" noodles give you a nice dose of complex carbohydrates for little or no fat and sugar. However, there are a few guidelines for sifting the wheat from the chaff when it comes to purchasing grains.

The Name Game

You can't tell a grain by its name. A bread labeled "Light Whole-Grain Sourdough" may sound like a 100 percent whole-grain product, but it actually contains mostly white flour with only a dusting of whole-grain flour. Some commercial breads with "Twelve Grain" in the name have little more fiber than white bread. Names like "Country," "Multigrain," and "Wheat" often are used for refined grains in disguise. A frozen waffle called "Fruit and Nut" may contain as little as 1/30 of an apple and 1/4 teaspoon of raisins as its fruit portion, while another brand of frozen waffles described as "Homestyle Blueberry" actually contains no blueberries at all.

When selecting products made from grains—from bread, frozen waffles, and crackers to noodles, rice, and bagels—ignore the name and go straight to the ingredients list. Purchase those products that list whole wheat flour (not wheat flour), brown rice, oats, or another whole grain or grain product as the first ingredient. If the label on a loaf of bread, a box of crackers, a bag of cookies, or a package of frozen pancakes does not read 100 percent whole wheat flour, assume the item is made primarily from refined flour. Granted, white bread is still a grain product, but its wholeness is gone. A slice of white bread has a fraction of the folic acid, chromium, selenium, and several other nutrients found in a slice of whole wheat bread.

Next, check the label for fiber content. While two slices of 100 percent whole wheat bread contain 4 grams of fiber, the same serving of sourdough bread contains almost none. Unfortunately, many manufacturers pump up their nutrient-poor white bread by merely adding processed fiber. So in addition to a high fiber content, you must find a whole-grain listing before you can assume the product is a reliable nutrition source.

Where's the Fat, Sugar, and Salt?

Check the fat and sugar content on food labels. By nature, grains are almost fat- and sugar-free. In general, the more processed a grain product is, the more likely it will be high in fat, sugar, and/or salt. Your best bet is to select only those cereals, crackers, and breads that contain 1 gram of fat or less for every 100 calories; at worst, select those with no more than 3 grams of fat for every 100 calories. Avoid products that have fatty additions, such as the cheese put into some crackers. Read the label and steer clear of any grain product—especially ready-to-eat cereals—that lists sugar (under any of its names) in the top three ingredients (see "Sweet Without Sugar," page 310).

Find out how much salt is in those packaged grain products, too. Did you know that many seasoned rice mixes contain more salt than canned soup—or as much as a teaspoon of salt per serving? You can avoid a salt overdose by selecting products that come with separate seasoning packages. Add only half the package (and none of the recommended fat), and you'll cut the salt in half. Skip the packaged rice that includes vegetables in the mix; usually the vegetable "crumbs" are mixed into the seasoning packet so you get a skimpy teaspoon of vegetables. You're better off buying brown rice and mixing it with plain vegetables at home. In fact, most packaged rice and noodle mixes are much more expensive and not as nutritious as the homemade version.

The Meat Market

Even as recently as a few years ago, meat held center stage at most meals. People planned their dinner around a main course of beef, pork, or other meats. A breakfast of bacon and eggs was considered a hearty way to start the day. Meat also was included in sandwiches, soups, and salads at lunch.

Times have changed. Although meat is an iron-rich food, it takes only 3 ounces a day (roughly the size of a deck of cards) to maximize all of its nutritional benefits. Consume any more and the increased intake of saturated fat, protein, and cholesterol will compromise your health by increasing your risk of developing heart disease, cancer, and other degenerative diseases. In fact, you could eliminate meat from your diet and replace it with more servings of cooked dried beans and peas with no harm to your nutritional status.

Sweet Without Sugar

Apple juice concentrate and pureed fruits such as bananas, apples, and prunes can be used to replace some of the fat and sugar in recipes. When you omit or reduce the sugar, honey, or other sweeteners, you can add sweetness with one of the following spices or with extracts that provide a sweet flavor, such as vanilla, almond, and cherry.

- *Allspice*. Use to season baked products such as muffins and breads; also vegetables such as carrots, winter squash, and sweet potatoes.
- *Anise*. These seeds give breads and desserts a unique licorice flavor.
- *Cardamom*. The unique flavor of this spice is good in curries or to flavor winter squash, sweet potatoes, breads, cakes, and cookies.
- *Cinnamon*. Use the sticks to give a spicy flavor to hot beverages; use ground cinnamon in baked goods, fruit sauces, stews, and puddings; also with carrots, sweet potatoes, and baked apples.
- *Cloves*. The most aromatic spice, it adds flavor to hot beverages, beets, carrots, sweet potatoes, winter squash, baked goods, meats, stews, and soups.
- *Coriander* (also called *cilantro*). Fresh coriander has a sharp, citrus-rind flavor that is good in salads and spicy casseroles, soups, and stews. The ground seeds impart a nutty flavor to rice, dried beans, shellfish, poultry, vegetables, salsa, and salads.
- *Ginger*. The fresh root is peeled and grated to add spice to marinades and with steamed vegetables, chicken, or fish. Use ground ginger in baking and marinades, rice dishes, and soups, and in preparing carrots, beets, and squash.
- *Mace*. Similar in taste to nutmeg but milder (it is the fibrous covering on the nutmeg seed), this spice enhances the flavor of broccoli, carrots, cauliflower, Brussels sprouts, baked goods, and puddings.
- *Mint*. Choose from more than thirty types of mint (fresh is most flavorful and sweet) to enhance grains, vegetable and fruit salads, iced teas, peas, corn, beans, cucumbers, carrots, and potatoes.
- *Nutmeg*. A nutty, versatile spice that brings out the best in spinach, broccoli, cauliflower, carrots, Brussels sprouts, onions, beans, and sweet potatoes; excellent in sauces, pasta, stews, and low-fat desserts.
- *Pumpkin pie spice*. A blend of nutmeg, cinnamon, cloves, and ginger that adds a sweet flavor to winter squash, sweet potatoes, and carrots, as well as fruit desserts such as baked apples.

If you do choose to eat meat, make sure it is extra-lean. Don't assume that ground chicken or turkey is low in fat. Purchase only ground meats with a fat content of 9 percent or less by weight (which means meat ground from chicken breast or turkey breast only).

Cast a wary eye at the meat department, and don't assume anything. For example, chicken and turkey were not created equal; chicken is one and a half times as fatty as turkey. Chicken also is not always leaner than beef. For example, a 4-ounce serving of chicken thigh meat contains more fat than an equal serving of fat-trimmed sirloin or chuck arm pot roast. In general, however, stick to white meats such as chicken and turkey breast. Avoid all products with a label that lists chicken or turkey, since they probably contain poultry parts, including the fatty skin. Instead, look for breast meat on the label.

Choose only beef with a grade of Select on the label. If there is no grade specified, the meat can have any fat content up to Prime or Choice, which signifies the highest grade and the fattiest cuts. Stick with round steak, including top, eye, bottom, and tip. Pork may be light in color, but it is not as lean as chicken or turkey, and may have a third or more of its calories from fat.

The Deli Dilemma

Nowhere in the grocery store is a wary eye more needed than at the deli meat case. Those hot dogs and other sandwich meats may have had a low-fat facelift, but don't take the label claims at face value. Turkey bologna, which in many cases advertises that it is 80 percent fat-free, actually may contain 12 grams of fat in two slices—or the equivalent of almost three teaspoons of grease.

Calculate the fat calories in the new turkey hot dogs. Even though the label reads 82 percent fat-free, these products can be 50 percent or more fat calories. Ignore the words *lite*, *healthy*, and *lean* on luncheon meats and hot dogs. They are no guarantee of a low-fat product. Steer clear of any product that does not provide fat information on the label, since not listing fat numbers suggests the manufacturer has something—like fat—to hide. Your best bet is to limit your choices to only those products that state 96 percent fat-free; even then, you'd be wise to calculate the fat to be sure there are no more than 3 grams of fat for every 100 calories. Fortunately for sandwich-meat lovers there are plenty of products that meet this standard.

The Dairy Case

The "purchase minimally processed food" rule does not apply to the dairy case. Left untouched, most dairy products contain more fat, especially saturated fat, than any other food except red meat. However, when some of the fat is removed, many items in the dairy case take on a new look. Low-fat milk (2 percent fat) has 1 teaspoon of fat for every cup; this is only a slight reduction from whole milk's 1½ teaspoons. On the other hand, 1 percent low-fat and nonfat milk and yogurt are low-fat nutritional powerhouses. Go easy on the fruited yogurts, however, since some contain more sugar than a candy bar. Your best bet is to purchase low-fat or nonfat plain yogurt and mix it with fresh fruit or a small amount of all-fruit jam.

In general, purchase milk in cartons, since milk in bottles and plastic jugs loses vitamin B2 when exposed to light. Always check the freshness date, examine the container for leakage or other damage, and refrigerate quickly after purchase.

When it comes to cheese, looks sometimes can be deceiving. Many of the "light" or "part-skim" cheeses have a fat content comparable to conventional cheeses. Other "reduced-fat" selections have lowered fat—say, from 9 grams to 5 grams—but 60 to 70 percent of the calories still come from fat. Still other cheeses have a fat content of 35 percent of total calories or less.

But how can you tell a "light" high-fat cheese from another low-fat product? Ignore the label on the front and go straight to the fat content listed on the back. A low-fat cheese will have 3 grams of fat or less per serving, or no more than 3 grams per ounce. A moderate-fat cheese will have 4 to 5 grams of fat per ounce, while a high-fat item contains 6 grams or more.

Cream cheese and sour cream are other dairy-case deceptions. Unless they are labeled as fat-free, assume the worst. Regular cream cheese is 90 percent fat calories and sour cream is 87 percent fat calories, with no redeeming qualities other than a smidgen of vitamin A. (You get more vitamin A in one carrot than in 24 ounces of cream cheese.) The "light" version of cream cheese—touted as half the fat of regular cream cheese—contains 75 percent fat calories, while a low-fat version of sour cream contains up to 51 percent fat calories. Not much to rave about!

Remember, butter is *all* fat. If you purchase butter, freeze three of the four sticks. You will be using this fat sparingly, and it is likely to turn rancid if left for long periods in the refrigerator.

Feeling Good About Grocery Shopping

Most people don't have time to read every label and investigate every food item at the grocery store. To minimize your shopping time and maximize your nutrition, organize your list before shopping. In addition, shop during off hours, if possible, to avoid congestion in the aisles and a lengthy line at the checkout. Lastly, never shop when hungry and try to avoid shopping with small children, both of which can lead to unplanned purchases.

Remember, one of the main premises of the Feeling Good Diet is to make dietary changes slowly. That also applies to shopping. Set small goals for yourself, such as scouting out certain sections of the grocery store each month, practicing label reading, or substituting a new, minimally processed food for a familiar high-fat or high-sugar food. Make copies of the Feeling Good Shopping List on pags 314–15 and keep a copy on the refrigerator, where you can mark down needed items. Shopping can be fun without being time-consuming if you plan ahead and focus on meeting your mental and physical health needs with nutrient-packed, wholesome foods.

Planning Your Meals and Snacks

Eating right does not begin at the stove or at the table. It starts with a plan. But the best-laid plans are worthless if they don't fit your activities and food preferences. Follow the three steps of the Feeling Good Diet and the Food-Family List in chapter 13 (pages 276 and 282–92) to plan the upcoming week. For examples and inspiration, review the sample menus beginning on page 329. These menus help translate the Food-Family List into real meals and snacks. The menus may not be a perfect fit for your tastes, so feel free to tailor them to your needs. Use the Menu Planning Worksheet on page 316 to plan your daily menus.

Planning your menus means more than just thinking about what you will eat; it means writing down your food choices on a day-by-day basis. The process should not feel overwhelming. If it does, reconsider the Feeling Good step you selected; perhaps you are making too many changes too quickly. Even so, in the beginning all this menu planning may feel odd or cumbersome. Remind yourself that any new skill, whether riding a bicycle or driving a car, will seem uncomfortable at first, but gets easier with practice. Eventually you will develop several sets of menus that suit your preferences and lifestyle.

The Feeling Good Shopping List

Use this sheet as a master copy. Keep a copy posted in the kitchen to circle needed items, then take the list with you when you shop.

The Produce Section

(vitamin C–rich selections are marked with an asterisk)
Fruit: Apples/Apricots/Bananas/Berries/*Cantaloupe/Casaba melon/Cherries/*Grapefruit/Grapes/*Kiwifruits/Kumquats/*Honeydew melon/Nectarines/*Oranges/*Papayas/Peaches/Pears/Pineapple/Plums/Pomegranates/Quince/*Tangerines/Watermelon
Other: ______________________________

(beta-carotene–rich vegetables are marked with an asterisk)
Vegetables: Artichokes/*Asparagus/Bean sprouts/Beets/*Broccoli/Brussels sprouts/Cabbage/*Carrots/Cauliflower/Celery/Cucumbers/*Chard/*Collards/Corn/*Dandelion greens/Eggplant/Green beans/*Kale/Leeks/Lettuce/Mushrooms/*Mustard greens/Okra/Onions/Parsnips/Peas/Peppers/Potatoes/Pumpkin/Rhubarb/Rutabaga/Snow peas/*Spinach/Summer squash or zucchini/*Sweet potatoes/Tomatoes/*Turnip greens/Winter squash/Yams
Other: ______________________________

Baked Goods

Bread: Whole wheat/Pumpernickel/Pita/Rye/Oat
Crackers: Ry-Krisp/Graham/Akmak/Saltines
Other: Bagels/English muffins/Rice cakes/Corn tortillas
Other: ______________________________

Dairy Case

Nonfat milk/Nonfat plain yogurt/Buttermilk/Low-fat and nonfat cheeses
Egg substitute
Other: ______________________________

Meat and Fish Department

Beef, extra-lean cuts only/Veal, extra-lean cuts only/Chicken/Turkey/Seafood/Luncheon meats, 95 percent fat-free
Other: ______________________________

Dry Goods

Powdered buttermilk/Powdered nonfat milk/Whole wheat flour/Dried beans and peas/Pasta/Brown rice/Wheat germ
Other: ______________________________

Canned Goods

Applesauce, no sugar added/Apricots, canned in own juice/Artichoke hearts, water-packed/Kidney, black, garbanzo beans/Carrot juice/Evaporated nonfat milk/Fruit cocktail, canned in own juice/100% fruit juices/Mandarin oranges, juice-packed/Peaches, canned in own juice/Peanut butter/Pears, canned in own juice/Pineapple chunks, canned in own juice/Salmon/Soups, low-fat/Spaghetti sauce, fat-free/Tomato juice/Tomato paste/Tomato sauce/Tuna, water-packed
Other: ______________________________

Breakfast Cereals

Cooked: Oatmeal/Barley/Farina
Ready-to-eat: Grape-Nuts/Shredded wheat/Nutri-Grain
Other: ______________________________

Frozen Foods

Desserts: Frozen fruit ice/Ice cream, fat- and sugar-free/Sherbet
Other: Vegetables/Whole wheat waffles
Other: ______________________________

Snack Items

Dried fruit/Nuts and seeds/Popcorn, plain/Potato chips, oven-baked, fat-free/Pretzels/Tortilla chips, oven-baked, fat-free
Other: ______________________________

Desserts

Angel food cake, no frosting/Sponge cake, no frosting/Animal crackers/Vanilla wafers
Other: ______________________________

Herbs, Oils, and Condiments

Active dry yeast/All-fruit jam/Baking powder/Baking soda/Catsup/Cornstarch/Herbs and spices/Lemon juice/Mustard/No-fat salad dressing/Olive or canola oil/Salsa/Unflavored gelatin/Vanilla/Vinegar
Other: ______________________________

WORKSHEET 14.1 The Menu Planning Worksheet

Plan your menus in the left-hand column and record differences if you did not eat as planned in the right-hand column for each day. This sheet provides space for two days of menus, including all meals and snacks. Use this sheet as a master and make additional copies.

	Date: ________		Date: ________	
	PLANNED	**ACTUAL**	**PLANNED**	**ACTUAL**
Breakfast				
Snack				
Lunch				
Snack				
Dinner				
Snack				

Ten Simple Guidelines

Simple is the key word when it comes to food preparation. Learning to eat right to feel your best initially takes some extra time and mental energy, but food preparation can be easy if you follow some easy guidelines:

1. *Limit your intake of fat and sugar*. Question the use of fat and sugar in everything you prepare and reduce or eliminate these two ingredients whenever possible (see "Alternatives for Health," page 320).

2. *Emphasize grains, vegetables, legumes, and fruits*. If you are following the Feeling Good Diet, these foods will constitute at least three-quarters of your meals.

3. *Stick to unprocessed foods*. Buy and serve foods as close to their original form as possible. In general, the more processed a food, the fewer nutrients and the more fat, sodium, and preservatives it contains. So choose fresh broccoli instead of frozen broccoli quiche, a baked potato instead of frozen scalloped potatoes or potato chips, and whole wheat bread instead of a croissant.

4. *Make nutritious foods readily available*. For example, clean and store enough raw vegetables to supply meals and snacks for up to three days. (Or purchase vegetables already washed and cut.) Freeze an extra loaf of whole wheat bread, stock extra cans of kidney beans, or purchase several cans of nonfat evaporated milk for use in recipes in case you run low on regular low-fat milk.

5. *Concentrate on food preparation only once or twice a week*. Plan one evening on the weekend and/or one evening during the week to cook enough foods to last the rest of the week. Soups, stews, and casseroles can be portion-packed, stored in the refrigerator or freezer, and reheated in the microwave. Also, cook enough of certain foods to use in more than one meal. For example, rice, dried peas and beans, pasta, potatoes, and marinara sauce are easy to prepare in large quantities. Chicken can be cooked, then used in sandwiches, pasta dishes, and snacks. Store the leftovers in the freezer in appropriate serving sizes for use in everything from burritos and side dishes to main meals.

6. *Keep it simple.* Unless you are a gourmet cook who loves to spend hours in the kitchen, avoid complicated recipes that require time, ingredients, and fancy equipment. You can prepare nutritious meals and snacks that take no more than five to thirty minutes. Have a set of simple meals that can be prepared in a flash.

7. *Make your meals attractive.* Consider eye appeal and the three T's—taste, texture, and temperature. Eating should be a pleasurable experience, not a medical one.

8. *Include vegetables in every meal.* Rather than 6-ounce pieces of beef and an iceberg lettuce salad, be creative. Add vegetables to your meals as follows:

- Spaghetti and pizza sauce: Stir in grated carrots, onions, mushrooms, peppers.
- Lasagna: Add a layer of broccoli or spinach in place of all or some of the meat and cheese.
- Casseroles: Add green peas, carrots, celery, onion, bell peppers, squash, or sweet potatoes to the mixture.
- Baked beans, chili, meatloaf: Include grated carrots, extra tomato sauce, canned tomatoes, or green beans to the recipe.
- Potato salad: Add carrots, peas, peppers, red onions.
- Canned soups: Include extra vegetables such as potatoes, corn, beans, peas, carrots, squash.
- Baked potato: Stuff with spinach and low-fat yogurt; broccoli, mushrooms, and part-skim ricotta cheese; or nonfat cottage cheese and salsa.
- Corn bread and muffins: Put grated carrots, zucchini, corn, or green chilies into the batter.
- Shish-kabob: Skewer at least twice as many vegetables—including mushrooms, carrots, eggplant, cherry tomatoes, zucchini, onion, or potato—as extra-lean meat, chicken, or shellfish.
- Tortillas: Fill with ricotta or cottage cheese and spinach sprinkled with nutmeg; black beans, plain nonfat yogurt, and salsa; grated carrot and zucchini, low-fat cheese, and green chili peppers; nonfat refried beans, cilantro, tomato, and grated carrot.

- Salads: Try carrot-raisin, Waldorf (apples, celery, green pepper, and nuts), spinach and orange slices, or marinated vegetables.

9. *Match the cooking technique to the food.* Broiling and barbecuing meats allows the fat to drip away, but will toughen less tender meats. Pound or marinate the latter. Cooking in a Crock-Pot or braising is ideal for tougher cuts of meat. Dried beans can be cooked quickly in a pressure cooker. Soaking time can be reduced; after rinsing, bring the beans and water to a boil in fresh water, turn off the heat, and let the pot sit for at least one hour, then continue to simmer until done, about two hours.
10. *Cook with vitamins in mind.* To retain nutrients during cooking, prepare fresh foods using the shortest cooking time and the least amount of water. In addition, wrap foods well and promptly refrigerate. Wash produce quickly; do not soak. Do not use baking soda when cooking vegetables because it destroys nutrients. Cook produce only until tender-crisp in a steamer or microwave. Use the liquid from cooking the vegetables for soups and sauces. Lastly, reheat only the portion of leftovers or prepared-ahead foods that will be eaten at that meal.

Determining the Correct Serving Sizes

Great meal plans can be undermined by a lack of attention to portion control. Underestimating the serving sizes specified in the Food-Family List may leave you hungry, while overestimating can result in exceeding your target calorie level and gaining weight. In particular, if the large serving is from the Nutritious Fatty Foods, Fats and Oils, or Guiltless Desserts family, you will eat too much fat or sugar and undermine your efforts. Portion awareness also is a way to wean yourself from troublesome foods. For example, instead of eating a dessert at one sitting, cut the portion into smaller pieces to enjoy throughout the day. The secret is to train your eyes to recognize common portion sizes and stick to them.

Besides the suggestions in "Portion Awareness," page 322, there are a few tips for improving your portion awareness. For example, ask the butcher at the meat counter to weigh your meat purchases so you know exactly what portions you are

Alternatives for Health

INSTEAD OF THIS . . .	DO THIS
Frying in fat	Bake, steam, grill, "fry" without oil in a nonstick pan or wok, or use nonstick cooking spray
Sautéing in oil	Cook in wine, lemon juice, vegetable juice, defatted stock
Putting butter on toast	Use low-sugar jam
Popping popcorn in oil	Air-pop popcorn
Grilling sandwiches or French toast in a skillet	Use nonstick pans or nonstick cooking spray
Using full-fat broths	Defat broths by cooling them in the refrigerator and discarding the fat that hardens on top, or use a gravy-fat separator
Cooking poultry with its skin	Remove skin from poultry before cooking
Cooking meats without trimming	Trim excess fats from meats before cooking
Following recipes for amounts of sugar and fat	Reduce the sugar and fat by half and continue to cut back as you reeducate your palate

buying. Use measuring cups and spoons to portion out your food until your awareness improves. Consider making some simple 2-, 3-, and 4-ounce food models from sponges or cardboard to make comparisons easier. Even when you are confident enough not to measure anymore, periodically check your accuracy.

Satisfying Snacks

Snacks play an important role in the Feeling Good Diet. When properly selected, snacks help control hunger by eliminating surges in your appetite-control chemicals. But before you race to the vending machine with a license to snack, keep in mind that healthful nibbling means following a few simple rules.

Rule #1: Keep it simple. A nutritious snack must be convenient, that is, it must be readily available, take little time to prepare, and taste great.

Rule #2: Include at least one fruit or vegetable at each snack, plus a nutritious second food, such as a whole grain, nuts and seeds, a nonfat milk product, cooked dried beans and peas, or extra-lean meat. For example, fruit slices dipped in nonfat yogurt with cinnamon or raw vegetables with a curried bean dip.

Rule #3: Minimally processed foods should outnumber highly processed snack items.

Prioritizing for Health

If you would rather hit the snooze button than eat breakfast, prefer to skip lunch and run one more errand, are too tired to eat right, or are so busy trying to have it all that you eat for convenience rather than for well-being, it's time to review your priorities. What you eat is one of the most important, but often most ignored, factors determining how you feel—physically, emotionally, and mentally. Although youth may mask the effects of poor nutrition, even small children show marked improvements in energy, concentration, intelligence, and mood when they eat right. Putting nutrition on the back burner will only escalate the problems as you age.

Yes, changing your dietary habits takes a little extra time and effort at first. Fortunately, it will pay off in the long run as you begin to feel, think, and look better. In addition, the process gets easier as old habits slowly drop by the wayside and are replaced with new, self-nurturing ways of living that help you reach your full emotional and physical potential. Remember, aim for progress, not perfection. View the Feeling Good Diet as a creative opportunity to refashion yourself into the best person you can be—a journey that begins today and continues for the rest of your life.

The Dining Out Dilemma

Most restaurants are willing to prepare a meal that meets the Feeling Good Diet guidelines if you ask for exactly what you want. In fact, a survey conducted by the National Restaurant Association showed that most restaurateurs are willing and able to alter their cooking or service methods on request. If a restaurant will not or cannot accommodate your needs, go elsewhere. (See "Common Myths About Restaurant Meals," page 324.)

Portion Awareness

The portions served in restaurants or packaged in processed foods are not necessarily normal serving sizes and are not reliable reference points. Here's how to improve your portion awareness:

Meats, poultry, and fish portions are the most challenging. Remember that 3 ounces is:

- The size of the palm of a woman's hand (fingers excluded)
- The amount in a typical fast-food restaurant hamburger (cooked)
- A chicken breast (3 inches across)
- The size of a deck of cards or the amount that would fill the lid of a mayonnaise jar

6 ounces equals:

- A restaurant-size chicken breast (6 inches across)
- The common cafeteria or luncheon portion

8 ounces equals:

- A common serving for a dinner meal at a restaurant

For cheese, 1 ounce equals:

- One slice on a sandwich or a hamburger
- One square inch cube or one wedge (airplane serving)
- The size of a Ping-Pong ball

For vegetables, 1/2 cup is the size of a tennis ball.

Potato servings are as follows:

- A small potato is 2 1/2 inches long (about 3 ounces)
- A medium potato is 4 inches long
- A large potato is 5 inches long (restaurant portion)
- An extra-large potato is 6 inches long (meal-in-one portion)

For fats, consider the following:

- 1 teaspoon of margarine or butter is 1 pat
- 1 tablespoon of mayonnaise is about the size of your thumb

For ice cream, 1/2 cup is 4 ounces or one scoop (the size of a tennis ball).

Your primary strategies for dining out are the same ones you use when dining at home:

1. Limit or avoid fat. For example, choose foods that have been broiled, poached, roasted, or steamed. Select items described as "garden fresh," "in a tomato base," "in broth," or cooked "in its own juice." On the other hand, avoid foods that are described as crisp, braised, buttered or buttery, creamed, scalloped, fried, à la mode, au gratin, au fromage, or refried; cooked in a butter, cheese, or cream sauce; served with gravy; or pan-fried, breaded, or sautéed.
2. Emphasize grains, vegetables, and fruits and use meat, chicken, fish, and dairy foods as condiments.
3. Choose foods that are as close to their original form as possible. Limit highly processed foods.
4. Have only the foods you intend to eat brought to your table. For example, ask the waiter to bring extra bread sticks, but not to bring the buttered garlic bread or the dessert tray.

In addition, you can choose restaurants that specialize in healthful foods. Look for establishments that have salad bars with a wide assortment of fresh produce; that serve low-fat pasta dishes and fresh fruit for dessert; and that poach, broil, or steam fish, seafood, chicken, and other meats. On the other hand, avoid restaurants that serve tempting but unhealthy foods such as baskets of fried tortilla chips at Mexican restaurants, gourmet chocolate desserts, or homemade cinnamon rolls and specialty coffees.

Ask whether special requests are honored before you make reservations. If you are not familiar with the restaurant, ask to see a menu so you can choose your meal and order it mentally before going to the restaurant. Request additional information about portion sizes, ingredients, preparation techniques, and accompaniments, such as side dishes or other items served with the entree. Then frequent restaurants where you have had success ordering the meal you want; you will know the menu and the servers will know your tastes.

At the restaurant, decide what you will order before you open the menu or order without looking at the menu. Certain foods may be available but not listed on the menu, such as baked fish or chicken, nonfat milk, baked potato, or a steamed vegetable plate. You should be able to assemble a low-fat meal from the

Common Myths About Restaurant Meals

Myth 1: All Chinese food is healthy because it is low in fat and sugar.
Fact: A stir-fried dish can contain anywhere from 1 to 9 teaspoons of fat per serving. Authentic Chinese dishes are mostly vegetables and very little animal protein, but Americanized versions usually are the reverse and often have too much added fat and sugary sweet-and-sour sauces. Ask that your food be prepared with minimal oil. Chinese food also may be high in MSG, unless you ask specifically that this additive not be used.

Myth 2: Fast-food chicken and fish sandwiches are lower in fat than a hamburger.
Fact: Breaded and fried fish or chicken sandwiches have more fat and calories than a hamburger. Choose grilled chicken and baked fish dishes, and request them without the mayonnaise-based sauce.

Myth 3: Italian food is high in fat. (Or Italian food is healthful.)
Fact: Spaghetti with a meatless marinara or red clam sauce is one of the lowest-fat meals you can order in a restaurant. With fresh Italian bread (no butter) and a salad (not antipasto), you have a low-fat feast. On the other hand, fettuccine Alfredo gets 58 percent of its calories from fat, and many restaurant lasagnas contain up to 11 teaspoons of fat per serving. If the restaurant cannot prepare a low-fat version of your order, ask for a double helping of pasta, a reduced portion of sauce, and extra portions of salad (dressing on the side), plain bread, and/or bread sticks to help cut the fat.

Myth 4: Chicken entrees are lowest in fat.
Fact: Chicken is as fat-laden or even fattier than other dishes if it has been breaded, deep-fat fried, or prepared with a cream sauce. Always identify how a chicken dish, or any meat dish, is prepared before ordering it.

appetizer, salad, and side-dish sections on the menu. For example, order two salads and split an entree with your dining partner. Order first to avoid being influenced by other diners at your table.

When ordering, always ask and never assume anything. A food described as grilled could be grilled with butter. When you order, specify how you want your food prepared—broiled instead of fried, grilled without butter, plain vegetables instead of the creamed version, no sugar for your tea, or fresh fruit instead of syrup for the pancakes.

Specify what you *don't* want. Learn to say "Hold the butter, margarine, cream, or cheese." Ask for salad dressing, gravy, sugar, jam, or syrup on the side. Rather than rely on willpower after the food arrives, ask that tempting foods be left in the kitchen. Send back anything that is prepared incorrectly. If there are droplets of oil on your vegetables, they were probably sautéed in oil rather than steamed. If your muffin tastes too sweet or leaves a slippery feel on your fingertips, it probably is high in sugar and/or fat.

When the meal is served, before you start to eat, put any foods or portions you are not going to eat into a doggie bag or on a side plate, and ask that it be removed. If necessary, bring your own low-fat or fat-free salad dressing packets in case low-fat dressings, vinegar, lemon, salsa, or other no-fat options are unavailable at the restaurant. If you want chicken, but a skinless entree is not available, remove the skin yourself when it is served.

Avoid drinking alcoholic beverages before and with your meal, or make selections very carefully. Alcohol stimulates the appetite and also may weaken your commitment to follow your diet when tempting foods are available.

Skip dessert unless it is fresh fruit, a low-sugar sorbet, or low-fat frozen yogurt. Split a dessert with a friend, or ask for a half-portion. Order tea, almond milk, fruit juice, or other low-fat, low-sugar beverages.

There are also steps you can take beyond these food choices. For example, go out for lunch rather than dinner; lunch entrees are smaller and less expensive.

Do not starve yourself in anticipation of a big restaurant meal. A regular pattern of breakfast, lunch, and snacks will prevent overindulging at the restaurant and will prevent your appetite-control chemicals from shifting into overdrive. Likewise, start the meal with volume (water, sparkling water, salad, raw vegetables, or clear soup) or have a snack before leaving home.

Take a break halfway through the meal. It takes about twenty minutes for the brain to receive the message that you are full. Push back from the table for a few moments to help your body attune to its signals. Focus on the people during the meal, not on the food. In other words, make dining a social event rather than an eating event.

Ethnic cuisines often are more creative with vegetables and grains than is standard American cooking. They frequently use smaller portions of fish, chicken, and meat and more grains, vegetables, and fruit. For tips on ordering meals in foreign restaurants, see "International Dining," page 327. In addition, the worksheet on page 326 will help you better plan your restaurant meals.

WORKSHEET 14.2 Dining Out Strategy Worksheet

To avoid last-minute decision making, plan your dining strategy before you leave home. Answer each of these questions. Use this sheet as a master to make copies.

The Event

1. Who will be there? Are they supportive or will they try to sabotage your efforts? ______

____

2. Who is providing the food? (Airline, restaurant, potluck, or hostess-served?) ______

____

3. What will be served? (If you don't know, can you call to find out? Can you request a special meal in advance?) ______

____

4. It is a sit-down meal or a buffet? ______

____

Your Strategy

1. What will you do if high-fat appetizers and cocktails are served? ______

____

2. How will you handle the food choices during the meal? ______

____

3. How will you deal with the food-pushers and other saboteurs? What can you do to foster support and discourage sabotage? ______

____

4. What are the payoffs for sticking with your diet? ______

____

International Dining

Mexican

- *Best choices*: Baked fish with pimientos; chili without meat; steamed corn tortillas; gazpacho; chicken in green sauce; mesquite-grilled chicken or seafood; Spanish rice without oil; steamed tacos or tostadas with low-fat fillings; enchiladas with low-fat fillings such as chicken, crab, tomato, onion, lettuce, chilies, and salsa; chicken or beef fajitas made with corn tortillas. For dessert, a small portion of flan.
- *Avoid*: Chiles rellenos, chimichangas, chorizo, flour tortillas, fried tacos and tostadas, guacamole, nachos, refried beans, tamales, fried tortilla chips.

Chinese

- *Tips*: Ask for "dry stir-fry" to reduce fat in cooking. Combine one cup of steamed rice for every cup of entree.
- *Best choices*: Soups made with chicken, seafood, vegetables, watercress; chicken or shrimp with snow peas and water chestnuts; lo mein noodles; tofu and vegetable stir-fries; moo goo gai pan; plain steamed rice; steamed vegetables; vegetarian or chicken chop suey; Szechuan shrimp.
- *Avoid*: Egg drop soup, egg rolls, barbecued spare ribs, chow mein noodles, fried wontons, duck, egg foo yung, fried rice, sweet and sour sauce.

Italian

- *Tips*: If you order pizza, ask for the number of slices you want and request that the rest be brought in a box when you are ready to leave.
- *Best choices*: Spaghetti with meat-free marinara or red clam sauce; minestrone soup; Italian bread without butter; chicken marsala without skin or oil; pasta with meatballs; seafood dishes; for dessert, fresh fruit whip or Italian ice.
- *Avoid:* Antipasto salad, creamed sauces (such as Alfredo), garlic bread with butter, pasta stuffed with meat and cheese, pesto, prosciutto, sausage dishes, veal parmigiana or scaloppine, lasagna.

Cajun

- *Best choices*: Red beans and rice without sausage, shrimp Creole, poultry or seafood jambalaya, blackened fish, boiled seafood; for dessert, split a serving of lemon coffee cake.
- *Avoid:* Hush puppies (fried corn bread), dirty rice (rice with gizzards), batter-fried seafood, cream soups such as bisque, and étouffée.

French

- *Best choices*: Salade niçoise, consommé and other stock-based soups, seafood stews such as bouillabaisse, ratatouille, poached or steamed fish or seafood, dishes with *coulis* (fresh vegetable sauce) or vegetable mélange, roast chicken, spinach braised with onions; for dessert, apples baked with rum, apricot sherbet, plums baked in custard, or fresh raspberries.
- *Avoid*: Cassoulet (bean and meat casserole) and gratins, quenelles, soufflés, quiche, Hollandaise and *beurre blanc* sauces, fatty meats such as sweetbreads and duck, pâté, rich desserts.

Greek

- *Best choices*: torato (cold soup with eggplant, pepper, and yogurt), skewered and grilled vegetables and meat dishes such as souvlaki and shish kebab, fish baked with plaki sauce; for dessert, split a serving of custard pie.
- *Avoid*: Stuffed pies, moussaka (eggplant pie), and meat-macaroni casseroles.

Indian

- *Best choices*: Lentil soups, mulligatawny, dal; tandoori chicken or fish; yogurt-based curries; baked breads such as chapati and kulcha; for dessert, a small serving of fresh fruit salad with thickened milk or pineapple fruit salad.
- *Avoid*: Fried breads such as poori and paratha; fried appetizers such as samosas and pakoras; any dish called kandhair, malai, or korma.

Middle Eastern

- *Best choices*: Hummus (mashed chick-peas), tabbouleh salad, lentil soup, kibbe (baked meat with wheat, onions, and pine nuts); for dessert, rice pudding.
- *Avoid*: Saganaki (fried cheese and butter), falafel (deep-fried chick-pea balls), kasseri (cheese and butter casserole).

Some Sample Menus

The following menus are based on the three-step approach of the Feeling Good Diet and provide a week's worth of eating plans. Keep in mind that these are only examples. You may follow these menus or use them as a guide for developing your own eating plan, tailored to your food preferences and habits.

Monday (Step 1)

BREAKFAST

1½ cups whole-grain cereal
8 walnut halves
1 tablespoon sugar
1 cup nonfat milk
1 banana
2 5-ounce cups of tea or coffee (optional)

LUNCH

SANDWICH
- 2 slices bread
- 3 ounces extra-lean roast beef
- 2 tablespoons mayonnaise
- 2 tomato slices
- 1 lettuce leaf

2 cups raw carrots and cauliflower
1 ounce cheese
1 diet cola (optional)
1 glass water

DINNER

4 ounces baked halibut, prepared with 1 tablespoon oil
⅔ cup cooked rice
1 cup steamed asparagus
1 tablespoon margarine
1 2-inch slice angel food cake
1 glass water

SNACK

1 cup plain yogurt
2 kiwifruit, sliced
7 vanilla wafers

Tuesday (Step 1)

BREAKFAST

1 bagel, toasted
2 tablespoons cream cheese
1 tablespoon jam
1 cup grapes
1 cup nonfat milk
2 5-ounce cups tea or coffee (optional)

LUNCH

TOSSED SALAD
- 2 cups mixed greens
- 2 ounces diced lean ham
- 1 ounce cheese, grated
- ¼ cup kidney beans
- ¼ cup grated carrot
- ¼ cup sliced tomato
- 2 tablespoons sunflower seeds
- 2 tablespoons salad dressing

1 slice bread
1 tablespoon margarine
1 medium orange
⅓ cup sherbet with 2 vanilla wafers
1 diet cola (optional)
1 glass water

DINNER

1 cup cooked spaghetti
⅔ cup marinara sauce with 3 ounces extra-lean beef
1 cup steamed broccoli
1 whole-grain roll
1 tablespoon margarine
1 glass water

SNACK

1 cup warmed nonfat milk flavored with almond extract to taste
1 3-inch slice angel food cake

Wednesday (Step 1)

BREAKFAST

1 English muffin, toasted
2 tablespoons peanut butter
2 tablespoons jam
1 medium orange
2 cups tea or coffee (optional)
1 glass water

LUNCH

2 cups low-fat beef vegetable soup
8 Ry-Krisp crackers
1 tablespoon margarine
1 cup milk
⅓ cup sherbet
1 diet cola (optional)

DINNER

3 ounces baked chicken breast, prepared with 1 tablespoon butter
1 medium baked sweet potato
1½ cups steamed spinach
1 dinner roll
2 tablespoons margarine
1 glass water

SNACK

1 cup plain yogurt
¾ cup fruit cocktail canned in own juice
20 animal crackers

Thursday (Step 1)

BREAKFAST

1½ cups whole-grain cereal
2 tablespoons almonds
1 tablespoon sugar
1 cup 1% low-fat milk
1 cup strawberries
½ cup orange juice
2 5-ounce cups tea or coffee (optional)

LUNCH

Tuna Salad Sandwich
- 2 slices bread
- 3 ounces water-packed tuna
- 2 tablespoons mayonnaise
- 2 tablespoons diced celery
- 2 slices tomato
- 1 lettuce leaf

2 medium raw carrots
⅓ cup ice cream
1 diet cola (optional)
1 glass water

DINNER

3 ounces broiled flank steak
1 cup steamed Brussels sprouts
1 cup cooked fettuccine noodles, tossed in 2 tablespoons olive oil
1 cup 1% low-fat milk
⅔ cup sherbet

SNACK

1 baked apple
1 tablespoon brown sugar
¼ teaspoon cinnamon
1 glass water

Friday (Step 1)

BREAKFAST

2 slices raisin toast
2 tablespoons cream cheese
1 cup nonfat milk
2 5-ounce cups of tea or coffee (optional)

LUNCH

3 ounces baked chicken breast
SPINACH SALAD
  3 cups fresh spinach
  ¼ avocado
  2 tablespoons salad dressing
1 medium orange
1 roll
½ tablespoon margarine
1 cup tomato juice
¾ cup fruit ice
1 diet cola (optional)
1 glass water

DINNER

3 ounces roast turkey
1 cup cooked brown rice
½ cup peas
1 tablespoon margarine
2 broiled grapefruit halves
1 tablespoon brown sugar
1 glass water

SNACK

5 vanilla wafers
1 tablespoon peanut butter
1 cup steamed nonfat milk flavored with vanilla extract and nutmeg to taste

Saturday (Step 1)

BREAKFAST

2 pancakes
1 teaspoon margarine
2 tablespoons syrup
1 ounce pork sausage, well drained
¾ cup applesauce
1 cup 1% low-fat milk
2 5-ounce cups of tea or coffee (optional)

LUNCH

TURKEY SANDWICH
  2 slices bread
  3 ounces turkey breast
  1 tablespoon mayonnaise
  2 tomato slices
  1 lettuce leaf
1 cup vegetable soup
⅔ cup Jell-O
1 diet cola (optional)
1 glass water

DINNER

3 ounces roasted pork loin
1 baked potato with 1 tablespoon margarine and 2 tablespoons sour cream
1½ cups cooked collard greens
1 glass water

SNACK

2 tangerines
1 cup plain low-fat yogurt
5 vanilla wafers
1 tablespoon peanuts

Sunday (Step 1)

BREAKFAST

1 whole wheat English muffin, toasted
2 tablespoons jam
½ tablespoon margarine
2 strips bacon, well drained
1 cup 1% low-fat milk
1 cup orange juice
2 5-ounce cups of tea or coffee (optional)

LUNCH

2 cups low-fat split-pea soup
4 Ry-Krisp crackers
2 ounces cheese
⅓ cup fruit ice
1 diet cola (optional)
1 glass water

DINNER

4 ounces sautéed red snapper, using ½ tablespoon olive oil
½ cup green peas
1 cup cooked pasta with 1 tablespoon butter
1 artichoke, steamed
1 tablespoon mayonnaise
1 glass water

SNACK

¾ cup low-fat cottage cheese
¾ cup pineapple chunks
20 animal crackers

Monday (Step 2)

BREAKFAST

1½ cups whole-grain cereal
8 walnut halves
1 tablespoon sugar
1 cup nonfat milk
1 banana
1 5-ounce cup of tea or coffee (optional)
1 glass water

LUNCH

Roast Beef Sandwich
- 2 slices bread
- 3 ounces extra-lean roast beef
- 1 tablespoon mayonnaise
- 2 tomato slices
- 1 lettuce leaf

2 cups raw carrots and cauliflower
1 ounce cheese
⅔ cup pear nectar
1 diet cola (optional)
1 glass water

SNACK

2 cups low-fat vegetable soup
1 glass water

DINNER

4 ounces baked halibut, prepared with 1 tablespoon oil
⅔ cup cooked brown and wild rice
1 cup steamed asparagus
1 tablespoon margarine
1 glass water

SNACK

1 cup nonfat plain yogurt
2 kiwifruit, sliced
7 vanilla wafers

Tuesday (Step 2)

BREAKFAST

1 whole wheat bagel, toasted
2 tablespoons cream cheese
1 cup grapes
1 cup nonfat milk
1 5-ounce cup of tea or coffee (optional)
1 glass water

LUNCH

Tossed Salad
- 2 cups mixed greens
- 2 ounces diced lean ham
- 1 ounce cheese, grated
- ¼ cup kidney beans
- ½ cup grated carrot

1 tomato slice
2 tablespoons sunflower seeds
1 tablespoon salad dressing
1 slice bread
½ tablespoon margarine
1 medium orange
1 diet cola (optional)
1 glass water

SNACK

¾ cup sliced peaches
5 vanilla wafers
1 glass water

DINNER

1 cup cooked spaghetti
⅔ cup marinara sauce with 3 ounces extra-lean beef
1 cup steamed broccoli
½ cup green peas
2 whole-grain rolls
½ tablespoon margarine
1 glass water

SNACK

1 cup warmed nonfat milk flavored with almond extract to taste
1 2-inch slice angel food cake

Wednesday (Step 2)

BREAKFAST

1 English muffin, toasted
2 tablespoons peanut butter
1 tablespoon jam
1 medium orange
1 5-ounce cup of tea or coffee (optional)
1 glass water

LUNCH

2 cups low-fat beef vegetable soup
8 Ry-Krisp crackers
½ tablespoon margarine
1 large raw carrot
1 cup 1% low-fat milk
1 diet cola (optional)
1 glass water

SNACK

1 apple
1 cup tomato juice
1 glass water

DINNER

3 ounces baked chicken breast, prepared with ½ tablespoon butter
1 medium baked sweet potato
1½ cups steamed spinach
1 whole-grain dinner roll
1 tablespoon margarine
1 glass water

SNACK

1 cup plain low-fat yogurt
¾ cup fruit cocktail canned in own juice
30 animal crackers

Thursday (Step 2)

BREAKFAST

1½ cups whole-grain cereal
2 tablespoons almonds
1 tablespoon sugar
1 cup nonfat milk
1 cup strawberries
½ cup orange juice
1 5-ounce cup of tea or coffee (optional)
1 glass water

LUNCH

Tuna Salad Sandwich
- 2 slices whole-grain bread
- 3 ounces water-packed tuna
- 1 tablespoon mayonnaise
- 2 tablespoons celery, diced
- 2 tomato slices
- 1 lettuce leaf

2 medium raw carrots
⅓ cup ice cream
1 diet cola (optional)
1 glass water

SNACK

1 large pear
1 glass water

DINNER

3 ounces broiled flank steak
1 cup steamed Brussels sprouts
1 cup beets
1 cup cooked fettuccine noodles, tossed with 1 tablespoon olive oil
1 cup 1% low-fat milk
½ cup sherbet
1 glass water

SNACK

1 baked apple
½ teaspoon ground cinnamon
¼ teaspoon vanilla extract

Friday (Step 2)

BREAKFAST

2 slices raisin toast
2 tablespoons cream cheese
¾ cup pineapple chunks
1 cup nonfat milk
1 5-ounce cup of tea or coffee (optional)
1 glass water

LUNCH

3 ounces baked chicken breast
SPINACH SALAD
  3 cups fresh spinach
  ¼ avocado
  1 tablespoon salad dressing
1 medium orange
1 whole-grain roll
1 cup tomato juice
½ cup fruit ice
1 diet cola (optional)
1 glass water

SNACK

2 cups raw vegetables
1 glass water

DINNER

3 ounces roast turkey
1 cup cooked brown rice
½ cup peas
1 tablespoon margarine
2 broiled grapefruit halves
1 glass water

SNACK

5 vanilla wafers
1 tablespoon peanut butter
1 cup warmed nonfat milk flavored with vanilla and nutmeg to taste

Saturday (Step 2)

BREAKFAST

2 pancakes
1 teaspoon margarine
2 tablespoons syrup
1 ounce pork sausage, well drained
¾ cup applesauce
1 cup 1% low-fat milk
1 5-ounce cup of tea or coffee (optional)
1 glass water

LUNCH

TURKEY SANDWICH
  2 slices whole wheat bread
  3 ounces turkey breast
  1 tablespoon mayonnaise
  2 tomato slices
  1 lettuce leaf
1½ cups vegetable soup
1 cup tomato juice
1 glass water

SNACK

1 cup grapefruit sections
4 graham crackers
1 diet cola (optional)
1 glass water

DINNER

3 ounces roasted pork loin
1 baked potato
1 tablespoon margarine
1 tablespoon low-fat sour cream
1½ cups cooked collard greens
1 glass water

SNACK

2 tangerines
1 cup plain nonfat yogurt
5 vanilla wafers
1 tablespoon peanut butter

Sunday (Step 2)

BREAKFAST

1 whole wheat English muffin, toasted
2 tablespoons jam
½ tablespoon margarine
2 strips bacon, well drained
1 cup orange juice
1 cup 1% low-fat milk
1 5-ounce cup of tea or coffee (optional)
1 glass water

LUNCH

2 cups low-fat split-pea soup
4 Ry-Krisp crackers
2 ounces cheese
1 apple
1 glass water

SNACK

2 cups raw vegetables
1 diet cola (optional)
1 glass water

DINNER

4 ounces sautéed red snapper, using ½ tablespoon olive oil
½ cup green peas
1½ cups cooked pasta
1 artichoke, steamed, with 1 tablespoon mayonnaise
1 glass water

SNACK

¾ cup low-fat cottage cheese
¾ cup pineapple chunks

Monday (Step 3)

BREAKFAST

1½ cups whole-grain cereal flakes
1 tablespoon sugar
1 cup nonfat milk
1 banana
1 5-ounce cup of tea or coffee (optional)
1 glass water

SNACK

1 cup fat-free cottage cheese
1 glass water

LUNCH

Sandwich
 2 slices bread
 3 ounces extra-lean roast beef
 2 teaspoons mayonnaise
 1 tablespoon mustard
 2 tomato slices
 1 lettuce leaf
2 cups raw carrots and cauliflower
1 ounce cheese
⅔ cup pear nectar
1 glass water

SNACK

2 cups low-fat vegetable soup
6 saltines
2 glasses water

DINNER

4 ounces baked halibut, prepared with
 1 teaspoon oil
⅔ cup cooked brown and wild rice
2 cups steamed asparagus
1 tablespoon margarine
1 glass water

SNACK

1 cup nonfat plain yogurt
2 kiwifruit, sliced
3 vanilla wafers

Tuesday (Step 3)

BREAKFAST

1 whole wheat bagel, toasted
2 tablespoons low-fat cream cheese
1 cup grapes
1 cup 1% low-fat milk
1 5-ounce cup of tea or coffee (optional)
1 glass water

SNACK

1 cup nonfat plain yogurt
4 graham crackers
2 glasses water

LUNCH

TOSSED SALAD
- 2 cups mixed greens
- 2 ounces diced lean ham
- 1 ounce cheese, grated
- ¼ cup kidney beans
- ½ cup grated carrot
- 1 tomato slice
- 1 tablespoon salad dressing

1 slice bread
1 medium orange
1 glass water

SNACK

¾ cup sliced peaches
1 glass water

DINNER

1 cup cooked spaghetti
⅔ cup marinara sauce with 3 ounces extra-lean beef
2 cups steamed broccoli
1 cup green peas
2 whole-grain rolls
1 glass water

SNACK

1 cup warmed nonfat milk flavored with almond extract to taste
1 2-inch slice angel food cake

Wednesday (Step 3)

BREAKFAST

1 English muffin, toasted
1 tablespoon peanut butter
1 cup nonfat milk
1 medium orange
1 5-ounce cup of tea or coffee (optional)
1 glass water

SNACK

¾ cup dry cereal
2 glasses water

LUNCH

2 cups low-fat beef vegetable soup
8 Ry-Krisp crackers
½ tablespoon margarine
1 large raw carrot
1 cup nonfat milk
1 glass water

SNACK

1 apple
2 cups raw vegetables
1 cup tomato juice
1 glass water

DINNER

3 ounces baked chicken breast, prepared with ½ tablespoon butter
1 medium baked sweet potato
1½ cups steamed spinach
1 whole-grain roll
1 tablespoon margarine
1 glass water

SNACK

1 cup plain nonfat yogurt
¾ cup fruit cocktail canned in own juice
20 animal crackers

Thursday (Step 3)

BREAKFAST

1½ cups whole-grain cereal flakes
2 tablespoons almonds
1 cup nonfat milk
1 cup strawberries
½ cup orange juice
1 5-ounce cup of tea or coffee (optional)
1 glass water

SNACK

2 rice cakes
1 cup tomato juice
2 glasses water

LUNCH

TUNA SALAD SANDWICH
- 2 slices whole-grain bread
- 3 ounces water-packed tuna
- 1 tablespoon mayonnaise
- 2 tablespoons diced celery
- 2 tomato slices
- 1 lettuce leaf

2 medium raw carrots
1 cup nonfat milk
1 glass water

SNACK

1 large pear
1 cup raw or lightly steamed broccoli
1 glass water

DINNER

3 ounces broiled flank steak
1 cup steamed Brussels sprouts
1 cup beets
1 cup cooked fettuccine noodles, tossed in 1 tablespoon olive oil
1 cup nonfat milk
½ cup sherbet
1 glass water

SNACK

1 baked apple
½ teaspoon ground cinnamon
¼ teaspoon vanilla extract

Friday (Step 3)

BREAKFAST

2 slices raisin toast
2 tablespoons low-fat cream cheese
¾ cup pineapple chunks
1 cup nonfat milk
1 5-ounce cup of tea or coffee (optional)
1 glass water

SNACK

2 cups air-popped popcorn
2 glasses water

LUNCH

3 ounces baked chicken breast
Spinach Salad
 3 cups fresh spinach
 ¼ avocado
 1 tablespoon salad dressing1 medium orange
2 whole-grain rolls
1 cup V8 juice
1 cup nonfat plain yogurt
1 glass water

SNACK

2 cups raw vegetables
1 glass water

DINNER

3 ounces roast turkey
1 cup cooked brown rice
2 medium carrots, steamed
½ cup peas
1 teaspoon margarine
2 broiled grapefruit halves
1 glass water

SNACK

5 vanilla wafers
1 cup warmed nonfat milk flavored with vanilla extract and nutmeg to taste

Saturday (Step 3)

BREAKFAST

2 pancakes
1 teaspoon margarine
1 tablespoon syrup
¾ cup applesauce
1 cup nonfat milk
1 5-ounce cup of tea or coffee (optional)
1 glass water

SNACK

¾ cup fat-free cottage cheese
2 medium tomatoes, sliced
2 glasses water

LUNCH

Sandwich
- 2 slices whole wheat bread
- 3 ounces turkey breast
- 2 teaspoons mayonnaise
- 1 tablespoon mustard
- 2 tomato slices
- 1 lettuce leaf

1½ cups vegetable soup
1 cup tomato juice
½ cup raw baby carrots
1 glass water

SNACK

1 cup grapefruit sections
4 graham crackers
1 glass water

DINNER

3 ounces roasted pork loin
1 baked potato
1 tablespoon low-fat sour cream
1½ cups cooked collard greens
1 whole-grain roll
1 glass water

SNACK

2 tangerines
1 cup plain nonfat yogurt
1 tablespoon peanut butter
3 vanilla wafers

Sunday (Step 3)

BREAKFAST

1 whole wheat English muffin, toasted
1 teaspoon margarine
1 cup orange juice
1 cup nonfat milk
1 5-ounce cup of tea or coffee (optional)

SNACK

3 medium pretzels
2 glasses water

LUNCH

2 cups low-fat split-pea soup
4 Ry-Krisp crackers
1 ounce cheese
1 apple
1 cup raw baby carrots
1 cup nonfat milk
½ cup fruit ice
1 glass water

SNACK

3 cups raw vegetables
2 glasses water

DINNER

4 ounces sautéed red snapper, prepared with 1 teaspoon olive oil
1½ cups cooked pasta
1 artichoke, steamed, with 1 tablespoon mayonnaise
1 cup green peas
1 glass water

SNACK

¾ cup nonfat cottage cheese
¾ cup pineapple chunks

CHAPTER FIFTEEN

Do You Need Supplements to Feel Good?

Movie stars, politicians, and physicians do it. Athletes, Ph.D.'s, and dietitians do it. In fact, four out of every ten Americans do it, even though many haven't a clue what they're doing.

Every day at health food stores, grocery stores, pharmacies, and discount department stores, people face a wall of vitamin and mineral supplements. A simple decision to take a supplement becomes a nightmare when you try to choose from thousands of powders, pills, potions, capsules, tablets, multiples, single nutrients, and day packs. Do you really need supplements? If so, what and how much do you need? And how can you be sure you're getting enough without getting too much? To test your knowledge of nutritional supplementation, take the quiz on page 346.

If you're confused and a bit overwhelmed by this subject, you're not alone. The committee that sets the Recommended Dietary Allowances (RDAs) admits that no one knows exactly how much of each nutrient promotes optimal health. Even less is known about how those nutrients work together to enhance or interfere with other nutrients in the body. Throw in the dramatic differences in nutritional needs that one person has compared to the next, and it is easy to see how difficult choosing a supplement can be. However, an educated guess is better than a shot in the dark, so this chapter offers an overview of nutritional supplementation, with guidelines to help you get the most from your supplement.

The Pros and Cons of Supplementation

Most people agree that wholesome foods are the best source of vitamins and minerals. National nutrition surveys report, however, that when it comes to vitamins and minerals, some people just don't get enough. For example, nine out of ten diets are marginal in chromium, a trace mineral essential for regulating blood sugar. More than 50 percent of all Americans consume half the recommended amount of magnesium and folic acid, nutrients found in whole-grain breads, nuts, and dark green leafy vegetables. Up to 80 percent of exercising women and many children are iron deficient. Other nutrients often found to be low in the American diet include the B vitamins, calcium, vitamin D, the trace minerals, vitamin E, and vitamin A.

In addition, many studies report that certain vitamins and minerals in amounts greater than current recommendations might help prevent premature aging and age-related disorders, including memory loss, mood swings associated with PMS and SAD, depression, cancer, and heart disease. Medication use, illness, and stress increase nutrient needs to levels difficult to obtain from even the best diet. For example, birth control pills might increase a woman's need for vitamin B6, while stress raises requirements for magnesium, vitamin C, and zinc. Intense exercise raises nutrient needs above what sedentary people require.

Despite this growing body of research showing that people do not consume even the recommended—let alone the optimal—quantities of certain nutrients, many nutrition advocates in the past considered vitamin and mineral supplements quackery. "Until recently, someone who took supplements was considered suspect," says William Pryor, Ph.D., Boyd Professor of Chemistry and Biochemistry at Louisiana State University in Baton Rouge. "Solid research supporting increased nutrient requirements has replaced the unscientific testimonials of the past, so people now are coming out of the closet and admitting they take supplements."

The potential need for supplements was reinforced by researchers at Harvard School of Public Health, who reported in a recent landmark study that 100 IU of vitamin E reduced the risk of developing heart disease by up to 40 percent. It is unrealistic to consider consuming this much in everyday meals, since it would take more than 1¼ cups of safflower oil, 22 cups of spinach, or 450 spears of

QUIZ 15.1 Your Supplements Know-How

Test your knowledge of supplements with the following quick quiz, then check your answers at the end.

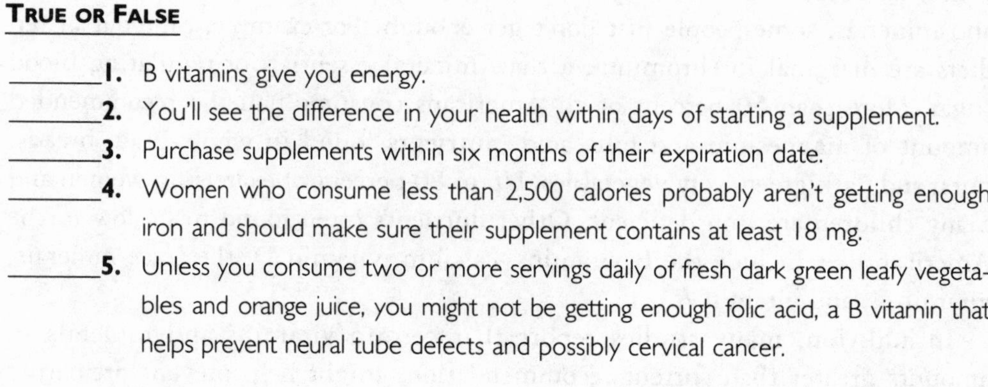

TRUE OR FALSE

_______**1.** B vitamins give you energy.

_______**2.** You'll see the difference in your health within days of starting a supplement.

_______**3.** Purchase supplements within six months of their expiration date.

_______**4.** Women who consume less than 2,500 calories probably aren't getting enough iron and should make sure their supplement contains at least 18 mg.

_______**5.** Unless you consume two or more servings daily of fresh dark green leafy vegetables and orange juice, you might not be getting enough folic acid, a B vitamin that helps prevent neural tube defects and possibly cervical cancer.

MULTIPLE CHOICE

6. While this vitamin can be toxic when consumed in large amounts, its building block (beta-carotene) is relatively safe even at high doses. The vitamin is:

a. vitamin D c. vitamin E e. all of the above

b. vitamin A d. vitamin B6

7. If your skin is not exposed regularly to sunshine, you do not consume at least three glasses of fortified milk each day, or you are middle-aged or older, you might need a supplement that contains 400 IU of which nutrient?

a. vitamin C c. vitamin A e. all of the above

b. calcium d. vitamin D

8. If you are a strict vegetarian (you avoid all meats and dairy products), your diet could be low in which of the following?

a. vitamin B2 c. vitamin B12 e. all of the above

b. zinc d. iron

Scoring:

1. F. The B vitamins help unleash energy from carbohydrates, protein, and fat, but they do not supply energy themselves.

2. F. Supplements provide the best protection against disease when they are taken regularly for years, not when they are taken on and off or for short periods of time.
3. F. For the best guarantee of freshness and potency, purchase supplements that are within nine months to one year of their expiration date.
4. T
5. T
6. b
7. d
8. e

---

asparagus to reach this level of vitamin E. In short, the problem is not whether some people might benefit from supplements, but how to sift through the supplement quagmire to find a worthy product.

Do You Need to Take a Supplement?

If you are following the Feeling Good Diet and consume at least 2,500 calories a day, you will at least meet the RDAs for all the vitamins and minerals. If your diet falls short of this mark, either in quality foods or in calories, then a multiple vitamin and mineral supplement can provide safe and inexpensive insurance. A multiple supplement supplies a balance of nutrients while avoiding secondary deficiencies that result when you take too much of one nutrient and crowd out another. For example, a woman who takes only iron to prevent anemia might become zinc deficient. A man who supplements his diet with only calcium could increase his risk of developing a magnesium deficiency. Excessive intake of folic acid could mask an underlying vitamin B12 deficiency.

On the other hand, many nutrients work in concert and should be provided as a group in the proper ratio for maximum effectiveness. For example, the B vitamins, including vitamin B1, vitamin B2, niacin, pantothenic acid, and biotin, work together to convert food components into energy. Supplementing with only one is unlikely to improve overall mental and emotional health.

Finally, if your diet is low in one nutrient, it probably is low in others. Foods provide a mixture of nutrients. A person who avoids meat and legumes is at risk of consuming inadequate amounts of iron, zinc, and the B vitamins. Too little milk in the diet and you're at risk for deficiencies of vitamin B2, vitamin D, and calcium. You are likely to be low in beta-carotene, vitamin C, folic acid, and some trace minerals if you don't consume at least two servings daily of dark green leafy vegetables and two servings of citrus fruits. It is virtually impossible to be deficient in just one nutrient. Consequently, even a multivitamin supplement is likely to provide incomplete nutrition without the accompanying minerals.

Most one-dose multiples don't contain enough calcium and magnesium, however. These minerals are important in the prevention of osteoporosis and possibly high blood pressure and heart disease. They are essential for optimal exercise performance, help prevent the mood swings associated with PMS, and improve a person's ability to cope with stress. So unless you consume at least three servings daily of low-fat milk products or other calcium-rich foods and a lot of magnesium-rich soybeans, nuts, bananas, dark green leafy vegetables, and wheat germ, you might consider an extra supplement of these two minerals. The best ratio for calcium and magnesium is two-to-one; that is, a supplement that provides at least 200 mg of calcium for every 100 mg of magnesium, with a maximum intake of 1,000 mg calcium and 500 mg magnesium (see also "The Best Bets," page 349).

The Right Dose

In general, choose a supplement that supplies 100 to 300 percent of the U.S. RDAs (U.S. Recommended Daily Allowances) for each nutrient. Megavitamin-mineral therapy—consuming ten times or more of the U.S. RDAs—is based on the belief that more is better or therapeutic, but usually it is a waste of money.

The body can use only so much of any one nutrient. At best, the excesses are excreted; at worst, they are stored in the body to potentially toxic levels. For example:

- As few as six high-potency iron pills can be poisonous to little children.
- High intakes of niacin can damage the liver and cause stomach problems.
- Excessive intake of selenium can damage tissues.

The Best Bets

You have several choices when designing a supplement program:

1. You can obtain all your vitamins and minerals from the Feeling Good Diet and skip the supplement aisle.
2. If you do not consume at least 2,500 calories of foods outlined in the Feeling Good Diet, consider taking a well-balanced multiple vitamin and mineral supplement, preferably one that can be taken in divided doses throughout the day.
3. If you are not selecting enough calcium- and magnesium-rich foods in the Feeling Good Diet, and your multiple doesn't contain RDA levels of calcium and magnesium, supplement your supplement with these two minerals in a ratio of 2 mg of calcium for every 1 mg of magnesium.
4. Consider taking extra antioxidants—vitamin C, vitamin E, and beta-carotene—with or without a multiple supplement.

- Long-term excessive intake of vitamin A (50,000 IU for an adult) can cause headaches, liver damage, bone damage, and diarrhea. Vitamin A overdose can cause birth defects if taken during pregnancy.
- Vitamin B6 in doses of 250 mg or higher (RDA is 2 mg) can cause weakness, numbness, and other symptoms of nerve damage if taken for extended periods of time.
- Long-term excessive intake of vitamin D can cause kidney damage and bone deformities.

In some cases—such as zinc—consuming too much can backfire. That is, a little zinc enhances the body's defense against disease, while too much might suppress immunity. By staying within 100 to 300 percent of the U.S. RDA, you obtain all you need without the risk of taking too much.

Exceptions to this rule are the antioxidant nutrients, which might be beneficial in doses several times the current U.S. RDA levels. Dr. Pryor recommends a modest supplement program of four pills a day. "Everyone should take a well-balanced multiple, plus the lowest-dose single supplements of vitamin C, beta-carotene, and vitamin E." For healthy adults, vitamin C appears safe in daily doses up to 500 mg, vitamin E is safe up to 400 IU, and beta-carotene is safe in amounts up to 15 mg or more. Many antioxidant supplements now contain these three nutrients in a one-a-day tablet.

Label Lingo

Although debate rages over which of what is best, when it comes to supplements, your best bet is to stick with the basics and avoid the glitz. Here's a crash course on label lingo.

Time-Release Vitamins: Theoretically, these supplements should raise and maintain blood levels of a vitamin better than regular supplements. In reality, most time-release tablets dissolve too slowly to be completely absorbed. Time-release forms of niacin are well absorbed, but might be more toxic to the liver than a similar amount of a non-time-release brand.

Chelated Minerals: A chelated mineral is chemically bound to another substance, usually an amino acid (the building blocks of protein). Examples include iron–amino chelate or chromium proteinate. Although manufacturers propose that chelation improves the absorption of a mineral, there is little proof that chelated minerals are absorbed any better than other supplements.

Synthetic Versus Natural Nutrients: The terms *organic* and *natural* have a wholesome sound, but in reality these products are more likely to tax your pocketbook than improve your health. First, in most cases, the body cannot distinguish a natural from a synthetic nutrient. Second, many products labeled as natural are actually synthetic vitamins mixed with small amounts of "natural" vitamins. For example, a natural vitamin C supplement contains mostly laboratory-made ascorbic acid with a small amount of vitamin C from rose hips or acerola berries.

Selenium, chromium, and vitamin E are exceptions to the rule. The "organic" forms of the trace minerals selenium and chromium are called selenium-rich yeast or L-selenomethionine and chromium-rich yeast. They are better absorbed and used by the body than the synthetic sodium selenite and chromic chloride and therefore are your best bets. Likewise, body tissues prefer the "natural" form of vitamin E, called d-alpha-tocopherol, to the synthetic counterpart, called dl-alpha- or all-rac-alpha-tocopherol, which is a mix of d-alpha-tocopherol plus seven less potent forms of vitamin E. In these three cases, a "natural" source of the nutrient might be your best bet.

Developing a Personalized Supplement Program

If you wish to devise you own supplementation program, there are ways to minimize waste and maximize benefits when choosing your vitamins and minerals. For example, choose a multiple vitamin-mineral preparation, rather than single supplements, unless prescribed by a dietitian or physician. Select a preparation that provides approximately 100 to 300 percent of the U.S. RDA for the following:

- *Vitamins:* Vitamins D, E, C, B1, B2, B6, and B12; niacin; folic acid; and pantothenic acid. (Avoid large doses of vitamin B1, vitamin B2, and niacin; a supplement manufacturer adds hefty amounts of these nutrients only because they are inexpensive, not because extra is better.)
- *Minerals:* Copper, iron (ferrous sulfate or ferrous fumarate are best absorbed), and zinc.

Your supplement should also offer 50 to 200 mcg of both chromium and selenium.

Avoid supplement claims of "natural," "organic," "therapeutic," "high-potency," "chelated," "time-release," or "stress-formulated." Also, avoid supplements that contain useless substances such as inositol, vitamin B15, PABA, or nutrients in amounts less than 25 percent of the RDA. The following nutrients are adequately supplied in the diet and are not needed in a supplement:

biotin	phosphorus
chloride	potassium
vitamin K	sodium

Vitamins C and E and beta-carotene can be consumed in amounts greater than the RDAs. Safe and potentially beneficial amounts of these nutrients are 250 to 500 mg of vitamin C, 100 to 400 IU of vitamin E, and 10 to 25 mg of beta-carotene. A mixture of carotenoids is better than beta-carotene alone.

TABLE 15.1 What to Look For: A Sample Supplement

Two to four tablets daily taken with meals supply the following:

NUTRIENTS	QUANTITY	% OF U.S. RDA
Vitamin A (retinol)	2,500 IU	50
Beta-carotene	15 mg	–
Vitamin D	400 IU	100
Vitamin E (d-alpha-tocopherol)	200 IU	600
Vitamin B1 (thiamin)	1.5 mg	100
Vitamin B2 (riboflavin)	1.7 mg	100
Niacin (niacinamide)	20 mg	100
Vitamin B6 (pyridoxine)	2 mg	100
Vitamin B12 (cobalamine)	6 mcg	100
Folic acid (folacin)	400 mcg	100
Pantothenic acid	10 mg	100
Vitamin C	250 mg	400
Calcium (calcium carbonate)	1,000 mg	100
Chromium (GTF-chromium)	200 mcg	*
Copper	2 mg	100
Iron (ferrous fumarate)	18 mg	100
Magnesium (magnesium citrate)	500 mg	125
Manganese	5 mg	*
Molybdenum	75–250 mcg	*
Selenium (L-selenomethionine)	200 mcg	*
Zinc	15 mg	100

*No U.S. RDA has been established for these nutrients. The amounts listed are based on the Food and Nutrition Board's Safe and Adequate daily amounts.

Consider a second supplement of calcium and magnesium if your diet and your multiple are low in these minerals. Your goals should be to consume at least 1,000 mg of calcium and 500 mg of magnesium from the combination of foods and supplement. Avoid calcium supplements that contain bonemeal, eggshell, or dolomite, since some of these products contain lead.

If you are willing to put up with the inconvenience, select a product that can be taken in several doses throughout the day, since nutrients are better absorbed when they are consumed in divided doses than when they are supplied in a one-shot supplement. For example, the body absorbs only about 100 mg of magnesium at one time. Doses greater than this are likely to be excreted. Multidose multiples also provide flexibility; you can reduce the number of tablets on days when your diet is optimal and increase the number on days you didn't have time to eat right.

Except for iron, which is best absorbed on an empty stomach, take your supplement with food and without coffee or tea.

In short, supplements support and reinforce the Feeling Good Diet, but they don't replace it. They cannot grant immunity to disease for a body that is otherwise unhealthy. In addition, many other substances in foods besides vitamins and minerals aid in the prevention of disease and the promotion of optimal emotional, physical, and mental health. Compounds called indoles, found in Brussels sprouts, broccoli, and other vegetables in the cabbage family, help prevent cancer. Ajoene and other substances in garlic enhance the body's natural defenses against colds, infections, and disease. None of these substances are found in vitamin and mineral supplements. In the future, even more food-related compounds that enhance well-being are likely to be identified. However, a well-balanced supplement plan is a safe and convenient form of nutritional insurance that fills in the gaps when eating habits fall short of perfect.

Glossary

Acetylcholine: A neurotransmitter in the brain that helps regulate memory. A dietary component called choline is the building block for acetylcholine.

Adenosine: A component of ATP (adenosine triphosphate), the primary storage form of quick energy in all body cells. Adenosine also inhibits some neurotransmitters that otherwise stimulate nerve cell activity.

Adrenal glands: The glands located near the kidneys that produce and secrete hormones, such as epinephrine (adrenalin) and norepinephrine.

Adrenalin: A hormone released by the adrenal glands during times of stress, also called epinephrine.

Aerobic exercise: Slow, steady, nonstop activities such as jogging, walking, biking, or swimming, which require a steady intake of oxygen and that use large muscle groups.

Allicin: A substance in garlic that is responsible for garlic's odor, inhibits the growth of bacteria, and strengthens the immune system.

Alliin: A compound in garlic that converts to allicin when garlic is chopped or crushed.

Alzheimer's disease: A degenerate nerve illness that affects the elderly and causes dementia and progressive memory loss.

Amenorrhea: Failure to menstruate.

Amino acids: The building blocks of proteins that make up hair, skin, blood, and other body tissues. Approximately twenty different amino acids are found in the protein of human tissues.

Ammonia: The toxic by-product of protein breakdown, converted to urea and excreted in urine.

Anaerobic exercise: Physical activity that requires short bursts of energy. Examples include football or sprinting.

Anaphylactic shock: A life-threatening, exaggerated allergic reaction to a substance to which the body has previously become sensitized.

Anemia: A change in the size, color, or number of red blood cells that results in reduced oxygen-carrying capacity of the blood.

Anorexia nervosa: Self-imposed food restriction that leads to severe weight loss of 15 percent or more of normal body weight and that is potentially life-threatening.

Antioxidant: A compound that reduces or prevents free-radical tissue damage otherwise associated with degenerative diseases such as heart disease and cancer, and premature aging.

Aspartame: A nonnutritive artificial sweetener more commonly known as NutraSweet or Equal.

Asthma: A chronic respiratory disease characterized by labored breathing and coughing, which alternate with symptom-free periods.

Atherosclerosis: Accumulation of fat in the artery wall. It is the underlying cause of cardiovascular disease.

Axon: The long "tail" of the nerve cell that conducts impulses from the body of the nerve cell toward the next nerve cell.

B-cells: A type of lymphocyte (white blood cell) in the immune system that circulates in the blood and destroys bacteria.

Beta-carotene: The building block for vitamin A that also functions as an antioxidant independent of its vitamin A activity and is found in dark green leafy or orange vegetables and in orange fruits.

Binge: A large intake of food in a short period of time, usually less than two hours.

Biofeedback: A stress-reduction technique that teaches a person how to control unconscious body functions.

Biotin: One of the B vitamins involved in the metabolism of amino acids, carbohydrates, and fats.

Bulimarexia: An eating disorder that combines binge-and-purge eating episodes with periods of self-starvation.

Bulimia: An eating disorder characterized by binge eating followed by purging with vomiting, laxative abuse, or the use of enemas.

Calorie: A measurement of energy in food. A calorie is the amount of heat energy required to raise the temperature of 1,000 grams of water 1 degree centigrade. Protein and carbohydrates in foods supply 4 calories per gram, fat supplies 9 calories per gram, and alcohol supplies approximately 7 calories per gram.

Cataract: A milky film that forms over the eye and is one of the most common causes of eyesight loss.

Cell membrane: The outer covering of each cell composed of fats and proteins.

Cesarean: Birth of a baby through a surgical incision in the abdomen.

Chelated: Describes a mineral combined with another compound, such as chromium picolinate.

Chinese restaurant syndrome: Condition marked by headaches, heart palpitations, and neck or chest pain that appears after eating foods containing MSG (monosodium glutamate), a flavor-enhancing additive.

Chlorinated hydrocarbon: Compounds used in decaffeinating coffee and suspected of causing cancer.

Cholecystokinin (CCK): A 33-amino acid hormone secreted from the digestive tract that has numerous effects on the digestive tract and central nervous system, including signaling fullness (satiety) after eating. The presence of food in the stomach triggers the release of CCK, which transmits messages to the central nervous system via the vagus nerve and results in reduced hunger.

Cholesterol: A noncaloric fatlike substance (called a sterol) found in foods of animal origin and produced by the liver. High levels of cholesterol in the blood are associated with heart disease.

Choline: A vitaminlike compound necessary for normal brain and nerve function. Choline is a building block for the neurotransmitter acetylcholine.

Chromic chloride: An inorganic form of chromium.

Chronic fatigue syndrome (CFS): A persistent condition characterized by lethargy, muscle aches and weakness, and mood swings.

Cognition: The mental process of knowledge acquisition; the process of knowing or perceiving.

Collagen: A protein in connective tissue and the organic substance in teeth and bones.

Complex carbohydrates: The nutrient-rich starches and fibers present in vegetables, some fruits, and cereals.

Compulsive eating: The feeling of an overwhelming urge or need to eat, not because of hunger but because of other factors, including emotions, habits, or appetite-control mechanisms in the body.

Corticotropic releasing hormone (CRH): A hormone from the hypothalamus in the brain that stimulates the release of other hormones such as adrenocorticotrop in (ACTH) from the pituitary gland in the brain that, in turn, affect the metabolism of glucose, proteins, and fats. CRH release also reduces appetite and hunger.

Cortisol: An adrenal gland hormone (called a glucocorticoid) that stimulates the body to manufacture glucose for energy. Cortisol is secreted in response to stress.

Cross-reactivity: Condition whereby a food allergy to one food increases the likelihood of an allergic reaction to other foods in that food family.

Cyclamates: Nonnutritive sweeteners suspected of causing cancer.

D-alpha-tocopherol: The natural form of vitamin E.

Dehydration: A loss of water from the body as a result of insufficient intake, excessive vomiting, or diarrhea.

Dendrites: Branches on neurons that receive messages.

D-fenfluramine: A drug that increases serotonin levels and helps curb hunger.

Diabetes: A hereditary disease resulting in abnormal insulin production or function and unregulated blood-sugar levels.

Diuretic: A substance that increases urinary excretion and decreases the amount of water in the body.

Dl-alpha-tocopherol: The synthetic form of vitamin E.

DNA: Deoxyribonucleic acid. The helix structure that carries the genetic information in the nucleus of all cells.

Dolomite: A mineral composed of calcium and magnesium. Dolomite supplements might contain lead.

Dopamine: A neurotransmitter and hormone and an intermediate product in the production of adrenalin. Dopamine also helps regulate mood and food intake. A dopamine deficiency results in Parkinson's disease, which is characterized by tremors and repetitive movements.

Electrolyte: A substance or salt, such as sodium, potassium, or chloride, that conducts an electrical charge. Electrolyte balance is the distribution of salts among the body fluids.

Electrolyte imbalance: Abnormal distribution of salts and other electrolytes in the body fluids.

Emotional eating: Eating in response to feelings, such as depression, anxiety, or anger, rather than in response to physical hunger.

Endocrine gland: A gland in the body that manufactures and secretes a hormone. Examples include the pancreas, the pituitary, the adrenals, and the ovaries.

Endorphins: The morphinelike neurotransmitter hormones that produce a pleasurable response and reduce pain sensations during stress and physical exertion. Endorphins also have a profound effect on food intake and the pleasure response related to eating.

Enriched: Describes the addition to processed foods of a few nutrients to bring the level back to the original vitamin or mineral content. Only four nutrients, vitamin B1, vitamin B2, niacin, and iron, are added back during enrichment, while many more nutrients are lost in processing.

Enzyme: A compound that acts as a catalyst in starting chemical reactions in the body.

Eosinophilia-myalgia syndrome: A rare disorder characterized by muscle pain, high white-blood-cell counts, cough, edema, fatigue, hypertension, oral ulcers, and nerve damage. An outbreak of EMS in the 1980s and early 1990s was linked to a batch of contaminated tryptophan supplements from Japan.

Epinephrine: A hormone secreted by the adrenal glands during times of stress or hypoglycemia. Also called adrenalin.

Esophageal perforation: A rip or tear in the esophagus, the muscular tube extending from the throat to the stomach.

Estrogen: A family of female reproductive hormones.

Fat calories: Calories that are derived from fat in a food or meal. Fat calories should not exceed 30 percent of total calories in the diet. Less is better. The percentage of fat calories is calculated by multiplying the total grams of fat in a food by 9 (fat supplies 9 calories per gram), dividing by the total calories in the food, and multiplying by 100.

Fatigue: Feelings of physical or mental weariness, tiredness, or weakness.

Fiber: The indigestible residue in food, composed of the carbohydrates cellulose, pectin, and hemicellulose; vegetable gums; and the noncarbohydrate lignin.

Flavonoids: A group of more than 200 compounds found in citrus fruits, leafy vegetables, red onions, and soybeans that may have antioxidant capability in protecting against free-radical damage to tissues.

Folic acid: A B vitamin essential for cell replication.

Follicle stimulating hormone (FSH): A hormone secreted from the pituitary in the brain that stimulates the ovaries to grow and eventually secrete estrogen in the woman and the testes to produce sperm in the man.

Food and Drug Administration (FDA): An agency in the U.S. government that monitors the safety of foods, drugs, and cosmetics.

Food Guide Pyramid: A dietary guideline proposed by the U.S. Department of Agriculture that emphasizes increased consumption of fruits, vegetables, and grains and reduced consumption of fatty foods.

Fortified: Describes the addition of vitamins or minerals to a processed food to levels greater than naturally found. Milk is fortified with vitamin D.

Free fatty acids: Fat fragments floating in the blood made up of a carbon chain with hydrogens attached and an acid group at the end. Three fatty acids combine with a molecule called glycerol to make a triglyceride.

Free radical: A damaging compound present in air pollution, radiation, tobacco smoke, UV sunlight, rancid fats, and made naturally in the body. Most free radicals are oxygen fragments.

Fructose: A sugar found in fruits and honey. Also called fruit sugar.

Fungus: A group of plants including yeasts, molds, and mushrooms.

GABA (gamma-amino-butyric acid): A neurotransmitter that inhibits message transmission from one nerve cell to another, which helps prevent the nerve cells from firing too fast and overloading the system. In essence, GABA helps balance other activating neurotransmitters such as acetylcholine.

Galactose: One of the simple-sugar units that make up milk sugar or lactose.

Galanin: A proteinlike chemical in the brain, in particular in the hypothalamus and possibly the amygdala, made up of 29 amino acids, that helps regulate the body's desire for and metabolism of fat.

Gamma linolenic acid (GLA): An omega-3 fatty acid.

Gastric atony: Reduced stomach muscle tone.

Glucagon: A hormone secreted by the pancreas that raises blood-sugar levels and that is essential to the metabolism of glycogen.

Glucocorticoids: Hormones secreted by the adrenal cortex that convert protein into carbohydrate and that regulate carbohydrate, fat, and protein metabolism.

Glucose: The carbohydrate that makes up sugar, blood sugar, and the building blocks of starch.

Glucose polymers: Manufactured strings of sugar molecules.

Glycogen: The storage form of glucose in the liver and muscles.

Gram: A unit of weight. Twenty-eight grams equal 1 ounce.

Growth hormone: A substance produced by the brain that promotes protein synthesis and tissue growth.

HDL-cholesterol: Cholesterol packaged in high-density lipoproteins (HDLs). HDL-cholesterol is composed of fats and protein, and serves as a means of transport for fats in the blood. A high level of HDL-cholesterol is associated with a reduced risk of developing cardiovascular disease.

Heartburn: A burning chest pain often caused by overeating, spicy food, or alcohol intake.

Hedonic: Relating to the pursuit of pleasure.

Hematocrit: A test for anemia that measures the percent volume of red blood cells in the blood.

Hemoglobin: The iron-rich protein in red blood cells that transports oxygen. A hemoglobin test measures the percentage of hemoglobin in the blood.

High-fructose corn syrup (HFCS): A sweetener commonly used in processed foods that contains 40 to 90 percent fructose.

Hormone: Chemical substance secreted by an endocrine gland, such as the adrenals, the pancreas, or the pituitary, that travels in the blood to other parts of the body to help regulate function.

Humors: Body elements, including fire, air, water, and earth, believed in ancient times to affect mood and health. Imbalances in these humors were thought to cause disease, mental disorders, and death.

Hyperactivity: A behavior pattern of high activity and lack of concentration in children.

Hypochondria: A condition characterized by morbid anxiety that the body is plagued by imaginary diseases.

Hypoglycemia: Low blood sugar.

Hysterectomy: Surgical removal of the uterus.

Immediate hypersensitivity: An allergic response that generates an immune reaction within minutes or hours of eating the offending food.

Immune system: The body's intricate defense system, composed of organs, tissues, and cells that fight against disease and infection.

Insomnia: Inability to fall or stay asleep.

Insulin: A hormone secreted by the pancreas that helps regulate blood-sugar levels by facilitating sugar into the cells when blood-sugar levels rise above normal.

Interferon: A substance released by the immune system that prevents an invading virus from multiplying.

International Unit (IU): An arbitrary measurement used for the fat-soluble vitamins A, D, and E. These units standardize the potency of the vitamin rather than measure it by weight. International Units can be converted to weight measurements; for example, 3.33 IU of vitamin A are equivalent to 1 mcg.

Intrinsic factor: A substance produced in the stomach that is essential for the absorption of vitamin B12 (extrinsic factor).

IQ (intelligence quotient): A number representing a person's level of intelligence. It is the mental age, as assessed by an intelligence test, multiplied by 100 and divided by a person's chronological age.

Irrational thoughts: Illogical beliefs, attitudes, or thinking patterns not founded in reality that fuel unhealthful behaviors, such as emotional eating.

Jet lag: The fatigue, insomnia, or impaired memory and thinking ability that results from flying across time zones.

Lactase: An enzyme in the small intestine that digests lactose or milk sugar.

Lactobacillus acidophilus: A bacteria found in some yogurts that might assist in lactose digestion and maintain a healthy environment in the digestive tract and vagina. Also called *L. acidophilus*.

Lactobacillus bulgarius: Bacteria found in yogurt that assists in lactose digestion.

Lactose: Milk sugar.

Lactose intolerance: The inability to digest the milk sugar lactose. The condition is characterized by abdominal bloating, cramping, intestinal gas, and diarrhea.

LDL-cholesterol: The low-density lipoprotein that transports cholesterol in the blood. High levels are associated with heart disease.

Lecithin: A substance with a fat-soluble side and a water-soluble side that is a component of cell membranes, is manufactured in the liver, and is obtained from foods. Lecithin contains choline, the building block for the neurotransmitter acetylcholine.

Legumes: Dried beans and peas, such as kidney or black beans, lentils, or split peas.

Lethargy: Tiredness, sluggishness, or fatigue.

Leukotrienes: Hormonelike compounds that are involved in the inflammation process and are manufactured in the body from polyunsaturated fats.

Linoleic acid: A polyunsaturated fatty acid essential to the body that must be obtained from the diet.

L-selenomethionine: The organic form of selenium.

Lupus: A group of chronic inflammatory diseases. For example, lupus erythematosus is an inflammation of the skin that can be fatal.

Lyme disease: A disease transmitted by ticks that causes flulike symptoms and inflammation.

Lymphokines: Proteins in the immune system that help facilitate communication and coordination of the body's immune defenses.

Macrophage: A large blood cell that aids in the immune response to disease and infection.

Magnesium: A major mineral essential for bone development, muscle relaxation, nerve transmission, and blood-sugar regulation.

Manganese: A trace mineral essential for the formulation of connective tissue, fat and cholesterol metabolism, bone development, and blood clotting.

MAO (monoamine oxidase) inhibitor: An antidepressant drug that prolongs the life of stimulating brain chemicals, such as serotonin and norepinephrine.

Mastalgia: Pain in the breasts.

Melatonin: A hormonelike substance secreted in the absence of light that produces drowsiness. Melatonin is similar in structure to serotonin and is manufactured in the pineal gland in the brain.

Menarche: The start of menstruation at puberty.

Menopause: The cessation of menstruation. Since a woman must be menstruation-free for twelve months, the diagnosis is made after the fact or is based on the typical signs and symptoms, such as hot flashes, and can be confirmed with a test that measures hormone levels, especially a female hormone called FSH (follicle stimulating hormone) that rises as estrogen levels fall.

Menstruation: The monthly discharge of the blood-enriched lining of the uterus. Also called menses.

Metabolic acidosis: An abnormal increased blood acidity as a result of excessive vomiting or diarrhea.

Metabolic rate: The amount of calories expended by basic body functioning and daily activities.

Metabolism: The sum of all chemical processes that convert food and its components to the fundamental chemicals that the body uses for energy or for repair, maintenance, and growth of tissues. Metabolism includes all the building-up processes, such as tissue growth, and all the tearing-down processes, such as breaking down glycogen for energy.

Metabolite: Any by-product of metabolism.

Microgram (mcg): A metric unit of weight equivalent to one one-thousandth of a milligram.

Milligram (mg): A metric unit of weight equivalent to one one-thousandth of a gram.

Mineral: An inorganic fundamental substance found naturally in the soil and taken up by plants and animals that has specific chemical and structural properties. Many minerals are essential nutrients for growth, maintenance, and repair of tissues.

Mini-goals: Divisions of a long-term plan into smaller weekly accomplishments.

Monocytes: A type of white blood cell active in the immune response.

Monosodium glutamate (MSG): A food additive that in some people causes an adverse reaction commonly called Chinese restaurant syndrome.

Multiple sclerosis: A progressive central-nervous-system disease that might lead to paralysis.

Myelin sheath: An insulating band around some nerve cells that speeds the conduction of nerve impulses down the axon.

Myoglobin: The iron-rich compound that holds and transports oxygen within the cell.

Narcolepsy: A sleep disorder causing uncontrollable episodes of sleep during the day.

Natural killer cells: A type of cell in the immune system that destroys microorganisms (germs) in the body.

Negative reinforcer: Something that reduces the likelihood that a person will repeat a behavior.

Nervous system: The brain and nerves that coordinate and control responses to stimuli and that condition behavior and all thinking processes.

Neural tube defects: A type of birth defect in the neural tube that becomes the spinal cord and brain in which this tube does not close in the developing embryo. Examples of neural tube defects include spina bifida, anencephaly, and encephalocoele. These birth defects result from both genetic and environmental factors, including poor maternal intake of folic acid during pregnancy.

Neuron: The smallest functioning unit of the nervous system. Also called the nerve cell.

Neuropeptide Y (NPY): A nerve chemical in the brain, in particular the hypothalamus, that regulates carbohydrate intake.

Neurotransmitter: A chemical that transmits messages between nerve cells or between nerve cells and organs or muscles.

Niacin: One of the B vitamins involved in the release of energy from amino acids, carbohydrates, and fats.

Nicotine: A stimulant and addictive drug found in tobacco.

Nitrites: Food additives that are converted to carcinogenic substances, called nitrosamines, in the stomach.

Norepinephrine: A neurotransmitter and hormone released by the adrenal glands and a small group of cells in the brain stem. Also called noradrenalin.

Nucleic acids: Components of DNA, the genetic code found in every cell and essential to cell replication and development.

Obesity: Body fat weight more than 20 percent above a desirable body weight. The body weight is excess fat, not muscle or lean tissue.

Olestra: A calorie-free artificial fat that may be added to foods in the future.

Organic brain syndromes: Disorders affecting consciousness, intellect, or mental functioning.

Orlistat: A compound that reduces the absorption of fat in the intestines.

Osteoporosis: A decrease in bone density resulting in brittle, porous bones that are susceptible to fractures.

Ovary: A glandular organ in the female reproductive system that produces the ovum (egg) and secretes the female hormones estrogen and progesterone. Loss of ovarian function is the deciding factor in menopause.

Ozone: A highly reactive form of oxygen in which the two atoms (0_2) are increased to three (0_3).

Pallor: Abnormally pale skin tone.

Palpitations: Rapid beating of the heart.

Pancreas: An endocrine gland in the abdomen that secretes a variety of hormones, including blood-sugar regulating hormones such as insulin and glucagon, and digestive enzymes such as pancreatic lipase.

Pancreatitis: Inflammation of the pancreas.

Panic disorder: A form of anxiety disorder characterized by repeated panic attacks that escalate during stress.

Pantothenic acid: One of the B vitamins involved in the metabolism of amino acids, carbohydrates, and fats.

Parotid glands: The salivary glands located in the neck.

Peptides: Short strings of amino acids.

Phenylalanine: An amino acid present in many foods.

Phenylethylamine (PEA): A substance present in chocolate that might release endorphins in the brain.

Phenylketonuria (PKU): An inherited intolerance of the amino acid phenylalanine that can result in retardation unless dietary intake of the amino acid is curtailed.

Phototherapy: Treatment of seasonal affective disorder (SAD) with sunlight or artificial light sources.

Pica: A desire to eat nonfood substances, such as chalk or soil.

Placebo: A medicine with no effect that is given to please or humor a patient.

Placenta: The organ that links the blood supply of a mother with the developing fetus.

Polyunsaturated fat: A triglyceride in which at least two of its three fatty acids are unsaturated (have room for the addition of more hydrogen atoms). Vegetable oils and fish oils are polyunsaturated fats.

Positive reinforcer: Something that increases the likelihood that a person will repeat a behavior.

Postpartum: Referring to after childbirth.

Premenstrual syndrome (PMS): A combination of physical and emotional symptoms present one to two weeks before menstruation.

Progesterone: A female reproductive hormone.

Prolactin: A hormone that stimulates milk secretion.

Prostaglandins: A group of hormonelike substances formed from polyunsaturated fatty acids that have a profound effect on the body, including contraction of smooth muscle and dilation or contraction of blood vessels in the regulation of blood pressure.

Protein: Compounds made up of amino acids found in many foods.

Rapid Eye Movement (REM): A stage of sleep characterized by heightened brain activity.

Recommended Dietary Allowance (RDA): Suggested amounts of most vitamins and minerals needed by healthy individuals to avoid clinical nutrient deficiencies, based on age, gender, and size.

Relapse: A return to old, unhealthful habits.

RNA (ribonucleic acid): Cellular compounds that transmit genetic information from DNA to the protein-forming system within the cell.

Saccharin: An nonnutritive artificial sweetener suspected of causing cancer.

Saturated fat: A triglyceride with the maximum possible number of hydrogen atoms. Saturated fats are solid at room temperature, such as butter and stick margarine, and are linked to an increased risk for developing heart disease and possibly breast cancer.

Schizophrenia: A group of disabling illnesses affecting cognition, emotions, and behavior.

Seasonal affective disorder (SAD): A disorder characterized by depression, increased food cravings, and fatigue that develop only during the winter months.

Self-talk: A person's internal dialogue; talking to yourself.

Senility: An age-related decline in mental ability that usually includes memory loss and reduced concentration.

Serotonin: A neurotransmitter in the brain that regulates sleep, mood, food intake, and pain.

Serum ferritin: The form of iron in the blood that is a sensitive indicator of tissue iron levels. A value less than 20 mcg/L indicates iron deficiency.

Simplesse: A fat substitute made from natural egg or milk protein and used in processed foods.

Sodium: An electrolyte that combines with chloride to make table salt.

Sodium selenite: An inorganic form of selenium.

Starch: Complex carbohydrates found in vegetables, some fruits, and cereals.

Streptococcus lactis: A bacteria found in some buttermilk that digests some of the milk sugar lactose.

Sucrose: Table sugar. A simple carbohydrate made up of two molecules, glucose and fructose.

Sugar: A sweet-tasting simple carbohydrate, such as sucrose, glucose, or fructose.

Synapse: The connection between two neurons where messages are transmitted from one nerve cell to the other.

Synaptic gap: The space between two neurons in which neurotransmitters are released and communication between two nerve cells occurs.

T-cells: A lymphocyte of the immune system that attacks bacteria and viruses within the cells.

Thought stopping: A technique to stop negative self-talk where the person silently says "STOP" whenever a negative thought occurs. A person then can replace the negative thought with a positive one.

Thyroxin: A hormone produced by the thyroid gland.

Tofu: A high-protein curd made from soybeans.

Toxemia: A potentially dangerous condition during pregnancy, characterized by elevated blood pressure. Also called eclampsia or pregnancy-induced hypertension.

Trace mineral: An essential mineral found in the body in amounts less than .0005 percent of body weight.

Trans fatty acids (TFA): Polyunsaturated fats formed during hydrogenation of vegetable oils to make margarine or shortening. The shape of these fats is different from other polyunsaturated fats, and it is suspected that they act more like saturated fats in the promotion of heart disease.

Tricyclics: Antidepressant medications that prolong the release of stimulating chemicals in the brain.

Triglyceride: The most common type of calorie-containing fat found in food, a person's fat tissues, and the blood.

Tryptophan: An amino acid that can be converted by the body to the B vitamin niacin or to the neurotransmitter serotonin.

Type A personality: A personality type that is time-conscious, impatient, competitive, and aggressive.

Type B personality: A personality type that is patient, relaxed, and slow-paced.

Tyramine: A chemical found naturally in foods such as aged cheeses that causes migraine headaches in some people.

Tyrosine: An amino acid converted by the body to the neurotransmitters dopamine and norepinephrine.

Unsaturated fat: A triglyceride that contains one or more fatty acids that could accept more hydrogen atoms. Unsaturated fats are liquid at room temperature. Examples include vegetable oils and fish oils.

Vasopressin: A hormone secreted by the pituitary gland in the brain that raises blood pressure and is an antidiuretic.

Virus: Any of a large group of minute particles that are capable of infecting plants, animals, and humans and causing disease.

Vitamin: An essential nutrient that must be obtained from the diet and is required by the body in minute amounts.

Waist-to-hip ratio (WHR): A measurement of regional distribution of body fat. A high WHR reflects excessive fat accumulation above the waist, which is associated with increased risk of heart disease, diabetes, cancer, and other disorders.

Whole grain: An unrefined grain that retains its edible outside layers (the bran) and the highly nutritious inner part, as in wheat germ.

Yeast: A type of fungus found naturally on the skin and other membranes of the body that when allowed to multiply can cause infection and disease.

Yo-yo dieting: Repeated attempts to lose weight, followed by a regain of the lost weight.

Recipes for Feeling Your Best

The following recipes are for dishes mentioned in this book.

Snacks and Side Dishes

Fruit Pops

½ cup orange juice
2 cups peeled and sliced nectarines or peaches
1 6-ounce can frozen unsweetened pineapple or pineapple-orange juice concentrate, thawed

Place juice, fruit, and concentrate in blender. Puree until smooth, then pour into molds and freeze overnight. Makes up to 12 pops.

Serving: 1 pop
Calories: 52
Percent calories from carbohydrates: 91
Percent calories from protein: 5
Percent calories from fat: 4
Fiber: 1 gram

Banana Pops

1 medium banana
1/4 cup orange juice
2 tablespoons coconut, low-fat granola, and/or wheat germ
2 Popsicle sticks
Waxed paper

Peel the banana and cut in half crosswise. Dip each half in the orange juice, then roll in the coconut, granola, and/or wheat germ. Stick a Popsicle stick into the end of each banana half. Wrap in waxed paper and freeze until solid, about 2 hours. Serve frozen. Makes 2 small pops.

Serving: 2 pops
Calories: 176
Percent calories from carbohydrates: 79
Percent calories from protein: 6
Percent calories from fat: 15
Fiber: 3 grams

Garlic Dip

This tasty dip takes only 5 minutes to make and is great with chips, raw vegetables, crackers, or French bread.

1 (8-ounce) package fat-free cream cheese, at room temperature
3 tablespoons evaporated nonfat milk
4–6 garlic cloves, minced
2 teaspoons dried parsley flakes
2 teaspoons chopped fresh chives
Salt
Paprika, for garnish

Blend the cream cheese and evaporated milk with a wire whisk or an electric mixer until smooth. Add the garlic, parsley, chives, and salt to taste; mix well. Pour into a serving dish and sprinkle with paprika. Refrigerate for at least 1 hour, then serve with fresh-cut vegetables such as carrot and celery sticks, green pepper slices, zucchini chunks, jicama slices, and broccoli flowerets. Makes about 1 cup.

Serving: ¼ cup
Calories: 65
Percent calories from carbohydrates: 36.4
Percent calories from protein: 63
Percent calories from fat: 0.6%
Fiber: less than 1 gram

Fresh Salsa

2 large fresh tomatoes, chopped
½ medium sweet onion (such as Bermuda or Walla Walla), minced
1 garlic clove, minced
½ cup chopped fresh cilantro
½ Anaheim chile, minced, or to taste
Salt and pepper

Place the ingredients in a bowl and mix well. Chill for 1 hour. Serve with oven-baked tortilla chips and/or Hot and Spicy Refried Beans (recipe follows). Makes 2½ to 3 cups.

Serving: ½ cup
Calories: 20
Percent calories from carbohydrates: 77
Percent calories from protein: 14
Percent calories from fat: 9
Fiber: 2 grams

Hot and Spicy Refried Beans

2 cups dried pinto beans, or 3 (16-ounce) cans cooked beans, rinsed and drained
½ teaspoon salt
¼ teaspoon black pepper
1½ cups chopped onions
3 garlic cloves
¼ cup chicken broth
½ teaspoon ground cumin

½ cup finely minced green chilies
Fresh Salsa (page 369)

If using dried beans, rinse and cover with water; soak 2 hours. Drain, cover with more water, then transfer to a saucepan, cover, and cook until soft, approximately 2 hours. Drain beans, place in a large bowl and add salt and pepper; mash, using a potato masher or large fork. Lightly cook the onions and garlic in the chicken broth with the cumin until onions are clear, about 3 minutes. Add the chilies, cover, and simmer for 5 minutes. Add vegetables to the beans and mix. Blend in salsa to taste. Serves 6.

Serving: about ⅔ cup
Calories: 103
Percent calories from carbohydrates: 73
Percent calories from protein: 21
Percent calories from fat: 6
Fiber: 5 grams

Cantaloupe Salad

½ medium cantaloupe, with seeds removed
1 6-ounce cup nonfat custard-style vanilla yogurt
½ cup fresh raspberries

Fill the center of the melon half with the yogurt and top with raspberries. Serves 1.

Serving: ½ cantaloupe, filled
Calories: 268
Percent calories from carbohydrates: 74
Percent calories from protein: 16
Percent calories from fat: 10
Fiber: 4.7 grams

Apple-Pineapple Salad

3 medium apples, cut into chunks
½ cup drained, crushed, unsweetened canned pineapple
¼ cup finely chopped celery
2 tablespoons raisins
5 tablespoons low-fat yogurt, or 4 tablespoons nonfat sour cream
1 tablespoon pineapple juice
⅛ teaspoon ground cinnamon
Dash of grated nutmeg

Combine all ingredients in a large bowl, toss, and serve. Serves 2.

Serving: 1½ cups
Calories: 205
Percent calories from carbohydrates: 88
Percent calories from protein: 5
Percent calories from fat: 7
Fiber: 6 grams

Green Mashed Potatoes

1 cup mashed potatoes
¼ cup skim milk
½ cup chopped cooked Swiss chard
2 teaspoons grated Parmesan cheese
Salt and pepper

Blend the potatoes with the milk, chard, cheese, and salt and pepper to taste until smooth. Serves 1.

Serving: 1½ cups
Calories: 189
Percent calories from carbohydrates: 79
Percent calories from protein: 13
Percent calories from fat: 8
Fiber: 6 grams

Nutrient Cocktails

The Brain Booster

This drink is high in vitamin C and beta-carotene, which are suspected to protect the brain's cells from free radical damage. No RDA has been set for beta-carotene or other carotenoids.

2 medium carrots
½ red bell pepper
2 tablespoons chopped fresh parsley
1 celery stalk
½ apple
½ large tomato
Optional:
1 garlic clove
1 green onion
Dash of Tabasco

Put ingredients in a juicer and process until smooth. Season to taste, adding optional items as desired. Serves 1.

Serving: approximately 2 cups
Calories: 168
Percent calories from carbohydrates: 87
Percent calories from protein: 8
Percent calories from fat: 6
Fiber: 2 grams

The Brain Energizer

This "milkshake" is high in the B vitamins, vitamin E, iron, magnesium, potassium, and zinc.

½ cup low-fat plain yogurt
¾ cup orange juice
½ cup chopped apple
1½ tablespoons peanut butter
¼ cup wheat germ

½ banana, peeled and sliced
½ teaspoon ground cinnamon
1 teaspoon vanilla extract
Ice cubes (optional)
Grated lemon peel (optional)

Place the ingredients in a blender and process until creamy. Serves 2.

Serving: 1 cup
Calories: 293
Percent calories from carbohydrates: 54
Percent calories from protein: 16
Percent calories from fat: 29
Fiber: 5.4 grams

The Anti–Brain Drainer

This drink supplies the B vitamins, vitamin C, magnesium, potassium, and selenium.

⅓ cucumber, peeled
1 cup crushed fresh pineapple
1 celery stalk
½ apple
Dash of Tabasco (optional)

In a juicer, liquefy all the ingredients. Serves 1.

Serving: 1½ cups
Calories: 136
Percent calories from carbohydrates: 89
Percent calories from protein: 4
Percent calories from fat: 6

The Quick Fix

This drink supplies the following percentages of the Recommended Dietary Allowances: Vitamin A and beta-carotene—41%; vitamin B1—62%; vitamin B2—36%; vitamin B6—33%; folic acid—77%; vitamin C—136%; vitamin E—121%; iron—24%; magnesium—49%; potassium—50%; selenium—62%; zinc—46%.

¼ cup nonfat milk
6 canned apricot halves in light syrup
1 medium orange
¼ cup pineapple chunks, fresh or canned, with juice
¼ cup wheat germ
Ice cubes (optional)

Combine all the ingredients in a blender and whip until creamy. Serves 1.

Serving size: approximately 1 cup
Calories: 346
Percent calories from carbohydrates: 75
Percent calories from protein: 16
Percent calories from fat: 9
Fiber: 9.9 grams

Light Meals

Vegetable Garlic Soup

This is a great soup any time of the year, especially for summer evenings or fall lunches. Serve with whole wheat rolls or sourdough bread.

2 teaspoons vegetable oil
6 garlic cloves, minced
1 cup finely chopped onion
2 large tomatoes, chopped
1 small can chopped green chilies
1½ tablespoons flour

2 quarts chicken stock
4 cups cubed peeled potatoes
3 medium carrots, sliced into thin rounds
1 medium zucchini, cut into cubes
1 medium yellow summer squash, cut into cubes
Salt and pepper
1 cup grated low-fat Monterey Jack cheese (nonfat Monterey Jack would reduce fat grams by almost half)

In a 3-quart saucepan, heat the oil and sauté the garlic, onion, tomatoes, and chilies for 3 minutes. Add the flour and stir. Slowly pour in the chicken stock while stirring. Add the potatoes and cook over low heat for 15 minutes. Add the carrots, zucchini, and squash and cook for 15 minutes more or until potatoes and vegetables are tender. Add salt and pepper to taste. Garnish with grated cheese. Serves 8.

Serving: 1½ cups
Calories: 225
Percent calories from carbohydrates: 45
Percent calories from protein: 26
Percent calories from fat: 30
Fiber: 5 grams

Crunchy Peanut Butter Sandwich

This sandwich supplies 25 to 50 percent of the daily need for folic acid, vitamin E, magnesium, selenium, and zinc, and is high in the B vitamins, iron, and other trace minerals.

2 tablespoons peanut butter
2 tablespoons wheat germ
1 tablespoon honey
2 slices whole wheat bread
1 small banana, sliced (optional)

Mix the peanut butter, wheat germ, and honey until smooth. Spread on the bread and top with banana slices. Serves 1.

Serving: 1 sandwich
Calories: 504
Percent calories from carbohydrates: 53
Percent calories from protein: 13
Percent calories from fat: 34
Fiber: 10 grams

Black Bean and Couscous Salad

3 teaspoons olive oil
4½ tablespoons red wine vinegar
½ tablespoon Worcestershire sauce
2 garlic cloves, chopped
1½ teaspoons ground cumin
3 cups cooked or canned black beans, drained
½ teaspoon dried oregano
2 tablespoons fresh lemon juice
¾ cup chicken broth
3 cups cooked couscous
½ red bell pepper, chopped
½ yellow bell pepper, chopped
½ green bell pepper, chopped
¾ cup chopped fresh parsley
½ cup chopped green onions
Salt and pepper

In a large bowl, mix 2 teaspoons of the olive oil, 2¼ tablespoons of the vinegar, the Worcestershire sauce, 1 garlic clove, and 1 teaspoon of the cumin. Add the beans and mix well. Chill.

In a large bowl, combine the remaining 2¼ tablespoons vinegar, 1 garlic clove, remaining ½ teaspoon cumin, the oregano, and the lemon juice. Set aside. In a 1-quart pan, heat the chicken broth and remaining 1 teaspoon olive oil until simmering. Stir in the couscous, cover, and remove from heat. Let stand 3 or 4 minutes, then stir with a fork to prevent clumping. Mix couscous into dressing and cool to room temperature.

Combine the marinated beans and couscous, then toss in the peppers, parsley, and green onions. Add salt and pepper to taste. Serve at room temperature or chilled. Serves 5.

Serving: ¾ cup
Calories: 310
Percent calories from carbohydrates: 70
Percent calories from protein: 19
Percent calories from fat: 11
Fiber: 10 grams

Veggie Burritos

1 cup no-fat refried beans
3 whole wheat tortillas
1 cup shredded zucchini
¾ cup shredded carrots
⅔ cup shredded low-fat cheddar cheese
⅔ cup salsa

Heat the beans in a saucepan until warmed through, about 5 minutes. Heat the tortillas in a dry cast-iron pan until warm. Fill tortillas with zucchini, carrots, beans, cheese, and salsa. Makes 3 burritos.

Serving: 1 burrito
Calories: 200
Percent calories from carbohydrates: 70
Percent calories from protein: 22
Percent calories from fat: 8
Fiber: 9 grams

Black Bean and Vegetable Chili

2½ cups dried black beans
2 cups chopped onions
8 garlic cloves, chopped
2 tablespoons safflower oil
⅓ cup chili powder
4 teaspoons ground cumin
Cayenne pepper
6 cups water
3 cups chicken broth

2 cups canned tomatoes
1 red bell pepper, chopped
1½ cups corn kernels
¾ cup bulgur
2 cups chunked zucchini
2 tablespoons Worcestershire sauce
Salt and pepper
⅓ cup chopped fresh cilantro

Rinse and soak the beans overnight in enough water to cover plus 2 inches, then drain. In a large cast-iron kettle, cook the onions and 5 garlic cloves in the oil until soft, about 5 minutes. Add the chili powder, cumin, and cayenne to taste and cook for 1 minute. Add the beans and water, and simmer for 1 hour or until beans are tender (add more water if needed to keep beans covered).

Stir in the broth, tomatoes, red pepper, and corn and simmer for 20 minutes, stirring occasionally. Add the bulgur, zucchini, and remaining garlic and cook until zucchini is tender, about 20 minutes. Season with the Worcestershire sauce and salt and pepper to taste. Simmer for 5 minutes. Garnish with cilantro. Serves 6.

Serving: 2 cups
Calories: 413
Percent calories from carbohydrates: 64
Percent calories from protein: 18
Percent calories from fat: 18
Fiber: 14 grams

Potato and Chicken Soup

4 medium potatoes, peeled and cubed
2½ cups chopped onions
4 cups chicken broth
½ cup chopped red bell pepper
3 cooked skinless chicken breasts, cut into large chunks
½ cup nonfat milk
Salt and pepper
3 tablespoons minced pimiento
½ cup nonfat sour cream

⅓ cup grated low-fat cheddar cheese
3 tablespoons chopped fresh chives

Combine the potatoes, onions, and broth in a large saucepan and cook until potatoes are tender, about 30 minutes. Place half the potato mixture in a blender and process until smooth. Stir the blended mixture back into the soup and add the red pepper, chicken, and milk. Cook over medium heat until red pepper is soft, about 5 minutes. Add salt and pepper to taste, then stir in the pimiento and garnish with sour cream, grated cheese, and chives. Serves 6.

Serving: 1⅓ cups
Calories: 264
Percent calories from carbohydrates: 43
Percent calories from protein: 37
Percent calories from fat: 20
Fiber: 2.8 grams

Linguini with Vegetables

1 cup low-fat ricotta cheese
⅓ cup grated Romano cheese, plus extra for topping
2½ cups cauliflower flowerets
2 cups broccoli flowerets
3 carrots, washed, peeled, and sliced into ¼-inch-thick slices
⅓ cup olive oil
10 garlic cloves, chopped
½ cup chicken broth
1 pound white mushrooms, washed and sliced
Salt and pepper
1 pound dry linguini

Combine the ricotta and Romano cheeses in a bowl and set aside. Steam the cauliflower, broccoli, and carrots until tender-crisp, about 8 minutes. Heat the oil in a large skillet and add the garlic. When garlic is golden, in about 3 minutes, add the broth, mushrooms, and salt and pepper to taste. Cook for 5 minutes, then stir in the cauliflower, broccoli, and carrots and cook another 10 minutes, adding more broth if mixture is too dry.

Cook linguini in rapidly boiling water until al dente, 10 to 12 minutes.

Drain and add pasta to vegetable mixture. Mix well, then serve topped with cheese mixture. Sprinkle on a little extra Romano. Serves 8.

Serving: 2 cups
Calories: 379
Percent calories from carbohydrates: 53
Percent calories from protein: 15
Percent calories from fat: 32
Fiber: 5.5 grams

Breakfast Options

Oatmeal Magic

¼ cup wheat germ
2 teaspoons brown sugar
¾ cup prepared oatmeal cooked in 1% low-fat milk
⅓ cup 1% low-fat milk

Stir the wheat germ and brown sugar into the cooked oatmeal. Top with milk. Serves 1.

Serving: ¾ cup
Calories: 281
Percent calories from carbohydrates: 62
Percent calories from protein: 21
Percent calories from fat: 18
Fiber: 7 grams

Quick 'n' Easy Blueberry Waffles

2 frozen whole wheat waffles
2 tablespoons nonfat sour cream
1 cup fresh or frozen blueberries

Toast the waffles according to package directions. Top with sour cream and blueberries. Serves 1.

Serving: 2 waffles
Calories: 311
Percent calories from carbohydrates: 60
Percent calories from protein: 12
Percent calories from fat: 28
Fiber: 6 grams

Sweet Muffins (Basic Recipe)

1 large egg
1 cup 1% low-fat milk
2½ tablespoons safflower oil
1¾ cups unbleached all-purpose flour
¼ cup wheat germ
¼ cup brown sugar
½ teaspoon salt
1 tablespoon baking powder

Preheat the oven to 400°F. Beat the egg in a large bowl. Add milk and oil, and blend. In another bowl, combine the flour, wheat germ, brown sugar, salt, and baking powder. Mix well, then add to egg mixture. Stir only until mixture is moistened; batter should be lumpy. Spray a 12-cup muffin tin with a thin film of oil. Then fill cups two-thirds full with batter. Bake for 25 minutes, or until center springs back when pushed with a fingertip. Serve with nonfat sour cream or apple butter. Makes 12 muffins.

Serving: 2 muffins
Calories: 253
Percent calories from carbohydrates: 66
Percent calories from protein: 11
Percent calories from fat: 23
Fiber: 2 grams

Variations

Apple-Cinnamon Muffins: Add 1 cup grated peeled apple and 1 teaspoon ground cinnamon to flour mixture before adding to egg mixture.

Blueberry Muffins: Add 1 cup fresh blueberries to flour mixture and 1 teaspoon vanilla extract to egg mixture.
Orange-Cranberry Muffins: Add 1½ tablespoons grated orange peel and 1 cup cranberries to flour mixture.

Holiday Fare

Harvest Dressing

To reduce calories by about 80 percent, bake the dressing for your holiday turkey in a covered baking dish instead of in the turkey. And roast the turkey in an oven roasting bag to maintain moisture.

¼ cup low-calorie margarine
2 medium onions, chopped
1½ cups chopped celery
3 cups chopped red and/or green tart apples
½ cup raisins
16 ounces herb-flavored stuffing mix (not butter basted)
½ cup chopped fresh parsley
¼ teaspoon salt
1 teaspoon freshly ground pepper
2½ cups apple cider

Preheat the oven to 350°F. Over medium-high heat, melt the margarine in a skillet. Add the onions, celery, apples, and raisins and cook for 5 minutes or until soft. Remove from heat and stir in the stuffing mix, parsley, salt, and pepper. Add cider to moisten. Spray a 2-quart baking dish with cooking spray and spoon in the dressing. Bake, covered, for 30 to 40 minutes. Remove the lid during the last 5 minutes to crisp the top. Serves 12.

Serving: approximately ½ cup
Calories: 234
Percent calories from carbohydrates: 79
Percent calories from protein: 8
Percent calories from fat: 13
Fiber: 1.7 grams

Baked Sweet Potatoes

6 medium sweet potatoes, peeled and cooked
2 tart apples, cored and cut into 1/4-inch rings
1/2 cup frozen unsweetened apple juice concentrate, thawed
1/4 cup brown sugar
1/4 teaspoon ground ginger
1/4 teaspoon ground cinnamon

Preheat the oven to 350°F. Cut the sweet potatoes into 1/4-inch slices. Layer them and the apples in an oblong baking dish (10 x 6 x 1 1/2 inches) that has been coated with cooking spray. Pour the apple juice concentrate over the potatoes and apples. In a bowl, mix brown sugar, ginger, and cinnamon; sprinkle over apples and spray lightly with cooking spray. Bake, uncovered, until apples are crisp-tender, about 30 minutes. Serves 8.

Serving: approximately ½ cup
Calories: 155
Percent calories from carbohydrates: 94
Percent calories from protein: 4
Percent calories from fat: 2
Fiber: 4 grams

Chunky Cranberry Sauce

2 cups fresh cranberries
2 large Red Delicious apples, cored and diced
1 cup frozen unsweetened apple juice concentrate, thawed
1/2 cup raisins
6 1/2 tablespoons lemon juice
4 tablespoons grated fresh ginger
5 tablespoons grated orange peel
2 teaspoons ground cinnamon
1 teaspoon ground allspice
Dash of cayenne pepper or grated horseradish (optional)

Combine all ingredients in a large saucepan over medium heat. Stir constantly until the mixture comes to a boil, then cover pan, reduce heat, and simmer for 1 hour. Serve warm or chilled. Makes 12 servings.

Serving: approximately 1/3 cup
Calories: 95
Percent calories from carbohydrates: 95
Percent calories from protein: 2
Percent calories from fat: 3
Fiber: 2.3 grams

Sugar-free Cranberry Chutney

2 cups fresh cranberries, cut into halves or left whole
⅔ cup frozen unsweetened orange juice concentrate
3 tablespoons fresh lemon juice
2 medium pears, peeled and chopped
2 tablespoons frozen unsweetened apple juice concentrate, thawed
½ teaspoon ground cloves
½ teaspoon ground coriander
½ teaspoon ground cinnamon

Combine all the ingredients in a large saucepan over medium heat. Stir constantly until mixture comes to a boil, then cover pan, reduce heat, and simmer for 20 minutes. Serve chilled. Makes 8 servings.

Serving: approximately ⅓ cup
Calories: 50
Percent calories from carbohydrates: 93
Percent calories from protein: 4
Percent calories from fat: 3
Fiber: 2.5 grams

Nonfat Whipped Topping

3 tablespoons sugar
1½ teaspoons unflavored gelatin
½ cup boiling water
½ cup cold water
¾ cup nonfat dry milk
1½ tablespoons lemon juice
1½ teaspoons vanilla extract

Mix the sugar and gelatin in a large bowl. Add boiling water and stir until gelatin is completely dissolved. Stir in cold water; let stand until room temperature. Add remaining ingredients, then beat with electric mixer on high speed until soft peaks form, about 3 minutes. Refrigerate until ready to serve. Stir before serving. Makes 5 cups.

Serving: ½ cup
Calories: 40
Percent calories from carbohydrates: 73
Percent calories from protein: 26
Percent calories from fat: 1
Fiber: less than 1 gram

Resources

AGING

The National Institute on Aging. Free booklet: "In Search of the Secrets of Aging"; call 800-222-2225, 8:30 A.M.–5 P.M. EST.

CHRONIC FATIGUE SYNDROME

CFS Society, P.O. Box 230108, Portland, OR 97223.

CFIDS (Chronic Fatigue and Immune Dysfunction Syndrome) Association of America, P.O. Box 220398, Charlotte, NC 28222-0016. Information packet available. Call 800-442-3437; or the information line, 900-896-2343, with a charge of $2.00 for the first minute and $1.00 for every minute after that.

National Chronic Fatigue Syndrome Association (NCFS), 3521 Broadway, Suite 222, Kansas City, MO 64111; 816-931-4777, or the CFS Activation Network (CAN), 212-627-5631.

DEPRESSION

Depression Awareness Recognition and Treatment (D/ART), a program of the National Institute of Mental Health. For free information, call 800-421-4211. For specific information, call 301-443-4140.

Depressives Anonymous, 329 East 62nd Street, New York, NY 10021. Send SASE for free information.

National Foundation for Depressive Illness. For a recorded message on symptoms of depression and available pamphlets and referrals, call 800-245-4381.

EATING DISORDERS

American Anorexia/Bulimia Association, 418 East 76th Street, New York, NY 10021; 212-734-1114. Mail SASE and $3.00 for information packet.

Anorexia Nervosa and Related Eating Disorders (ANRED), P.O. Box 5102, Eugene, OR 97405; 503-344-1144. Free information available.

Food Addicts Anonymous, 4623 Barthill, Suite 111-5, West Palm Beach, FL 33415; 407-967-3871.

National Anorexic Aid Society, 5796 Karl Road, Columbus, OH 43229; 614-436-1112.

National Association of Anorexia Nervosa and Associated Disorders, P.O. Box 7, Highland Park, IL 60035; 708-831-3438.

EXERCISE

American Alliance for Health, Physical Education, Recreation, and Dance, 1900 Association Drive, Reston, VA 22091; 703-476-3400.

President's Council on Physical Fitness and Sports, 701 Pennsylvania Avenue, NW, Suite 250, Washington, DC, 20024; 202-272-3421.

FOOD ALLERGIES

American Academy of Allergy and Immunology. Free brochure: "Adverse Reactions to Foods"; call 800-822-2762.

American Academy of Pediatrics. For a free brochure, send SASE to: Allergies in Children: Plain Talk for Parents, Dept. C, Academy of Pediatrics, P.O. Box 927, Elk Grove Village, IL 60009-0927.

American Council on Science and Health, 1995 Broadway, 2nd floor, New York, NY 10023-5860. Booklet: "Food Allergies"; $3.85.

American Dietetic Association. Booklet: "Food Allergies" by Merri Lou Dobler, $5.50; 800-745-0775, ext. 5000.

Food Allergy Network. Offers a bimonthly newsletter (with recipes) and other information. Send a SASE to: Food Allergy Network, 4744 Holly Avenue, Fairfax, VA 22030.

General Foods, Consumer Response & Information Center, 250 North Street, White Plains, NY 10625. Free booklet: "Food Allergies & Intolerances."

Department of Agriculture, Superintendent of Documents, U.S. Government Printing Office, Washington, DC 20402. Booklet: "Cooking for People with Food Allergies," G-246; $1.50.

The Milk-Free Kitchen, by Beth Kidder. New York: Henry Holt & Co., Inc.; $16.95.

FOOD SAFETY

Food and Drug Administration, Consumer Inquiry Section, 5600 Fishers Lane, Rockville, MD 20857; 301-443-1544; or in some areas, 800-426-3758.

American Council on Science and Health, 1995 Broadway, 2nd floor, New York, NY 10023-5860. Booklet: "Pesticides and Food Safety"; $3.85.

General Foods, Consumer Response & Information Center, 250 North Street, White Plains, NY 10625. Free booklet: "Additives."

HEADACHES

American Association for the Study of Headaches, 875 Kings Highway, West Deptford, NJ 08096; 609-845-0322.

National Headache Foundation, 5252 N. Western Avenue, Chicago, IL 60625. Send a SASE for free information, or upon request they will send a list of physicians specializing in headache treatment in your area; 312-878-7715 or 800-843-2256.

HEALTHFUL EATING

American Diabetes Association, 18 East 48th Street, New York, NY 10017.

American Dietetic Association, 216 West Jackson Boulevard, Suite 800, Chicago, IL 60606-6995. Hotline (National Center of Nutrition and Dietetics, 800-366-1655, 10 A.M.–5 P.M. EST, Monday–Friday). Prerecorded messages 9 A.M.–9 P.M. seven days a week.

American Heart Association, 7272 Greenville Avenue, Dallas, TX 75231-4596; 800-242-8721. Booklet: "An Eating Plan for Healthy Americans," free with SASE.

Bulletin Office, 10B Agriculture Hall, Michigan State University, East Lansing, MI 48824. Booklet: "Shop Smart" #5; 10¢.

Community Nutrition Institute, 2001 South Street, NW, Suite 530, Washington, DC 20009; 202-462-4700.

Consumer Information Center, Superintendent of Documents, Department 150-Y, Pueblo, CO 81009. Booklet: "Dietary Guidelines for Americans," free with SASE. Also Booklet: "The Food Guide Pyramid," $1.00 check or money order.

National Cancer Institute, 9000 Rockville Pike, Building 31, Room 10A24, Bethesda, MD 20892. Booklet: "Eat More Fruits & Vegetables: Five-a-Day for Better Health," free with SASE.

Food and Drug Administration, Office of Consumer Affairs, Public Inquiries, 5600 Fishers Lane (HFE-88), Rockville, MD 20857; 301-443-1544.

Food Marketing Institute, 800 Connecticut Avenue, NW, Washington, DC 20006. Booklet: "The Food Guide Pyramid: Beyond the Basic 4," 50¢ with SASE.

Food and Nutrition Information Center, National Agriculture Library, Room 304, 10301 Baltimore Blvd., Beltsville, MD 20705; 301-504-5414.

"Light, Lean & Low Fat," P.O. Box 741021, Department W, Houston, TX 77274. Booklet free with SASE.

LEAD TOXICITY

Lead Testing Kit, Frandon Pace Environs, 81 Finchden Square, Scarborough, Ontario, Canada M1X 1B4; 416-293-4955. Kits available for testing water and for testing surfaces such as ceramic cookware.

LEARNING DISABILITIES

National Center for Learning Disabilities, 381 Park Avenue S., New York, NY 10016.

American Academy of Ophthalmology, P.O. Box 7424, San Francisco, CA 94120-7424. Brochure: "Learning Disabilities: Dyslexia, Reading, and Perceptual Problems," free with SASE.

American Academy of Pediatrics, Department of Publications, 141 Northwest Point Blvd., P.O. Box 927, Elk Grove Village, IL 60009. Booklet: "Learning Disabilities and Children: What Parents Need to Know," free with SASE.

MENTAL HEALTH

National Institute of Mental Health, Alcohol, Drug Abuse and Mental Health Administration, U.S. Department of Health and Human Services, 5600 Fishers Lane, Rockville, MD 20857; 310-443-4513.

National Mental Health Association, Information Center, 1021 Prince Street, Alexandria, VA 22314; 703-684-7722. 9 A.M.–5 P.M. EST, Monday–Friday. Information available on clinical depression, the warning signs of mental illness, and local mental health services.

NEUROLOGICAL DISORDERS

National Institute of Neurological Disorders and Stroke; 800-352-9424.

OTHER DISORDERS

National Organization for Rare Disorders; 800-999-NORD.

PANIC ATTACKS

National Institute of Mental Health. Panic hotline: 800-64-PANIC.

PREMENSTRUAL SYNDROME

PMS Access, P.O. Box 9326, Madison, WI 53715; 608-833-4767 or 800-222-4PMS; to talk with a pharmacist: 800-558-7046. Although a product-oriented company (the product is a PMS supplement called Pro Cycle), this service also provides coping tips, answers to questions, information packets, and charts to track symptoms. You also can order a free copy of "Women's Health Access," a newsletter that contains articles on PMS.

SLEEP DISORDERS

American Sleep Disorders Association, 1610 14th Street NW, Suite 300, Rochester, MN 55901; 507-287-6006.

National Sleep Foundation, 122 South Robertson Boulevard, 3rd floor, Department FC, Los Angeles, CA 90048.

WEIGHT CONTROL

Overeaters Anonymous, 383 Van Ness Avenue, Suite 1601, Torrance, CA 90501; 310-618-8835.

Weight Watchers International, 10 South Middleneck Road, Great Neck, NY 11021; in some areas, 800-333-3000.

References

INTRODUCTION: WHY MOST DIETS MAKE US CRAZY

Ackroff K, Sclafani A: Sucrose-induced hyperphagia and obesity in rats fed a macronutrient self-selection diet. *Physl Behav* 1988;44:181–187.

Ames H, Gee M, Hawrysh Z: Taste perception and breast cancer: Evidence of a role for diet. *J Am Diet A* 1993;93:541–546.

Anderson G, Hrboticky N: Approaches to assessing the dietary component of the diet-behavior connection. *Nutr Rev* 1986;44 (Suppl May):42–50.

Anderson R, Kozlovsky A, Moser P: Effects of diets high in simple sugars on urinary chromium excretion of humans. *Fed Proc* 1985;44:751.

Baghurst K, Baghurst P, Record S: Demographic and nutritional profiles of people consuming varying levels of added sugars. *Nutr Res* 1992;12:1455–1465.

Block G, Dresser C, Hartman A, et al: Nutrient sources in the American diet: Quantitative data from the NHANES II survey. 2. Macronutrients and fat. *Am J Epidem* 1985;122(1):27–40.

Brewster L, Jacobson M: *The Changing American Diet: A Chronicle of American Eating Habits from 1910–1980*. Washington, DC, Center for Science in the Public Interest, 1983.

deWolfe J, Shannon B: Factors affecting fat consumption of university students: Testing a model to predict eating behaviour change. *J Can Diet* 1993;54(3):132–137.

Gibson S: Consumption and sources of sugars in the diets of British schoolchildren: Are high-sugar diets nutritionally inferior? *J Hum Nu Di* 1993;6(4):355–371.

Gondal J, Myers A, MacArthy P, et al: Effects of dietary sucrose on blood pressure and other cardiovascular parameters in spontaneously hypertensive rats (SHR) (Meeting abstract). *J Am Col N* 1993;12(5):592.

Heaton K: The sweet road to gall stones. *Br Med J* 1984;288:1103–1104.

Katschinski B, Logan R, Edmond M, et al: Duodenal ulcer and refined carbohydrate intake: A case-control study assessing dietary fibre and refined sugar intake. *Gut* 1990;31:993–996.

Katschinski B, Logan R, Edmond M, et al: Dietary fiber, sugar, and the risk of duodenal ulcer. *Gastroenty* 1987;92:1460.

Kavanagh M, Prendiville V, Buxton A, et al: Does sucrose damage kidneys? *Br J Urol* 1986;58:353–357.

Krebs-Smith S, Cronin F, Haytowitz D, et al: Food sources of energy, macronutrients, cholesterol, and fiber in diets of women. *J Am Diet A* 1992;92:168–174.

Kruis W, Forstmaier G, Scheurlen C, et al: Effect of diets low and high in refined sugars on gut transit, bile acid metabolism, and bacterial fermentation. *Gut* 1991;32(4): 367–371.

Lawton C, Burley V, Wales J, et al: Dietary fat and appetite control in obese subjects: Weak effects on satiation and satiety. *Int J Obes* 1993;17(7):409–416.

Lenders C, Hediger L, Scholl T, et al: Dietary sugar in adolescent pregnancy: Effect on maternal blood pressure and intrauterine growth (Meeting abstract). *J Am Col N* 1993;12(5):605.

Lewis C, Park Y, Dexter P, et al: Nutrient intakes and body weights of persons consuming high and moderate levels of added sugars. *J Am Diet A* 1992;92:708–713.

New Food: 1992 new product totals by category. *New Product News* January 8, 1993.

Pivonka E, Grunewald K: Aspartame- or sugar-sweetened beverages: Effects on mood in young women. *J Am Diet A* 1990;90:250–254.

Rogers P, Blundell J: Uncoupling sweet taste and calories: Effects of saccharine on hunger and food intake in human subjects. *Ann NY Acad* 1989;575:569–571.

Sparks J, Sparks C, Kritchevsky D: Hypercholesterolemia and aortic glysosaminoglycans of rabbits fed semi-purified diets containing sucrose and lactose. *Atheroscler* 1986;60:183–196.

Tucker D, Penland J, Sandstead H, et al: Nutrition status and brain function in aging. *Am J Clin N* 1990;52:93–102.

Young S: The use of diet and dietary components in the study of factors controlling affect in humans: A review. *J Psych Neu* 1993;18(5):235–244.

Yudkin J, Eisa O, Kang S, et al: Dietary sucrose affects plasma HDL cholesterol concentration in young men. *Ann Nutr M* 1986;30:261–266.

CHAPTER 1: HOW FOOD AFFECTS YOUR MOOD

Abou-Saleh M, Coppen A: The biology of folate in depression: Implications for nutritional hypotheses of the psychoses. *J Psychiat R* 1986;20(2):91–101.

Atkinson R, Berke L, Drake C, et al: Effects of long-term therapy with naltrexone on body weight in obesity. *Clin Pharm* 1985;38:419–422.

Bakshi V, Kelley A: Feeding induced by opioid stimulation of the ventral striatum: Role of opiate receptor subtypes. *J Pharm Exp* 1993;265(3):1253–1260.

Baptista T, Parada M, Hernandez L: Long-term administration of some antipsychotic drugs increases body weight and feeding in rats: Are D2 dopamine receptors involved? *Pharm Bio B* 1987;27:399–405.

Beck B, Burlet A, Bazin R, et al: Elevated neuropeptide Y in the arcuate nucleus of young obese Zucker rats may contribute to the development of their overeating. *J Nutr* 1993;123:1168–1172.

Bell I: Vitamin B12 and folate in acute geropsychiatric inpatients. *Nutr Rep* 1991;9(1): 1, 8.

Bell I, Edman J, Morrow F, et al: Brief communication: Vitamin B1, B2, and B6 augmentation of tricyclic antidepressant treatment in geriatric depression with cognitive dysfunction. *J Am Col N* 1992;11(2):159–163.

Bell I, Edman J, Morrow F, et al: B complex vitamin patterns in geriatric and young adult inpatients with major depression. *J Am Ger So* 1991;39:252–257.

Bender D: B vitamins in the nervous system: A review. *Neurochem I* 1984;6:297–321.

Benton D, Cook R: The impact of selenium supplementation on mood. *Biol Psychi* 1991;29:1092–1098.

Blass E, Jackson A, Smotherman W: Milk-induced, opioid-mediated antinociception in rats at the time of cesarean delivery. *Behav Neuro* 1991;105(5):677–687.

Blum I, Vered Y, Graff E, et al: The influence of meal composition on plasma serotonin and norepinephrine concentrations. *Metabolism* 1992;41(2):137–140.

Blundell J: Nutritional manipulations for altering food intake: Towards a causal model of experimental obesity. *Ann NY Acad* 1987;499:144–155.

Blundell J, Latham C, Leshem M: Differences between the anorexic actions of amphetamine and fenfluramine: Possible effects on hunger and satiety. *J Pharm* 1976; 28:471–477.

Brewerton T, Heffernan M, Rosenthal N: Psychiatric aspects of the relationship between eating and mood. *Nutr Rev* 1986;44 (Suppl May):78–88.

Burger S, Haas J, Habicht J: Testing the effects of nutrient deficiencies on behavioral performance. *Am J Clin N* 1993;57 (Suppl):295S–302S.

Capuano C, Leibowitz S, Barr G: The pharmaco-ontogeny of the perifornical lateral hypothalamic beta 2-adrenergic and dopaminergic receptor systems mediating epinephrine- and dopamine-induced suppression of feeding in the rat. *Brain Res Dev* 1992;70(1):1–7.

Christensen L, Redig C: Effect of meal composition on mood. *Behav Neuro* 1993;107(2): 346–353.

Dagnault A, Deshaies Y, Richard D: Effects of the 5-hydroxytryptamine agonist d,1-fenfluramine on energy balance in rats: Influence of gender. *Int J Obes* 1993;17:367–373.

deGraaf C: The validity of appetite ratings. *Appetite* 1993;21:156–160.

DeJong A, Strubbe J, Steffens A: Hypothalamic influence on insulin and glucagon release in the rat. *Am J Physl* 1977;233:E380–E388.

de la Morena E: Efficacy of CDP-choline in the treatment of senile alterations in memory. *Ann NY Acad* 1991;640:233–236.

DeLong G: Effects of nutrition on brain development in humans. *Am J Clin N* 1993;57: 286S–290S.

Dietary choline and synaptic morphology in mice. *Nutr Rev* 1987;45(1):25–27.

Does dietary tryptophan influence serotonin release from brain neurons? *Nutr Rev* 1987; 45(3):87–89.

Dunant Y, Israel M: The release of acetylcholine. *Sci Am* 1985;252(4):58–67.

Eastman C, Gullarte T: Vitamin B6, kynurenines, and central nervous system function: Developmental aspects. *J Nutr Bioc* 1992;3:618–631.

Eipper B, Mains R: The role of ascorbate in the biosynthesis of neuroendocrine peptides. *Am J Clin N* 1991;54:1153S–1156S.

Fernstrom J: Acute and chronic effects of protein and carbohydrate ingestion on brain tryptophan levels and serotonin synthesis. *Nutr Rev* 1986;44 (Suppl May):25–36.

Fernstrom J: Dietary amino acids and brain function. *J Am Diet A* 1994;94:71–77.

Garattini S, Bizzi A, Caccia C, et al: Progress in assessing the role of serotonin in the control of food intake. *Clin Neuropharm* 1988;11 (Suppl):S8–S32.

Garattini S, Mennini T, Samanin R: Reduction of food intake by manipulation of central serotonin. *Br J Psychi* 1989;155 (Suppl 8):41–51.

Gelenberg A, Wojcik J, Falk W, et al: Tyrosine for depression: A double-blind trial. *J Affect D* 1990;19:125–132.

Giugliano D, Cozzolino D, Salvatore T, et al: Physiological elevations of plasma beta-endorphin alter glucose metabolism in obese, but not normal-weight, subjects. *Metabolism* 1992;41(2):184–190.

Godfrey P, Toone B, Carney M, et al: Enhancement of recovery from psychiatric illness by methylfolate. *Lancet* 1990;336:392–395.

Grantham-McGregor S: Assessments of the effects of nutrition on mental development and behavior in Jamaican studies. *Am J Clin N* 1993;57 (Suppl):303S–309S.

Harrell R, Capp R, Davis D, et al: Can nutritional supplements help mentally retarded children? An exploratory study. *P NAS US* 1981;78(1):574–578.

Harris R, Martin R: Lipostatic theory of energy balance: Concepts and signals. *Nutr Behav* 1984;1:253–275.

Hartmann E: Effect of l-tryptophan and other amino acids on sleep. *Nutr Rev* 1986;44 (Suppl May):70–73.

Jenkins P, Grossman A: The control of the gonadotropin-releasing hormone pulse generator in relation to opioid and nutritional cues. *Hum Repr* 1993;8(S2):154–161.

Krassner M: Diet and brain function. *Nutr Rev* 1986;44 (Suppl May):12–15.

Kyrkouli S, Stanley B, Leibowitz S: Differential effects of galanin and neuropeptide Y on extracellular norepinephrine levels in the paraventricular hypothalamic nucleus of the rat: A microdialysis study. *Life Sci* 1992;51(3):203–210.

Lappalainen R, Sjoden P, Hursti T, et al: Hunger/craving responses and reactivity to food stimuli during fasting and dieting. *Int J Obes* 1990;14:679–688.

Leathwood P: Neurotransmitter precursors: From animal experiments to human application. *Nutr Rev* 1986;44 (Suppl May):193–204.

Lehnert H, Wurtman R: Amino acid control of neurotransmitter synthesis and release: Physiological and clinical implications. *Psychoth Ps* 1993;60(1):18–32.

Leibowitz S: Neurochemical-neuroendocrine systems in the brain controlling macronutrient intake and metabolism. *Trends Neur* 1992;15(12):491–497.

Leibowitz S: Neurochemical control of macronutrient intake, in Domura Y, Tarui S, Dnoue S, et al (eds): *Progress in Obesity Research*. London, John Libbey, 1991, pp 13–18.

Leibowitz S: Hypothalamic neuropeptide Y in relation to energy balance. *Ann NY Acad* 1990;611:284–301.

Leibowitz S, Kim T: Impact of a galanin antagonist on exogenous galanin and natural patterns of fat ingestion. *Brain Res* 1992;599:148–152.

Leibowitz S, Lucas D, Leibowitz K, et al: Developmental patterns of macronutrient intake in female and male rats from weaning to maturity. *Physl Behav* 1991;50(6):1167–1174.

Leibowitz S, Weiss G, Shor-Posner G: Hypothalamic serotonin: Pharmacological, biochemical and behavioral analysis of its feeding-suppressive action. *Clin Neurop* 1988;11 (Suppl 1):S51–S71.

Leibowitz S, Xuereb M, Kim T: Blockage of natural and neuropeptide Y-induced carbohydrate feeding by a receptor antagonist PYX-2. *Neuroreport* 1992;3(11): 1023–1026.

Leiter L, Haboticky N, Anderson G: Effects of l-tryptophan on food intake and selection in lean men and women. *Ann NY Acad* 1987;499:327–328.

Li E, Anderson G: Amino acids in the regulation of food intake. *Rev Clin N* 1983;53:169–181.

Lieberman H, Spring B, Garfield G: The behavioral effects of food constituents: Strategies used in studies on amino acids, protein, carbohydrate, and caffeine. *Nutr Rev* 1986;44 (Suppl May):61–70.

Lieberman H, Wurtman J, Chew B: Changes in mood after carbohydrate consumption among obese individuals. *Am J Clin N* 1986;44(6):772–778.

Lovenberg W: Biochemical regulation of brain function. *Nutr Rev* 1986;44 (Suppl May):6–11.

Lyons P, Truswell A: Serotonin precursor influenced by type of carbohydrate meal in healthy adults. *Am J Clin N* 1988;47(3):433–439.

Maggio C, Presta E, Bracco E, et al: Naltrexone and human eating behavior: A dose-ranging inpatient trial in moderately obese men. *Brain Res B* 1985;14: 657–661.

Martineua J, Barthelemy C, Lelord G: Long-term effects of combined vitamin B6-magnesium administration in an autistic child. *Biol Psychi* 1986;21:511–518.

Melchior J, Rigaud D, Colas-Linhard N, Petiet A, et al: Immunoreactive beta-endorphin increases after an aspartame chocolate drink in healthy human subjects. *Physl Behav* 1991;50:941–944.

Metz J: Cobalamine deficiency and the pathogenesis of nervous system disease. *Ann R Nutr* 1992;12:59–79.

Moller S: Serotonin, carbohydrates, and atypical depression. *Pharm Tox* 1992;71(S1): 61–71.

Moller S: Carbohydrate/protein selection in a single meal correlated with plasma tryptophan and tyrosine ratios to neutral amino acids in fasting individuals. *Physl Behav* 1986;38:175–183.

Morley J: Appetite regulation by gut peptides. *Ann R Nutr* 1990;10:383–395.

Nagai I, Thibault L, Mishikawa K, et al: Effect of glucagon in macronutrient self-selection: Glucagon-enhanced protein intake. *Brain Res B* 1991;27:409–415.

Norton P, Falciglia G, Gist D: Physiologic control of food intake by neural and chemical mechanisms. *J Am Diet A* 1993;93:450–454.

Paez X, Stanley B, Leibowitz S: Microdialysis analysis of norepinephrine levels in the paraventricular nucleus in association with food intake at dark onset. *Brain Res* 1993;606:167–170.

Philen R, Hill R, Flanders W, et al: Tryptophan contaminants associated with eosinophilia myalgia syndrome. *Am J Epidem* 1993;138(3):154–159.

Podell R: Nutritional precursors and the treatment of depression. *Postgr Med* 1983; 73(3):99–103.

Pollitt E: Iron deficiency and cognitive function. *Ann R Nutr* 1993;13:521–537.

Read N, French S, Cunningham K: The role of the gut in regulating food intake in man. *Nutr Rev* 1994;52(1):1–10.

Rude R: Magnesium metabolism and deficiency. *End Metab C* 1993;22(2):377–395.

Russ M, Ackerman S, Banay-Schwartz M, et al: Plasma tryptophan to large neutral amino acids ratios in depressed and normal subjects. *J Affect D* 1990;19(1):9–14.

Sabelli H: Rapid treatment of depression with selegiline-phenylalanine combination (letter). *Clin Psych* 1991;52:137.

Sabelli H, Fawcell J, Gusovsky F, et al: Clinical studies on the phenylethylamine hypothesis of affective disorder: Urine and blood phenylacetic acid and phenylalanine dietary supplements. *J Clin Psy* 1986;47:66–70.

Sandyk R: L-tryptophan in neuropsychiatric disorders: A review. *Int J Neurs* 1992; 67(1–4):127–144.

Schimizu H, Bray G: Effects of neuropeptide Y on norepinephrine and serotonin metabolism in rat hypothalamus in vivo. *Brain Res B* 1989;22:945–950.

Schweiger U, Laessle R, Pirke K: Macronutrient intake and mood during weight-reducing diets. *Ann NY Acad* 1987;499:335–337.

Shepard G: Microcircuits in the nervous system. *Sci Am* 1978;238(2):93–103.

Shide D, Blass E: Opioid mediation of odor preferences induced by sugar and fat in 6-day-old rats. *Phsyl Behav* 1991;50(5):961–966.

Shideler C: Vitamin B6: An overview. *Am J Med Te* 1983;49:17–22.

Shimizu N, Oomura Y, Novin D, et al: Functional correlations between lateral hypothalamic glucose-sensitive neurons and hepatic portal glucose-sensitive units in rats. *Brain Res* 1983;265:49–54.

Silverstone T: Mood and food: A psychopharmacological enquiry. *Ann NY Acad* 1987;499:264–268.

Smith B, Stevens K, Torgerson W, et al: Diminished reactivity of postmature human infants to sucrose compared with term infants. *Devel Psych* 1992;28(5):811–820.

Spring B, Chiodo J, Bowen D: Carbohydrates, tryptophan and behavior: A methodological review. *Psych B* 1987;102:234–256.

Spring B, Lieberman H, Swope G, et al: Effects of carbohydrates on mood and behavior. *Nutr Rev* 1986;44 (Suppl May):51–60.

Spring B, Maller O, Wurtman J, et al: Effects of protein and carbohydrate meals on mood and performance: Interactions with sex and age. *J Psych Res* 1983;17(2):155–167.

Stanley B, Magdalin W, Seirafi A, et al: Evidence for neuropeptide Y mediation of eating produced by food deprivation and for a variant of the Y1 receptor. *Peptides* 1992;13(3):581–587.

Steffens A: Neuroendocrine mechanisms involved in regulation of body weight, food intake, and metabolism. *Neurosci B* 1990;14:305–313.

Stricker E, Verbalis J: Control of appetite and satiety: Insights from biologic and behavioral studies. *Nutr Rev* 1990;48(2):49–56.

Tempel D, Leibowitz S: Diurnal variations in the feeding responses to norepinephrine, neuropeptide Y and galanin in the PVN. *Brain Res B* 1990;25(6):821–825.

Tempel D, Leibowitz S: Galanin inhibits insulin and corticosterone release after injection into the PVN. *Brain Res* 1990;536(1–2):353–357.

Tempel D, McEwen B, Leibowitz S: Effects of adrenal steroid agonists on food intake and macronutrient selection. *Phsyl Behav* 1992;52(6):1161–1166.

Trulson M: L-tryptophan-induced liver toxicity: A new look at the "natural" sleeping aid. *Nutr Rep* 1987;5(6):40,48.

Uvnas-Moberg K: Endocrinologic control of food intake. *Nutr Rev* 1990;48(2):57–63.

Venero J, Herrera A, Machado A, et al: Changes in neurotransmitter levels associated with the deficiency of some essential amino acids in the diet. *Br J Nutr* 1992: 68(2):409–420.

Wilber J: Neuropeptides, appetite regulation, and human obesity. *J Am Med A* 1991: 266(2):257–259.

Wood D, Reimherr F, Wender P: Treatment of attention deficit disorder with dl-phenylalanine. *Psychiat R* 1985;16:21–26.

Woodbury M, Woodbury M: Neuropsychiatric development: Two case reports about the use of dietary fish oils and/or choline supplementation in children. *J Am Col N* 1993;12(3):239–245.

Woods S, Gibbs J: The regulation of food intake by peptides. *Ann NY Acad* 1987; 499:236–243.

Wurtman J: The involvement of brain serotonin in excessive carbohydrate snacking by obese carbohydrate cravers. *J Am Diet A* 1984;84(9):1004–1007.

Wurtman R: Food & mood. *Nutr Action* 1992;19(7):1,5–7.

Wurtman R: Nutrients that modify brain function. *Sci Am* 1982;April:50–59.

Wurtman R, Fernstrom J: Control of brain monoamine synthesis by diet and plasma amino acids. *Am J Clin N* 1975;28:638–647.

Wurtman R, Wurtman J: Carbohydrates and depression. *Sci Am* 1989;January: 21–33.

Yogman M, Zeisel S, Roberts C: Assessing effects of serotonin precursors on newborn behavior. *J Psych Res* 1983;17:123–133.

York D: Metabolic regulation of food intake. *Nutr Rev* 1990;48(2):64–70.

Young J, Troisi R, Weiss S, et al: Relationship of catecholamine excretion to body size, obesity, and nutrient intake in middle-aged and elderly men. *Am J Clin N* 1992;56:827–834.

Young R, Bach F, Vannorman A, et al: Release of beta endorphin and methionine enkephalin into cerebrospinal fluid during deep brain stimulation for chronic pain: Effects of stimulation locus and site of sampling. *J Neurosurg* 1993;79(6): 816–825.

Young S: Some effects of dietary components (amino acids, carbohydrate, folic acid) on brain serotonin synthesis, mood, and behavior. *J Psych Res* 1986;20(2): 91–101.

Young S: The effects on aggression and mood of altering tryptophan levels. *Nutr Rev* 1986;44 (Suppl May):112–122.

Zeisel S: Choline: An important nutrient in brain development, liver function and carcinogenesis. *J Am Col N* 1992;11(5):473–481.

Zeisel S, DaCosta K, Franklin P, et al: Choline, an essential nutrient for humans. *FASEB J* 1991;5:2093–2098.

CHAPTER 2: DO YOU CRAVE CARBOHYDRATES?

Accardo P, Lindsay R: Nutrition and behavior: The legend continues. *Pediatrics* 1994;93(1):127–128.

Beck B, Burlet A, Bazin R, et al: Elevated neuropeptide Y in the arcuate nucleus of young obese Zucker rats may contribute to the development of their overeating. *J Nutr* 1993;123:1168–1172.

Blackburn G, Wilson G, Kanders B, et al: Weight cycling: The experience of human dieters. *Am J Clin N* 1989;49:1105–1109.

Blank D, Mattes R: Sugar and spice: Similarities and sensory attributes. *Nurs Res* 1990;39(5):290–292.

Blass E, Shide D, Weller A: Stress-reducing effects of ingesting milk, sugars, and fat. *Ann NY Acad* 1989;575:292–305.

Blum I, Nessiel L, Graff E, et al: Food preferences, body weight, and platelet-poor plasma serotonin and catecholamines. *Am J Clin N* 1993;57:486–489.

Blum I, Vered Y, Graff E, et al: The influence of meal composition on plasma serotonin and norepinephrine concentrations. *Metabolism* 1992;41(2):137–140.

Blume E: Do artificial sweeteners help you lose weight? *Nutr Action HealthLetter* 1987;May 1;4–5.

Blundell J: Paradoxical effects of an intense sweetener (aspartame) on appetite. *Lancet* 1986;I:1092.

Brownell K: *Lifestyle, Exercise, Attitudes, Relationships, Nutrition: The LEARN Program of Weight Control*. Philadelphia, University of Pennsylvania, 1988.

Caballero B: Brain serotonin and carbohydrate craving in obesity. *Int J Obes* 1987;11 (Suppl 3):179–183.

Christensen L: Effects of eating behavior on mood: A review of the literature. *Int J Eat D* 1993;14(2):171–183.

Council on Scientific Affairs: Aspartame: Review of safety issues. *J Am Med A* 1985;254:400.

Dakshinamurti K, Sharma S, Bonke D: Influence of B vitamins on binding properties of serotonin receptors in the CNS of rats. *Klin Woch* 1990;68:142–145.

deGraaf C, Jas P, vander Kooy K, et al: Circadian rhythms of appetite at different stages of a weight loss programme. *Int J Obes* 1993;17(9):521–526.

deGraaf C, Schreurs A, Blauw Y: Short-term effects of different amounts of sweet and non-sweet carbohydrates on satiety and energy intake. *Physl Behav* 1993;54: 833–843.

Dews P: Meeting report: Summary report of an international aspartame workshop. *Food Chem T* 1987;25:549–552.

deZwaan M, Mitchell J: Binge eating in the obese. *Ann Med* 1992;24:303–308.

deZwaan M, Mitchell J: Opiate antagonists and eating behavior in humans: A review. *J Clin Phar* 1992;32(12):1060–1072.

Drewnowski A: Sensory preferences for fat and sugar in adolescence and adult life. *Ann NY Acad* 1989;561:243–250.

Drewnowski A, Holden-Wiltse J: Taste responses and food preferences in obese women: Effects of weight cycling. *Int J Obes* 1992;16(9):639–648.

Drewnowski A, Kurth C, Holden-Wiltse J, et al: Food preferences in human obesity: Carbohydrates versus fats. *Appetite* 1992;18(3):207–221.

Drewnowski A, Kurth C, Rahaim J: Taste preferences in human obesity: Environmental and familial factors. *Am J Clin N* 1991;54(4):635–641.

Drewnowski A, Massien C, Louis-Sylvestre J, et al: Comparing the effects of aspartame and sucrose on motivational ratings, taste, preferences, and energy intakes in humans. *Am J Clin N* 1994;59:338–345.

Flatt J: Dietary fat, carbohydrate balance, and weight maintenance: Effects of exercise. *Am J Clin N* 1987;45:296–306.

Garattini S, Mennini T: Reduction of food intake by manipulation of central serotonin. *Br J Psych* 1989;155 (Suppl):41–51.

Giugliano D, Cozzolino D, Salvatore T, et al: Physiological elevations of plasma beta endorphin alter glucose metabolism in obese, but not normal-weight, subjects. *Metabolism* 1992;41(2):184–190.

Harvey J, Wing R, Mullen M: Effects on food cravings of a very low calorie diet or a balanced, low-calorie diet. *Appetite* 1993;21:105–115.

Hill A, Blundell J: Sensitivity of the appetite control system in obese subjects to nutritional and serotoninergic challenges. *Int J Obes* 1990;14:219–233.

Hill A, Weaver C, Blundell J: Food craving, dietary restraint, and mood. *Appetite* 1991;17(3):187–197.

Horton J, Yates A: The effects of long-term high and low refined-sugar intake on blood glucose regulation, mood, bodily symptoms and cognitive functioning. *Behav Res T* 1987;25(1):57–66.

Kehoe P, Blass E: Conditioned opioid release in ten-day-old rats. *Behav Neuro* 1989;103:423–428.

Kyrkouli S, Stanley B, Leibowitz S: Differential effects of galanin and neuropeptide Y on extracellular norepinephrine levels in the paraventricular hypothalamic nucleus of the rat: A microdialysis study. *Life Sci* 1992;51(3):203–210.

Lappalainen R, Sjoden P, Hursti T, et al: Hunger/craving responses and reactivity to food stimuli during fasting and dieting. *Int J Obes* 1990;14(8):679–688.

Lieberman H, Wurtman J, Chew B: Changes in mood after carbohydrate consumption among obese individuals. *Am J Clin N* 1986;44(6):772–778.

Marlatt G, Gordon J: *Relapse Prevention*. New York, Guilford Press, 1985.

Murakawa T, Altura B, Carella A, et al: Importance of magnesium and potassium concentration on basal tone and 5-HT-induced contractions in canine isolated coronary artery. *Br J Pharm* 1988;94:325–334.

Norton P, Falciglia G, Gist D: Physiologic control of food intake by neural and chemical mechanisms. *J Am Diet A* 1993;93:450–454,457.

Pijl H, Kippeschaar H, Cohen A, et al: Evidence of brain serotonin-mediated control of carbohydrate consumption in normal weight and obese humans. *Int J Obes* 1993;17:513–520.

Renwich A: Intense sweeteners, food intake, and the weight of a body of evidence. *Physl Behav* 1994;55(1):139–143.

Rodin J: Effects of pure sugar vs. mixed starch fructose loads on food intake. *Appetite* 1991;17:213–219.

Rodin J: Comparative effects of fructose, aspartame, glucose, and water preloads on calorie and macronutrient intake. *Am J Clin N* 1990;51:428–435.

Rodin J: Metabolic effects of fructose and glucose: Implications for food intake. *Am J Clin N* 1988;47:683–689.

Rumessen J: Fructose and related food carbohydrates. *Sc J Gastro* 1992;27:819–828.

Rushforth J, Levene M: Effect of sucrose on crying in response to heel jab. *Arch Dis Ch* 1993;69:388–389.

Schlundt D, Virts K, Sbrocco T, et al: A sequential behavioral analysis of craving sweets in obese women. *Addict Beha* 1993;18(1):67–80.

Shaywitz B, Sullivan C, Anderson G, et al: Aspartame, behavior, and cognitive function in children with attention deficit disorder. *Pediatrics* 1994;93(1):70–75.

Shide D, Blass E: Opioid mediation of odor preferences induced by sugar and fat in 6-day-old rats. *Physl Behav* 1991;50:961–966.

Shukla A, Agarwal K, Chansuria J, et al: Effect of latent iron deficiency on 5-hydroxytryptamine metabolism in rat brain. *J Neurochem* 1989;52:730–735.

Smith B, Fillion T, Blass E: Orally mediated sources of calming in 1- to 3-day-old human infants. *Devel Psych* 1990;26:731–737.

Smith B, Stevens K, Torgerson W, et al: Diminished reactivity of postmature human infants to sucrose compared with term infants. *Devel Psych* 1992;28:811–820.

Spiegel T, Kaplan J, Tomassini A, et al: Bite size, ingestion rate, and meal size in lean and obese women. *Appetite* 1993;21:131–145.

Stanley B, Magdalin W, Seirafi A, et al: Evidence for neuropeptide Y mediation of eating produced by food deprivation and for a variant of the Y1 receptor mediating this peptide's effect. *Peptides* 1992;13(3):581–587.

Swanson J, Laine D, Thomas W, et al: Metabolic effects of dietary fructose in healthy subjects. *Am J Clin N* 1992;55:851–856.

Tollefson L, Barnard R: An analysis of FDA passive surveillance reports of seizures associated with consumption of aspartame. *J Am Diet A* 1992;92:598–601.

Torii K, Mimura T, Takasaki Y, et al: Dietary aspartame with protein on plasma and brain amino acids, brain monoamines, and behavior in rats. *Physl Behav* 1986;36:765–771.

Walton R: Seizure and mania after high intake of aspartame. *Psychosomat* 1986;27: 218–219.

Watanabe Y, Kobayashi B: Differential release of calcium, magnesium and serotonin by rabbit and human platelets. *J Pharmacob* 1988;11:268–276.

Wilber J: Neuropeptides, appetite regulation, and human obesity. *J Am Med A* 1991;266(2):257–259.

Worthington-Roberts B, Little R, Lambert M, et al: Dietary cravings and aversions in the postpartum period. *J Am Diet A* 1989;89:647–651.

Wurtman J: Depression and weight gain: The serotonin connection. *J Affect D* 1993;29:183–192.

Wurtman J: Carbohydrate cravings: A disorder of food intake and mood. *Clin Neurop* 1988;1:S139–S145.

Wurtman J: Recent evidence from human studies linking central serotoninergic function with carbohydrate intake. *Appetite* 1987;8(3):211–213.

Wurtman J: The involvement of brain serotonin in excessive carbohydrate snacking by obese carbohydrate cravers. *J Am Diet A* 1984;84(9):1004–1007.

Wurtman J, Moses P, Wurtman R: Prior carbohydrate consumption affects the amount of carbohydrate rats choose to eat. *J Nutr* 1983;113:70–78.

Wurtman R: Aspartame effects on brain serotonin. *Am J Clin N* 1987;45:799–801.

Wurtman R: Aspartame: Possible effect on seizure susceptibility. *Lancet* 1985;II: 1060.

Wurtman R, Wurtman J: Carbohydrates and depression. *Sci Am* 1989; January:21–33.

Yokogoshi H, Roberts C, Caballero B, et al: Effects of aspartame and glucose administration on brain and plasma levels of large neutral amino acids and brain 5-hydroxyindoles. *Am J Clin N* 1984;40:1–7.

CHAPTER 3: OTHER FOOD CRAVINGS

Abbott W, Howard B, Ruotolo G, et al: Energy expenditure in humans: Effects of dietary fat and carbohydrate. *Am J Physl* 1990;258(2):E347–E351.

Anderson J, Akanji A: Dietary fiber: An overview. *Diabet Care* 1991;14(12):1126–1131.

Astrup A, Buemann B, Western P, et al: Obesity as an adaptation to a high-fat diet: Evidence from a cross-sectional study. *Am J Clin N* 1994;59:350–355.

Birch L, Johnson S, Jones M, et al: Effects of a nonenergy fat substitute on children's energy and macronutrient intake. *Am J Clin N* 1993;58:326–333.

Braaten J, Wood P, Scott F, et al: Oat gum lowers glucose and insulin after an oral glucose load. *Am J Clin N* 1991;53:1425–1430.

Canty D, Chan M: Effects of consumption of caloric vs noncaloric sweet drinks on indices of hunger and food consumption in normal adults. *Am J Clin N* 1991;53: 1159–1164.

Caputo F, Mattes R: Human dietary responses to perceived manipulation of fat content in a midday meal. *Int J Obes* 1993;17(4):237–240.

Caputo F, Mattes R: Human dietary responses to covert manipulations of energy, fat, and carbohydrate in a midday meal. *Am J Clin N* 1992;56(1):36–43.

Choi P, Van Horn, Picker D, et al: Mood changes in women after an aerobics class: A preliminary study. *Health Care Women Int* 1993;14:167–177.

Corwin R, Robinson, Crawley J: Galanin antagonists block galanin-induced feeding in the hypothalamus and amygdala of the rat. *Eur J Neuro* 1993;5:1528–1533.

deWolfe J, Shannon B: Factors affecting fat consumption of university students: Testing a model to predict eating behavior change. *J Can Diet* 1993;54(3):132–137.

Drewnowski A: Dietary fats: Perceptions and preferences. *J Am Col N* 1990;9(4): 431–435.

Drewnowski A: The new fat replacements. *Postgr Med* 1990;87(6):111–121.

Drewnowski A: Sensory preferences for fat and sugar in adolescence and adult life. *Ann NY Acad* 1989;561:243–249.

Drewnowski A: Food perceptions and preferences of obese adults: A multidimensional approach. *Int J Obes* 1985;9(3):201–212.

Drewnowski A, Brunzell J, Sande K, et al: Sweet tooth reconsidered: Taste responsiveness in human obesity. *Physl Behav* 1985;35(4):617–622.

Drewnowski A, Holden-Wiltse J: Taste responses and food preferences in obese women: Effects of weight cycling. *Int J Obes* 1992;16(9):639–648.

Drewnowski A, Krahan D, Demitrac M: Taste responses and preferences for sweet high-fat foods: Evidence for opioid involvement. *Physl Behav* 1992;51(2):371–379.

Drewnowski A, Kurth C, Holden-Wiltse J, et al: Food preferences in human obesity: Carbohydrates versus fats. *Appetite* 1992;18(3):207–221.

Drewnowski A, Kurth C, Rahaim J: Taste preferences in human obesity: Environmental and familial factors. *Am J Clin N* 1991;54(4):635–641.

Flatt J: Dietary fat, carbohydrate balance, and weight maintenance. *Ann NY Acad* 1993;683:122–140.

Goldfarb A, Harfield B, Potts J, et al: Beta endorphin time course response to intensity of exercise: Effect of training. *Int J Spt Med* 1991;12:264–268.

Gosnell B, Krahn D: The effects of continuous morphine infusion on diet selection and body weight. *Physl Behav* 1993;54:853–859.

Griffiths R, Woodson P: Reinforcing effects of caffeine in humans. *J Pharm Exp* 1988;246(1):21.

Harold M, Reeves R, Bolze M, et al: Effect of dietary fiber in insulin-dependent diabetics: Insulin requirements and serum lipids. *J Am Diet A* 1985;85:1455–1460.

Hill J, Lin D, Yakubu F, et al: Development of dietary obesity in rats: Influence of amount and composition of dietary fat. *Int J Obes* 1992;16:321–333.

Kern D, McPhee L, Fisher J, et al: The postingestive consequences of fat condition preferences for flavors associated with high dietary fat (Meeting abstract). *FASEB J* 1993;7(3):A90.

Klesges R, Klesges L, Haddock C, et al: A longitudinal analysis of the impact of dietary intake and physical activity on weight change in adults. *Am J Clin N* 1992;55: 818–822.

Kyrkouli S, Stanley B, Leibowitz S: Differential effects of galanin and neuropeptide Y on extracellular norepinephrine levels in the paraventricular hypothalamic nucleus of the rat: A microdialysis study. *Life Sci* 1992;51(3):203–210.

Leibowitz S, Kim T: Impact of a galanin antagonist on exogenous galanin and natural patterns of fat ingestion. *Brain Res* 1992;599:148–152.

Leibowitz S, Xuereb M, Kim T: Blockade of natural and neuropeptide Y-induced carbohydrate feeding by a receptor antagonist PYX-2. *Neuroreport* 1992;3(11):1023– 1026.

Lester D, Bernard D: Liking for chocolate, depression, and suicidal preoccupation. *Psychol Reports* 1991;69:570.

Marano H: Chemistry and craving. *Psychol Tod* 1993;January/February:30–36.

Mattes R: Fat preference and adherence to a reduced-fat diet. *Am J Clin N* 1993;57(3):373–381.

Melchior J, Rigaud D, Colas-Linhart N, et al: Immunoreactive beta-endorphin increases after an aspartame chocolate drink in healthy human subjects. *Physl Behav* 1991;50:941–944.

Miller W: Diet composition, energy intake, and nutritional status in relation to obesity in men and women. *Med Sci Spt* 1991;23(3):280–284.

Mullen B, Martin R: The effect of dietary fat on diet selection may involve central serotonin. *Am J Physl* 1992;263(3):R559–R563.

Pasquali R, Casimirri F, Cantobelli S, et al: Beta-endorphin response to exogenous corticotrophin-releasing hormone in obese women with different patterns of body fat distribution. *Int J Obes* 1993;17:593–596.

Pi-Sunyer F: Effect of the composition of the diet on energy intake. *Nutr Rev* 1990;48(2):94–105.

Prewitt T, Schmeisser D, Bowen P, et al: Changes in body weight, body composition, and energy intake in women fed high- and low-fat diets. *Am J Clin N* 1991;54: 304–310.

Reilly M, Dunlop D, Lajtha A: Dietary phenylalanine: does it affect brain function? (Meeting abstract) *J Neurochem* 1993;61(S):S102.

Reimer L: Role of dietary fat in obesity: Fat is fattening. *J Florida M A* 1992; 79(6):382–384.

Rising R, Alger S, Boyce V, et al: Food intake measured by an automated food-selection system: Relationship to energy expenditure. *Am J Clin N* 1992;55:343–349.

Rogers P, Richardson N: Why do we like drinks that contain caffeine? *Trends Food Sci Tech* 1993;April (4):108–111.

Rolls B: Effects of intense sweeteners on hunger, food intake, and body weight: A review. *Am J Clin N* 1991;53:872–878.

Rolls B, Jacobs L, Hetherington M: Sweeteners and energy regulation. *Appetite* 1986;7:291.

Rolls B, Shide D: The influence of dietary fat on food intake and body weight. *Nutr Rev* 1992;50(10):283–290.

Rossignol A, Bonnlander H: Prevalence and severity of the premenstrual syndrome: Effects of foods and beverages that are sweet or high in sugar content. *J Repro Med* 1991;36(2):131–136.

Rozin P, Levine E, Stoess C: Chocolate cravings and liking. *Appetite* 1991;17(3):199–212.

Sardesai V, Waldshan T: Natural and synthetic intense sweeteners. *J Nutr Bioc* 1991;2:236.

Schlundt D, Hill J, Pope-Cordle J, et al: Randomized evaluation of a low fat ad libitum carbohydrate diet for weight reduction. *Int J Obes* 1993;17:623–629.

Schlundt D, Virts K, Sbrocco T, et al: A sequential behavioral analysis of craving sweets in obese women. *Addict Beha* 1993;18(1):67–80.

Schwartz L, Kindermann W: Changes in beta endorphin levels in response to aerobic and anaerobic exercise. *Sport Med* 1992;13(1):25–36.

Sunday S, Einhorn A, Halmi K: Relationship of perceived macronutrient and caloric content to affective cognitions about food in eating-disordered, restrained, and unrestrained subjects. *Am J Clin N* 1992;55:362–371.

Suter P, Schutz Y, Jequier E: The effect of ethanol on fat storage in healthy subjects. *N Eng J Med* 1992;326:983–987.

Swinburn B, Ravussin E: Energy balance or fat balance? *Am J Clin N* 1993;57 (Suppl):766S–771S.

Thomas C, Peters J, Reed G, et al: Nutrient balance and energy expenditure during ad libitum feeding of high-fat and high-carbohydrate diets in humans. *Am J Clin N* 1992;55:934–942.

Tucker L, Kano M: Dietary fat and body fat: A multivariate study of 205 adult females. *Am J Clin N* 1992;56:616–622.

Walter J, Soliah L, Dorsett D: Preliminary study of sweetener preference among college-age females. *Health Values* 1993;17(5):27–32.

Warwick Z, Hall W, Pappas T, et al: Taste and smell sensations enhance the satiating effect of both a high-carbohydrate and high-fat meal in humans. *Physl Behav* 1993;53(3):553–563.

Weingarten H, Elston D: Food cravings in a college population. *Appetite* 1991;17(3): 167–175.

Weingarten H, Elston D: The phenomenology of food cravings. *Appetite* 1990;15: 231–246.

CHAPTER 4: NO ENERGY?

Atkinson H: *Women and Fatigue*. New York, Pocket Books, 1985.

Baghurst K, Baghurst P, Record S: Demographic and nutritional profiles of people consuming varying levels of added sugars. *Nutr Res* 1992;12:1455–1465.

Ballin A, Berar M, Rubinstein U, et al: Iron state in female adolescents. *Am J Dis Ch* 1992;146(7):803–805.

Barclay C, Loisell D: Dependence of muscle fatigue on stimulation protocol: Effect of hypocaloric diet. *J Appl Phys* 1992;72(6):2278–2284.

Bonnet M, Arand D: Caffeine use as a model of acute and chronic insomnia. *Sleep* 1992;15(6):526–536.

Borch-Johnsen B, Meltzer H, Stenberg V, et al: Bioavailability of daily low dose iron supplements in menstruating women with low iron stores. *Eur J Clin N* 1990; 44(1):29–34.

Campbell P, Gerich J: Mechanisms for prevention, development and reversal of hypoglycemia. *Adv Intern* 1988;33:205–230.

Canners C: *The Effect of Breakfast on the Cardiac Response and Behavior of Children*. Minneapolis, MN, Society for Psychophysiological Research, 1982.

Chen M: The epidemiology of self-perceived fatigue among adults. *Prev Med* 1986;15(1):74–81.

Cheraskin E, Ringsdorf W, Medford F: Daily vitamin C consumption and fatigability. *J Am Ger So* 1976;24(3):136–137.

Chou T: Wake and smell the coffee: Caffeine, coffee, and medical consequences. *West J Med* 1992;157:544–553.

Christensen L: The roles of caffeine and sugar in depression. *Nutr Rep* 1991;9(3): 16,24.

Christensen L, Burrows R: Dietary treatment of depression. *Behav Ther* 1990;21: 183–193.

Christensen L, Krietsch K, White B, et al: Impact of a dietary change on emotional distress. *J Abn Psych* 1985;94(4):565–579.

Cox I, Campbell J, Dowson D: Red blood cell magnesium and chronic fatigue syndrome. *Lancet* 1991;337:757–760.

Danowski T, Nolan S, Stephan T: Hypoglycemia. *World Rev Nutr Dietetics* 1975;22:288–303.

Dawson D, Sabin T: *Chronic Fatigue Syndrome*. Boston, Little, Brown, 1993.

Defining the chronic fatigue syndrome. *Arch In Med* 1992;152:1569–1570.

de Graaf C, Jas P, van der Kooy K, et al: Circadian rhythms of appetite at different stages of a weight loss programme. *Int J Obes* 1993;17:521–526.

Deulofeu R, Gascon J, Gimenez N, et al: Magnesium and chronic fatigue syndrome. *Lancet* 1991;338:641.

Dyment P: Frustrated by chronic fatigue? *Phys Sportsmed* 1993;21(11):47–54.

Fairweather-Tait S, Piper Z: The effect of tea on iron and aluminum metabolism in the rat. *Br J Nutr* 1991;65:61–68.

Gin W, Christiansen F, Peter J: Immune function and the chronic fatigue syndrome. *Med J Aust* 1989;151:117–118.

Hallberg L, Brune M, Rossander L: The role of vitamin C in iron absorption, in Walter P, et al (eds): Elevated Dosages of Vitamins. *Int J Vit N*, Toronto, Hans Huber Publishers, 1989, p 103.

Hallberg L, Hulten L, Lindstedt G, et al: Prevalence of iron deficiency in Swedish adolescents. *Pediat Res* 1993;34(5):680–687.

Hallberg L, Rossander-Hulten L: Iron requirements in menstruating women. *Am J Clin N* 1991;54:1047–1058.

Hill A, Blundell J: Sensitivity of the appetite control system in obese subjects to nutritional and serotoninergic challenges. *Int J Obes* 1990;14:219–233.

Hofeldt F, Dippe S, Forsham P: Diagnosis and classification of reactive hypoglycemia based on hormonal changes in response to oral and intravenous glucose administration. *Am J Clin N* 1972;25:1193–1201.

Horswill C, Hickner R, Scott J, et al: Weight loss, dietary carbohydrate modifications, and high intensity, physical performance. *Med Sci Spt* 1990;22(4):470–476.

Influence of tea on iron and aluminum bioavailability in the rat. *Nutr Rev* 1991;49(9): 287–289.

Johnson J, Walker P: Zinc and iron utilization in young women consuming a beef-based diet. *J Am Diet A* 1992;92:1474–1478.

Katon W, Russo J: Chronic fatigue syndrome criteria. *Arch In Med* 1992;152: 1604–1609.

Krebs-Smith S, Cronin F, Haytowitz D, et al: Food sources of energy, macronutrients, cholesterol, and fiber in diets of women. *J Am Diet A* 1992;92:168–174.

Kroenke K: Chronic fatigue syndrome: Is it real? *Postgr Med* 1991;89(2):44–55.

Krupp L, Jandorf L, Coyle P, et al: Sleep disturbance in chronic fatigue syndrome. *J Psychosom* 1993;37(4):325–331.

Lamanca J, Haymes E, Daly J, et al: Sweat iron loss of male and female runners during exercise. *Int J Sp M* 1988;9:52–55.

Lewis C, Park Y, Dexter P, et al: Nutrient intakes and body weights of persons consuming high and moderate levels of added sugars. *J Am Diet A* 1992;92:708–713.

Lieberman H, Corkin S, Spring B, et al: Mood, performance, and pain sensitivity: Changes induced by food constituents. *J Psych Res* 1982/1983:17:135–145.

Lieberman H, Spring B, Garfield G: The behavioral effects of food constituents: Strategies used in studies of amino acids, protein, carbohydrate and caffeine. *Nutr Rev* 1986;May (Suppl):61–70.

Lieberman H, Wurtman J, Chew B: Changes in mood after carbohydrate consumption among obese individuals. *Am J Clin N* 1986;44(6):772–778.

Little K, Castellanos X, Humphries L, et al: Altered zinc metabolism in mood disorder patients. *Biol Psychi* 1989;26:646–648.

Lopez I, de Andraca I, Perales C, et al: Breakfast omission and cognitive performance of normal, wasted and stunted schoolchildren. *Eur J Cl N* 1993;47(8):533–542.

Manore M, Besenfelder P, Wells C, et al: Nutrient intakes and iron status in female long-distance runners during training. *J Am Diet A* 1989;89(2):257–259.

Monsen E, Breskin M, Worthington-Roberts B: Iron status of women and its relation to habitual dietary sources of protein. *Fed Proc* 1986;45(4):978.

Morris D, Lubin A: A review of the symposium "Diet and Behavior"—a multidisciplinary evaluation. *Cont Nutr* 1985;10(5):1–2.

Newhouse I, Clement D, Lai C: Effects of iron supplementation and discontinuation on serum copper, zinc, calcium, and magnesium levels in women. *Med Sci Spt* 1993;25(5):562–571.

Newsholme E, Calder P, Yaquoob P: The regulatory, informational, and immunomodulatory roles of fat fuels. *Am J Clin N* 1993;57 (Suppl):738S–751S.

Pattini A, Schena F: Effects of training and iron supplementation on iron status of cross-country skiers. *J Sport Med* 1990;30(4):347–353.

Politt E: *Research Strategies for Assessing the Behavioral Effects of Foods and Nutrition*. Cambridge, MA, MIT Press, 1982, pp 132–144.

Prasad M, Pratt C: The effects of exercise and two levels of dietary iron on iron status. *Nutr Res* 1990;10(11):1273–1283.

Pratt C: Moderate exercise and iron status in women. *Nutr Rep* 1991;9(7):48,56.

Reid M, Feldman H, Miller M: Isometric contractile properties of diaphragm strips from alcoholic rats. *J Appl Phys* 1987;63(3):1156–1164.

Risser W, Risser J: Iron deficiency in adolescents and young adults. *Phys Sportmed* 1990;18(12):87–88,91,94,96–98,101.

Rogers P, Edwards S, Green M, et al: Nutritional influences on mood and cognitive performance: The menstrual cycle, caffeine, and dieting. *P Nutr Soc* 1992;51:343–351.

Salonen J, Nyyssonen K, Korpela H, et al: High stored iron levels are associated with excess risk of myocardial infarction in eastern Finnish men. *Circulation* 1992;86: 803–811.

Schlundt D, Hill J, Sbrocco T, et al: The role of breakfast in the treatment of obesity: A randomized clinical trial. *Am J Clin N* 1992;55:645–651.

Schwartz J, Jandorf L, Krupp L: The measurement of fatigue: A new instrument. *J Psychosom* 1993;37(7):753–762.

Siegenberg D, Baynes R, Bothwell T, et al: Ascorbic acid prevents the dose-dependent inhibitory effects of polyphenols and phytates on nonheme-iron absorption. *Am J Clin N* 1991;53:537–541.

Silverman K, Evans S, Strain E, et al: Withdrawal syndrome after the double-blind cessation of caffeine consumption. *N Eng J Med* 1992;327(16):1109–1114.

Smith A, Kendrick A, Maben A: Use and effects of food and drink in relation to daily rhythms of mood and cognitive performance. *P Nutr Soc* 1992;51:325–333.

Smith A, Ralph A, McNeill G: Influences of meal size on post-lunch changes in performance efficiency, mood, and cardiovascular function. *Appetite* 1991;16:85–91.

Smith C: Exercise: Practical treatment for the patient with depression and chronic fatigue. *Prim Care* 1991;18(2):271–281.

Spring B, Maller O, Wurtman J, et al: Effects of protein and carbohydrate meals on mood and performance: Interactions with sex and age. *J Psych Res* 1982/3;17(2): 155–167.

Stoner B, Corey G: Chronic fatigue syndrome: A practical approach. *NC Med J* 1992;53(6):267–270.

Thayer R: Energy, tiredness, and tension effects of a sugar snack versus moderate exercise. *J Pers Soc* 1987;52(1):119–125.

Turconi G, Bazzano R, Caramello R, et al: High-calorie, fiber-rich breakfast: Its effect on satiety. *J Hum Nu Di* 1993;6(3):245–252.

Wadden T, Stunkard A, Smoller J: Dieting and depression: A methodological study. *J Cons Clin* 1986;54:869–871.

Weissenburger J, Rush J, Giles D, et al: Weight change in depression. *Psychi Res* 1986;17:275–283.

Wurtman J: Depression and weight gain: The serotonin connection. *J Affect D* 1993; 29:183–192.

CHAPTER 5: PMS AND SAD

Abraham G: Nutritional factors in the aetiology of the premenstrual tension syndromes. *J Repro Med* 1983;28:446–464.

Abraham G, Lubran M: Serum and red cell magnesium levels in patients with premenstrual tension. *Am J Clin N* 1981;34:2364–2366.

Bancroft J, Cook A, Davidson D, et al: Blunting of neuroendocrine responses to infusion of L-tryptophan in women with perimenstrual mood change. *Psychol Med* 1991; 21(2):305–312.

Bancroft J, Cook A, Williamson L: Food craving, mood and the menstrual cycle. *Psychol Med* 1988;18(4):855–860.

Bancroft J, Williamson L, Warner P, et al: Perimenstrual complaints in women complaining of PMS, menorrhagia, and dysmenorrhea: Toward a dismantling of the premenstrual syndrome. *Psychol Med* 1993;55:133–145.

Barr W: Pyridoxine supplements in premenstrual syndrome. *Practition* 1984;228: 425–427.

Blum I, Vered Y, Graff Y, et al: The influence of meal composition on plasma serotonin and norepinephrine concentrations. *Metabolism* 1992;41:137–140.

Boyce P, Parker G: Seasonal affective disorder in the Southern Hemisphere. *Am J Psychi* 1988;145(1):96–99.

Brzezinski A, Wurtman J, Wurtman R, et al: d-fenfluramine suppresses the increased calorie and carbohydrate intake and improves the mood of women with premenstrual depression. *Obstet Gyn* 1990;76:296–301.

Brush M, Perry M: Pyridoxine and the premenstrual syndrome. *Lancet* 1985;I:1399.

Brush M, Watson S, Horrobin D, et al: Abnormal essential fatty acid levels in plasma of women with premenstrual syndrome. *Am J Obst G* 1984;150:363–366.

Caan B, Duncan D, Hiatt R, et al: Association between alcoholic and caffeinated beverages and premenstrual syndrome. *J Repro Med* 1993;38(8):630–636.

Chakmakjian Z: A critical assessment of therapy for the premenstrual tension syndrome. *J Repro Med* 1983;28:532–538.

Christensen L: Effects of eating behavior on mood: A review of the literature. *Int J Eat D* 1993;14(2):171–183.

Christensen L, Burrows R: Dietary treatment of depression. *Behav Ther* 1990;21: 183–193.

Christensen L, Krietsch K, White B, et al: Impact of a dietary change on emotional distress. *J Abn Psych* 1985;94(4):565–579.

Christianson A, Oei T, Callan V: The relationship between premenstrual dysphoria and daily ratings dimensions. *J Affect D* 1989;16(2–3):127–132.

Chung Y, Daghestani A: Seasonal affective disorder: Shedding light on a dark subject. *Postgr Med* 1989;86(5):309–314.

Chuong C, Coulman C, Kao P, et al: Neuropeptide levels in premenstrual syndrome. *Fert Steril* 1985;44:760–765.

Chuong C, Dawson E, Smith E: Vitamin E levels in premenstrual syndrome. *Am J Obst G* 1990;163:1591–1595.

Colditz G, Giovannucci E, Rimm E, et al: Alcohol intake in relation to diet and obesity in women and men. *Am J Clin N* 1991;54:49–55.

Dalton K: Pyridoxine overdose in premenstrual syndrome. *Lancet* 1985;I:1168.

Dalton K: *The Premenstrual Syndrome and Progesterone Therapy*. Chicago, Year Book Medical Publishers, 1984, pp 10–38.

Dalvit S: The effect of the menstrual cycle on patterns of food intake. *Am J Clin N* 1981;34:1811.

Day J: Clinical trials in the premenstrual syndrome. *Curr Med R* 1979;6:40–45.

Delitala G, Masala A, Algana S, et al: Effects of pyridoxine on human hypophyseal trophic hormone release: A possible stimulation of hypothalamic dopaminergic pathway. *J Clin End* 1976;42:603–606.

Endicott J: The menstrual cycle and mood disorders. *J Affect D* 1993;29:193–200.

Fong A, Kretsch M: Changes in dietary intake, urinary nitrogen, and urinary volume across the menstrual cycle. *Am J Clin N* 1993;57:43–46.

Garvey M, Wesner R, Godes M: Comparison of seasonal and nonseasonal affective disorders. *Am J Psychi* 1988;145(1):100–102.

Girdler S, Pedersen C, Stern R, et al: Menstrual cycle and premenstrual syndrome: Modifiers of cardiovascular reactivity in women. *Health Psyc* 1993;12(3):180–192.

Goei G, Abraham G: Effect of nutritional supplement Optivite on symptoms of premenstrual tension. *J Repro Med* 1983;28:527–531.

Grunberg N: The effects of nicotine and cigarette smoking on food consumption and taste preferences. *Addict Beh* 1982;7:317–331.

Gunn A: Vitamin B6 and the premenstrual syndrome (PMS), in Hanck A, Hornig D (eds): Vitamins: Nutrients and Therapeutic Agents. *Int J Vit N*, Basle, Switzerland, Hans Huber Publishers, 1985, pp 213–224.

Hagen I, Nesheim B, Tuntland T: No effect of vitamin B6 against premenstrual tension. *Act Obst Sc* 1985;64:667–670.

Halliday A, Bush B, Cleary P, et al: Alcohol abuse in women seeking gynecologic care. *Obstet Gyn* 1986;68(3):322–326.

Harrison W, Sharpe L, Endicott J: Treatment of premenstrual symptoms. *Gen Hosp Ps* 1985;7:54–65.

Helvacioglu A, Yeoman R, Hazelton J, et al: Premenstrual syndrome and related hormonal changes. *J Repro Med* 1993;38:864–870.

Hitzig P: Combined dopamine and serotonin agonists: A synergistic approach to alcoholism and other addictive behaviors. *MD Med J* 1993;42:153–157.

Horrobin D: The role of essential fatty acids and prostaglandins in the premenstrual syndrome. *J Repro Med* 1983;28:465–468.

Isaacs G, Stainer T, Sensky T, et al: Phototherapy and its mechanism of action in seasonal affective disorder. *J Affect D* 1988;14:13–19.

Jias L, Ellison G: Chronic nicotine induces a specific appetite for sucrose in rats. *Pharm Bioc B* 1990;35:489–491.

Johnson B: Nutrient intake as a time signal for circadian rhythm. *J Nutr* 1992;122(9): 1753–1759.

Jorgensen J, Rossignol A, Bonnlander H: Evidence against multiple premenstrual syndromes: Results of a multivariate profile analysis of premenstrual symptomatology. *J Psychosom* 1993;37(3):257–263.

Kasper S, Wehr T, Bartko J, et al: Epidemiological findings of seasonal changes in mood and behavior. *Arch G Psyc* 1989;46:823–833.

Kendall K, Schnurr P: The effects of vitamin B6 supplementation on premenstrual symptoms. *Obstet Gyn* 1987;70:145–149.

Kerr G: The management of the premenstrual syndrome. *Curr Med R* 1977;4:29–34.

Kizilay P: Predictors of depression in women. *Women Heal* 1992;27(4):983–993.

Krauchi K, Wirz-Justice A: The four seasons: Food intake frequency in seasonal affective disorder in the course of a year. *Psychi R* 1988;25:323–338.

Krauchi K, Wirz-Justice A, Graw P: High intake of sweets late in the day predicts a rapid and persistent response to light therapy in winter depression. *Psychiat R* 1993;46(2):107–117.

Lebrun C: Effect of the different phases of the menstrual cycle and oral contraceptives on athletic performance. *Sport Med* 1993;16(6):400–430.

Lee K, Rittenhouse C: Prevalence of perimenstrual symptoms in employed women. *Women Heal* 1991;17(3):17–32.

Lieberman H, Wurtman J, Chew B: Changes in mood after carbohydrate consumption among obese individuals. *Am J Clin N* 1986;44:772–778.

Liebowitz M, Klein D: Hysteroid dysphoria. *Psych Cl N* 1979;2:255.

Lissner L, et al: Variation in energy intake during the menstrual cycle: Implications for food intake research. *Am J Clin N* 1988;48:956.

London R, Bradley L, Chiamori N: Effect of a nutritional supplement on premenstrual symptomatology in women with premenstrual syndrome: A double-blind longitudinal study. *J Am Col N* 1991;10(5):494–499.

London R, et al: The effect of alpha-tocopherol on premenstrual symptomatology: A double-blind study. *J Am Col N* 1983;2:115.

Mason R: Circadian variation in sensitivity of suprachiasmatic and lateral geniculate neurons to 5-hydroxytryptamine in the rat. *J Physl* 1986;377:1–13.

Mathus-Vliegen L, Res A: Dexfenfluramine influences dietary compliance and eating behavior, but dietary instruction may overrule its effect on food selection in obese subjects. *J Am Diet A* 1993;93:1163–1164.

Mauri A, Martellotta M, Melis M, et al: Plasma alpha-melanocyte-stimulating hormone during the menstrual cycle in women. *Hormone Res* 1990;34:66–70.

McGrath R, Buckwald B, Resnick E: The effect of l-tryptophan on seasonal affective disorder. *J Clin Psy* 1990;51:162–163.

Mello N, Mendelson J, Lex B: Alcohol use and premenstrual symptoms in social drinkers. *Psychopharm* 1990;101(4):448–455.

Mello N, Mendelson J, Palmieri S: Cigarette smoking by women: Interactions with alcohol use. *Psychopharm* 1987;93(1):8–15.

Mills J: Is it my period or is it my life? *Shape* 1991;November:86–90.

Moline M: Pharmacologic strategies for managing premenstrual syndrome. *Clin Pharm* 1993;12:181–196.

Moos R: The development of a menstrual distress questionnaire. *Psychos Med* 1968;30: 853.

Morton J, Additon H, Addison R, et al: A clinical study of premenstrual tension. *Am J Obst G* 1953;65:1182–1191.

Murphy D, Abas M, Winton F, et al: Seasonal affective disorder: A neurophysiological approach, in Thompson C, Silverstone T (eds): *Seasonal Affective Disorders*. London, Farand Press, 1989.

Nduka E, Agbedana E: Total cholesterol, high density lipoprotein cholesterol and steroid hormone changes in normal weight women during the menstrual cycle. *Int J Gyn Obst* 1993;41:265–268.

O'Rourke D: Treatment of seasonal depression with d-fenfluramine. *J Clin Psych* 1989;50(9):343–347.

Partonen T: Effects of morning light treatment of subjective sleepiness and mood in winter depression. *J Affect D* 1994;30:47–56.

Partonen T, Lonnqvist J: Effects of light on mood. *Ann Med* 1993;25:301–302.

Penland J, Hunt J: Nutritional status and menstrual-related symptomatology (Meeting abstract). *FASEB J* 1993;7:A379.

Penland J, Johnson P: Dietary calcium and manganese effects on menstrual cycle symptoms. *Am J Obst G* 1993;168:1417–1423.

Puolakka J, Makarainen L, Viinikka L, et al: Biochemical and clinical effects of treating the premenstrual syndrome with prostaglandin synthesis precursors. *J Repro Med* 1985;30(3):149–153.

Pye J, Mansel R, Hughes L: Clinical experience of drug treatments for mastalgia. *Lancet* 1985;August 17:373–376.

Rapkin A: The role of serotonin in premenstrual syndrome. *Clin O Gyne* 1992;35(3): 629–636.

Reid R: Premenstrual syndrome. *N Eng J Med* 1991;324(17):1208–1210.

Reid R: Premenstrual syndrome: A time for introspection. *Am J Obst G* 1986;155:921.

Rogers P, Edwards S, Green M, et al: Nutritional influences on mood and cognitive performance: The menstrual cycle, caffeine, and dieting. *P Nutr Soc* 1992;51:343–351.

Rosenstein D, Elin R, Hosseini J, et al: Magnesium measures across the menstrual cycle in premenstrual syndrome. *Biol Psychi* 1994;35(8):557–561.

Rosenthal N: Psychobiological effects of carbohydrate- and protein-rich meals in patients with seasonal affective disorder and normal controls. *Biol Psychi* 1989;23:1029–1040.

Rosenthal N, Blehar M (eds): *Seasonal Affective Disorders and Phototherapy*. New York, Guilford Press, 1989.

Rosenthal N, Genhart M, Callabero B, et al: Psychobiological effects of carbohydrate- and protein-rich meals in patients with SAD and normal controls. *Biol Psychi* 1989;25:1029–1040.

Rosenthal N, Genhart M, Jacobsen F, et al: Disturbances of appetite and weight regulation in seasonal affective disorder. *Ann NY Acad* 1987;569:216–230.

Rossignol A: Caffeine-containing beverages and premenstrual syndrome in young women. *Am J Pub He* 1985;75:1335.

Rossignol A, Bonnlander H: Prevalence and severity of the premenstrual syndrome: Effects of food and beverages that are sweet or high in sugar content. *J Repro Med* 1991;36(2):131–136.

Rossignol A, Bonnlander H: Caffeine-containing beverages, total fluid consumption, and premenstrual syndrome. *Am J Pub He* 1990;80(9):1106–1110.

Rubin R, Heist E, McGeoy S, et al: Neuroendocrine aspects of primary endogenous depression. XI. Serum melatonin measures in patients and matched control subjects. *Arch G Psychi* 1992;49(7):558–567.

Rubinow D: The premenstrual syndrome: New views. *J Am Med A* 1992;268(14):1908–1912.

Sack L, Blood M, Lewy A: Melatonin rhythm in night shift workers. *Sleep* 1992;15: 434–441.

Seelig M: Interrelationship of magnesium and estrogen in cardiovascular and bone disorders, eclampsia, migraine and premenstrual syndrome. *J Am Col N* 1993; 12(4):442–458.

Severino S, Yonkers K: A literature review of psychotic symptoms associated with the premenstruum. *Psychosomat* 1993;34(4):299–306.

Sherwood R, Rocks B, Stewart A, et al: Magnesium and the premenstrual syndrome. *Ann Clin Bi* 1986;23:667–670.

Smallwood J, Ah-Kye D, Taylor I: Vitamin B6 in the treatment of pre-menstrual mastalgia. *Br J Clin P* 1986;40(12):532–534.

Smith S, Sauder C: Food cravings, depression, and premenstrual problems. *Psychosom Med* 1969;31(4):281–287.

Somer E: *Nutrition for Women: The Complete Guide*. New York, Henry Holt & Company, 1993, pp 364–369.

Steinberg S, Sylvester W, Dean C: Pharmacologic management of premenstrual syndrome. *Can Pharm J* 1985;118(4):150–164.

Taylor R, James G: The clinician's view of patients with premenstrual syndrome. *Curr Med R* 1979;6:46–51.

Thompson C, Silverstone T (eds): *Seasonal Affective Disorders*. London, CNS Neuroscience Press, 1990.

Thys-Jacobs S, Ceccarelli S, Bierman A, et al: Calcium supplementation in premenstrual syndrome: A randomized crossover trial. *J Gen Int M* 1989;4:183–189.

Tomelleri R, Granulate K: Menstrual cycle and food cravings in young college women. *J Am Diet A* 1987;87(3):311–315.

van der Ploeg H, Lodder E: Longitudinal measurement of diagnostics of the premenstrual syndrome. *J Psychosom* 1993;37(1):33–38.

Wehr T, Giesen H, Schulz P, et al: Contrasts between symptoms of summer depression and winter depression. *J Affect D* 1991;23(4):173–183.

Weingarten H, Elston D: The phenomenology of food cravings. *Appetite* 1990;15:231–246.

Williams M, Harris R, Dean B, et al: Controlled trial of pyridoxine in the premenstrual syndrome. *J Int Med R* 1985;13:174–179.

Winton F, Corn T, Huson W, et al: Effects of light treatment upon mood and melatonin in patients with seasonal affective disorder. *Psychol Med* 1989;19:585–590.

Wirz-Justice A, van der Velde P, Bucher A, et al: Comparison of light treatment with citalopram in winter depression: A longitudinal single case study. *Int Clin Ps* 1992;7(2):109–116.

Wurtman J, Brzenzinski A, Wurtman R, et al: Effect of nutrient intake on premenstrual depression. *Am J Obst G* 1989;161:1228–1234.

Yung L, Gordis E, Holt J: Dietary choices and likelihood of abstinence among alcoholic patients in an outpatient clinic. *Drug Al Dep* 1983;12:355–362.

CHAPTER 6: FOOD AND THE BLUES

Abou-Saleh M, Coppen A: The biology of folate in depression: Implications for nutritional hypothesis of the psychoses. *J Psych Res* 1986;20(2):91–101.

Bantle J: Clinical aspects of sucrose and fructose metabolism. *Diabet Care* 1989;12 (Suppl 1):56–61.

Bell I: Vitamin B12 and folate in acute geropsychiatric inpatients. *Nutr Rep* 1991;9(1):1,8.

Bell I, Markley E, King D, et al: Polysymptomatic syndromes and autonomic reactivity to nonfood stressors in individuals with self-reported adverse food reactions. *J Am Col N* 1993;12(3):227–238.

Bell I, Edman J, Morrow F, et al: Brief communication: Vitamin B1, B2, and B6 augmentation of tricyclic antidepressant treatment in geriatric depression with cognitive dysfunction. *J Am Col N* 1992;11:159–163.

Bell I, Edman J, Morrow F, et al: B complex vitamin patterns in geriatric and young adult inpatients with major depression. *J Am Ger So* 1991;39:252–257.

Bender D: B vitamins in the nervous system: A review. *Neurochem I* 1984;6:297–321.

Benton D, Cook R: The impact of selenium supplementation on mood. *Biol Psychi* 1991;29:1092–1098.

Berger A, Schaumburg H, Schroeder C, et al: Dose response, coasting, and differential fiber vulnerability in human toxic neuropathy. *Neurology* 1992;42:1367–1370.

Blank D, Mattes R: Sugar and spice: Similarities and sensory attributes. *Nurs Res* 1990;32:290–292.

Blom W, van den Berg G, Huijmans J: Successful nicotinamide treatment in an autosomal dominant behavioral and psychiatric disorder. *J Inh Met D* 1985;8:107–108.

Blum I, Vered Y, Graff E, et al: The influence of meal composition on plasma serotonin and norepinephrine concentrations. *Metabolism* 1992;41(2):137–140.

Brinsmead M, Smith R, Singh B, et al: Peripartum concentrations of beta endorphin and cortisol and maternal mood states. *Aust N Z J O* 1985;25(3):194–197.

Byrne A, Byrne D: The effect of exercise on depression, anxiety, and other mood states: A review. *J Psychosom* 1993;37(6):565–574.

Carney M: Vitamin deficiency and mental symptoms. *Br J Psychi* 1990;156:878–882.

Chouvinard G, Young S, Annable L, et al: Tryptophan dosage critical for its antidepressant effect. *Br Med J* 1978;I:1422.

Christensen L: The roles of caffeine and sugar in depression. *Nutr Rep* 1991; 9(3):16,24.

Christensen L, Burrows R: Dietary treatment of depression. *Behav Ther* 1990; 21:183–193.

Christensen L, Krietsch K, White B, et al: Impact of a dietary change on emotional distress. *J Abn Psych* 1985;94(4):565–579.

Christensen L, Redig C: Effect of meal composition on mood. *Behav Neuro* 1993; 107(2):346–353.

de Geus E, vanDoornen L, Orlebeke J: Regular exercise and aerobic fitness in relation to psychological make-up and physiological reactivity. *Psychos Med* 1993;55: 347–363.

Desharnais R, Jobin J, Cote C: Aerobic exercise and the placebo effect: A controlled study. *Psychos Med* 1993;55:149–154.

Drewnowski A, Schwartz M: Invisible fats: Sensory assessment of sugar/fat mixtures. *Appetite* 1990;14(3):203–217.

Eastman C, Gultarte T: Vitamin B6, kynurenines, and central nervous system function: Developmental aspects. *J Nutr Bioc* 1992;3:618–631.

Eipper B, Mains R: The role of ascorbate in the biosynthesis of neuroendocrine peptides. *Am J Clin N* 1991;54 (Suppl):1153S–1156S.

Gelenberg A, Wojcik J, Falk W: Tyrosine for depression: A double-blind trial. *J Affect D* 1990;19(2):125–132.

Gjerdingen D, Froberg D, Kochevar L: Changes in women's mental and physical health from pregnancy through six months postpartum. *J Fam Pract* 1991;32(2):161–166.

Godfrey P, Toone B, Carney M, et al: Enhancement of recovery from psychiatric illness by methylfolate. *Lancet* 1990;336:392–395.

Groves P, Schlesinger K: *Introduction to Biological Psychology, ed 2.* Dubuque, IA, Wm. C. Brown Co., 1982.

Hancock M, Hullin R, Aylard P, et al: Nutritional state of elderly women on admission to mental hospital. *Br J Psychi* 1985;147:404–407.

Hannah P, Adams D, Lee A, et al: Links between early post-partum mood and post-natal depression. *Br J Psychi* 1992;160:777–780.

Harris B: Post-partum thyroid dysfunction and post-natal depression. *Ann Med* 1993;25:215–216.

Heller W: Gender differences in depression: Perspectives from neuropsychology. *J Affect D* 1993;29:129–143.

Hertzman P, Blevins W, Mayer J, et al: Association of the eosinophilia-myalgia syndrome with the ingestion of tryptophan. *N Eng J Med* 1990;322(13):869–873.

Heseker H, Kubler W, Pudel V, et al: Psychological disorders as early symptoms of a mild to moderate vitamin deficiency. *Ann NY Acad* 1992;669:352–357.

Kehoe P, Blass E: Conditioned opioid release in ten-day-old rats. *Behav Neuro* 1989;103:423–428.

Kehoe P, Blass E: Behaviorally functional opioid systems in infant rats: II. Evidence for pharmacological, physiological, and psychological mediation of pain and stress. *Behav Neuro* 1986;100:624–630.

Kendall K, Schnurr P: The effects of vitamin B6 supplementation on premenstrual symptoms. *Obstet Gyn* 1987;70:145–149.

Kessler R, McGonagle K, Swartz M, et al: Sex and depression in the National Comorbidity Survey I: Lifetime prevalence, chronicity and recurrence. *J Affect D* 1993;29:85–96.

Kizilay P: Predictors of depression in women. *Women Heal* 1992;27(4):983–993.

Knight R, Thirkettle J: The relationship between expectations of pregnancy and birth, and transient depression in the immediate post-partum period. *J Psychosom* 1987;31(3):351–357.

L Tryptophan "Peak E" identified by Showa Denko researchers. *Food Chem News* 1990; October 8:44–45.

Lewis C, Park Y, Dexter P, et al: Nutrient intakes and body weights of persons consuming high and moderate levels of added sugars. *J Am Diet A* 1992;92:708–713.

Littlefield V, Chang A, Adams B: Participation in alternative care: Relationship to anxiety, depression, and hostility. *Res Nurs H* 1990;13(1):17–25.

Lozoff B, Jimenez E, Wolf A: Long-term developmental outcome of infants with iron deficiency. *N Engl J Med* 1991;325:687–694.

Matchar D, Feussner J, Watson D, et al: Significance of low serum vitamin B12 levels in the elderly. *J Am Ger So* 1986;34:680–681.

McCance-Katz E, Price L: Depression associated with vitamin A intoxication. *Psychosomat* 1992;33(1):117.

McCullough A, Kirksey A, Wachs T, et al: Vitamin B6 status of Egyptian mothers: Relation to infant behavior and maternal-infant interactions. *Am J Clin N* 1990;51:1067–1074.

Mebert C: Dimensions of subjectivity in parents' rating of infant temperament. *Child Dev* 1991;62(2):352–361.

Moller S: Carbohydrate/protein selection in a single meal correlated with plasma tryptophan and tyrosine ratios to neutral amino acids in fasting individuals. *Physl Behav* 1986;38:175–183.

Moller S: Tryptophan to competing amino acids ratio in depressive disorder: Relation to efficacy of antidepressant treatments. *Acta Psyc Sc* 1985;325(72):7–31.

Pedersen C, Stern R, Pate J, et al: Thyroid and adrenal measures during late pregnancy and the puerperium in women who have been major depressed or who become dysphoric postpartum. *J Affect D* 1993;29:201–211.

Pierce T, Madden D, Siegel W, et al: Effects of aerobic exercise on cognitive and psychosocial functioning in patients with mild hypertension. *Health Psyc* 1993;12(4): 286–291.

Podell R: Nutritional precursors and the treatment of depression. *Postgr Med* 1983; 73(3):99–103.

Pop V, Essed G, deGeus C, et al: Prevalence of post partum depression: Or is it post-puerperium depression? *Act Obst Sc* 1993;72:354–358.

Repetti R: Short-term effects of occupational stressors on daily mood and health complaints. *Health Psyc* 1993;12(2):125–131.

Ruble D, Greulich F, Pomerantz E, et al: The role of gender-related processes in the development of sex differences in self-evaluation and depression. *J Affect D* 1993;29:97–128.

Sabelli H, Fawcell J, Gusovsky F, et al: Clinical studies on the phenylalanine hypothesis of affective disorder: Urine and blood phenylacetic acid and phenylalanine dietary supplements. *J Clin Psy* 1986;47:66–70.

Shide D, Blass E: Opioid mediation of odor preferences induced by sugar and fat in 6-day-old rats. *Physl Behav* 1991;50:961–966.

Simons A, Angell K, Monroe S, et al: Cognition and life stress in depression: Cognitive factors and the definition, rating, and generation of negative life events. *J Abn Psych* 1993;102(4):584–591.

Stern G, Kruckman L: Multi-disciplinary perspectives on post-partum depression: An anthropological critique. *Social Sci M* 1983;17(15):1027–1041.

Trulson M: L-tryptophan-induced liver toxicity: A new look at the "natural" sleeping aid. *Nutr Rep* 1987;5(6):40, 48.

Tsukasaki M, Ohta Y, Oishi K, et al: Types and characteristics of short-term course of depression after delivery: Using Zung's Self-Rating Depression Scale. *Jpn J Psy N* 1991;45(3):565–576.

Weissman M, Bland R, Joyce P, et al: Sex differences in rates of depression: Cross-national perspectives. *J Affect D* 1993;29:77–84.

Wieland R: Vitamin B12 deficiency in the nonanemic elderly. *J Am Ger So* 1986;34:690.

Wolman W, Chalmers B, Hofmeyr G, et al: Postpartum depression and companionship in the clinical birth environment: A randomized, controlled study. *Am J Obst G* 1993;168:1388–1393.

Worthington-Roberts B, Little R, Lambert M, et al: Dietary cravings and aversions in the postpartum period. *J Am Diet A* 1989;89:647–651.

Wurtman J: Depression and weight gain: The serotonin connection. *J Affect D* 1993;29:183–192.

Wurtman J: The involvement of brain serotonin in excessive carbohydrate snacking by obese carbohydrate cravers. *J Am Diet A* 1984;84(9):1004–1007.

Young S: Some effects of dietary components (amino acids, carbohydrate, folic acid) on brain serotonin synthesis, mood, and behavior. *Can J Phys* 1991;69:893–903.

CHAPTER 7: STRESS AND DIET

Ackroff K, Sclafani A: Sucrose-induced hyperphagia and obesity in rats fed a macronutrient self-selection diet. *Physl Behav* 1988;44:181–187.

Anderson R, Kozlovsky A, Moser P: Effects of diets high in simple sugars on urinary chromium excretion of humans. *Fed Proc* 1985;44:751.

Baghurst K, Baghurst P, Record S: Demographic and nutritional profiles of people consuming varying levels of added sugars. *Nutr Res* 1992;12:1455–1465.

Bender D: B vitamins and the nervous system. *Neurochem I* 1984;6(3):297–321.

Blass E, Shide D, Weller A: Stress-reducing effects of ingesting milk, sugars, and fat. *Ann NY Acad* 1989;575:292–306.

Byrne A, Byrne D: The effect of exercise on depression, anxiety, and other mood states: A review. *J Psychosom* 1993;37(6):565–574.

Caster W: Effect of diet and stress on the thiamin and pyramin excretion of normal young men maintained on controlled intakes of thiamin. *Nutr Res* 1991;11:549–558.

Chandra R: The role of trace elements and immune function. *Nutr Rep* 1987;5(4):24, 32.

Christensen L, Krietsch K, White B, et al: Impact of a dietary change on emotional distress. *J Abn Psych* 1985;94:565–579.

Classen H: Stress and magnesium. *Artery* 1981;9(3):182–189.

Couzy F, Lafargue P, Guezennec C: Zinc metabolism in the athlete: Influence of training, nutrition and other factors. *Int J Sp M* 1990;11(4):263–266.

DiPlama J: Magnesium replacement therapy. *Am Fam Phys* 1990;42(1):173–176.

Dryburgh D: Vitamin C and chiropractic. *J Manip Phy* 1985;8(2):95–103.

Eaton W, McLeod J: Consumption of coffee and tea and symptoms of anxiety. *Am J Pub He* 1984;74(1):66–68.

Ericsson Y, Angmar-Mansson B, Flores M: Urinary mineral ion loss after sugar ingestion. *Bone Miner* 1990;9:233–237.

Fawaz F: Zinc deficiency in surgical patients: A clinical study. *J Parent En* 1985;9:364–369.

Fine K, Santa Ana C, Porter J, et al: Intestinal absorption of magnesium from food and supplements. *J Clin In* 1991;88:396–402.

Fowkes F, Leng G, Donnan P, et al: Serum cholesterol, triglycerides, and aggression in the general population. *Lancet* 1992;340:995–998.

Gallacher J, Fehily A, Yarnell J, et al: Type A behaviour, eating pattern and nutrient intake: The Caerphilly Study. *Appetite* 1988;11:129–136.

Gebhart K, Gridley D, Stickney D, et al: Enhancement of immune status by high levels of dietary vitamin B6 without growth inhibition of human malignant melanoma in athymic nude mice. *Nutr Cancer* 1990;14:15–26.

Glueck C, Tieger M, Kunkel R, et al: Improvement in symptoms of depression and in an index of life stressors accompany treatment of severe hypertriglyceridemia. *Biol Psychi* 1993;34(4):240–252.

Hambridge K: The role of zinc and other trace minerals in pediatric nutrition and health. *Ped Clin NA* 1977;24:95.

Herbert T, Cohen S: Stress and immunity in humans: A meta-analytic review. *Psychos Med* 1993;55:364–379.

Hess J, Prasad A, Kaplan J: Zinc nutrition and cellular immunity in the elderly. *J Am Ger So* 1987;35:91.

House J: Occupational stress and coronary heart disease: A review and theoretical integration. *J Health So* 1974;15(March):12–26.

Houston B, Chesney M, Black G, et al: Behavioral clusters and coronary heart disease risk. *Psychos Med* 1992;54:447–461.

Jabaaij L, Grosheide P, Heijtink R, et al: Influence of perceived psychological stress and distress on antibody response to low dose rDNA hepatitis B vaccine. *J Psychosom* 1993;37(4):361–369.

Jayo J, Shively C, Kaplan J, et al: Effects of exercise and stress on body fat distribution in male cynomolgus monkeys. *Int J Obes* 1993;17:597–604.

Joborn H, Hjemdahl P, Larsson P, et al: Effects of prolonged adrenaline infusion and of mental stress on plasma minerals and parathyroid hormone. *Clin Phys B* 1990;10:37–53.

Jootsen E, van den Berg A, Riezler R, et al: Metabolic evidence that deficiencies of vitamin B12 (cobalamin), folate, and vitamin B6 occur commonly in elderly people. *Am J Clin N* 1993;58:468–476.

Joseph M, Kennett G: Stress-induced release of 5-HT in the hippocampus and its dependence on increased tryptophan availability: An in vivo electrochemical study. *Brain Res* 1983;270(2):251–257.

Kallner A: Influence of vitamin C status on the urinary excretion of catecholamines in stress. *Hum Nutr-Cl* 1983;37:405–411.

Kaplan J, Manuck S, Shively C: The effects of fat and cholesterol on social behavior in monkeys. *Psychos Med* 1991;53:634–642.

Kinsella J: Dietary polyunsaturated fatty acids affect inflammatory and immune functions. *Nutr Rep* 1990;8(10):72, 80.

Klatsky A, Friedman G, Armstrong M: Coffee use prior to myocardial infarction restudied: Heavier intake may increase the risk. *Am J Epidem* 1990;132(3):479–488.

Kor H, Scimeca J: Influence of dietary fat replacement on immune function. *FASEB* 1991;5(5):A565.

Kramer T, Udomkesmalee E, Dhanamitta S, et al: Lymphocyte responsiveness of children supplemented with vitamin A and zinc. *Am J Clin N* 1993;58:566–570.

Lampe J, Slavin J, Apple F: Poor iron status of women runners training for a marathon. *Int J Sp M* 1986;7:111–114.

Lehrman N: Pleasure heals: The role of social pleasure, love in its broadest sense, in medical practice. *Arch In Med* 1993;153:929–934.

Levenstein S, Prantera C, Varvo V, et al: Development of the perceived stress questionnaire: A new tool for psychosomatic research. *J Psychosom* 1993;37(1):19–32.

Lewis C, Park Y, Dexter P, et al: Nutrient intakes and body weights of persons consuming high and moderate levels of added sugars. *J Am Diet A* 1992;92:708–713.

Liebler D: The role of metabolism in the antioxidant function of vitamin E. *Cr R Toxic* 1993;23(2):147–169.

Little K, Castellanos X, Humphries L, et al: Altered zinc metabolism in mood disorder patients. *Biol Psychi* 1989;26:646–648.

Littman A, Fava M, Halperin P, et al: Physiological benefits of a stress reduction program for healthy middle-aged army officers. *J Psychosom* 1993;37(4):345–354.

Marano H: Chemistry and cravings. *Psych Today* 1993;January/February:30–36, 74.

McEwen B, Stellar E: Stress and the individual: Mechanisms leading to disease. *Arch In Med* 1993;153:2093–2101.

Miller L, Kerkvliet N: Effect of vitamin B6 on immunocompetence in the elderly. *Ann NY Acad* 1990;587:49–54.

Miller P, Light K, Bragdon E, et al: Beta-endorphin response to exercise and mental stress in patients with ischemic heart disease. *J Psychosom* 1993;37(5):455–465.

Moore R, Friedl K, Tulley R, et al: Maintenance of iron status in healthy men during an extended period of stress and physical activity. *Am J Clin N* 1993;58:923–927.

Morgan R, Palinkas L, Barrett-Connor E, et al: Plasma cholesterol and depressive symptoms in older men. *Lancet* 1993;341:75–79.

Muldoon M, Bachen E, Manuck S, et al: Acute cholesterol responses to mental stress and change in posture. *Arch In Med* 1992;152:775–780.

Muldoon M, Manuck S, Matthews K: Lowering cholesterol concentrations and mortality: A quantitative review of primary prevention trials. *Br Med J* 1990;301: 309–314.

Muldoon M, Rossouw J, Manuck S, et al: Low or lowered cholesterol and risk of death from suicide and trauma. *Metabolism* 1993;42(9):45–56.

Nehlig A, Daval J, Debry G: Caffeine and the central nervous system: Mechanisms of action, biochemical, metabolic, and psychosomatic effects. *Brain Res R* 1992;17(2): 139–169.

Nielsen F: New essential trace elements for the life sciences. *Biol Tr El* 1990;26–27:599–611.

Nieman D, Miller A, Henson D, et al: Effects of high- vs moderate-intensity exercise on natural killer cell activity. *Med Sci Spt* 1993;25(10):1126–1134.

Nirgiotis J, Hennessey P, Black C, et al: Low-fat, high-carbohydrate diets improve wound healing and increase protein levels in surgically stressed rats. *J Ped Surg* 1991;26(8):925–929.

Parker C: Environmental stress and immunity: Possible implications for IgE-mediated allergy. *Persp Biol* 1991;34(2):197–212.

Patterson B, Cornell C, Carbone B, et al: Protein depletion and metabolic stress in elderly patients who have a fracture of the hip. *J Bone-Am V* 1992;74(2):251–260.

Peretz A, Neve J, Desmedt J, et al: Lymphocyte response is enhanced by supplementation of elderly subjects with selenium-enriched yeast. *Am J Clin N* 1991;53: 1323–1328.

Pratt C: Moderate exercise and iron status in women. *Nutr Rep* 1991;9(7):48,56.

Pryor W: Can vitamin E protect humans against the pathological effects of ozone in smog? *Am J Clin N* 1991;53:702–722.

Puccio E, McPhillips J, Barrett-Connor E, et al: Clustering of atherogenic behaviors in coffee drinkers. *Am J Pub He* 1990;80:1310–1313.

Radanov B, diStefano G, Schnidrig A, et al: Psychosocial stress, cognitive performance and disability after common whiplash. *J Psychosom* 1993;37(1):1–10.

Rall L, Meydani S: Vitamin B6 and immune competence. *Nutr Rev* 1993;51(8): 217–234.

Resina A, Fedi S, Gatteschi L, et al: Comparison of some serum copper parameters in trained runners and control subjects. *Int J Sp M* 1990;11:58–60.

Robinson S, Arnold H, Spear N, et al: Experience with milk and an artificial nipple promotes conditioned opioid activity in the rat fetus. *Devel Psych* 1993;26(7):375–387.

Scherwitz L, Perkins L, Chesney M, et al: Hostility and health behaviors in young adults. The CARDIA Study. *Am J Epidem* 1992;136(2):136–145.

Schleifer S, Keller S, Stein M: Stress effects on immunity. *Psychiat J* 1985;10(3):125–131.

Seelig M: Cardiovascular consequences of magnesium deficiency and loss: Pathogenesis, prevalence, and manifestations—Magnesium and chloride loss in refractory potassium repletion. *Am J Card* 1989;63:4G–21G.

Shekelle R, Vernon S, Ostfeld A: Personality and coronary heart disease. *Psychos Med* 1991;53:176–184.

Sherman A: Zinc, copper, and iron nutriture and immunity. *J Nutr* 1992;122:604–609.

Singh A, Smoak B, Patterson K, et al: Biochemical indices of selected trace minerals in men: Effects of stress. *Am J Clin N* 1991;53:126–131.

Stone A, Bovbjerg D, Neale J, et al: Development of common cold symptoms following experimental rhinovirus infection is related to prior stressful life events. *Behav Med* 1992;18:115–120.

Sugawara N, Sugawara C, Maehara N, et al: Effect of acute stresses on Zn-thionein production in rat liver. *Eur J A Phy* 1983;51(3):365–370.

Superko H, Bortz W, Williams P, et al: Caffeinated and decaffeinated coffee effects on plasma lipoprotein cholesterol, apolipoproteins, and lipase activity: A controlled, randomized trial. *Am J Clin N* 1991;54:599–605.

Turner R, Finch J: Selenium and immune response. *P Nutr Soc* 1991;50:275–285.

Weidner G, Connor S, Hollis J, et al: Improvements in hostility and depression in relation to dietary change and cholesterol lowering. *Ann In Med* 1992;117:820–823.

CHAPTER 8: SMART FOODS

Abe E, Murai S, Masuda Y, et al: Reversal by 3,3',5-triido-L-thyronine of the working memory deficit, and the decrease in acetylcholine, glutamate and gamma amino butyric acid induced by ethylcholine aziridinium ion in mice. *Naunyn Schmiedebergs Arch Pharmacol* 1992;346(2):238–242.

Algeri S: Potential strategies against age-related brain deterioration. Dietary and pharmacological approaches. *Ann NY Acad* 1992;663:376–383.

Ames B, Shigenaga M, Hagen T: Oxidants, antioxidants, and the degenerative diseases of aging. *P NAS US* 1993;90(17):7915–7922.

Ballin A, Berar M, Rubinstein U, et al: Iron state in female adolescents. *Am J Dis Ch* 1992;146(7):803–805.

Beard J, Connor J, Jones B: Brain iron: Location and function. *Prog Food N* 1993; 17(3):183–221.

Ben-Shachar D, Livne E, Spanier I, et al: Iron modulates neuroleptic-induced effects related to the dopaminergic system. *Isr J Med S* 1993;29(9):587–592.

Benton D: Vitamin-mineral supplements and intelligence. *P Nutr Soc* 1992;51:295–302.

Berger A, Schaumburg H, Schroeder C, et al: Dose response, coasting, and differential fiber vulnerability in human toxic neuropathy. *Neurology* 1992;42:1367–1370.

Blom W, vanden Berg G, Huijmans J: Successful nicotinamide treatment in an autosomal dominant behavioral and psychiatric disorder. *J Inh Met D* 1985; 8:107–108.

Booth D, French J, Wainwright C, et al: Personal benefits from post-ingestional actions of dietary constituents. *P Nutr Soc* 1992;51(3):335–341.

Borel M, Smith S, Brigham D, et al: The impact of varying degrees of iron nutriture on several functional consequences of iron deficiency in rats. *J Nutr* 1991; 121:729–736.

Branconnier R, Dessain E, Cole J, et al: An analysis of dose-response of plasma choline to oral lecithin. *Biol Psychi* 1984;19(5):765–770.

Carney M: Vitamin deficiency and mental symptoms. *Br J Psychi* 1990;156:878–882.

Castano A, Cano J, Machado A: Low selenium diet affects monoamine turnover differentially in substantia nigra and striatum. *J Neurochem* 1993;61:1302–1307.

Cavan K, Gibson R, Grazioso C, et al: Growth and body composition of periurban

Guatemalan children in relation to zinc status: A longitudinal zinc intervention trial. *Am J Clin N* 1993;57(3):344–352.

Christensen H, Mackinnon A: The association between mental, social and physical activity and cognitive performance in young and old subjects. *Age Aging* 1993; 22:175–182.

Chrobak J, Walsh T: Dose- and delay-dependent working/episodic memory impairments following intraventricular administration of ethylcholine aziridinium ion (AF64A). *Behav Neur* 1991;56(2):200–212.

Claggett M: Nutritional factors relevant to Alzheimer's disease. *J Am Diet A* 1989; 89:392–396.

Clarkson T: Metal toxicity in the central nervous system. *Envir H Per* 1987;75:59–64.

Coyle J, Price D, LeLong M: Alzheimer's disease: A disorder of cortical cholinergic innervation. *Science* 1983;219:1184–1190.

Craig A: Acute effects of meals on perceptual and cognitive efficiency. *Nutr Rev* 1986;May (Suppl):163–171.

Crombie I, Todman J, McNeill G, et al: Effect of vitamin and mineral supplementation on verbal and non-verbal reasoning of schoolchildren. *Lancet* 1990;335(8692): 1158–1160.

Deijen J, vander Beek E, Orlebeke J, et al: Vitamin B-6 supplementation in elderly men: Effects on mood, memory, performance, and mental effort. *Psychophar* 1992; 109(4):489–496.

Deinard A, List A, Lindgren B, et al: Cognitive deficits in iron-deficient and iron-deficient anemic children. *J Pediat* 1986;108(5 pt 1):681–689.

DeLong G: Effects of nutrition on brain development in humans. *Am J Clin N* 1993;57 (Suppl):286S–290S.

Desharnais R, Jobin J, Cote C, et al: Aerobic exercise and the placebo effect: A controlled study. *Psychos Med* 1993;55:149–154.

Dietary choline and synaptic morphology in mice. *Nutr Rev* 1987;45(1):25–27.

Dunbar G, Rylett R, Schmidt B, et al: Hippocampal choline acetyltransferase activity correlates with spatial learning in aged rats. *Brain Res* 1993;604(1–2):266–272.

Dustman R, Ruhling R, Russell E, et al: Aerobic exercise training and improved neuropsychological function of older individuals. *Neurobiol A* 1984;5:35–42.

Eastman C, Guilarte T: Vitamin B6, kynurenines, and central nervous system function: Developmental aspects. *J Nutr Bioc* 1992;3:618–631.

Elias M, Wolf P, D'Agostino R, et al: Untreated blood pressure level is inversely related to cognitive functioning: The Framingham Study. *Am J Epidem* 1993;138(6): 353–364.

Fairweather-Tait S, Piper Z, Fatemi S, et al: The effect of tea on iron and aluminum metabolism in the rat. *Br J Nutr* 1991;65:61–68.

Farkas C, LeRiche W: Effect of tea and coffee consumption on non-haem iron absorption. *Hum Nutr-Cl* 1987;41C(2):161–163.

Foley D, Hay D, Mitchell R: Specific cognitive effects of mild iron deficiency and associations with blood polymorphisms in young adults. *Ann Hum Bio* 1986;13(5): 417–425.

Freedman M, Tighe S, Amato D, et al: Vitamin B12 in Alzheimer's disease. *Can J Neur* 1986;13:183.

Gorelick P, Bozzola F: Alzheimer's disease: Clues to the cause. *Postgr Med* 1991; 89(4):231–240.

Grantham-McGregor S: Assessments of the effects of nutrition on mental development and behavior in Jamaican studies. *Am J Clin N* 1993;57:303S–309S.

Grunewald R: Ascorbic acid in the brain. *Brain Res R* 1993;18(1):123–133.

Guilarte T: Vitamin B6 and cognitive development: Recent research findings from human and animal studies. *Nutr Rev* 1993;51(7):193–198.

Harrell R, Capp R, Davis D, et al: Can nutritional supplements help mentally retarded children? An exploratory study. *P NAS US* 1981;78(1):574–578.

Heseker H, Kubler W, Pudel V, et al: Psychological disorders as early symptoms of a mild-to-moderate vitamin deficiency. *Ann NY Acad* 1992;669:352–357.

Influence of tea on iron and aluminum bioavailability in the rat. *Nutr Rev* 1991;49(9): 287–289.

Idjradinata P, Pollitt E: Reversal of developmental delays in iron-deficient anaemic infants treated with iron. *Lancet* 1993;341(8836):1–4.

Imagawa M, Naruse S, Tsuji S, et al: Coenzyme Q10, iron, and vitamin B6 in genetically-confirmed Alzheimer's disease. *Lancet* 1992;340(8820):671.

Jacqmin H, Commenges D, Letenneur L, et al: Components of drinking water and risk of cognitive impairment in the elderly. *Am J Epidem* 1994;139:48–57.

Jensen G, Pakkenberg B: Do alcoholics drink their neurons away? *Lancet* 1993;342: 1201–1203.

Joosten E, vanden Berg A, Riezler R, et al: Metabolic evidence that deficiencies of vitamin B12 (cobalamine), folate, and vitamin B6 occur commonly in elderly people. *Am J Clin N* 1993;58:468–476.

Kanarek R, Swinney D: Effects of food snacks on cognitive performance in male college students. *Appetite* 1990;14(1):15–27.

Kohlschutter A: Vitamin E and neurological problems in childhood: A curable neurodegenerative process. *Develop Med* 1993;35(7):642–646.

Krause K, Bonjour J, Berlit P, et al: Biotin status of epileptics. *Ann NY Acad* 1985; 447:297–313.

Krestch M, Sauberlich H, Newbrun E: Electroencephalographic changes and periodontal status during short-term vitamin B6 depletion of young, nonpregnant women. *Am J Clin N* 1991;53:1266–1274.

Levitt A, Karlinsky H: Folate, vitamin B12, and cognitive impairment in patients with Alzheimer's disease. *Act Psyc Sc* 1992;86(4):301–305.

Lieberman H, Wurtman R, Emde G, et al: The effects of low doses of caffeine on human performance and mood. *Psychopharm* 1987;90:120–125.

Lione A, Allen P, Smith J: Aluminum coffee percolators as a source of dietary aluminum. *Food Chem T* 1984;22:265–268.

Loy R, Heyer D, Williams C, et al: Choline-induced spatial memory facilitation correlates with altered distribution and morphology of septal neurons. *Adv Exp Med Biol* 1991;295:373–382.

Lozoff B, Brittenham G: Behavioral aspects of iron deficiency. *Prog Hematol* 1986;14:23–53.

Lozoff B, Jimenez E, Wolf A: Long-term developmental outcome of infants with iron deficiency. *N Eng J Med* 1991;325:687–694.

Maloney G, Salbe A, Levander O: Selenium (Se) as sodium selenate (NaSeO4) is more toxic than selenium as L-selenomethionine (SeMet) in methionine deficient rats. *Clin Res* 1988;36:A763.

Matchar D, Deussner J, Watson D, et al: Significance of low serum vitamin B12 levels in the elderly. *J Am Ger So* 1986;34:680–681.

McCance-Katz E, Price L: Depression associated with vitamin A intoxication. *Psychosomat* 1992;33(1):117.

Meador K, Loring D, Nichols M, et al: Preliminary findings of high-dose thiamine in dementia of Alzheimer's type. *J Ger Psy N* 1993;6(4):222–229.

Meador K, Loring D, Rivner M, et al: The effects of high-dose thiamine in dementia of Alzheimer's type. *Ann Neurol* 1990;28:261.

Means L, Higgins J, Fernandez T: Mid-life onset of dietary restriction extends life and prolongs cognitive functioning. *Physl Behav* 1993;54:503–508.

Meck W, Smith R, Williams C: Pre- and postnatal choline supplementation produces long-term facilitation of spatial memory. *Devel Psych* 1988;21(4):339–353.

Messer W, Stibbe J, Bohnett M: Involvement of the septohippocampal cholinergic system in representational memory. *Brain Res* 1991;564(1):66–72.

Metz J: Cobalamin deficiency and the pathogenesis of nervous system disease. *Ann R Nutr* 1992;12:59–79.

Miguel J, Fleming J: Antioxidation, metabolic rate, and aging in Drosophila. *Arch Ger G* 1982;1:159.

Muller J, Steinegger A, Schlatter C: Contribution of aluminum from packaging materials and cooking utensils to the daily aluminum intake. *Z Lebensmit* 1993; 197(4):332–341.

Nakajima M, Furukawa S, Hayashi K, et al: Age-dependent survival-promoting activity of vitamin K on cultural CNS neurons. *Dev Brain R* 1993;73(1):17–23.

Nakamura S, Tani Y, Maezono Y, et al: Learning deficits after unilateral AF64A lesions in the rat basal forebrain: Role of cholinergic and noncholinergic systems. *Pharm Bio B* 1992;42(1):119–130.

Nelson M: Vitamin and mineral supplementation and academic performance in schoolchildren. *P Nutr Soc* 1992;51(3):303–313.

Newhouse J, Clement D, Lai C: Effects of iron supplementation and discontinuation on serum copper, zinc, calcium, and magnesium levels in women. *Med Sci Spt* 1993;25: 562–571.

Oster O, Drexler M, Schenk J, et al: The serum selenium concentration of patients with acute myocardial infarction. *Ann Clin R* 1986;18:36–42.

Pirttila T, Salo J, Laippala P, et al: Effect of advanced brain atrophy and vitamin deficiency on cognitive functions in nondemented subjects. *Act Neur Sc* 1993;87(3): 161–166.

Pollitt E: Iron deficiency and cognitive development. *Ann R Nutr* 1993;13:521–537.

Pollitt E, Gorman K, Engle P, et al: Early supplementary feeding and cognition: Effects over two decades. *Mon S Res C* 1993;58(7):1–118.

Pollitt E, Saco-Pollitt C, Leibel R, et al: Iron deficiency and behavioral development in infants and preschool children. *Am J Clin N* 1986;43(4):555–565.

Prasad P, Bamji M, Lakshmi A, et al: Functional impact of riboflavin supplementation in urban school children. *Nutr Res* 1990;10:275–281.

Preuss H: A review of persistent, low-grade lead challenge: Neurological and cardiovascular consequences. *J Am Col N* 1993;12(3):246–254.

Priest N: Satellite symposium on Alzheimer's disease and dietary aluminum. *P Nutr Soc* 1993;52:231–240.

Rogers P, Edwards S, Green M, et al: Nutritional influences on mood and cognitive performance: The menstrual cycle, caffeine, and dieting. *P Nutr Soc* 1992;51:343–351.

Rogers P, Green M: Dieting, dietary restraint and cognitive performance. *Br J Cl Psy* 1993;32:113–116.

Rosenberg I, Miller J: Nutritional factors in physical and cognitive functions of elderly people. *Am J Clin N* 1992;66 (Suppl):1237S–1243S.

Sanchez C, Hooper E, Garry P, et al: The relationship between dietary intake of choline, choline serum levels, and cognitive function in healthy elderly persons. *J Am Ger So* 1984;32(3):208–212.

Sandyk R, Kanofsky J: Vitamin C in the treatment of schizophrenia. *Int J Neurs* 1993;68(1–2):67–71.

Sasaki H, Matsuzaki Y, Meguro K, et al: Vitamin B12 improves cognitive disturbance in rodents fed a choline-deficient diet. *Pharm Bio B* 1992;43(2):635–639.

Schaie K, Willis S: Can decline in adult intellectual functioning be reversed? *Devel Psych* 1986;22:223–232.

Scott J: Folate-vitamin B12 interrelationships in the central nervous system. *P Nutr Soc* 1992;51(2):219–224.

Smart J: Behavioral consequences of undernutrition. *P Nutr Soc* 1993;52:189–199.

Soemantri A, Pollitt E, Kim I: Iron deficiency anemia and educational achievement. *Am J Clin N* 1985;42:1221.

Southon S, Wright A, Finglas P, et al: Micronutrient intake and psychological performance of schoolchildren: Consideration of the value of calculated nutrient intakes for the assessment of micronutrient status in children. *P Nutr Soc* 1992; 51(2):315–324.

Spring B, Maller O, Wurtman J, et al: Effects of protein and carbohydrate meals on mood and performance: Interactions with sex and age. *J Psych Res* 1982/1983;17(2): 155–167.

Tarricone B, Keim S, Simon J, et al: Intrahippocampal transplants of septal cholinergic neurons: High-affinity choline uptake and spatial memory function. *Brain Res* 1991;548(1–2):55–62.

Taylor G, Ferrier I, McLoughlin I, et al: Gastrointestinal absorption of aluminum in Alzheimer's disease: Response to aluminum citrate. *Age Aging* 1992;21:81–90.

Thomas D, Chung-A-On K, Dickerson J, et al: Tryptophan and nutritional status of patients with senile dementia. *Psychol Med* 1986;16:297–305.

Tucker D, Penland J, Sandstead H, et al: Nutrition status and brain function in aging. *Am J Clin N* 1990;52:93–102.

Turley C, Brewster M: Alpha-tocopherol protects against a reduction in adenosylcobalamin in oxidatively stressed human cells. *J Nutr* 1993;123:1305–1312.

Vitamin E deficiency and neurological dysfunction. *Nutr Rev* 1986;44(8):268–269.

von Allworden H, Horn S, Kahl J, et al: The influence of lecithin on plasma choline concentrations in triathletes and adolescent runners during exercise. *Eur J A Phy* 1993;67(1):87–91.

Wachs T, Moussa W, Bishry Z, et al: Relations between nutrition and cognitive performance in Egyptian toddlers. *Intelligenc* 1993;17(2):151–172.

Wazniak D, Cicero T, Kettinger L, et al: Paternal alcohol consumption in the rat impairs spatial learning performance in male offspring. *Psychopharm* 1991;105(2):289–302.

Wood S, Hendrickson D, Schvanevey N, et al: A longitudinal study of the influence of iron status on mental and motor development of infants and toddlers. *Nutr Res* 1993;13(12):1367–1378.

Woodbury M, Woodbury M: Neuropsychiatric development: Two case reports about the use of dietary fish oils and/or choline supplementation in children. *J Am Col N* 1993;12(3):239–245.

Wurtman R: The choline-deficient diet. *FASEB J* 1991;5(11):2612.

Zaman Z, Roche S, Fielden P, et al: Plasma concentrations of vitamins A and E and carotenoids in Alzheimer's disease. *Age Aging* 1992;21:91–94.

Zeisel S: Choline: An important nutrient in brain development, liver function and carcinogenesis. *J Am Col N* 1992;11:473–481.

CHAPTER 9: CAN'T SLEEP?

Adam K: Brain rhythm that correlates with obesity. *Br Med J* 1977;2:234.

Akata T, Sekiguchi S, Takahashi M, et al: Successful combined treatment with vitamin B12 and bright artificial light of one case with delayed sleep phase syndrome. *Jpn J Psy N* 1993;47(2):439–440.

Anderson E, Petersen S, Wailoo M: Factors influencing the body temperature of 3–4 month old infants at home during the day. *Arch Dis Ch* 1990;65(12):1308–1310.

Baumann P, Steinberg R, Koeb L, et al: Long-term treatment of hyposomnia with L-tryptophan. *Experientia* 1985;41:1214.

Bhanot J, Chhina G, Singh B, et al: REM sleep deprivation and food intake. *I J Physl Pharm* 1989;33(3):139–145.

Dahlitz M, Alvarex B, Vignau J, et al: Delayed sleep phase syndrome response to melatonin. *Lancet* 1991;337:1121–1124.

Danguir J: Cafeteria diet promotes sleep in rats. *Appetite* 1987;8(1):49–53.

Devoe L, Murray C, Youssif A, et al: Maternal caffeine consumption and fetal behavior in normal third-trimester pregnancy. *Am J Obst G* 1993;168:1105–1112.

Everson C, Wehr T: Nutritional and metabolic adaptations to prolonged sleep deprivation in the rat. *Am J Physl* 1993;264 (2 pt 2):R376–R387.

Fagioli I, Baroncini P, Ricour C, et al: Decrease of slow-wave sleep in children with prolonged absence of essential lipids intake. *Sleep* 1989;12(6):495–499.

Fenster L, Eskenazi B, Windham G, et al: Caffeine consumption during pregnancy and fetal growth. *Am J Pub He* 1991;81:458–461.

Green J, Pollak C, Smith G: Meal size and intermeal interval in human subjects in time isolation. *Physl Behav* 1987;41(2):141–147.

Groves P, Schlesinger K: *Introduction to Biological Psychology, ed 2.* Dubuque, IA, W. C. Brown Co., 1982.

Hartmann E: Effect of L-tryptophan and other amino acids on sleep. *Nutr Rev* 1986;44(suppl):70–73.

Hartmann E: L-tryptophan: The sleeping pill of the future. *Psychol Tod* 1978;December:180.

Hilton C, Mizuma H: Bioactive peptides in food. *Ann Med* 1993;25:427–428.

Investigation of normal flatus production in healthy volunteers. *Gut* 1991;32(6):665–669.

Johnson B: Nutrient intake as a time signal for circadian rhythm. *J Nutr* 1992;122(9):1753–1759.

Karklin A, Driver H, Buffenstein R: Restricted energy intake affects nocturnal body temperature and sleep patterns. *Am J Clin N* 1994;59:346–349.

Kirschstein R: From the National Institutes of Health. *J Am Med A* 1993;270(10):1172.

Koral A: The enemies of sleep. *Psychol Tod* 1982;March:71.

Krupp L, Jandorf L, Coyle P, et al: Sleep disturbance in chronic fatigue syndrome. *J Psychosom* 1993;37(4):325–331.

Lacey J, Crisp A, Kalucy R, et al: Weight gain and the sleeping electroencephalogram: Study of ten patients with anorexia nervosa. *Br Med J* 1975;4:556–558.

Levy A, Dixon K, Schmidt H: Sleep architecture in anorexia nervosa and bulimia. *Biol Psychi* 1988;23:99–101.

Levy A, Dixon K, Schmidt H: REM and delta sleep in anorexia nervosa and bulimia. *Psychiat Res* 1987;20:189–197.

Lucero K, Hicks R: Relationship between habitual sleep duration and diet. *Perc Mot Sk* 1990;71(3 pt 2):1377–1378.

Maurizi C: The therapeutic potential for tryptophan and melatonin: Possible roles in depression, sleep, Alzheimer's disease and abnormal aging. *Med Hypoth* 1990;31: 233–242.

McGrath R, Buckwald B, Resnick E: The effect of L-tryptophan on seasonal affective disorders. *J Clin Psy* 1990;51:162–163.

Mullen P, Linsell C, Parker D: Influence of sleep disruption and calorie restriction on biological markers for depression. *Lancet* 1986;Nov 8;2(8515):1051–1055.

Murphy J, Thome L, Michals K, et al: Folic acid responsive rages, seizures and homocystinuria. *J Inh Met D* 1985;8:109–110.

Neumann M, Jacobs K: Relationship between dietary components and aspects of sleep. *Perc Mot Sk* 1992;75(3 pt 1):873–874.

Ohta T, Ando K, Iwata T, et al: Treatment of persistent sleep-wake schedule disorders in adolescents with methylcobalamin (vitamin B12). *Sleep* 1991;14(5):414–418.

Okawa M, Mishima K, Nanami T, et al: Vitamin B12 treatment for sleep-wake rhythm disorders. *Sleep* 1990;13(1):15–23.

Penland J: Effects of trace element nutrition on sleep patterns in adult women. *FASEB J* 1988;2:A434.

Pivonka E, Grunewald K: Aspartame- or sugar-sweetened beverages: Effects on mood in young women. *J Am Diet A* 1990;90(2):250–254.

Pollak C, Green J: Eating and its relationships with subjective alertness and sleep in narcoleptic subjects living without temporal cues. *Sleep* 1990;13(6):467–478.

Pollet P, Leathwood P: The influence of tryptophan on sleep in man. *Int J Vit N* 1983;53:223.

Rakel R: Insomnia: Concerns of the family physician. *J Fam Pract* 1993;36(5):551–558.

Russ M, Ackerman S, Banzy-Schwartz M, et al: Plasma tryptophan to large neutral amino acid ratios in depressed and normal subjects. *J Affect D* 1990;19:9–14.

Sack R, Lewy A: Human circadian rhythms: Lessons from the blind. *Ann Med* 1993;25:303–305.

Sloan E, Hauri P, Bootzin R, et al: The nuts and bolts of behavioral therapy for insomnia. *J Psychosom* 1993;37 (Suppl 1):19–37.

Smidt L, Cremin F, Grivetti L, et al: Influence of thiamin supplementation on the health and general well-being of an elderly Irish population with marginal thiamin deficiency. *J Gerontol* 1991;46(1):M16–22.

Spinweber C: L-tryptophan administration to chronic sleep-onset insomniacs: Late-appearing reduction of sleep latency. *Psychophar* 1986;90:151–155.

Spring B, Chiodo J, Harden M, et al: Psychobiological effects of carbohydrates. *J Clin Psy* 1989;50 (Suppl):27–34.

Walsh B, Goetz R, Roose S, et al: EEG-monitored sleep in anorexia nervosa and bulimia. *Biol Psychi* 1985;20:947–956.

Your Answers on Sleep Survey. *Self* 1993;October:44.

Zammit G, Ackerman S, Shindledecker R, et al: Postprandial sleep and thermogenesis in normal men. *Physl Behav* 1992;52(2):251–259.

CHAPTER 10: NOT FEELING UP TO PAR?

Bahna S: Critique of various dietary regimens in the management of food allergy. *Ann Allergy* 1986;57(1):48–52.

Bell I, Markley E, King D, et al: Polysymptomatic syndromes and autonomic reactivity to nonfood stressors in individuals with self-reported adverse food reactions. *J Am Col N* 1993;12(3):227–238.

Belluardo N, Mudo G, Bindoni M: Effects of early destruction of the mouse arcuate nucleus by monosodium glutamate on the age-dependent natural killer activity. *Brain Res* 1990 Nov 26;534(1–2):225–233.

Binkley K: Role of food allergy in atopic dermatitis. *Int J Derm* 1992;31(9):611–614.

Bjorkstein B: Does breast-feeding prevent the development of allergy? *Immunol Tod* 1983;4(8):215–217.

Blume E: MSG adds flavor—and problems—to food. *Nutr Action* 1987;September:8–9.

Brankack J, Klingberg F: Visually evoked responses in the primary cortex of rats are permanently changed by early postnatal treatment with monosodium-L-glutamate. *Biomed Bioc* 1990;49(6):473–480.

Butkus S, Mahan L: Food allergies: Immunological reactions to food. *J Am Diet A* 1986;86:601–608.

Chandra R: Food allergy: 1992 and beyond. *Nutr Res* 1992;12:93–99.

Conners C: Food additives and hyperkinesis: A controlled, double-blind experiment. *Pediatrics* 1976;58(2):154–166.

Cornwell N, Clarke L, VanNunen S: Intolerance to dietary chemicals in recurrent idiopathic headache. *Clin Pharm* 1987;41:201.

David T: Anaphylactic shock during elimination diets for severe atopic eczema. *Arch Dis Ch* 1984;59:983–986.

Diagnosing food allergies. *Nutr Action* 1981;May:10.

Douglas J, Logan R, Gillon J, et al: Sarcoidosis and coeliac disease: An association? *Lancet* 1984;July 7:13.

Drewnowski A: Genetics of taste and smell. *World Rev Nutr Diet* 1990;63:194–208.

Feingold B: *Why Your Child Is Hyperactive.* New York, Random House, 1975.

Fisher K, Turner R, Pineault G, et al: The postweaning housing environment determines expression of learning deficit associated with neonatal monosodium glutamate (MSG). *Neurotox T* 1991 Sep–Oct;13(5):507–513.

Food additives and hyperactive children. *FDA Consumer.* HEW Publication No. (FDA) 77-2080, US Department of Health, Education, and Welfare, Public Health Administration, Food and Drug Administration, Office of Public Affairs. March, 1977.

Gastrointestinal permeability in food-allergic children. *Nutr Rev* 1985;43(8):233–235.

Goldman M, Stowe G: The modifying influence of aging on behavior in mice neonatally injected with monosodium glutamate. *Psychophar* 1985;86(3):359–364.

Harley J: Hyperkinesis and food additives: Testing the Feingold hypothesis. *Pediatrics* 1978;61:818.

Harley J: Synthetic food colors and hyperactivity in children. *Pediatrics* 1978;62:975.

Jessop D, Chowdrey H, Biaswas S, et al: Substance P and substance K in the rat hypothalamus following monosodium glutamate lesions of the arcuate nucleus. *Neuropeptid* 1991;18(3):165–170.

Joneja J: Management of food allergy: Personal perspectives of an allergy dietitian. *J Can Diet* 1993;54(11):15–16.

Kawamura M, Azuma N: Morphological studies on cataract and small lens formation in neonatal rats treated with monosodium-L-glutamate. *Ophthal Res* 1992;24(5): 289–297.

Klingberg H, Brankack J, Klingberg F: Long-term effects on behavior after postnatal treatment with monosodium-L-glutamate. *Biomed Bioch* 1987;46(10):705–711.

LaDu B: The role of genetics in idiosyncratic reactions or adverse reactions to foods. *World Rev Nutr Diet* 1990;63:209–219.

Lessof M: Reactions to food additives. *J Roy S Med* 1992;85:513–515.

Megavitamins and the hyperactive child. *Nutr Rev* 1985;43:105.

Monte T: The Feingold diet: Still hazy after all these years. *Nutr Action* 1979;December.

Parker S, Krondl M, Coleman P: Foods perceived by adults as causing adverse reactions. *J Am Diet A* 1993;93:40–44.

Pearson D: Pseudo food allergy. *Br Med J* 1986;292:221.

Pennington J (ed): *Bowes and Church's Food Values of Portions Commonly Used, ed 15.* New York, HarperPerennial, 1989.

Position of the American Dietetic Association: Promotion and support of breast-feeding. *J Am Diet A* 1993;93(4):467–469.

Sampson H, Metcalfe D: Food allergies. *J Am Med A* 1992;268(20):2840–2844.

Taylor S: Food allergies and sensitivities. *J Am Diet A* 1986;86:599–600.

Taylor S, Bush R: Sulfites as food ingredients. *Cont Nutr* 1986;11(10):1–2.

Toth L, Karcsu S, Feledi J, et al: Neurotoxicity of monosodium-L-glutamate in pregnant and fetal rats. *Acta Neurop* 1987;75(1):16–22.

van de Perre P, Simonon A, Hitimana D, et al: Infective and anti-infective properties of breastmilk from HIV-1-infected women. *Lancet* 1993;341:914–918.

Wilkin J: Does monosodium glutamate cause flushing (or merely "glutamania")? *J Am Acad D* 1986 Aug:15(2 pt 1):225–230.

Zaloga G, Hierlwimmer U, Engler R: Anaphylaxis following psyllium ingestion. *J Allerg Cl* 1984;74:79–80.

CHAPTER 11: MOOD, FOOD, AND EATING DISORDERS

Abraham H, Joseph A: Bulimic vomiting alters pain tolerance and mood. *Int J Psy M* 1987;16(4):311.

Abrams S, Silber T, Esteban N, et al: Mineral balance and bone turnover in adolescents with anorexia nervosa. *J Pediat* 1993;123:326–331.

Abou-Saleh M, Chung-A-On K: Folate and vitamin B12 in eating disorders. *Br J Psychi* 1987;150:133.

Abou-Saleh M, Coppen A: The biology of folate in depression: Implications for nutritional hypotheses of the psychoses. *J Psych Res* 1986;20(2):91–101.

Adams L, Antonow D, Humphries L, et al: Zinc nutriture in eating disorders. *Clin Res* 1984;32:A745.

Ainley C: Zinc state in anorexia nervosa. *Br Med J* 1986;293:992–993.

Ainley C, Cason J, Slavin B, et al: The influence of zinc status and malnutrition on immunological function in Crohn's disease. *Gastroenty* 1991;100:1616–1625.

Alger S, Schwalberg M, Bigauouette J, et al: Effect of a tricyclic antidepressant and opiate antagonist on binge-eating behavior in normoweight bulimic and obese, binge-eating subjects. *Am J Clin N* 1991;53:865–871.

American Psychiatric Association: *Diagnostic and Statistical Manual of Mental Disorders, ed 3.* Washington, DC, American Psychiatric Association, 1980.

Arnow B, Kenardy J, Argas W: Binge eating among the obese: A descriptive study. *J Behav Med* 1992;15:155–169.

Bakan R: Anorexia and zinc deficiency. *Lancet* 1984;II:1162.

Bakan R: The role of zinc in anorexia nervosa: Etiology and treatment. *Med Hypoth* 1979;5:731–736.

Bakshi V, Kelley A: Feeding induced by opioid stimulation of the ventral striatum: Role of opiate receptor subtypes. *J Pharm Exp* 1993;265(3):1253–1260.

Baranowska B: Are disturbances in opioid and adrenergic systems involved in the hormonal dysfunction of anorexia nervosa? *Psychoneuro* 1990;15(5&6):371–379.

Beumont P, Chambers T, Rouse L, et al: The diet composition and nutritional knowledge of patients with anorexia nervosa. *J Hum Nu D* 1981;35:265–273.

Beumont P, Russell J, Touyz S: Treatment of anorexia nervosa. *Lancet* 1993;341: 1635–1640.

Blouin A, Blouin J, Bushnik T, et al: A double-blind placebo-controlled glucose challenge in bulimia nervosa: Psychological effects. *Biol Psychi* 1993;33:160–168.

Blum K, Trachtenberg M, Cook D: Neuronutrient effects on weight loss in carbohydrate bingers. An open clinical trial. *Curr Ther R* 1990;48:217–233.

Boothe D: Mood- and nutrient-conditioned appetites: Cultural and physiological bases for eating disorders. *Ann NY Acad* 1989;575:122–134.

Brambilla F, Cavagnini F, Invitti C, et al: Neuroendocrine and psychopathological measures in anorexia nervosa: Resemblances to primary affective disorders. *Psychiat R* 1985;16:165–176.

Brambilla F, Cocchi D, Nobile P, et al: Anterior pituitary responsiveness to hypothalamic hormones in anorexia nervosa. *Neuropsychob* 1981;7:225–237.

Brambilla F, Ferrari E, Panerai A, et al: Psychoimmunoendocrine investigation in anorexia nervosa. *Neuropsychob* 1993;27:9–16.

Brambilla F, Ferrari E, Petraglia F, et al: Peripheral opioid secretory pattern in anorexia nervosa. *Psychiat R* 1991;39:115–127.

Brewerton T, Mueller E, Brandt H, et al: Dysregulation of 5-HT function in bulimia nervosa. *Ann NY Acad* 1989;575:500–502.

Brewerton T, Mueller E, Lesem M, et al: Neuroendocrine responses to m-chlorophenylpiperazine and l-tryptophan in bulimia. *Arch G Psyc* 1992;49: 852–861.

Bryce-Smith D: Anorexia and zinc deficiency. *Lancet* 1984;II:1162.

Bryce-Smith D, Simpson R: Case of anorexia nervosa responding to zinc sulphate. *Lancet* 1984;August 11:350.

Caspar R: An evaluation of trace metals, vitamins and taste function in anorexia nervosa. *Am J Clin N* 1980;33:1810–1818.

Caspar R: Zinc and copper status in anorexia nervosa. *Psychoph B* 1978;14:53–54.

Casper R, Eckert E, Halmi K, et al: Bulimia: Its incidence and clinical importance in patients with anorexia nervosa. *Arch G Psyc* 1980;37:1030–1035.

Casper R, Kirschner B, Sandstead H, et al: An evaluation of trace metals, vitamins, and taste function in anorexia nervosa. *Am J Clin N* 1980;33:1801–1808.

Cole W, Lapierre Y: The use of tryptophan in normal-weight bulimia. *Can J Psych* 1986;31:755–756.

Coiro V, Capretti L, Volpi R, et al: Growth hormone responses to growth hormone-releasing hormone, clonidine and insulin-induced hypoglycemia in normal weight bulimic women. *Neuropsychob* 1990;23:8–14.

Crisp A, Stonehill H: Aspects of the relationship between sleep and nutrition: A study of 375 psychiatric out-patients. *Br J Psychi* 1973;122:379–394.

Crowther J, Post G, Zaynor L: The prevalence of bulimia and binge eating in adolescent girls. *Int J Eat D* 1985;4:29–42.

Curran-Celentano J, Erdman J, et al: Alterations in vitamin A and thyroid hormone status in anorexia nervosa and associated disorders. *Am J Clin N* 1985;42:1183–1191.

Dalvit-McPhillips S: A dietary approach to bulimia treatment. *Physl Behav* 1984;33:769–775.

Davidson A, Anisman P, Eshaghpour E: Heart failure secondary to hypomagnesemia in anorexia nervosa. *Pediat Card* 1992;13:241–242.

deGraaf C, Schreurs A, Blauw Y: Short-term effects of different amounts of sweet and nonsweet carbohydrates on satiety and energy intake. *Physl Behav* 1993; 54:833–843.

DeMarinis L, Mancini A, D'Amico C, et al: Influence of naloxone infusion on prolactin and growth hormone response to growth hormone-releasing hormone in anorexia nervosa. *Psychoneuro* 1991;16(6):499–504.

Demitrack M, Putnam F, Brewerton T, et al: Relation of clinical variables to dissociative phenomena in eating disorders. *Am J Psychi* 1990;147:1184–1188.

Devlin M, Walsh T, Katz J, et al: Hypothalamic-pituitary gonadal function in anorexia nervosa and bulimia. *Psychiat R* 1989;28:11–24.

deZwaan M, Mitchell J: Opiate antagonists and eating behavior in humans: A review. *J Clin Phar* 1992;32(12):1060–1072.

Dinsmore W, Alderdice J, McMaster D, et al: Zinc absorption in anorexia nervosa. *Lancet* 1985;May 4:1041–1042.

Doerries L, Aravich P, Metcalf A, et al: Beta-endorphin and activity-based anorexia in the rat. *Ann NY Acad* 1989;575:609–611.

Drewnowski A: Sensory preferences for fat and sugar in adolescence and adult life. *Ann NY Acad* 1989;575:243–250.

Drewnowski A: Taste responsiveness in eating disorders. *Ann NY Acad* 1989;575: 399–407.

Drewnowski A, Bellisle F, Aimez P, et al: Taste and bulimia. *Physl Behav* 1987;41(6): 621–626.

Drewnowski A, Hopkins S, Kessler R: The prevalence of bulimia nervosa in the US college student population. *Am J Pub He* 1988;78(10):1322–1325.

Drewnowski A, Yee K: Men and body image: Are males satisfied with their body weight? *Psychos Med* 1987;49(6):626–634.

Drewnowski A, Yee K, Krahan K: Bulimia in college women: Incidence and recovery rates. *Am J Psychi* 1988;145(6):753–755.

Emerson E, Stein D: Anorexia nervosa: Empirical basis for the restricting and bulimic subtypes. *J Nutr Ed* 1993;25:329–336.

Enns M, Drewnowski A, Grinker J: Body composition, body size estimation, and attitudes towards eating in male college athletes. *Psychos Med* 1987;49(1):56–64.

Esca S, Brenner W, Mach K, et al: Kwashiorkor-like zinc deficiency syndrome in anorexia nervosa. *Act Der-Ven* 1979;59:361–364.

Fonseca V, D'Souza V, Houlder S, et al: Vitamin D deficiency and low osteocalcin concentrations in anorexia nervosa. *J Clin Path* 1988;41:195–197.

Fonseca V, Harvard C: Electrolyte disturbances and cardiac failure with hypomagnesemia in anorexia nervosa. *Br Med J* 1985;291:1680–1682.

Fornari V, Sandberg D, Lachenmeyer J, et al: Seasonal variations in bulimia nervosa. *Ann NY Acad* 1989;575:509–511.

Garfinkel P, Garner D: *Anorexia Nervosa: A Multidimensional Perspective.* New York, Brunner/Mazel, 1982.

Garner D: Pathogenesis of anorexia nervosa. *Lancet* 1993;341:1631–1640.

Geracioti T, Liddle R: Impaired cholecystokinin secretion in bulimia nervosa. *N Eng J Med* 1988;319:683–688.

Geliebter A, Aversa A: Eating in response to emotional states and situations in overweight, normal weight and underweight individuals. *Int J Obes* 1991;15 (Suppl 3):9.

Geliebter A, Melton P, Roberts D, et al: The stomach's role in appetite regulation of bulimia. *Ann NY Acad* 1989;575:512–513.

Gillman M, Lichtigfeld F: The opioids, dopamine, cholescystokinin, and eating disorders. *Clin Neurop* 1986;9(1):91–97.

Gleaves D, Williamson D, Barker S: Additive effects of mood and eating forbidden foods upon the perceptions of overeating and bingeing in bulimia nervosa. *Addict Beha* 1993;18:299–309.

Goldfein J, Walsh B, Lachaussen J, et al: Eating behavior in binge eating disorder. *Int J Eat D* 1993;14(4):427–431.

Gormally J, Rardin D, Black S: Correlates of successful response to a behavioral weight control clinic. *J Coun Psyc* 1980;27:179–191.

Gosnell B, Krahn D: The effects of continuous morphine infusion on diet selection and body weight. *Physl Behav* 1993;54:853–859.

Gren J, Woolf A: Hypermagnesemia associated with catharsis in a salicylate-intoxicated patient with anorexia nervosa. *Ann Emerg M* 1989;February:200.

Gwirtsman H, Kaye W, Obarzanek E, et al: Decreased caloric intake in normal-weight patients with bulimia: Comparison with female volunteers. *Am J Clin N* 1989;49: 86–92.

Hall R, Hoffman R, Beresford T, et al: Hypomagnesemia in patients with eating disorders. *Psychosomat* 1988;29(3):264–272.

Hall R, Hoffman R, Beresford T, et al: Refractory hypokalemia secondary to hypomagnesemia in eating-disorder patients. *Psychosomat* 1988;29(4):435–437.

Halmi K, Sunday S, Puglisi A, et al: Hunger and satiety in anorexia and bulimia nervosa. *Ann NY Acad* 1989;575:431–444.

Hill A: Causes and consequences of dieting and anorexia. *P Nutr So* 1993;52:211–218.

Hill K, Hill D, McClain M, et al: Serum insulin-like growth factor-I concentrations in the recovery of patients with anorexia nervosa. *J Am Col N* 1993;12(4):475–478.

Hiller W, Zaudig M: Comorbidity of eating disorders in comparison with mood disorders. *Ann NY Acad* 1989;575:532–534.

Holland A, Sicotte N, Treasure J: Anorexia nervosa: Evidence for a genetic basis. *J Psychosom* 1988;32:561–571.

Howat P, Varner L, Hegsted M, et al: The effect of bulimia upon diet, body fat, bone density, and blood components. *J Am Diet A* 1989;89:929–934.

Humphries L, Vivian B, Stuart M: Zinc deficiency and eating disorders. *J Clin Psy* 1989;50(12):456–459.

Jimerson D, Lesem M, Kaye W, et al: Eating disorders and depression: Is there a serotonin connection? *Biol Psychi* 1990;28:443–454.

Jimerson D, Lesem M, Kaye W, et al: Symptom severity and neurotransmitter studies in bulimia. *Psychopharm* 1988;96:124.

Johnson C, Larson R: Bulimia: An analysis of moods and behavior. *Psychos Med* 1982;44(4):341–350.

Johnson E: Elevated vasopressin and bulimia. *J Am Med A* 1992;268(7):854.

Jonas J, Gold M: The use of opiate antagonists in treating bulimia: A study of low-dose versus high-dose naltrexone. *Psychiat R* 1988;24:195–199.

Jonas J, Gold M: Treatment of antidepressant resistant bulimia with naltrexone. *Int J Psy M* 1987;16:305–309.

Kales E: A laboratory study of cognitive factors in bulimia: Abstinence violation effect. *Ann NY Acad* 1989;575:535–537.

Katz R, Keen C, Litt I, et al: Zinc deficiency in anorexia nervosa. *J Adoles H* 1987;8:400–406.

Kaye W, Berrettini W, Gwirtsman H, et al: Altered cerebrospinal fluid neuropeptide Y and peptide YY immunoreactivity in anorexia and bulimia nervosa. *Arch G Psyc* 1990;47:548–556.

Kaye W, Gwirtsman H, Brewerton T, et al: Bingeing behavior and plasma amino acids: A possible involvement of brain serotonin in bulimia nervosa. *Psychiat R* 1988;23:31–43.

Kaye W, Gwirtsman H, George D: The effect of bingeing and vomiting on hormonal secretion. *Biol Psychi* 1989;25:768–780.

Kaye W, Gwirtsman H, Lake R, et al: Disturbances of norepinephrine metabolism and adrenergic receptor activity in anorexia nervosa: Relationship to normal state. *Psychoph B* 1985;21:419–423.

Kaye W, Pickar D, Naker D, et al: Cerebrospinal fluid opioid activity in anorexia nervosa. *Am J Psychi* 1982;139:643–645.

Kaye W, Rubinow D, Gwirtsman H, et al: CSF somatostatin in anorexia nervosa and bulimia: Relationship to the hypothalamic pituitary-adrenal cortical axis. *Psychoneuro* 1988;13(3):265–272.

Kaye W, Weltzin T: Neurochemistry of bulimia nervosa. *J Clin Psy* 1991;52 (10 suppl):21–28.

Kiriike N, Iketani K, Nakanishi S, et al: Reduced bone density and major hormones regulating calcium metabolism in anorexia nervosa. *Acta Psyc Sc* 1992;86: 358–363.

Kiyohara K, Tamai H, Karibe C, et al: Serum thyrotropin (TSH) responses to thyrotropin-releasing hormone (TRH) in patients with anorexia nervosa and bulimia: Influence of changes in body weight and eating disorders. *Psychoneuro* 1987;12(1): 21–28.

Krahn D, Hasse S, Ray A: Caffeine consumption in patients with eating disorders. *Hosp Commun* 1991;42(3):313–315.

Kramlik S, Altemus M, Castonguay T: The effects of the acute administration of RU 486 on dietary preference in fasted lean and obese men. *Physl Behav* 1993;54:717–724.

Kreip R, Hicks D, Rosier R, et al: Preliminary findings on the effects of sex hormones on bone metabolism in anorexia nervosa. *J Adoles H* 1993;14(4):319–324.

Krieg J, Roscher S, Strian F, et al: Pain sensitivity in recovered anorexics, restrained and unrestrained eaters. *J Psychosom* 1993;37(6):595–602.

Lacy J, Crisp A, Kalucy R, et al: Weight gain and the sleeping electroencephalogram: Study of ten patients with anorexia nervosa. *Br Med J* 1975;4:556–558.

Lacy A, Dixon K, Schmidt H: REM and delta sleep in anorexia nervosa and bulimia. *Psychiat R* 1987;20:189–197.

Langan S, Farrell P: Vitamin E, vitamin A and essential fatty acid status of patients hospitalized for anorexia nervosa. *Am J Clin N* 1985;41:1054–1060.

Leibowitz S: Hypothalamic neuropeptide Y, galanin, and amines: Concepts of coexistence in relation to feeding behavior. *Ann NY Acad* 1989;575:221–231.

Levine A, Billington C: Opioids: Are they regulators of feeding? *Ann NY Acad* 1989;575:209–219.

Little K, Castellanos X, Humphries L, et al: Altered zinc metabolism in mood disorder patients. *Biol Psychi* 1989;26:646–648.

Marcos A, Varela P, Santacruz I, et al: Nutritional status and immunocompetence in eating disorders: A comparative study. *Eur J Cl N* 1993;47(11):787–793.

Marrazzi M, Luby E: Anorexia nervosa as an auto-addiction: Clinical and basic studies. *Ann NY Acad* 1989;575:545–547.

McClain C, Humphries L, Hill K, et al: Gastrointestinal and nutritional aspects of eating disorders. *J Am Col N* 1993;12(4):466–474.

McClain C, Stuart M, Kasarskis E, et al: Zinc, appetite regulation and eating disorders, in Prasad A (ed): *Essential and Toxic Trace Elements in Human Health and Disease: An Update.* New York, Wiley Liss, 1993;380:47–64.

McClain C, Stuart M, Vivian B, et al: Zinc status before and after zinc supplementation of eating disorder patients. *J Am Col N* 1992;11:694–700.

McManus M, Comerci G: Financial barriers in the care of adolescents with anorexia nervosa and bulimia. *Sem Adol Med* 1986;2:89–92.

Melchior J, Rigaud D, Colas-Linhart N, et al: Negative allesthesia and decreased endogenous opiate system activity in anorexia nervosa. *Pharm Bio B* 1990;35:885–888.

Mira M, Stewart P, Abraham S: Vitamin and trace element status of women with disordered eating. *Am J Clin N* 1989;50:940–944.

Mitchell J, Laine D, Morley J, et al: Naloxone but not CCK-8 may attenuate binge-eating behavior in patients with the bulimia syndrome. *Biol Psychi* 1986;21: 1399–1406.

Morley J: Appetite regulation by gut peptides. *Ann R Nutr* 1990;10:383–395.

Mount J, Heduan E, Herd C, et al: Adaptation of coenzyme stimulation assays for the nutritional assessment of vitamins B1, B2, and B6 using the Coas Bio centrifugal analyzer. *Ann Clin Bi* 1987;24:41–46.

Newman M, Halmi K, Satinoff E, et al: Sleep states and body temperatures in patients with anorexia nervosa. *Ann NY Acad* 1989;575:559–560.

Newton J, Freeman C, Hannan W, et al: Osteoporosis and normal weight bulimia nervosa: Which patients are at risk? *J Psychosom* 1993;37(3):239–247.

Patton G: Eating disorders: Antecedents, evolution and course. *Ann Med* 1992; 24:281–285.

Phillipp E, Pirke K, Kellner M, et al: Disturbed cholecystokinin secretion in patients with eating disorders. *Life Sci* 1991;48:2443–2450.

Pierce B, Halmi K, Sunday S: Relationship between taste and food preferences in eating disorders. *Ann NY Acad* 1989;575:564–566.

Raphael F, Lacey J: Sociocultural aspects of eating disorders. *Ann Med* 1992;24:293–296.

Rathner G, Bonsch C, Maurer G, et al: The impact of a guided self-help group on bulimic women: A prospective 15 month study of attenders and non-attenders. *J Psychosom* 1993;37(4):389–396.

Ruggiero L, Williamson D, Davis C, et al: Forbidden food survey: Measure of bulimic's anticipated emotional reactions to specific foods. *Addict Behav* 1988;13:267–274.

Safai-Kutti S: Zinc supplementation in anorexia nervosa. *Am J Clin N* 1986;44:581–582.

Safai-Kutti S, Kutti J: Zinc therapy in anorexia nervosa. *Am J Psychi* 1986;143:1059.

Safai-Kutti S, Kutti J: Zinc and anorexia nervosa. *Ann Int Med* 1984;100:317–318.

Salisbury J, Mitchell J: Bone mineral density and anorexia nervosa in women. *Am J Psychi* 1991;148(6):768–774.

Saloff-Coste C, Hamburge P, Herzog D: Nutrition and psychotherapy: Collaborative treatment of patients with eating disorders. *B Menninger* 1993;57(4):504–516.

Scheiger U, Pirke K, Laessle R, et al: Gonadotropin secretion in bulimia nervosa. *J Clin End* 1992;74:1122–1127.

Simon Y, Bellisle F, Monneuse M, et al: Taste responsiveness in anorexia nervosa. *Br J Psychi* 1993;162:244–246.

Smith J, Waldorf V, McNamara C: Use of implosive therapy scenes to assess the fears of women with bulimia in two response modes. *Behav Ther* 1993;24:601–618.

Sunday S, Einhorn A, Halmi K: Relationship of perceived macronutrient and caloric content to affective cognitions about food in eating-disordered, restrained, and unrestrained subjects. *Am J Clin N* 1992;55:362–371.

Telch C, Agras W: The effects of a very low calorie diet on binge eating. *Behav Ther* 1993;24(2):177–193.

Tepper R, Weizman A, Apter A, et al: Elevated plasma immunoreactive beta-endorphin in anorexia nervosa. *Clin Neurop* 1992;15(5):387–391.

Thibault L, Roberge A: The nutritional status of subjects with anorexia nervosa. *Int J Vit N* 1987;57:447–452.

Turner M, Foggo M, Bennie J, et al: Psychological, hormonal and biochemical changes following carbohydrate bingeing: A placebo controlled study in bulimia nervosa and matched controls. *Psychol Med* 1991;21:123–133.

van Binsbergen C, Hulshof K, Webel M, et al: Food preferences and aversions and dietary pattern in anorexia nervosa patients. *Eur J Clin N* 1988;42:671–678.

Van Voorhees A, Riba M: Acquired zinc deficiency in association with anorexia nervosa: Case report and review of the literature. *Pediat Derm* 1993;9(3):268–271.

Varela P, Marcos A, Navarro M: Zinc status in anorexia nervosa. *Ann Nutr M* 1992;36:197–202.

Wadden T, Stunkard A, Smoller J: Dieting and depression: A methodological study. *J Cons Clin* 1986;54:869–871.

Weingarten H, Elston D: The phenomenology of food cravings. *Appetite* 1990;15:231–246.

Wilson G: Relation of dieting and voluntary weight loss to psychological functioning and binge eating. *Ann Int Med* 1993;119(7):727–730.

Woods S, Gibbs J: The regulation of food intake by peptides. *Ann NY Acad* 1989;575:236–242.

Wurtman R, O'Rourke D, Wurtman J: Nutrient imbalances in depressive disorders: Possible brain mechanisms. *Ann NY Acad* 1989;575:75–82.

CHAPTER 12: FOOD ABUSE

Ames H, Gee M, Hawrysh Z: Taste perception and breast cancer: Evidence of a role for diet. *J Am Diet A* 1993;93(5):541–546.

Blair A, Lewis V, Booth D: Does emotional eating interfere with success in attempts at weight control? *Appetite* 1990;15:151–157.

Borah-Giddens J, Falciglia G: A meta-analysis of the relationship in food preferences between parents and children. *J Nutr Educ* 1993;25:102–107.

Caputo F, Mattes R: Human dietary responses to perceived manipulation of fat content in a midday meal. *Int J Obes* 1993;17(4):237–240.

Drewnowski A: Genetics of taste and smell. *World Rev Nutr Diet* 1990;63:194–208.

Falciglia G, Norton P: Evidence for a genetic influence on preference for some foods. *J Am Diet A* 1994;94:154–158.

Grunberg N, Straub R: The role of gender and taste class in the effects of stress on eating. *Health Psyc* 1992;11(2):97–100.

Hill A, Weaver C, Blundell J: Food craving, dietary restraint and mood. *Appetite* 1991;17(3):187–197.

Horner T, Utermohlen V: A multivariate analysis of the psychological factors related to body mass index and eating preoccupation in female college students. *J Am Col N* 1993;12(4):459–465.

Kalodner C, DeLucia J: The individual and combined effects of cognitive therapy and nutrition education as additions to a behavior modification program for weight loss. *Addict Beha* 1991;16:255–263.

Lavery M, Loewy J: Identifying predictive variables for long-term weight change after participation in a weight loss program. *J Am Diet A* 1993;93:1017–1024.

Lawton C, Burley V, Wales J, et al: Dietary fat and appetite control in obese subjects: Weak effects on satiation and satiety. *Int J Obes* 1993;17:409–416.

Merker L: Childhood sexual abuse as an antecedent to obesity. *Obesity & Health* 1992;6(4):66–68.

Parham E: Enhancing social support in weight loss management groups. *J Am Diet A* 1993;93:1152–1156.

Rolls B: Sensory-specific satiety. *Nutr Rev* 1986;44(3):93–101.

Rosenbloom C, Whittington F: The effects of bereavement on eating behaviors and nutrient intakes in elderly widowed persons. *J Gerontol* 1993;48(4):S223–S229.

Schiffman S, Garlin C: Clinical physiology of taste and smell. *Ann R Nutr* 1993;13:405–436.

Schlundt D, Virts K, Sbrocco T, et al: A sequential analysis of craving sweets in obese women. *Addict Beha* 1993;18(1):67–80.

Similarity of children's and their parents' food preferences. *Nutr Rev* 1987;45(5):134–137.

Stone L, Pangborn R: Preferences and intake measures of salt and sugar, and their relation to personality traits. *Appetite* 1990;15:63–79.

Wayler A: Fear of food, compulsive eating, and extreme anger scar ex-liquid dieters. *Obesity & Health* 1992;6(2):50–51.

Wing R: Behavioral treatment of severe obesity. *Am J Clin N* 1992;55:545S–551S.

CHAPTER 13: THE FEELING GOOD DIET

Blank D, Mattes R: Sugar and spice: Similarities and sensory attributes. *Nurs Res* 1992;September:290–293.

Diet and human health: A 90s perspective. Summary of proceedings from the conference held in New Orleans, November 15, 1992.

Lowe M: The effects of dieting on eating behavior: A three-factor model. *Psychol B* 1993;114(1):100–121.

Medeiros L, Shipp R, Taylor D: Dietary practices and nutrition beliefs through the adult life cycle. *J Nutr Ed* 1993;25(4):201–204.

Miller W, Wallace J, Eggert K, et al: Cardiovascular risk reduction in a self-taught, self-administered weight-loss program called the nondiet diet. *Med Ex Nutr He* 1993;2:218–223.

Miller W, Wallace J, Linderman A, et al: The non-diet diet: A 100-point scoring system for monitoring weight loss behavior. *J Am Diet A* 1991;91(8):973–975.

CHAPTER 14: PUTTING THE FEELING GOOD DIET INTO PRACTICE

Beare-Rogers J, Gray L, Hollywood R: The linoleic acid and trans fatty acids of margarine. *Am J Clin N* 1979;32:1805–1809.

Blume E: Poisoned peaches, toxic tomatoes: Reckoning pesticide risks. *Nutr Action* 1987;October:8–9.

Dining out with a healthy appetite. *FDA Consumer* 1987;March:5–7.

Dragsted L, Strube M, Larsen J: Cancer protective factors in fruits and vegetables: Biochemical and biological background. *Pharm Tox* 1993;72(S1):S116–S135.

Enig M, Atal S, Keeney M, et al: Isomeric trans fatty acids in the U.S. diet. *J Am Col N* 1990;9(5):471–486.

Environmental Protection Agency: *The EBDC Pesticides and EPA's Proposed Regulatory Decision: Facts for Consumers.* December 4, 1989.

FDA's final regulations on health claims for foods. *Nutr Rev* 1993;51(3):90–93.

Food label as nutrition policy. *Nutr Rev* 1992;50(2):58–60.

Greene G: How to eat healthy at New York's great restaurants. *New York Magazine,* August 15, 1988.

Ippolitto P, Mathios A: New food labeling regulations and the flow of nutrition information to consumers. *J Publ Pol* 1993;12(2):188–205.

Kummerow F: Dietary effects of trans fatty acids. *J Env P Tox* 1986;6(3–4):123–149.

Lefferts L: Pesticides: Fact vs fantasy. *Nutr Action* 1989;June:8–9.

Mandatory nutrition labeling: FDA's final rule. *Nutr Rev* 1993;51(4):101–105.

Mela D: Consumer estimates of the percentage energy from fat in common foods. *Eur J Cl N* 1993;47:735–740.

Mensink R, Zock P, Katan M, et al: Effect of dietary cis and trans fatty acids on serum lipoprotein[a] levels in humans. *J Lipid Res* 1992;33(10):1493–1501.

Montgomery A: America's pesticide-permeated food. *Nutr Action* 1987;June:1,4–7.

National Research Council: *Regulating Pesticides in Food: The Delaney Paradox.* Washington, DC, National Academy Press, 1987.

Natural Resources Defense Council: *Intolerable Risk: Pesticides in Our Children's Food.* New York, Natural Resources Defense Council, February 27, 1989.

Pass the pesticides. *Nutr Action* 1989;April:5–7.

Patterson B, Black G, Rosenberger W, et al: Fruit and vegetables in the American diet: Data from the NHANES II survey. *Am J Pub He* 1990;80(12):1443–1449.

Saltos E: The food pyramid–food label connection. *FDA Consumer* 1993;June:17–21.

Schrijver R, Privell O: Energetic efficiency and mitochondrial function in rats fed trans fatty acids. *J Nutr* 1984;114:1183–1191.

Stehlin D: A little "lite" reading. *FDA Consumer* 1993;June:12–16.

Troisi R, Willett W, Weiss S: Trans fatty acid intake in relation to serum lipid concentrations in adult men. *Am J Clin N* 1992;56:1019–1024.

United States Nutrition Labeling and Education Act of 1990. *Nutr Rev* 1991;49(9):273–276.

Willett W, Stampfer M, Manson J, et al: Intake of trans fatty acids and risk of coronary heart disease among women. *Lancet* 1993;341 (March 6):581–585.

Wood R, Kubena K, O'Brien B, et al: Effect of butter, mono- and polyunsaturated fatty acid-enriched butter, trans fatty acid margarine, and zero trans fatty acid margarine on serum lipids and lipoproteins in healthy men. *J Lipid Res* 1993;34(1):1–11.

CHAPTER 15: DO YOU NEED SUPPLEMENTS TO FEEL GOOD?

Anderson R, Kozlovsky A: Chromium intake, absorption and excretion of subjects consuming self-selected diets. *Am J Clin N* 1985;41:1177–1183.

Bender M, Levy A, Schucker R, et al: Trends in prevalence and magnitude of vitamin and mineral usage and correlation with health status. *J Am Diet A* 1992;92:1096–1101.

Bendich A: Safety issues regarding the use of vitamin supplements. *Ann NY Acad* 1992;669:300–312.

Bendich A: Vitamins and immunity. *J Nutr* 1992;122:601–603.

Chandra R: Excessive intake of zinc impairs immune responses. *J Am Med A* 1984;252:1443–1446.

Classen H: Stress and magnesium. *Artery* 1981;9(3):182–189.

Couzy F, Lafargue P, Guezennec C: Zinc metabolism in the athlete: Influence of training, nutrition and other factors. *Int J Sp M* 1990;11(4):263–266.

Dietary Intake Source Data: United States 1976–1980. Data from the National Health Survey, Series 11, No. 231, DHHS Publication No (PHS) 83-1681, March 1983.

Diplock A: Antioxidant nutrients and disease prevention: An overview. *Am J Clin N* 1991;53:189S–193S.

Ericsson Y, Angmar-Mansson B, Flores M: Urinary mineral ion loss after sugar ingestion. *Bone Miner* 1990;9:233–237.

Fine K, Santa Ana C, Porter J, et al: Intestinal absorption of magnesium from food and supplements. *J Clin Inv* 1991;88:396–402.

First Health and Nutrition Examination Survey. Public Health Service, Health Resources Administration, US Department of Health, 1971–1972.

Heimburger D: Localized deficiencies of folic acid in aerodigestive tissues. *Ann NY Acad* 1992;669:87–96.

Horwitt M: The promotion of vitamin E. *J Nutr* 1986;116:1371–1377.

Horwitt M, Elliott W, Kanjanangulpan P, et al: Serum concentrations of alpha-tocopherol after ingestion of various vitamin E preparations. *Am J Clin N* 1984;40:240.

Hu J, Zhao X, Jia J, et al: Dietary calcium and bone density among middle-aged and elderly women in China. *Am J Clin N* 1993;58:219–227.

Kallner A: Influence of vitamin C status on the urinary excretion of catecholamines in stress. *Hum Nutr-Cl* 1983;37:405.

Knopp R, Ginsaber J, Albers J, et al: Contrasting effects of unmodified and time-release forms of niacin on lipoproteins in hyperlipidemic subjects: Clues to the mechanism of action of niacin. *Metabolism* 1985;34:642–650.

Krehl W: Vitamin supplementation—A practical view. *Vit Nutr Info Serv* 1984;4:8–11.

Leklem J: Vitamin B6 requirements and oral contraceptive use: A concern? *J Nutr* 1986;116(3):475–477.

Mareschi J, Magliola C, Couzy F, et al: The well-balanced diet and the "at risk" micronutrients: A forecasting nutritional index. *Int J Vit N* 1987;57:79–85.

Nationwide Food Consumption Survey, Spring 1980. US Department of Agriculture, Science and Education Administration, Beltsville, MD.

Newhouse I, Clement D, Lai C: Effects of iron supplementation and discontinuation on serum copper, zinc, calcium, and magnesium levels in women. *Med Sci Spt* 1993;25: 562–571.

O'Dell B: Mineral interactions relevant to nutrient requirements. *J Nutr* 1989;119: 1832–1838.

Paolisso G, D'Amore A, Giugliano D, et al: Pharmacologic doses of vitamin E improve insulin action in healthy subjects and non-insulin-dependent diabetic patients. *Am J Clin N* 1993;57:650–656.

Pennington J: Total diet study: nutritional elements. *Nutr Rep* 1992 May;10(5):33,40.

Pennington J, Young B, Wilson D, et al: Mineral content of foods and total diets: The selected minerals in foods survey, 1982 to 1984. *Am J Diet A* 1986;86:876–890.

Reaven P, Witztum J: Comparison of supplementation of RRR-alpha-tocopherol and racemic alpha-tocopherol in humans. *Arter Throm* 1993;13:601–608.

Schectman G: Estimating ascorbic-acid requirements for cigarette smokers. *Ann NY Acad* 1993;686:335–346.

Seelig M: Cardiovascular consequences of magnesium deficiency and loss: Pathogenesis, prevalence and manifestations—magnesium and chloride loss in refractory potassium repletion. *Am J Card* 1989;63:4G–21G.

Stampfer M, Hennekens C, Manson J, et al: Vitamin E consumption and the risk of coronary disease in women. *N Eng J Med* 1993;328:1444–1449.

Subar A, Block G: Use of vitamin and mineral supplements: Demographic and amounts of nutrients consumed. *Am J Epidem* 1990;132:1091–1101.

Supplementation with vitamin D3 and calcium prevents hip fractures in elderly women. *Nutr Rev* 1993;51:183–185.

Tamura T: Folic acid. *Nutr MD* 1984;10:1–2.

Thomson C, Robinson M, Butler J, et al: Long-term supplementation with selenate and selenomethionine: Selenium and glutathione peroxidase (EC 1.11.1.9) in blood components of New Zealand women. *Br J Nutr* 1993;69:577–588.

Wolff M, Toniolo P, Lee E, et al: Blood levels of organochlorine residues and risk of breast cancer. *J Nat Canc* 1993;85:648–652.

Index

Entries in boldface refer to illustrations, tables, and worksheets. Entries in italics refer to recipes.